The Birth of the Gods and the Origins of Agriculture

Jacques Cauvin has worked on the beginnings of the Neolithic in the Near East for twenty years, excavating key sites and developing new ideas to explain the hugely significant cultural, social and economic changes involved in the transformation of mobile hunter-gatherers into the first village societies and farmers in the world. This book is the confident synthesis of his mature understanding of the process that began around 14,000 years ago. Cauvin challenges the ecological and materialist interpretations, and argues for a quite different kind of understanding that is influenced by the ideas of structuralist archaeologists such as André Leroi-Gourhan and members of the French Annales school of historians. He defines the Neolithic Revolution as essentially a restructuring of the human mentality that is expressed in terms of new religious ideas and symbols. The survey ends around 9,000 years ago, when the developed religious ideology, the social practice of village life and the economy of mixed farming had become established throughout the Near East and east Mediterranean, and was already spreading powerfully into Europe.

JACQUES CAUVIN is Directeur de Recherches émérite of the CNRS. He is the founder of a CNRS-funded multidisciplinary research team that has worked at the Institut de Préhistoire Orientale at Jalès for more than twenty years on the beginnings of sedentary village life and the origins of farming in the Near East.

NEW STUDIES IN ARCHAEOLOGY

Series editors
Wendy Ashmore, *University of Pennsylvania*
Clive Gamble, *University of Southampton*
John O'Shea, *University of Michigan*
Colin Renfrew, *University of Cambridge*

Archaeology has made enormous advances recently, both in the volume of discoveries and in its character as an intellectual discipline: new techniques have helped to further the range and rigour of inquiry, and encouraged inter-disciplinary communication.

The aim of this series is to make available to a wider audience the results of these developments. The coverage is worldwide and extends from the earliest hunting and gathering societies to historical archaeology.

For a list of titles in the series please see the end of the book.

JACQUES CAUVIN

The Birth of the Gods and the Origins of Agriculture

Translated by
TREVOR WATKINS

CAMBRIDGE
UNIVERSITY PRESS

CAMBRIDGE UNIVERSITY PRESS
Cambridge, New York, Melbourne, Madrid, Cape Town, Singapore, São Paulo

Cambridge University Press
The Edinburgh Building, Cambridge CB2 8RU, UK

Published in the United States of America by Cambridge University Press, New York

www.cambridge.org
Information on this title: www.cambridge.org/9780521651356

Originally published in French as *Naissance des divinités, naissance de l'agriculture.
La révolution des symboles au Néolithique* by CNRS editions 1994

First published in English by CNRS editions and Cambridge University Press
as *The birth of the gods and the origins of agriculture* 2000
English translation © CNRS editions and Cambridge University Press 2000
Reprinted 2002, 2003

This digitally printed version 2007

A catalogue record for this publication is available from the British Library

Library of Congress Cataloguing in Publication data

Cauvin, Jacques.
    The Birth of the gods and the origins of agriculture /
Jacques Cauvin; translated by Trevor Watkins.
        p.   cm. – (New studies in archaeology)
    Includes bibliographical references.
    ISBN 0 521 65135 2 hb
    1. Neolithic period – Middle East.   2. Religion, Prehistoric –
Middle East.   3. Agriculture – Origin.   4. Middle East – Antiquities.
I. Watkins, Trevor, 1938–.   II. Title.   III. Series.
GN776.32.N4C38   2000
939.4 – dc21   99-33530 CIP

ISBN 978-0-521-65135-6 hardback
ISBN 978-0-521-03908-6 paperback

CONTENTS

PLATES

FIGURES

The purpose of this English language edition of Jacques Cauvin's book is to make it accessible to a wider international readership. While many of us will read an article or a short report in a language that is not our own, most of us, I am sure, balk at reading a whole book. I have known the work of Jacques Cauvin for a long time. I have been interested in very much the same field of research for many years, and it has been a pleasure and a gesture of homage to translate his important book. Jacques Cauvin's work is always original, based on a vast knowledge, deeply thought, deeply felt and passionately written.

Which is better? To have a translation that is professionally done by someone who does not know the author's subject at all intimately, or one that is written by an amateur translator who is fairly conversant with the sites, the technical literature, the ideas and the arguments? This translation is the latter. And since Jacques' book is centrally concerned with a rereading of a great deal of detailed information in order to criticise many of the ideas of the rest of us and propose a case for some very individual ideas of his own, it seems to me to make sense that the translator should be sensitive to what the author is thinking and talking about, as much as the specific words that he uses.

I had the very great advantage of being able to discuss this translation with Darren Noyes, whose knowledge of French is much greater than mine will ever be. And finally, in a return visit to the Institut de Préhistoire Orientale at Jalès in Ardèche, I was able to work through the translation with Jacques Cauvin himself, making final corrections, adjustments and additions to ensure that the text is exactly as he would wish it to be. Where the English translation departs from the French edition for the sake of clarity and readability in English, the reader can be assured that the author has read the translation with meticulous care and approved. He has also saved the translator from a number of errors and infelicities. I was particularly keen that Jacques should have the opportunity to take note of new information and important publications that had come into print since he revised the French edition (completed in 1996). Some of these new references and further pieces of relevant information have been put into place in the text. And Jacques has also added a Postscript (completed 13 November 1998) which summarises further considerations that have arisen since the French original was published.

The only liberties I have taken have been to substitute spellings for site names more usually seen in English language books than some of the francophone renderings of Arabic, and, very occasionally, to use an equivalent term rather than a literal translation. There are many places in the text, where, as an archaeologist, I would have wanted to put things differently, but that amounts to taking a different view from Jacques Cauvin, which is not the translator's job. I have also added a small number of references to publications more recent than the second French edition, where authors cited by Jacques Cauvin have published more up-to-date information or advances on the account of their own views.

One or two words in Jacques Cauvin's vocabulary deserve comment. He uses the word *néolithisation* frequently to mean the process of becoming Neolithic, essentially beginning to cultivate crops and to herd animals, and the term 'neolithisation' is the practically unpronounceable English equivalent. Because Cauvin defines the Neolithic in terms of subsistence strategy, he is left with a period which is neither Palaeolithic (or Epi-palaeolithic for the last millennia of the Palaeolithic) nor yet Neolithic, because the Palaeolithic conventionally ends in step with the geological Pleistocene period. He therefore uses the term Mesolithic, as it is used in Britain and Europe, for the pre-agricultural times at the beginning of the Holocene period. Others use the term Mesolithic for the final millennia of the Pleistocene, because they consider the cultures equivalent to the European Mesolithic cultures of the early Holocene, but Cauvin observes the more usual convention of labelling these final Palaeolithic cultures Epi-palaeolithic. I have also chosen to use the spelling Çatalhöyük, the form preferred in Turkey and in use by the new Çatalhöyük Research Project, for the site more widely known in the archaeological literature as Çatal Hüyük. The site of 'Ain Mallaha or Eynan, with an Arabic and a Hebrew name, always causes difficulties for those unfamiliar with it. Cauvin usually uses the Arabic name, but I think that the site is better known among English-speaking archaeologists as Eynan, and I have usually used that form.

Trevor Watkins

FOREWORD TO THE SECOND FRENCH EDITION

The present edition appeared only three years after the first. The framework of the book and its general conclusions have scarcely been modified. However, that a revised edition was already necessary is some measure of how 'things change fast' in Near Eastern prehistory and how excavations and discoveries continue to accumulate rapidly.

The main events since 1994 that bear on the Near Eastern Neolithic have been on the one hand the renewal of salvage excavations at aceramic Neolithic settlements on the Middle Euphrates in northern Syria, where another new dam was being built, and where Spanish, French and Franco-Syrian teams have worked; and on the other hand the discovery of a phase of occupation on the island of Cyprus several centuries earlier than the Khirokitia culture, previously thought to be the oldest occupation of the island, which is very important for the understanding of the diffusion of the Neolithic; and finally, the spectacular advances in research in Anatolia achieved by Turkish and German teams. These new facts have led us to overhaul certain chapters quite significantly, in particular chapters 4, 9 and especially 15. Otherwise, there are corrections of detail that have been made in response to suggestions that have been made to me.

I thank Thomas Mourier, the editor of CNRS Editions, for his understanding and his patience in the face of all the corrections and Jacqueline Traincat who took care of the finalisation of the text at our Institute of Near Eastern Prehistory, Jalès.

I also thank my colleagues Jean Guilaine, Miguel Molist, Eric Coqueugniot, Danielle Stordeur, Harald Hauptmann and Paul Sanlaville for having kept me regularly informed of the advances in their research and their still unpublished results.

JACQUES CAUVIN
Jalès, December 1996

It is important to me that I have this opportunity to present this synthesis to anglo-phone readers, who are generally accustomed to an interpretation of prehistory that is more strictly socio-economic than this. Without seeking to bring into question the results that have been obtained by means of that perspective, I have tried by contrast to incorporate a cultural perspective on the Neolithic Revolution in the Near East that is concerned with the propensities of the human mind. This complementary component is important: it gives greater place in the transformation of the affairs of our species to human agency and to human cognitive and psychological dispositions. It may go some way to serving as a useful corrective to today's economic 'fatalism' which is the source of so much pessimism about the future.

When the second French edition was published in 1997, it was necessary to bring the book up to date, and this present edition requires some more up-dating. There are now many archaeologists working in the Near East, and their discoveries and most recent publications need to be included here. I have chosen the path of not modifying the text of the 1997 edition, excepting some new references here and there among the notes at the end of each chapter. The general bibliography has been augmented, and the most important advances in research during the last two or three years have been dealt with in a 'Postscript' at the end of the book. They have generally given support to the views I had expressed, and have required only a few corrections of detail to the essential thesis of this work.

I am particularly glad that this English edition has been translated by my colleague and friend Trevor Watkins. He also works on the recent prehistory of the Near East and is also concerned with the less material indications of the data that he recovers. He knows the subject treated here very well, and I have found agreement and confidence in the ability to discuss freely with him some of the French passages that are difficult to translate. He has my warm gratitude for his efficiency and patience.

Jacques Cauvin
Jalès, November 1998

PREFACE

Among the great turning points in human history, the one called the Neolithic Revolution is one of the most critical: it concerned the beginning of the first manipulations of the natural environment by our species, and it lies directly at the origins of our present power. The analysis of this metamorphosis, its circumstances and its causes, is therefore an indispensable first stage for those who are interested in how civilisation began. This event occurred first in the Near East, before radiating directly to other regions, or giving place to later imitations elsewhere.

This book is therefore first and foremost the synthesis of recent research on the Neolithic of the Near East. By 'Near East', a region whose extent fluctuates according to the author, I mean the territory designated by that name by UNESCO, that is to say the Levant (Syria, Lebanon, Israel and Jordan) and the Anatolian peninsula (Turkey).

The period covered is from about 12,000 to 6300 BC, when the transition of prehistoric communities of hunter-gatherers into the first farmers and the first herders was effected in stages, earlier in this part of the world than anywhere else, together with technical and ideological changes which accompanied and sometimes preceded the process.

For readers already somewhat familiar with this subject, these dates will be a surprise: they will appear older than those which they have read elsewhere, including in my own work *Les premiers villages de Syrie-Palestine*, published in 1978. Prehistoric chronology relies on radiocarbon dates, which we now know need to be 'calibrated', that is, corrected as a function of the history of cosmic radiation and its variation (see the Chronological table, pp. xvii).

Now, the calibration tables have only recently extended to periods as ancient as the Near Eastern Neolithic: this synthesis is therefore the first to take account of this revision. I am grateful to Jacques Evin, director of the radiocarbon laboratory of the University of Lyon-1, for having made all the necessary corrections to my text.

Like any history, that of the Neolithic is first of all a narrative, but I wanted to set a theoretical discussion on this narrative, in so far as the events described have had an impact on the rest of human evolution and its significance right up to our form of civilisation today. It was Goëry Delacote, then the director of scientific and technical information at the CNRS, who encouraged me in 1989 to undertake this task of elucidation. I am deeply grateful for his confidence and his interest: this work would not have seen the light of day without him.

Marie-Claire Cauvin and Danielle Stordeur have helped me continually with their reading of what I have written, their corrections and their advice. I have been able to take advantage of my friend Raymond Vogel with his extensive knowledge of philosophy and epistemology to make sure of the theoretical background on which my analyses of the archaeology were founded. I am also obliged to Patricia Anderson, Olivier Aurenche, Nur Balkan-Atli, Claude Boisson, Daniel Helmer, Jacobus Roodenberg, Paul Sanlaville and George Willcox, consulted on this or that part of the work, for reducing the errors I committed. To all of them I express my gratitude.

Claudine Maréchal had the most sustained and irreplaceable task of rendering the text on to personal computer and, having done that, making me aware of the basic errors into which I had slipped. Her efforts in the finishing of the text and her knowledge of Near Eastern prehistory have been invaluable. I owe the maps to Christine Chataigner, and to Gérard Deraprahamian the rest of the illustrations, both the originals and those redrawn from elsewhere. They have my appreciation and gratitude.

Finally I thank my colleagues Ofer Bar-Yosef, Harald Hauptmann, Alain Le Brun, Jean Perrot, Gary Rollefson, Maurits van Loon and François Valla who kindly allowed me to reproduce photographs.

Calibrated dates and ^{14}C dates

Since about 1950 its has been known that absolute dates may be proposed, based on the principle of the continuous decay of radiocarbon (^{14}C) that is contained in all organic matter. Little by little, after the death of the organism, this radioactive carbon is transformed into non-radioactive carbon (^{12}C). For a long time it was considered that the quantity of radioactive carbon in the atmosphere and absorbed by living organisms was constant, and therefore it was thought that the residual radioactivity of the samples measured in the laboratory could give a measure of absolute age, within a certain margin of error.

Dating methods such as dendrochronology have subsequently revealed that the flux of cosmic radiation that is the origin of the formation of radioactive carbon had varied over the millennia. This necessitates a calibration of the ^{14}C dates to take account of these variations. This calibration has resulted in dates 'BC' that are absolutely exact, which is not the case for dates 'BP' (before present) and 'bc' (before Christ, but not calibrated). Until quite recently, the impossibility of calibrating by means of dendrochronology alone dates as ancient as those of the Neolithic of the Near East has made it necessary to retain a 'traditional' ^{14}C chronology, that is, one that is not calibrated. This is the situation in all syntheses of Near Eastern prehistory that have appeared until now.

A short while ago, thanks to the application of other methods, calibration became possible up to 20,000 years before the present. This synthesis is therefore the first to give true dates for the Near East for the period covered.

The chronological scheme established by the Maison de l'Orient

A collective enterprise has been under way since 1975 at the Maison de l'Orient in Lyons with the objective of offering an up-to-date synthesis of the evolution of the whole of the Near East from the time of the last hunter-gatherer communities of the Upper Palaeolithic period down to the emergence of urban civilisation. This enterprise has produced a scheme of chronological periods. These are of unequal length, and have been determined on the basis of archaeological and radiometric criteria. The early periods of this scheme each represent a stage in the process of neolithisation.

Callibrated dates BC	Radiocarbon dates BP	Maison de l'Orient periods	Western Anatolia	Central Anatolia	Phoenician (coast) and Cyprus	Arid zone of the Southern Levant Transjordan Negev–Sinai	Levantine core — Jordan valley Damascus basin	Levantine core — Middle Euphrates	Eastern Taurus	Syrian Desert	Sinjar	Zagros
6000	7000 BP	6	Ilipinar	Haçılar	Lustrous pottery cultures — Amuq A-B; Ras Shamra VB-A; Byblos Early Neolithic	*YARMUKIAN* — Shaar Ha Golan; 'Ain Ghazal	*NOMADS* ?	Sabi Abyad	?	*ACERAMIC* Neolithic nomads — El Kowm 2 "PNA"	*HASSUNA CULTURE*	*ACERAMIC of the ZAGROS*
7000	7600 BP	5		Çatalhöyük	*KHIROKITIA CULTURE*	*Final PPNB of the Black Desert* 'Ain Ghazal 'PPNC'	Ashkelon; Ramad III	Abu Hureyra 2C; Damishliya		*Final PPNB* sedentary: El Kowm 2; nomads: Qdeir 1	Kültepe (nomads); Sotto; Umm Dabaghiyah	Jarmo
8000	8000 BP	4		*ASIKLI CULTURE*	*Late PPNB* Shilourokambos; Labwe; Ras Shamra VC; Tell aux Scies	*Late PPNB* 'Ain Ghazal	*Late PPNB* Abu Gosh; Ramad I-II; Beisamoun	*Late PPNB* Tell Assouad?; Abu Hureyra 2B; Halula		*Late PPNB* Bouqras	*Late PPNB of the Sinjar* Magzalia	Aceramic Jarmo; Ali Kosh; Ganj Dareh
8600	8600 BP	3		?		*Khiamian* Abu Madi I (Levels 5–12)	*Middle PPNB of Palestine* Jericho PPNB; Munhata — *SULTANIAN* Jericho PPNA; Netiv Hagdud	*Middle PPNB* Abu Hureyra 2A; Halula; Mureybet IV B — *Early PPNB* Mureybet IV A — *Late MUREYBETIAN* Mureybet III B; Cheikh Hassan, Jerf el Ahmar — *Early MUREYBETIAN* Mureybet III A	*PPNB of the Taurus* Cafer Höyük; Nevali Çori; Çayönü — Basal Çayönü — ?		*NEMRIKIAN* Nemrik	?
9000	9600 BP	2			*KHIAMIAN of Lebanon* Sables de Beyrouth	*Recent NATUFIAN of the Negev* Rosh Zin; Rosh Horesha	*KHAMIAN* El Khiam, Salibiyeh IX; Hatoula — *Final NATUFIAN* Tor Abou Sif — *Late NATUFIAN* Eynan, upper levels	*KHIAMIAN* Mureybet II; Mureybet I B — *Final NATUFIAN* Mureybet I A; Abu Hureyra I C — *Late NATUFIAN* Abu Hureyra I A–B	Hallam Cemi Tepesi		*QERMEZIAN* Qermez Dere	?
10,000	10,300 BP	1			*Late NATUFIAN of Lebanon* Sables de Beyrouth; Saayideh	?	*Early NATUFIAN* Eynan; El Wad; Hayonim	*Early NATUFIAN*		*Early NATUFIAN of* El Kowm		Zawi Chemi Shanidar
11,000	12,000 BP	0			*GEOMETRIC KEBARAN* Abri Bergy	*GEOMETRIC KEBARAN*	*GEOMETRIC KEBARAN*	*GEOMETRIC KEBARAN*		*GEOMETRIC KEBARAN*		*ZARZIAN*
12,000												

Man, the 'king of creation' who manipulates the rest of creation for his benefit, the pinnacle of biological evolution, 'master and possessor' of the other biological orders, who has multiplied the species that he has domesticated and decimated those which have remained wild, drawing energy from inert matter, overturning whole landscapes and transforming the planet – this is our portrait of ourselves at the end of the twentieth century, when abuse of our privileges has begun to stir disquiet.

But the emergence of the human species reaches back at least three million years. The origins of that supremacy can of course be found in those remote periods, where the development of specific human faculties made it possible, in the ability to stand upright, which liberated the hands and favoured the growth of the brain and in the first tools thanks to which the ingenuity of our species began little by little to compensate for the physical handicaps of the 'naked ape'. There was then an enormous period of latency, that of the Palaeolithic in its entirety, hundreds of millennia that separate the emergence of man from his taking charge of his environment, which appears normal today. This is the fruit of a last-minute process which unfolded in the Near East scarcely 12,000 years ago, when there occurred what, since Gordon Childe, we have called the Neolithic Revolution.

Whatever the considerable period that separates the clumsy tools made on cobbles that constitute the African *pebble culture* of 2 million years ago from the much more elaborate industry of tools made of stone or bone and the artistic products of the Magdalenian culture of only 18,000 years ago, a common trait exists between these two extremes in the Palaeolithic period: human groups hunted, fished and gathered. That is to say they drew from nature the basic foods necessary for their survival according to their needs, just like any other predatory species. Family-based 'micro-bands' used their mobility to compensate for the temporary exhaustion of wild resources in an area, except perhaps where these resources, especially the plants, were available throughout the year; knowing that they were particularly fertile and able to recover year after year; they did not yet create any fixed installations, nor did they alternate the strategies of acquisition according to the seasons.

But they could only acquire what nature presented them with. Abundance and shortage were spontaneous phenomena whose origin was thought to be beyond man's control and among the hazards of life. In spite of the development of mental ability and of technological ability, and in spite of the observation that he must have made of the natural processes of reproduction, Palaeolithic man never himself undertook the proliferation of the animals and plants that he consumed.

However, his unique superiority within the animal kingdom was manifest from an early stage. Humans have been burying their dead for over 100,000 years. Whether this is evidence of a belief in survival beyond physical extinction, or simply the ability to maintain a memory of the departed for some time, one senses that there already existed here the power of human thought to separate itself from the natural cycle of the generations, to meditate on its own condition and to bear witness through practices that are unique among animals that mankind is not an animal like the others. Moreover, people of the Upper Palaeolithic period prove by their art that for them nature had become a spectacle for observation, that bison, horses or mammoths were not only in the last resort foodstuffs but also 'forms' that their hands could reproduce on the walls of caves to constitute an imagery which expressed some sense for them. A conception of their world comes through from beneath these juxtapositions of images which are not simply coincidence and hazard: an act of ordering the natural abundance of living forms. In brief, although he had not left us any visible traces for a very long time, man was now capable of making and conveying sense.

But if we return from that mental supremacy to the demands of everyday life, the hunter has to go and search for animals and plants wherever he can find them in order to survive, to follow the herds of bison, as the American Indians did until very recently in their spontaneous shifts of camp; he needs to go and watch near the rock of Solutré for the herds of wild horses migrating through an essential narrow passageway, in order to take his toll of them; or, as a fisher, he needs to wait in his rock-shelter in the Vézère valley for the salmon that return to the river each year at a certain time. In brief, while utilising for his profit natural phenomena of which he has great experience, he does not have the power to change them, nor even to intervene in their course. His supremacy in the bosom of nature is a sort of certificate of excellence; he remains without power over nature.

For a long time now we have appreciated, by contrast, the extraordinary revolution that the Neolithic invention of cultivation and herding represents in this context. The analysis of its effects has become commonplace: resources that were from this time 'products', that is to say in large measure removed from the hazards of competing in their environment (to some extent, for climate and natural disasters have never been mastered); a food reserve, constituted of cultivated plants and domesticated animals, extendible and renewable, and therefore dependent on simple human initiative and a function of the needs and technical possibilities of the ever more numerous human communities; a new mastery of time as represented by the preferential choice among plant species thus exploited of those, such as the cereals, which can be stored, thereby assuring regular provision of supply throughout the seasons; the possibility that is afforded by certain animal species which are naturally gregarious and migratory, once herding allows their control and the direction of their herd movements, for the mastery of space as it is exercised by pastoral nomads. The new possibilities that were opened up by subsistence production could be detailed: in brief they consisted of a considerable and rapid rise in the power of humanity in the face of ecological constraints from which it could now begin to emancipate itself step by step. Little by little a portion of soil was set aside from its wild state, at first minimal but always being extended, worked, 'civilised' and refashioned by human activity and exploitation; a process of extension of control was set in motion which has with time resulted in what geographers say of today's world, a world in which almost none of our landscape resembles the natural environment that it must have once been. The destruction of the Amazonian rain-forest that is now in progress is without doubt the last, disturbing avatar of that process.

On the time-scale of the history of our species, very little time in fact separates the first village farming communities from the first urban civilisations, and then from the first industrial societies. If one admits that, in our domination of the world, the decisive step was taken in the Neolithic period and that we are the inheritors and the direct result of that critical turning-point, it is to that point that we must take our 'history' back.

It is usual, of course, to oppose the 'historical' civilisations, those which have known writing, to the 'peoples without a history' who preceded them or who remained ignorant of writing. That is why, as some believe, 'History begins at Sumer.' However, that is a presupposition of the epigraphists and historians who are totally absorbed in their interpretation of texts, veneering the study of the past with the careful distinctions that exist between university disciplines. In fact, before and after writing, we have other methods of investigation. The prehistoric archaeologist, without the help of written texts, turns to other disciplines, including the natural, physical and chemical sciences, to assist in the dating and analysis of change. Now, these changes in the Neolithic period are important and rapid. Above all, one of the intentions of this book will be to demonstrate that it is actually in the Neolithic Revolution that we find the roots of the present state of the human race, not only in its domination and exploitation of the environment, but also, it will be suggested, in the very foundations of our culture and mentality.

That is why the interrogation of the past, in prehistory no less than in other times, is not neutral. Every civilisation, especially in times of crisis, seeks its origins in the depths of the past in order to understand itself. For us in the West, classical antiquity has long played this role of justifying foundation and fascinating origin: it is well known to what extent the imagination of the French revolutionaries of 1789 drew their models from that source, in exactly the same way as the humanist tradition which has for so long nurtured our educational ideas.

In the face of our fears and our questioning of even the most fundamental assumptions of our millennial times, is there anything more than a phenomenon of fashion in the vogue for prehistory? Is it necessary to reach back further and further in order to understand where we are, that is to say where the mutation was produced that is the source of our power? This comes close to making of the prehistorian the instrument of a recall, anamnesis in an almost psychoanalytical sense.

This analogy between archaeology and psychoanalysis is nothing new. Freud himself had recourse to prehistory in order to understand the nature of psychoanalysis. One attends to a neurosis, he said, through an 'archaeology' of the individual, which brings back to the conscious mind the forgotten memories of infancy, when the mental and emotional attitudes were fixed which with time have become repetitive and disturbing, precisely because their source has become unconscious. The difference between psychoanalysis and archaeology, he added however, is that Agamemnon and Clytemnestra are no longer here to draw benefit from this pushing back of anamnesis. One might respond that humanity, in as much as it is the genuine collective subject of this descent to its origins, is always here, and that while putting in parallel that which is appropriate to the individual and that which is appropriate to the species, as is also often done in other domains, it is necessary to keep the two sides of the analogy in station and distinct to the very end. It can thus be said that a function of 'collective psychology' exists in archaeological research, in as much as the knowledge that we gain from archaeology allows us to shed real light on our present condition.

However, it is not sufficient, in effect, to situate the premises and the process of the Neolithic Revolution in time and space, nor to enumerate the ecological effects of these new strategies: this work is already well advanced. The transformation with which we are concerned does not consist only of subsistence production and the subsequent modifications of the landscape. Every sector of human life was involved, from the most material to the most symbolic. Habitat, technology, demography, social organisation, settlement and the use of space, and artistic and religious expressions were equally involved. These numerous parameters of what was a total metamorphosis are thoroughly enmeshed with each other to the extent that it is very difficult to order them in relative significance, to distinguish effects from causes, or to render their relationships intelligible. The difficulty is increased by the fact that the 'neolithisation' of various parts of the world was effected in different ways, in part by decisive, localised changes in particular centres of innovation, and in part by diffusion of their attributes very far from the centres of origin. The neolithisation of Europe, for example, is indeed the result of one of these diffusions, and it was there that the Neolithic was first defined and studied by western researchers at the beginning of this century. All its traits had come from elsewhere, whether economic, like cultivation and herding, or technical, like polished and ground stone or pottery, and it appeared simultaneously, combined with an overlay of local cultural persistence and autonomous stylistic creations, forming a whole that is difficult to unravel. In so far as it may be said to be a typical example of 'secondary neolithisation', the European Neolithic furnishes all the elements that allow us to investigate the mechanisms of diffusion, but it offers us much less help in giving an account of the Neolithic Revolution itself, in much the same way as the industrialisation of Japan does not tell us a great deal about the European Industrial Revolution which was its source.

From that observation comes the interest in studying the phenomenon in the Near East, for it was in that part of the world that it first arose, without any assistance or external influence to set it off or precipitate it. The other centres of neolithisation that exist in the world all seem to be later, given the present state of our knowledge. Above all, if in 1925 Gordon Childe was able to situate 'the dawn of European civilisation' in the Near East, it was because it is there that we can see its origins and at the same time the origins of a model of civilisations which has not ceased to diffuse itself since to the point that it has become global, from the point of view both of its intellectual and technical attributes and of its ultimate 'neurotic' effects: the malaise of a third world progressively deracinated from its own past furnishes us with a spectacular illustration of this in our own times. That is why one can speak of a collective anamnesis that is of interest to all modern humanity when we focus on the remembrance of the infancy of our civilisation.

Since the first excavations in the Neolithic levels of Jericho, and despite fifty years of research in the Near East, we are still a long way from seeing things clearly. For a start, as in all research where the documentation remains poor, the explanations remain largely hypothetical, the researchers papering over the gaps in their factual knowledge with a theoretical apparatus that most often reflects the popular ideology and ideas of the day. Thus, Childe was already able to sustain the thoroughly defensible view that the origins of the European Neolithic was oriental, because it was there that the wild progenitors of the principal species that were domesticated were to be found: but in order to explain domestication itself, he could only follow the model then in vogue, a simplified 'historical materialism', according to which the emergence of an economy of production represented *a priori* the sole fundamental change that was the basis for all the others and which itself could only be explained in terms of environmental determinism.

Now, at that time rather numerous facts were available concerning the European Neolithic, while the Near East was known only from sparse excavations of sites in Egypt or in Mesopotamia later than the sixth millennium BC, which could not therefore provide information on the actual origins of the process, which was more than 3,000 years earlier.

This situation has changed. From about 1950, relaunched by the discoveries at Jericho as well as by the thinking of Gordon Childe, research in the Near and Middle East has not stopped intensifying. Teams from many countries have contributed their efforts, the region being a privileged and universally attractive arena for the study of neolithisation, just as East Africa is for human evolution. Once rather thin and scattered, now the archaeological information base has become dense, above all for the countries of the Levant which are the focus of this work.

What about our theoretical approaches? Implicitly and imposing so many constraints, the same old 'materialist' model remains dominant today. Its strength can be seen in the way it governs the questions that are posed more than in the answers. What are investigated above all are the facts of nature which may have stimulated humans to take recourse to cultivation and herding in order to survive. The American expeditions led by Robert Braidwood since 1950 associated for the first time numerous natural scientists with the archaeologists in this objective in the Near East. Wild cereals are found today growing spontaneously in a semi-arid band bordering the 'Fertile Crescent' from the Dead Sea to the Iranian plateau (Fig. 1), and it was in the central part of the 'nuclear zone', that is to say in the Zagros mountains in NE Iraq, that Braidwood chose to investigate the traces of the very first agricultural experiments. He did not find them, or at least he found nothing as old as Jericho or the other village–farming communities that have been found

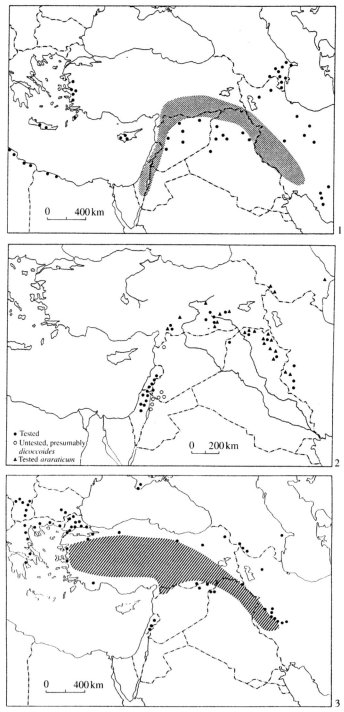

Fig. 1 Maps of the present distribution of wild cereals, after D. Zohary: 1 Barley (*Hordeum spontaneum*); 2 emmer (*Triticum dicoccoides*); 3 Einkorn (*Triticum boeoticum*). The hachured areas define the zones where the species are massively present.

more recently in the Levant. Some important parameter must have been missing from his prognosis. In the face of the manifest lateness of domestication relative to the emergence of a climatically and botanically favourable environment about 15,000 years ago, he did suppose that there was a certain autonomy in the cultural factors and their own evolution, but he could not see what this interesting intuition implied.

Around 1970, an intense theoretical renewal was brought about by the anglophone New Archaeology movement. It introduced the preoccupations of American anthropology concerning the processes that operate in human societies and the evolution of their social systems into an archaeology that up to that time had been too simply descriptive. However, nothing new appeared concerning our central theme. When one of the principal theoreticians affirms that culture in man is only 'the sum of his extra-somatic means of adaptation to his environment',[1] it is not surprising that the natural environment takes the initiative in the dialogue. That means that social and cultural changes must be triggered by that within us which is rooted deepest within our biological nature and is most sensitive to its changes, that is to say our bodies and their need for food. This 'ecology', which only confirmed the direction of research that had been initiated by Childe, still remains at the base of most of the questions that are posed.

So this conception, founded on unverified 'materialist' premises concerning human nature, is no more than a postulation, that is, in a truly scientific perspective, no more than a hypothesis to be examined. The principal scientific advances are known to come not so much from the linear accumulation of new facts but rather from the periodic questioning of its least criticised premises.[2] Unless knowledge is defined as the endless accumulation of factual information, it is pointless to ask of prehistoric archaeology only that it confirms what we have already 'known' since the middle of the nineteenth century, or one is confusing science with ideology. One may add that such a standstill in knowledge is of little value for philosophy and history, for it is not in projecting our own economic obsessions by a dotted line back into the past that we shall understand better what brought them into being.

Now, however, several voices are making themselves heard that underline the fact that the dominant model does not explain everything. From 1955 onwards a village of hunter-gatherers was excavated by Jean Perrot in the Jordan valley (Eynan-Mallaha), a settlement two millennia older than any cultivation or herding; other discoveries of the same kind followed. An important sociological phenomenon, settlement in village communities, was thereby found removed from its traditional theoretical status as a consequence of the productive economy of farming. We have shown that major changes in ideology, a sort of 'revolution of symbolism', had also preceded the adoption of a farming economy. The Neolithic Revolution, a chain reaction where every sector of human life at some time finds itself transmuted, when it is studied where it was born no longer appears to follow the expected sequence in the succession of changing components: cultural transformations in particular refuse to keep their place in a 'superstructure' based on economic changes, a demented stratigraphy sometimes inflicted on the expected order of cause and effect. This makes a general rereading of the available information essential rather than the short-term plastering over of the cracks in the existing theory.

By means of this rereading I shall endeavour to outline a very different theoretical option in the pages that follow, without disguising the fact that it will remain to be better supported in the future, because the facts that could sustain it have not always been observed with sufficient attention. It is true that one can often 'see' only what one thinks one is looking for, and nothing inhibits us more in this connection than a dogmatic presupposition so submerged in the unconscious of the searcher that its veracity does not even pose a problem. If we succeed in shaking some of these pseudo-facts as we make our way, the enterprise will have achieved its objective.

PART 1

The origins of agriculture

1

Natural environment and human cultures on the eve of the Neolithic

When people seek to explain the precociousness of the Neolithic Revolution in the Near East in relation to other regions of the world, it is the remarkably favourable environmental conditions that are most often invoked. What is still called the 'Fertile Crescent', the gentle arc from the Dead Sea to the Iranian plateau, between the summits of the Lebanon and Amanus mountains and the eastern Taurus and Zagros mountains on the one hand and the desert interior on the other, is an intermediary zone of sedimentary plains and hill country that is highly favourable for human life, covered by dense steppe vegetation and often forested, and frequented by an abundant and varied wild fauna. There are found the majority of the botanical and zoological species that the people of the Neolithic domesticated: not only the cereals, barley and wild rye and two species of wild wheat (emmer and wild einkorn) (Fig. 1), but also leguminous plants such as peas, lentils, beans, vetches and chickpeas, and among the animal species goats, mouflon (wild sheep), aurochs (wild cattle) and wild boar which, transformed by herding, still remain at the basis of our meat diet.

However, while this concentration of useful species is in itself remarkable, the Near East is far from owning exclusive rights over many of them: wild einkorn has crossed the straits between Asia and Europe and is also found in Macedonia, aurochs and wild boar were practically omnipresent at the end of the Pleistocene period almost all around the Mediterranean basin, and wild lentils were pushing forward in temperate Europe. Nevertheless these species do not seem to have been domesticated in these other regions. In the Near East itself, they were exploited for a long time by the traditional strategies of hunting and gathering, well before people began to control reproduction of them.

Climatic change on the eve of the Neolithic
The biological component of the environment, it is true, is not the only cause. It is itself the product of climatic change.[1] Cereals, which are particularly important, could only have occupied their present ecological habitat from the end of the Pleistocene period, about 15,000 years ago, as one consequence among others of a more general process: the global warming of climate at the end of the glacial period. However, if this climatic evolution was worldwide, the Near East experienced a singular version of the event. On the one hand, taking into account its latitude and the distance from glacial areas, the Near East had never known the rigours of the cold that was felt further north in the European Palaeolithic. On the other hand,

the process towards today's climatic situation was progressive, in other words less traumatic for mankind than in some other parts of the planet.

In Europe, the warming process had begun about 20,000 years ago, but it was slowed down by the maintenance of the cold climatic conditions that characterise the final glacial episode, known as Würm IV or simply Final Glacial. It is thought that the melting of the inland seas of polar ice, which had trapped enormous quantities of water in the form of ice up to that time, would have had the effect not only of raising the sea-level and of drowning large surfaces of inhabited land, but also, through the multiplication of icebergs, of cooling the ocean itself and land bordering rivers. It was thus that France, for example, experienced a tundra landscape, frequented by herds of reindeer, the typical fauna of the Final Glacial, and it was thus that the Magdalenian culture developed a remarkable adaptation to this new landscape, quite comparable with that of today's Inuit peoples. The reindeer, the species that was most hunted and that became fairly familiar, was followed in its seasonal migrations. This adaptation was apparently too absolute, because the Magdalenians did not survive further changes of climate. As the return to a warmer climate ran its course, rather than staying where they were, the Magdalenians preferred to follow the reindeer as their herds retreated towards the Scandinavian plains. In temperate Europe, by now quite well forested and dissected by lakes and marshes, the Mesolithic way of life would be seen to survive, in small isolated cultural groups, in communities that were perforce reduced by the Magdalenian exodus.

Nothing of this kind occurred in the Near East. Between 20,000 and 16,000 BC, the cold climate of the Final Glacial phase made itself felt, but less vigorously than in Europe, and it was followed by a steady and uninterrupted rewarming. However, particular processes are appropriate in northern Africa and western Asia: they depend on cyclonic phenomena and a regime of winds that themselves determine the rainfall patterns, rather than the general, global temperature. These are of major importance at this latitude; and because of them, regional 'climatic crises'[2] can make different sub-regions quite singular from the point of view of their precipitation levels. Thus the Near East, from the Zagros mountains to the Gulf, would remain semi-desert until about 9,000 years ago, not only because the Gulf region, a natural conservator of rainfall, had been dry for a long time, but also because the summer monsoon that brings rains from the Indian Ocean was absent.[3] Further west, by contrast, the Levant, better watered thanks to the winds from the Mediterranean, had escaped this aridity. A much more moist episode than the present continued between 16,000 and 13,000 BC, when regions that are normally very arid, such as Sinai, the Negev and the Syrian desert, saw a *floruit* of innumerable hunter-gatherer camps of the 'Geometric Kebaran' culture. When the climatologists agree in detecting a climatic desiccation in the Natufian period around 12,500 BC, it is in fact a situation quite similar to today that was establishing itself.

At that time, 12,000 years ago, the people of the Near East as far as their neolithisation is concerned, had already known for several millennia exceptionally clement natural conditions: they were sheltered from the most severe variations of temperature, from destructive marine transgressions which elsewhere accompanied the rise in sea-levels, because the coastal chain of hills of the Levant protected the hinterland, and they were protected from the persistent aridity of the Middle East. This benevolent environment however in no way explains the fundamental transformation that we shall be describing. Indeed, it may have favoured a prolonged hunting and gathering economy rather than the strategy of farming production that was to follow. The climatic history, like the list of potential domesticates, explains to an extent certain modalities of the process of neolithisation in this part of the world rather than what actually triggered the process itself. Thus one can understand why the Zagros mountains and lower Mesopotamia can be said to be retarded in relation to the regions on the Mediterranean façade: the Fertile Crescent took a long time to extend to its eastern extreme. Too arid a terrain constitutes an obstacle but favourable conditions play a permissive role. Let us now recapitulate once more the last millennia of the Pleistocene period, this time examining what people did with those circumstances.

Cultural evolution before 12,500 BC
The importance of the Near East in prehistory does not begin with the Neolithic. Welded to Africa by the Arabian peninsula, a million years ago the Near East was adopted by the earliest humanity *(Homo erectus)* in his diffusion towards Asia and Europe and away from his African cradle. It was also through the Levant that our fellow-man, *Homo sapiens sapiens*, must have transited. He was fully modern in morphology, had also come from Africa, and is well dated in Israel (at Qafzeh) at around 90,000 years ago. In the area of the evolution of technical ability, the invention of blade industries in chipped stone is attributed to him, dated at the Syrian oasis site of El Kowm to 80,000 years ago, the very beginning of the Middle Palaeolithic. This method of working flint produced long, parallel-sided blanks, called blades by archaeologists; these blanks were more regular than simple flakes and well thought out for the fashioning of certain types of tool.

In the Upper Palaeolithic, the Levantine Aurignacian, dated between 45,000 and 20,000 years ago, shows close parallels with the European Aurignacian, with which contacts must have existed. Tools and weapons of stone and of bone began to diversify and become specialised for particular tasks. It is clear, however, that the 'microlithic tendency' appeared in the Near East from the Aurignacian period, much earlier than anywhere else. Production of Microliths is an advanced technique found in many parts of the world which reduces the weight of flint armatures, the flints being reduced to very small elements which were mounted as composites in tools of other materials (wood or bone). However, in the following period, when the Solutrean culture was flourishing in the west of Europe with its brilliant skills in lithic technology and artistic creativity, the Kebaran of the Levant was very far from attaining a comparable blossoming. More often encountered so far in caves and natural shelters in the Mediterranean façade of the Levant and southern Anatolia than in the regions of the interior, which were perhaps less hospitable during a climatic episode that was relatively cold and dry,[4] the Kebaran perpetuates and develops the microlithic tradition that it had inherited: almost all of its toolkit was fashioned on fine blades or bladelets which began to take on geometric forms (scalene triangles in particular), in a direct line of descent that leads, by about 15,000 BC, to the 'Geometric Kebaran'. But its communities seem to have been small, their material creations limited in range, their working of bone rare and production of works of art absent. The Near East seems to bear witness at that time to no more than an advanced evolutionary stage. At least that is how it appears if we follow the criteria that are generally used to evaluate human cultures in terms of their technical performance.

The Geometric Kebaran which follows the Kebaran between about 15,500 and 12,500 BC takes to the point of extravagance, as its name suggests, the tendency to geometrics, its microlithic armatures being mostly fashioned in the form of rectangles or trapezes. Climatic improvement, as we have seen, opens up the whole of the Levant to this culture, which is present from the Euphrates to Sinai, and from the Mediterranean to the desert oases. Camps in caves become rare, but there are numerous open-air sites, which suggest the existence of communities that are more substantial than before and less mobile: 'base camps' attain areas of 2,000 m², with indications of zoning of activities that suggests relative stability.[5] Several examples of habitation structures built in circular depressions are known, notably at Kharaneh in Jordan and in the Sinai. These 'round houses' have so far been encountered only once in what is thought of as the core territory of the Kebaran, namely at Ein Gev in Israel and in the cave of Jiita in the Lebanon. They are not yet sufficiently numerous to form villages, but they prefigure what will be the Natufian villages of the following period. At the same time, equipment for pounding and grinding (mortars), long thought to be a Natufian innovation, make their first appearance in the Geometric Kebaran period.

All of this is witness to a progressive cultural maturing, where the improvement in the stone tool assemblage is, naturally, accompanied by improvement in the living environment. What 'characterises' a period is almost always prefigured in the period that precedes it. The cultural blossoming of the last hunter-gatherer cultures which would contribute to the Natufian culture was the product of this continuity.

2

The first pre-agricultural villages: the Natufian

Between about 12,500 and 10,000 BC, the Natufian culture extended over almost the whole of the Levant, from the Euphrates to Sinai (Fig. 2). The Natufian has long been considered as the pivotal period when the process of neolithisation was prepared. That has been traditionally understood as the process in the course of which human communities passed from hunting and gathering to the production of their subsistence base. In the 1930s, the direct and precocious switch to agriculture was attributed to the Natufian. The excavation of Eynan-Mallaha, a village in the upper Jordan valley, begun in 1955, showed that subsistence still depended on hunting and gathering, but it introduced the new idea of pre-agricultural sedentism in the Near East. Other discoveries in the southern Levant and in the Euphrates valley soon produced confirmation. The absence of palaeobotanical information on the subsistence strategy of the Natufians at that time was compensated for by their apparent concentration in the semi-arid zone where wild cereals were at home. That, together with the presence of storage pits at Eynan, suggested that these villages should be defined not only as the first sedentary communities in the Levant, but as 'harvesters of cereals', that is, genuine specialists who by making these plants an essential resource had prepared for their next step forward.

Research was intensified. Teams from many different countries multiplied the number of excavations and presented their results. Their analysis of the material culture was refined, and analysis of the palaeobotanical remains began to be undertaken. As a result we now have a picture of the Natufian that has been greatly changed.[1]

First, on the cultural plane: when it was first described as being restricted to a zone that included only the southern Levant (Mount Carmel and the Jordan valley), the Natufian culture appeared to present a definite suite of regularly associated characteristics.[2] The houses that were discovered were in open settlements and grouped, thus qualifying as 'villages'; they were semi-subterranean, being built in shallow circular pits whose sides were supported by dry-stone retaining walls; they had one or two hearths and traces of concentric circles of posts that attest (at Eynan-Mallaha) to the construction of a really robust framework to support the roof (pl. I). In the lithic toolkit, geometric microliths now take the form of segments of a circle, in strict contrast with the trapezes or triangles of the Geometric Kebaran, but they continue to arm composite tools for hunting or fishing. An important component is the heavy ground stone tools (deep mortars, pestles and occasionally mill-stones) which were designed for pounding and grinding. Above all, there is a remarkable bone industry

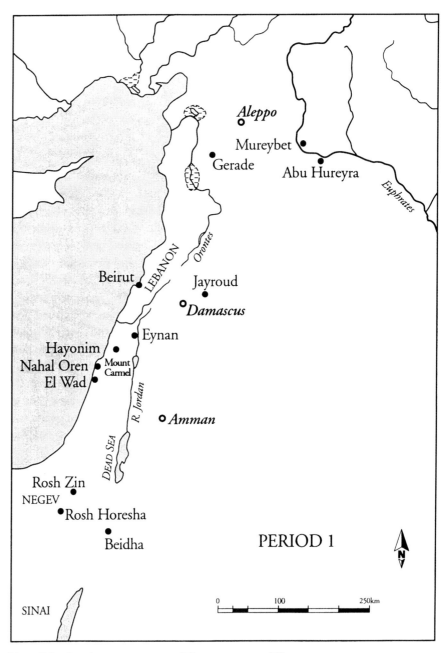

Fig. 2 Map of Natufian sites, 12,500–10,000 BC, 12,000–10,300 BP.

(fish-hooks, harpoons both barbed and plain, the bodies of composite tools, cutting implements and various perforated objects) which can be compared only with the Magdalenian of Europe for their high degree of elaboration. Single or collective burials, both primary and secondary, were interred under houses or grouped outside in genuine cemeteries. The dog, the only animal domesticated at this time, sometimes accompanied its master in the tomb, both at Mallaha and at Hayonim, allowing us a view of burials that are for the first time supported by sacrificial practices.[3] Some of the buried bodies also produced elaborate ornaments composed of shells (especially of *dentalium*) and bone. At the end of the Natufian period some ornaments are made of polished stone, where the technique of polishing by abrasion that has always been taken as a characteristic of the Neolithic makes a precocious appearance.[4] There are portable art objects, some naturalistic, some schematic, in bone or in stone, whose subject material is essentially zoomorphic (Fig. 3); they represent small herbivores, deer or gazelles, but very rarely human forms, the latter depicted in summary form with no indication of sex. Although the houses may not have been very numerous (five or six maximum according to François Valla), the solidity of their construction converges with the heavy equipment and the abundance of burials to suggest hamlets where occupation was permanent, that is, sedentary communities, in spite of the absence of any subsistence production.

It was very early noted that, over the course of the 2,500 years that the Natufian lasted, there was clearly development of the culture through time in the direction of simplification. For example there was a progressive reduction of its most sophisticated elements,[5] seen equally in the mode of retouch on the microlithic tools and in the impoverishment of the bone industry, which loses its most complex tools, and in the near disappearance of portable art objects. This cultural development has been confirmed by recent work in the Mediterranean zone of the southern Levant.[6] Even more evidence has come from the extension of research to the Negev, Jordan and the northern Levant, which has shown that these regions can provide a comparable indication[7] and also suggests the extension of a single, unique culture to the whole of the Levant. It is true to say that only the recent and final phases of the Natufian are at present well known in these regions, thanks to the excavation of sites in the Negev (Rosh Zin and Rosh Horesha) and in the Syrian middle Euphrates region (Abu Hureyra and Mureybet). The oldest phase of the culture, although its presence is known from surface surveys in Lebanon and Syria,[8] is much less well known.

As one goes further from the relatively well watered Mediterranean zone, where the Natufian was initially defined by archaeologists, towards the steppe country of the interior, it is to be expected that the way of life will change with the landscape. While it is well established for the moister zones of Israel, sedentary village occupation is less certain for the sites of the Negev or southern Jordan (Beidha), which are set in a more arid environment and which lack burials; perhaps these sites were seasonal occupations. It is very probably the opposite case on the middle Euphrates, where the absence of burials at Abu Hureyra and Mureybet could be explained by the excavation of too small areas of these early periods.

However, the retention of the 'first villages' as an essential trait of the Natufian is justified by the evidence and the relative novelty of the phenomenon. But that does not signify that all Natufians were villagers. In the coastal zone many small surface sites indicate ephemeral camp-sites used by small groups. These groups could have emanated from the villages where, since their territory was fixed, the food quest had to remain relatively itinerant, for lack of cultivation. But it is more probable that in

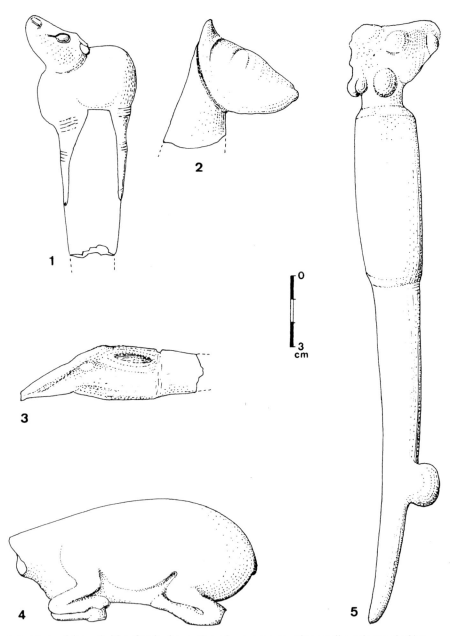

Fig. 3 Art objects of the early Natufian in the southern Levant representing small ruminants: haftings for knives from Mount Carmel (1, 3, 5); bone figurine from Nahal Oren (2); stone statuette from the Judaean desert (4). After D. Garrod, M. Stekelis and R. Neuville.

the steppe zones, drier and less rich in vegetable foods, a more radical nomadism would have remained the rule. Besides, it is there that the flint segments, which are related to hunting activities,[9] are the most numerous and that the 'lustred blades' that relate to the cutting of plant stems are the most rare. The model of the Natufian sedentary village remains confined to the richer environments, the coastal regions, the edges of rivers or lakes, where the regular contribution of aquatic resources (fish, shell-fish, water-fowl, etc.), which are always well represented in the faunal remains, helped to make year-round occupation feasible and stable.[10]

The Natufian economy in general has been defined as a 'broad spectrum' hunting and gathering economy, that is, a very eclectic strategy that exploited a varied selection of wild food resources. The examples of sedentary occupation appear to be supported by this variety, with resources sufficiently spread throughout the year to render longer-distance food-gathering expeditions unnecessary. This model, once rather hypothetical, seems to be consolidated with the progress of excavation experience.

However, this is a very important point where we can modify our conceptions: it is here that one may learn that it is possible to discern 'cultural preferences' operating on the margins of that eclecticism, in the area of meat in favour of hunting gazelle and among the harvested plants for cereals. If there are always gazelles represented among the faunal remains, it is because gazelle was omnipresent throughout the Levant. It is quite enough that it may have been a little less abundant than other animals in any locality, and that these other species effectively dominate the kitchen waste (for example, goat at Beidha, and birds at Hayonim). There was thus no 'cultural filter' (D. O. Henry) in favour of gazelle; still less were there attempts at the domestication of the species, attempts that some have thought they were able to deduce without other evidence of this preference.

The case of the cereals is still more eloquent. At Abu Hureyra between 11,000 and 10,000 BC the Natufians intensively harvested wild cereals. However, at the end of the occupation of this site,[11] as with the final Natufian of Mureybet,[12] these plants became rare and it was other species (knot grass (*Polygonum*) and milk vetch (*Astragalus*)) that were exploited en masse. A phase of climatic desiccation, felt throughout the whole of the Levant, modified the environment for a time after 9,800 BC. Diet was therefore adjusted according to what the environment offered. People were only 'harvesters of cereals' in so far as these were abundant sufficiently close to their village. There was still no phenomenon of deliberate specialisation. The corollary is seen in the microscopic analysis of wear traces on the lustred blades and bladelets, which has shown that in different localities they served either for the harvesting of wild cereals or for cutting of other species (reeds, canes, etc.) with no presumption that they were used exclusively in the food quest.[13] Their precise function can in fact vary according to the locality, as can their relative frequency in the toolkit. One can only draw conclusions on their significance with detailed case by case analysis.

The harvesting of wild cereals thus appears only as a general characteristic of the Natufian economy, and is not even particularly frequently found. The limits of this cultural group somewhat exceed the natural habitat of these plants, since at present one finds the Natufian just as often in the oasis areas of the arid desert as in the north Mediterranean zone that is too moist for them to grow spontaneously.

In other words, if one considers as 'cultural' the adaptive behaviour of a human group in relation not to its particular physical environment, but only to those aspects of it that contribute to a socially transmitted knowledge (the 'interior environment' of André Leroi-Gourhan) relatively independent of the chances of the physical environment, it appears that the harvesting of cereals did not play a part in Natufian 'culture'. Their way of life was varied, as were species that they hunted and ate. Among them figured those which would later be domesticated, sometimes in much smaller quantities than others which would never be domesticated. Prescience concerning future choices should not be attributed to the Natufians, any more than the effective presence of the complete 'typically agricultural' tool assemblage that would be used later by the Neolithic farmers should trouble us. These include sickles, grinding and pounding equipment, and even, in the Natufian of Mureybet, adzes or hoes flaked from flint identical to those which would exist 3,000 years later at the Hassunan sites of north Iraq or in the southern Mesopotamian Ubaid culture.[14] At Mureybet these were wood-working tools[15] which no-one had yet thought of using for working the soil. In exactly the same way, the Natufian grinding stones, according to the use traces that have been observed, were utilised for the grinding of ochre rather than vegetable materials. These tools only became agricultural by means of a particular adaptation or some specialisation of their original functions. Until the much later invention of the plough and animal traction, the people of the Neolithic had no new tool to invent in order to pursue their strategy of farming production: everything they needed already existed in the Natufian culture, and sometimes even earlier, among the hunter-gatherers of the advanced Palaeolithic. We can detect not so much as a single element that prefigures a techno-economic context still to come.

Such is the important correction that recent research imposes on our conception of the immediately pre-Neolithic period in the Levant. On the environmental plane as in the stone tool assemblage, the Natufian already includes the majority of the elements which, put into the different structural perspective of farming practices of the future, will be fundamental to the point of characterising these new times of the Neolithic. But in the Natufian they still remain sparse and intermittent, and they tell us nothing of the origin of these farming practices.

The originality of the Natufian lies elsewhere. Its technical capacities were not fundamentally revolutionary, but the historical importance of the phenomenon of sedentary villages deserves emphasis. It is an important step in the tendency of humans to group themselves into ever larger communities. It also supposes a reorganisation of social structures so as better to ensure the continuity of this permanent coexistence.

By means of their sedentary settlement, these larger communities also put down roots in a stable, permanent social environment, where the company of the dead, of which we see witness in the first cemeteries that are mingled with the houses of the living, reinforces metaphorically the community of the living[16] and can legitimate in some way its permanence. Agriculture will of course be an invention of sedentary villagers and it was the Natufians in the Levant who developed the sociological framework within which their descendants, both biological and cultural, inaugurated new strategies whose emergence we shall shortly seek to explain. By restricting this question to the level of biological needs, the explanatory models that have been tried till now have simply invoked a greater number of mouths to feed. We shall see that it was not that simple.

In any case, we should recall that 25,000–30,000 years ago, long before the Natufian therefore, there already existed in the Gravettian and Pavlovian cultures of central Europe, contemporary with the Aurignacian of the Levant, groups with remarkably well-constructed sedentary settlements, sometimes accompanied by collective or individual burials, where no process of neolithisation was effected. The human tendency to sociability is very general and is a part of our species. The Near East in no way played the part of precursor in this aspect of evolution. With regard to central Europe, it was a case of making up for lost time.

The particular dynamic which brought about the villages of the Levant, and from these particular village communities the special framework of the first Neolithic Revolution, remains still to be elucidated. The precise analysis of the different developments which constituted sedentary village life and their placing in order in time is thus the next task to be undertaken.

3

The Revolution in Symbols and the origins of Neolithic religion

The episode known as the Khiamian phase, which occurred between 10,000 and 9500 BC, at first seemed simply to mark the transition between the Natufian and the following chronological horizon, in the Levant labelled PPNA (Pre-Pottery Neolithic A). But it remains without a doubt much closer in terms of its material culture to what preceded it than to what followed. Initially, it is solely the appearance of the first projectile points, a type with lateral notches that is known as the 'Khiam point' after the Palestinian site of that name, which engendered the generic title of 'Khiamian' to indicate all the sites producing such points. These sites are numerous between the Israeli littoral, the Dead Sea and the Jordan valley, but they also occur on the Euphrates (Mureybet), in some Jordanian oases (Azraq), in the Anti-Lebanon (Nasharini) and in the south as far as Sinai (Abu Madi) (Fig. 4). There, too, recent excavations have fixed the date and the stratigraphic position of the Khiamian: the principal sites are Mureybet (phases IB and II),[1] Salabiyah IX in the Jordan valley[2] and Hatoula in the Judaean hills.[3]

The arrow-head took over from the microlithic segment only little by little for the arming of projectiles, and the Khiam point therefore began everywhere by coexisting alongside declining numbers of Natufian microliths before supplanting them completely (by Mureybet II). In this case it was a simple technical advance in a particular domain, that of hunting. The rest of the toolkit followed the preceding tradition in its essentials, with local variants such as the presence of flint hoes at Mureybet prolonging the pre-existing tradition of the final Natufian on the same site, and the existence of a particularly skilled bone industry that produced denticulated tools (Fig. 5: 5 and 7), needles with eyes and small sleeves for holding an axe in its wooden haft (Fig. 5: 6).

Another area of technical progress saw the light of day in another domain, that of architecture. The villages were scarcely different or more important than in the Natufian period, save that their basic element, the round house (whether circular or oval) might from now on come out of its original pit and be constructed directly on the surface of the ground (Mureybet II, Abu Madi). That implies the use of clay as a building material, whether to constitute the wall itself (*pisé*), or simply as mortar holding the stones together. Hunting, fishing and gathering appear as diversified as before.[4]

This episode would scarcely merit being made the first stage in neolithisation if it had not produced another type of transformation, which we think the critical one and which we have called the 'revolution of symbols'.[5] Symbolism has rarely been

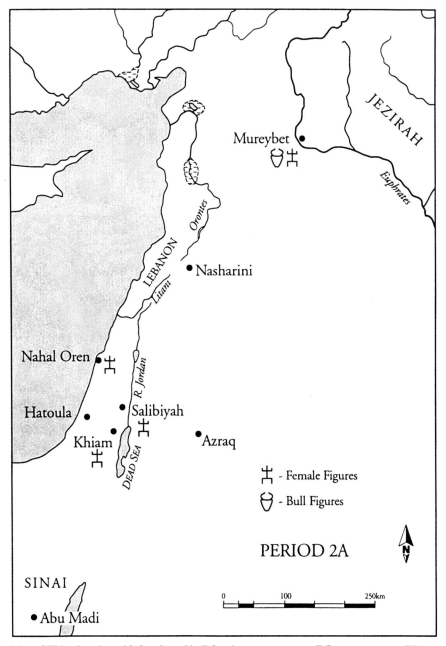

Fig. 4 Map of Khiamian sites with female and bull figurines, 10,000–9500 BC, 10,300–10,000 BP.

tackled in prehistoric archaeology. The work of André Leroi-Gourhan, seeking to reconstruct the structural system of mental imagery of the Upper Palaeolithic hunter-gatherers of western Europe from their art, is well known.[6] We suggested in 1978 that it was a change in collective psychology which must have preceded and engendered all the others in the matter of the process of neolithisation.[7] In much the

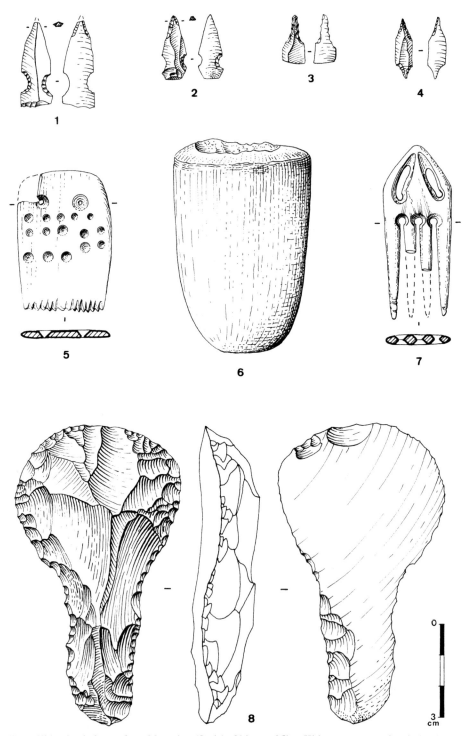

Fig. 5 Khiamian industry from Mureybet (Syria). Objects of flint: Khiam type arrow-heads (1–2); micro-borers (3–4); hoe (8). Objects of bone: serrated plaque (5); sleeve for hafting an axe (6); ornamental comb (7).

same way British researchers under the influence of Hodder[8] have recently sought by means of 'symbolic archaeology' to penetrate beyond the empirical and adaptational purposes of archaeological objects to the underlying structures which operate in every culture to effect a dynamic cohesion. We shall more than once pose questions of this kind in these pages.

Among all the information we have at our disposal, art therefore introduces those things which have the least practical utility but which are by contrast, thanks to the imagery that they develop, well able to set us on the track of the 'symbolic systems' (Claude Lévi-Strauss) which under-pin them. In this sense the period from about 10,000 to 9000 BC, that is, the period that includes the Khiamian and the four or five following centuries just preceding the emergence of village–farming societies, witnesses important changes. It is in effect our good fortune to have a figurative art, before and during this period of change, that permits us to perceive its real content.

The woman and the bull

Natufian art, as we have seen, was essentially zoomorphic (Fig. 3), exactly comparable to the Franco-Cantabrian art of Western Europe, with which it was partly contemporary. Gazelles and deer (fallow deer?) were the principal species represented, on small portable objects.[9] This subject is more or less recognisable as long as the art itself was naturalistic or schematic, for both these styles coexisted. The representation of a bird is also known (at Wadi Hammeh), and another of a dog-like animal (at Nahal Oren). We must take account of these hard facts, for the finding of portable art is very often haphazard; its animal representations and the very rare asexual human heads or silhouettes that are occasionally found[10] are each discovered in isolation, deprived by the chances of their deposition of spatial relationship, of contiguities or reciprocal exclusions, all of which allowed Leroi-Gourhan, when studying Palaeolithic cave-painting, to deduce a significant arrangement of species and certain thought structures expressed in this art.

Thus the principal change in the Khiamian period seems to concern its art. Limestone figurines from the Jordan valley (Salibiyah IX and Gilgal) are representations of female forms, though still schematic (Fig. 6); comparable pieces come from Mount Carmel (Nahal Oren) and the shores of the Dead Sea (El Khiam), and another, broken example from the Khiamian phase at Mureybet (phase II). By contrast, no representation of an animal is known in the Levant for this period.

A little later, between 9500 and 9000 BC, but still on the eve of the appearance of an agricultural economy in the Euphrates valley, the site of Mureybet (in phase IIIA) produces still more explicit documents. Eight figurines (Figs. 7 and 8), in stone or baked clay, are female representations. The majority, whether they are naturalistic or schematic, have clear indications of their sex. Two of them, anthropomorphic but still more simplified, do not exhibit any clear sexual character. They represent, without a doubt, the same reality, but in a more allusive fashion. There is no masculine figurine among them, and just one zoomorphic figure; the latter represents a nocturnal raptor. The spectacular humanisation of this art is thus the first recorded

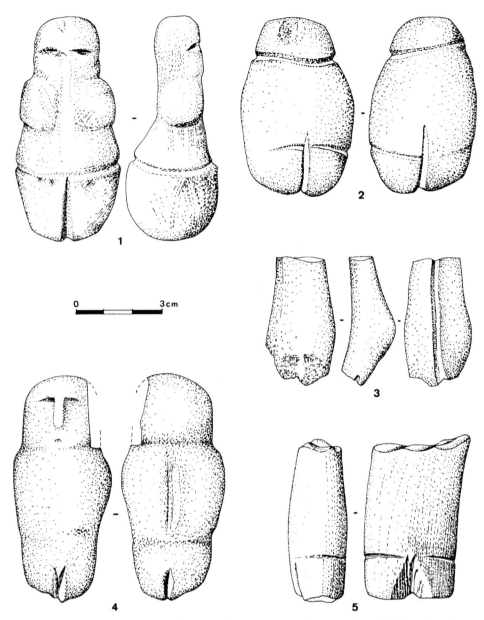

Fig. 6 Stone statuettes of the Khiamian culture from the tenth millennium BC: 1 Salabiyah IX (after O. Bar-Yosef); 2 Nahal Oren (after M. Stekelis and T. Yizraeli); 3 El Khiam (after J. G. Echegaray); 4 Gilgal (after T. Noy); 5 Mureybet (after J. Cauvin).

trait, and whenever there is sufficient realism to permit the definition of the sex, what it shows is a female figure.

However, at least in the northern Levant, not all representation of animals is absent from this symbolic repertoire, but its thematic content appears to differ completely from that of Natufian art. Besides the raptor statuette from Mureybet already mentioned, which may mark the first appearance in the Levant of a theme that later becomes very widespread in Near Eastern symbolism,[11] the animal kingdom is

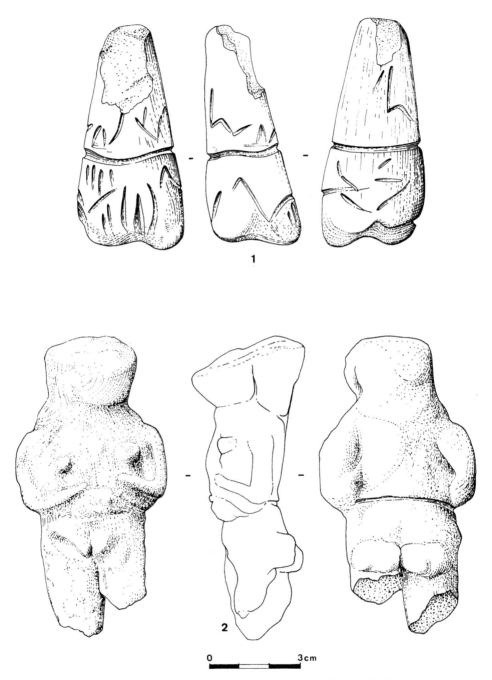

Fig. 7 Female statuettes in stone from the early Mureybetian period (Syria, end of the tenth millennium BC).

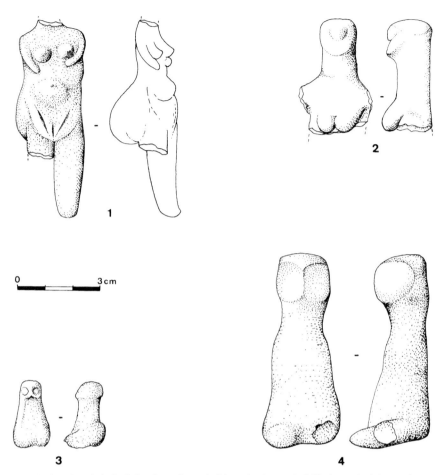

Fig. 8 Female figurines in baked clay from the early Mureybetian period (Syria, end of the tenth millennium BC).

represented by the bull, but not yet in an 'artistic' style. From the beginning of the Khiamian, around 10,000 BC, some skulls of aurochs are buried in houses, complete with their horns; they are reported to have been found inside clay 'benches' and associated specifically with the shoulder-blades of bovids and equids. Later, lasting throughout the history of the occupation of Mureybet, horns of bulls are repeatedly found buried in walls.[12] Although there is no question here of figurative representations like those that abound later, these deliberate deposits bear witness to a symbolic dimension. The Khiamian villagers at Mureybet, like the Natufians, hunted various herbivores of the steppe (gazelles and equid species) for their food needs, but very rarely the wild cattle that were present in the gallery forest on the edges of the Euphrates, no doubt for lack of audacity or the appropriate techniques for capturing them. These bull skulls are not a reflection of practical familiarity.

From that time on, about 9500 BC, in a still unchanged economic context of hunting and gathering that is just on the eve of its complete disruption, what we see dawning for the first time in the Levant are these two dominant symbolic figures, the Woman and the Bull. They will keep their leading roles throughout the whole of the Near Eastern Neolithic and Bronze Age periods, including the religion of the pre-hellenic eastern Mediterranean. Here again it is primarily the problem of portable objects, and they will present the same difficulties of interpretation as those of the Natufian, if we may be allowed to take advantage of what we know of their later history in the same cultural region.

A new religion

The female representations will in fact multiply very quickly throughout the whole Near Eastern Neolithic. From that time their economic context will be one of farming. At the same time, on the basis of their simple realisation and their material environment, their meaning will often be better perceived. However, we shall leave till later the account of the diffusion of the Neolithic from its source in the northern Levant into Anatolia. But here let us note that in the seventh millennium, in the civilisation of Çatalhöyük[13] that derives directly from this stream of diffusion, the woman and the bull will be predominant because of the number of their representations. They will manifest themselves in the heart of the exceptionally well-preserved architecture of the settlement, whether as painted frescoes, modelled relief sculptures or statuettes. Then we can deepen our analysis by taking into account the enlightening relationships suggested by the thematic and spatial study of these structured assemblages.[14] There we can perceive that this 'woman' is truly a goddess: in the schematic monumental relief sculptures she dominates the north or west wall of the domestic sanctuaries of Çatalhöyük, arms and legs spread, giving birth to bulls (or exceptionally rams) whose sculpted bucrania, set below her, seem to emanate from her (Fig. 9: 2). Paintings and mural reliefs attach a significant retinue to her. There are the jaws of carnivores (weasels and foxes), wild boar tusks or beaks of vultures, all carnivorous or dangerous animals, disguised inside female 'breasts' that are modelled in clay and protrude from walls in a curious combination of simultaneously nutritious and lethal symbolism. There are also raptors (vultures) in the painted frescoes, perching with extended wings on top of little match-stick men without heads. James Mellaart, the excavator of Çatalhöyük, quite rightly underlined the funerary association of this imagery, the Mistress of Life also ruling the dead. In the portable art, the very numerous female figurines of Çatalhöyük and Haçilar, another Anatolian site of the seventh millennium, may be seen as simply the descendants of those of Mureybet, as far as the most simple of them are concerned, with the same exaggeration of the hips symbolising fertility. But there also exist more complex realisations in Anatolia, revealing 'associations of ideas' of which the portable art very often deprives us. Thus, there is the celebrated statuette of Çatalhöyük (Fig. 9: 1), the Goddess, obese, giving birth, seated on panthers that serve as her throne; at Haçilar, the same person, equally seated on a panther, holds in her arms sometimes an infant, sometimes a young feline. Thus, in surreal assemblages which bring evidence of the world of the imagination, there are ideas of fertility, of maternity, of royalty and of being the mistress of wild animals. Here are all the traits of the

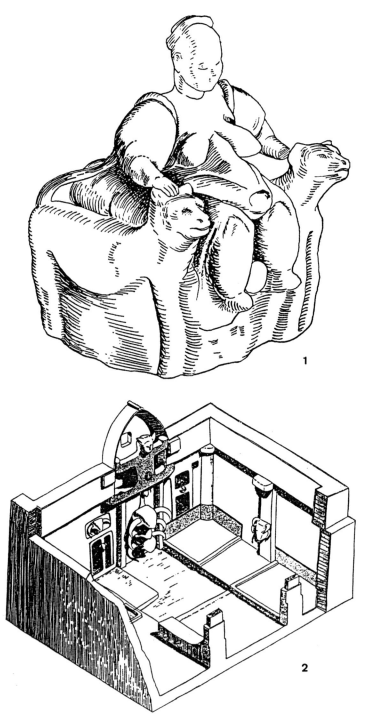

Fig. 9 The mother goddess of Çatalhöyük (Turkey, seventh millennium BC): 1 statuette of the goddess with felines, reconstruction, 16.5 cm without the head; 2 reconstruction of a domestic sanctuary with goddess in high relief giving birth, and bulls' heads. After J. Mellaart.

0   50 cm

Fig. 10 Painted fresco from Çatalhöyük: bull and armed men (Turkey, seventh millennium BC). After J. Mellaart.

Mother-Goddess who dominates the oriental pantheon right up to the time of the male-dominated monotheism of Israel.

The image of the bull is equally an almost obsessive theme at Çatalhöyük. From the simple texture of the first bucrania found at Mureybet,[15] still quite 'natural' in their style, they have become works of art in which the head is modelled in clay and attached to a wall; but they are always real horn-cores that finish off the objects. Equally, in the sanctuaries, horn-cores project from the multiple pillars and benches, while on the wall murals themselves an enormous silhouette of a bull frequently occupies the totality of a wall, modelled in relief and incised or painted. On several of these frescoes (e.g. Fig. 10), the beast is surrounded by men in movement, armed with bows and throwing-sticks; these men, represented at a very reduced scale in proportion to the bull, emphasise its enormity by the contrast. It is one of the first known scenes of the bull-contest, whose later history in the eastern Mediterranean we know well in the Minoan ceremonies. Above all, as with the Goddess, here are relevant facts for the contextual analysis, the placing and the association of the figures, the contrasts in size that show the hierarchy of respective values, which put us on the track of a structured symbolic thought-system in which the simple quantitative predominance of these representations with which we must elsewhere content ourselves takes shape and is made clear.

In order that the mural paintings and reliefs can be known to us it is a presupposition that the walls themselves were still standing when the archaeologist intervened. At Mureybet, where only the bases of the walls survived, the germ of the ideas in the painted frescoes of geometric decoration may be detected, but we shall never know anything more. By contrast, after the appearance of pottery, one Near Eastern culture at the end of the seventh millennium, known as the Halaf culture, would cover the sides of its pots with naturalistic decoration, which has come down to us. Female silhouettes and bucrania form dominant and repetitive motifs; above all at the site of Arpachiyah in Iraq, just as at Çatalhöyük, structured scenes have been recovered where one can recognise at once the theme of the goddess and the scene of the hunt.[16]

Throughout the total duration of the Neolithic across the whole of the Near and Middle East, a unique 'ideology' is found, expressed through different modes and artistic styles that at times contribute to the differentiation of cultures; and we shall see other examples. It is organised around two key symbols: one, female, has already taken human form. Can she perhaps be derived from the first female statuettes known in the Upper Palaeolithic of Europe and spread as far as Siberia? But these at that time counted for very little in relation to the huge predominance of animal representations. What is new at this time is their number, and also the indication that she was not only a 'fertility symbol' but a genuine mythical personality, conceived as a supreme being and universal mother, in other words a goddess who crowned a religious system which one could describe as 'female monotheism' in the sense that all the rest remained subordinated to her. The other, incarnate in the form of the Bull, is male but in an essentially zoomorphic expression.[17] At Çatalhöyük he appears subordinated to the Goddess by filial relationship, but he nevertheless ranks as the second supreme figure, made immediately and absolutely clear by the intensity of his depiction, the privileged size and the placing of his image. It is possible, as J. Mellaart has suggested, that a symbolic system which knew the mythology of the son who is also the spouse already existed in the Neolithic, analogous to what the much later texts of the tablets of the Mesopotamian Bronze Age reveal to us, but at this date with nothing in the religious art yet so specifically indicated. The Bull may be born of the Goddess, but no married couple, no 'divine couple' in the proper sense, was yet explicit.[18]

What recent research in the Near East has shown and what is important to us here is that this system with two persons began to be put in place around 9500 BC among the last hunter-gatherers of the Khiamian of the Levant. Without doubt this is the epoch when the first experiments in bringing wild cereals into cultivation may have been taking place in what is for us a marginal and imperceptible fashion (see below, p. 00). We shall see that it must have taken some considerable time for these experiments to achieve regular cultivation in our sense of the term. In the same way, it is not certain that the recasting of the symbolic repertoire that has been described would have straightaway attained the explicitly 'theological' form that the iconography of Çatalhöyük allows us to assert. At this stage nothing more than the promotion of new 'dominant symbols' can be proved. This change, whose historical importance has been underlined because of the germ of all the later constructions of mythic thought of the Near East and the east Mediterranean that it contained, occurs at this initial stage as a purely mental development. It is out of the question to seek to derive it from some transformation of the material infrastructure, following a line of reasoning that has become too classical. The strategies of subsistence were in no way agricultural, and the bull can be defined as economically insignificant, since that species, which was present sporadically among the hunted fauna, was not yet preferred to other game. That only became the case at Mureybet after 9000 BC, some time before the species was finally domesticated.

On the other hand, the emergence of this symbolic system is not identical in the southern Levant and the northern Levant. Only the Euphrates region appears to present the two components of the Khiamian epoch. Up to the present, the Jordan valley has furnished us only with female figurines. We only begin to see representations of bulls somewhat later, at the same time that there appeared a certain progressive and very partial 'humanisation' of the male personality, but we are not there yet and shall return to this subject later.

4

The first farmers: the socio-cultural context

We have seen that from the end of the Palaeolithic the Levant was the arena for continuous and progressive cultural evolution, but at this stage it was not particularly precocious in its economic and technical advances, notably with regard to Europe. On the other hand, we have not detected any determining external influence which could have acted upon this evolution.

These innovators were the direct heirs of the Khiamians who were to found the first farming economy in the Levant around 9000 BC, again based in a local evolution. We shall situate this process geographically and culturally, and make clear the methods by which we can detect and demonstrate the progression which appears to us to tie it back to the 'revolution of symbols', since in our view the farming economy is the second and not the first step in the process of neolithisation.

The cultural lineage from Natufian to Khiamian next engenders three distinct cultural groups: the Sultanian, the Aswadian and the Mureybetian, respectively discovered in the southern Levant (Israel, Jordan), in the central Levant (the area around Damascus) and on the middle Euphrates (Fig. 11). These three have generally been confused under the term 'Pre-Pottery Neolithic A' (PPNA), using the nomenclature invented by Kathleen Kenyon for Jericho when PPNA designated only a simple chronological horizon without precise cultural significance. Although these three cultures may have had the same Khiamian origin, the regional diversifications become more pronounced and from this stage on the individual traits of each outweigh their common traits. At the same time, the first traces of agriculture can be detected at the heart of these three cultures. This applies not throughout the Levant, but rather in an alluvial band which runs from the Jordan to the Euphrates valley, passing through the oasis of Damascus; Ofer Bar-Yosef has called this crucial region 'the Levantine corridor'.

The Sultanian
The Sultanian was first discovered and called the Pre-Pottery Neolithic A by Kathleen Kenyon,[1] when she dug the basal levels of Jericho (Tell es-Sultan) in the lower Jordan valley during the 1950s. There it lay over an early Natufian stratum, but a significant stratigraphic lacuna separated the two chronologically. There appears to have been no later Natufian or Khiamian at Jericho. The Sultanian assemblage covers the period 9500–8300 BC. Its oldest phase, called 'Protoneolithic', remains poorly known because the area excavated was too confined (5 m^2). The following phase by contrast was found in several large trenches at different points on the site.

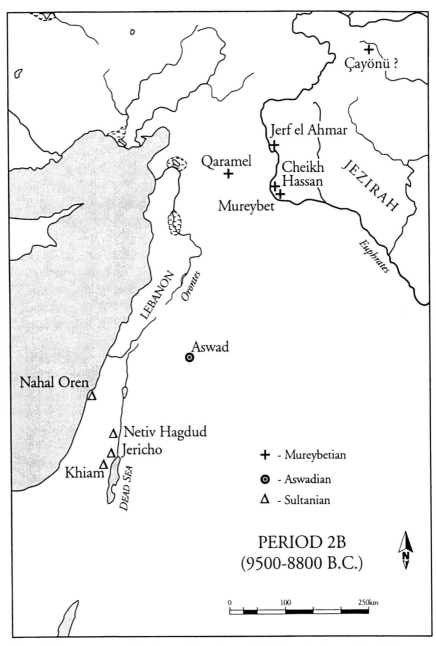

Fig. 11 Map of villages mentioned in the text belonging to the PPNA period, 9500–8300 BC, 10,000–9600 BP.

Jericho was a Neolithic village extending over more than 2 hectares. The Natufian tradition of the semi-subterranean round house was perpetuated, but the walls were built with mud bricks which were plano-convex in section and laid with mud mortar. The floors were paved and access to the interior was by means of a ramp or steps. The inhabitants invested their settlement with an impressive wall built of unshaped stones and 3 m thick, which must represent a collective construction; in this respect architecture for the first time steps beyond the uniquely private and family sphere of the domestic house. At one point a tower was attached to the encircling wall; it was 10 m in diameter at its base and preserved to a height of about 8.5 m, and it had an internal staircase. At first the wall was interpreted as a defensive system., but it has since been shown that the tower was some sort of monument and the wall perhaps a protection against floods.[2] Whatever their function, these were constructions for collective use with all the community organisation of labour for their construction that this implies.

The less extensive site of Netiv Hagdud[3] presents the same sort of houses with paved floors, but the foundations of the walls are built of stone. We see similar houses at Gilgal I[4] and Gesher, all three sites in the lower Jordan valley, and in the upper level at Hatoula[5] in the Judaean hills. In the PPNA levels of Nahal Oren[6] near the coast in northern Israel the majority of the fourteen houses excavated belong probably to the Sultanian period.

As well as an important suite of grinding implements, Sultanian sites produce an original chipped stone industry (Fig. 12: 1–5). Khiam points for arming arrows are still there, though rather less numerous (Fig. 12: l-2). Scrapers and burins are not specially characteristic, but a more heavy toolkit makes its appearance, formed of bifacial *tranchet* blades, which are types of flint axe or adze whose cutting edges have been created by transverse flake removals. On some sites, the first polished axes made in other kinds of stone join the repertoire. A new type of flint sickle-blade, named after the site of Beit Taamir (Fig. 12: 3), also helps to characterise the Sultanian, while a little obsidian, imported from Cappadocia, occurs on most sites in the form of bladelets. The bone industry is rich and diversified, and it includes tools that are novel and typical of this culture, notably implements for working animal hides (Fig. 12: 6), which are very similar in their form to the *tranchet* blades in flint. Finally, three distinct techniques of basketry (corded, spiral and superimposed sheets) make their appearance at this period, detectable by their imprints. In this group, the presence of corded basket-work seems to establish a quite new tradition in the southern Levant which is not found further north.[7]

Funerary rites are well known only at Jericho, where there are secondary burials in pits and also the custom of separately inhuming groups of skulls, prefiguring what will be the 'skull cult' of the PPNB in the eighth millennium. Finally, Netiv Hagdud has produced some very stylised female figurines (Fig. 13) whose hips, upper torso and eyes are the only details explicitly indicated in an otherwise highly abstracted body.

Together these facts reveal some salient features on the socio-cultural plane that we need to relate to the simultaneous transformation of the strategy of subsistence.

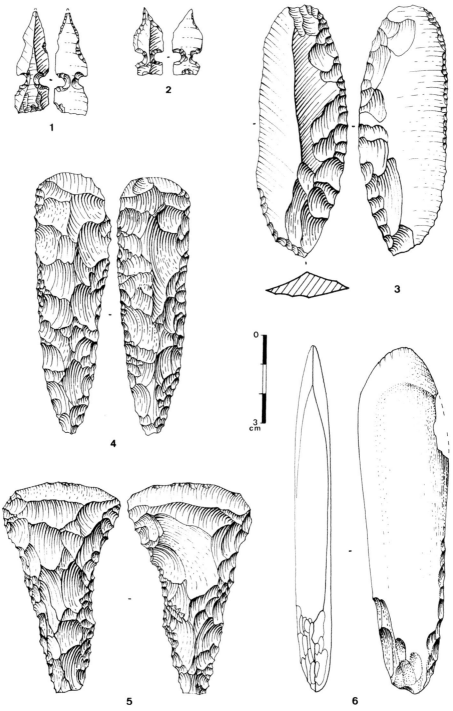

Fig. 12 Sultanian industry (southern Levant, ninth millennium BC). Flint: El Khiam points (1–2), after O. Bar-Yosef *et al.*; 'Beit Taamir knife' (3) after J. Crowfoot-Payne; bifacial *tranchet* axes (4–5). Bone: polished *tranchet* (6) after D. Stordeur.

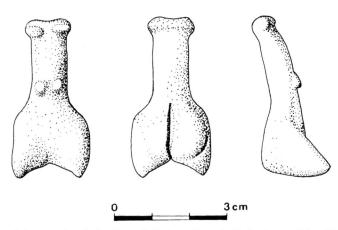

0   3 cm

Fig. 13 Schematic female figurine in baked clay from the Sultanian period at Netiv Hagdud (Israel), ninth millennium BC. After O. Bar-Yosef.

In fact, one is struck not just by a perfecting of techniques and an apparent diversification of the activities of transformation, or at least of the typical and specialised tools that are related to it: that aspect continues to develop in a progressive evolution. The important point is the sudden emergence of large human settlements, like Jericho, which do not bear comparison with the modest hamlets of the Natufian and Khiamian periods. More people cohabit in these larger settlements and now they are sufficiently well organised to join together in the building of monumental architecture with a collective purpose. A third trait concerns the total territory occupied. This phenomenon is certainly not exclusive to the southern Levant, but, thanks to the length of time and the intensity with which research has been in progress, it is there that the density of the human population and its growth may best be estimated. On the one hand the more arid zones (Negev and Transjordan) are thinly inhabited at the time, but on the other hand, even in the best-watered regions, between the Jordan river and the Mediterranean, the number of archaeological sites is very low at the beginning of the ninth millennium compared with what it was before and what it would be later.[8] As usual in archaeology, there are more sites to be discovered and we shall never know them all. But in the course of scientific conferences, one notes the same disproportion between the discoveries announced concerning this period and those which frame it. Indeed, there is certainly a correlation between these two observations, that is, of settlements becoming larger, but less numerous. One can think of it, as we have suggested,[9] as a spectacular progress in sedentarisation and at the same time as a regrouping of populations moving into a particular ecological zone in which they live in more substantial communities, while the dispersed traces of small more or less mobile groups that were still the majority in the Natufian almost disappear from the record.

These phenomena are significant and novel. They reveal original modalities in the form of the occupation of space by people and the community's social coherence in a single place, but they do not in any way indicate a general demographic expansion on the scale of the Near East. The traditional attribution of the invention of agriculture to a growing human population and to a consequent exhausting of the supply of wild resources does not stand up against a simple look at the general distribution map of these settlements.

The Aswadian

The prehistoric village of Tell Aswad is to be found in the Damascus oasis, on the eastern margin of the Anti-Lebanon. It was dug by Henri de Contenson by means of soundings.[10] The settlement was established by farmers of the PPNA horizon, a little before 9000 BC. The tell covers no less than 7 hectares, but the area of the initial settlement described here is certainly much less although it cannot be accurately estimated. The Aswadian culture, defined at present by this one village, consists of small semi-subterranean round houses (2 to 3 m in diameter), flanked by cylindrical pits of smaller diameter that were possibly used as silos. Although mud brick was utilised, notably for floors and platforms, the debris of burned huts strewn everywhere suggests that lighter materials (reeds coated with clay) were used for walls and roofs.

The lithic industry[11] is original, comprising arrow-heads ('Aswad points') that are derived from the Khiam points; they are larger and more elaborate (Fig. 14: l-3), but similar in terms of the way that the head was fixed to the shaft by means of lateral notches. The blades with a lustred edge ('sickle-blades') are larger than those of the Sultanian, and finely denticulated. This last is the best-represented category of tool, and is securely and directly related to the practice of agriculture, whose presence the botanists also confirm.[12] The other tools of stone and bone are less numerous and less diagnostic. Baked clay figurines that look like conical pawns may perhaps be anthropomorphic, at least in the eyes of their users, but they are too schematised for us to be able to affirm this. They exist alongside animal figurines.

The Mureybetian

The Mureybetian culture is contemporary with those previously described, and is exclusive to the northern Levant (Fig. 11). It was first recognised at two sites on the Syrian middle Euphrates, Mureybet (phase III), dug first by Maurits Van Loon[13] and then by us,[14] and Sheikh Hassan.[15] A new site is now under excavation further upstream at Jerf el Ahmar,[16] and further examples may possibly exist in the Aleppo region (e.g. Tell Qaramel) known from surface survey, and probably as far as southeast Anatolia, at the base of the prehistoric tell of Çayönü, on a tributary of the upper Tigris. It is probable that its distribution covered all the Syro-Turkish Jezirah between the Euphrates and the eastern Taurus mountains, but no systematic research has yet been conducted in this region.

Phase III at Mureybet lasted from around 9500 to 8700 BC, but no farming economy is evident, so far as one can see, until the second part of the period (phase IIIB), after 9000. Architecture continues to develop in the tradition of round houses inherited from the Khiamian period, but, in phase IIIA, they can be more spacious (6 m in diameter), semi-subterranean or constructed with walls of *pisé* on the

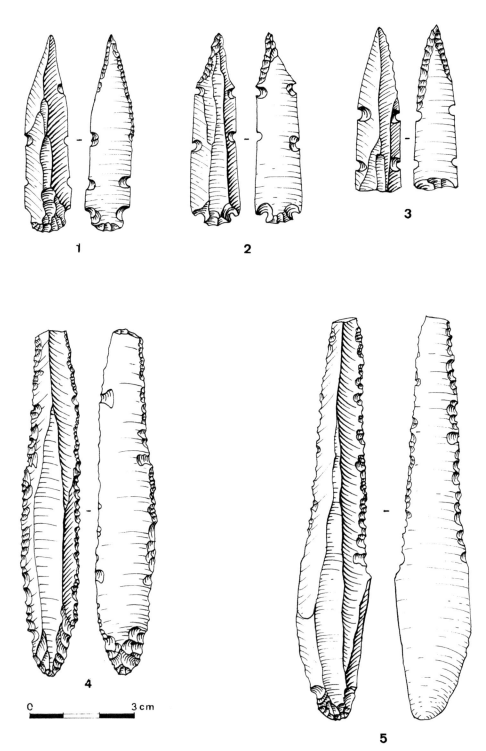

Fig. 14 Aswadian flint industry (Damascus region, Syria, ninth millennium BC): arrow-heads with multiple notches, called 'Aswad points' (1–3); sickle-blades (4–5). After M.-C. Cauvin.

surface. In contrast with the Sultanian and Aswadian houses, where the domestic space is not subdivided, the house of the Mureybetian facies is now strongly differentiated[17] (Fig. 15). In the best-preserved house, a raised sleeping area occupies the whole of the far end, opposite the entrance, while in the front part, to right and left of a central corridor, low internal walls divide the space into small rectangular cells. One of these contains a hearth while others, too small to serve as living space, must have been storage facilities for foodstuffs. Storage constructions were found in the form of charred wood in the corridor, associated with a remarkable concentration of flint and bone tools, often absolutely new and apparently not yet used, plus a wooden vessel. A flat mud roof covered the whole building. It rested on jointed joists, themselves borne on beams radiating towards the sides from a major lintel situated at the end of the corridor area. These houses were already quite sophisticated in themselves, and could be agglutinated and made partly contiguous with one another. Besides these there were other, smaller round houses one of which produced traces of a painted fresco decoration with geometric black and perhaps also red chevrons on a white background,[18] the earliest dawning of an art that is integral to the architecture in the Levant. Between the houses, communal open spaces contain several large 'fire-pits'. These pits are of a type that is frequently encountered in the whole of the Near Eastern Neolithic.[19] They are cylindrical or basin-shaped, and are found packed full of pebbles. They may have functioned on the model of the Polynesian oven, where the pebbles store the heat of a fire lit on their surface, and then give off that heat over a long period. The fire-pits of Mureybet are generally surrounded with animal bones that are to a greater or lesser degree charred. Their utilisation for the communal cooking of meat seems reasonably probable.

The end of the Mureybetian (phase IIIB), both at Mureybet and at Sheikh Hassan, sees the beginning of an important change in the architectural domain whose symbolic significance we shall consider later. It is at this point that the first rectangular constructions known in the Near East, or in the world, appear. Built of lumps of soft chalk chipped into a cigar shape and bonded with mortar, these constructions are divided internally into little square cells which are often scarcely more than a metre square[20] (Fig. 16). Their probable function as silos at Mureybet follows from their cramped scale, while the round houses, now rather smaller (3 to 4 m in diameter) and not internally subdivided, coexist alongside them. These latter must have had the sole function of providing shelter for people, while the storing of foodstuffs was now organised outside the domestic quarters. As for Jerf el Ahmar, which is dated to the end of the tenth millennium and the beginning of the ninth, there is a probable correspondence to the earlier and later Mureybetian phases at Mureybet. For a start, outside a house that is semi-circular in plan and very similar to House XLVII at Mureybet, one can see another form of building transitional between a round structure and a building with rectilinear walls: these are rectangular houses with rounded corners, their walls constructed of chalk blocks chipped into cigar shapes.

The extent of the village at Mureybet is poorly known for Phase IIIA, but from

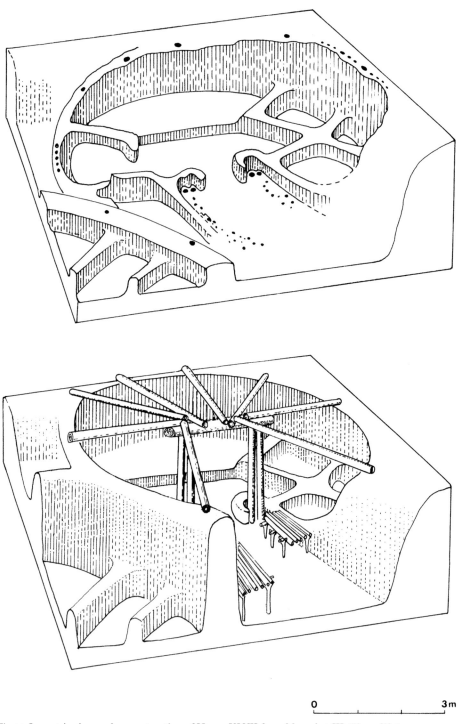

Fig.15 Isometric view and reconstruction of House XLVII from Mureybet III (Phase III A, Mureybetian, Syria).

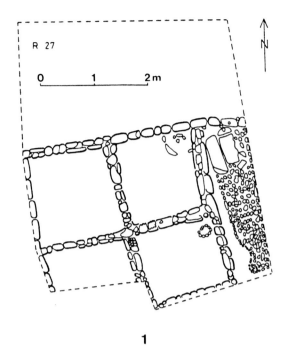

1

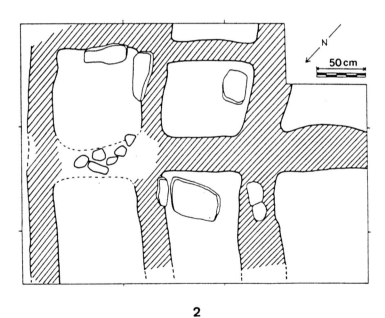

2

Fig. 16 The first rectangular structures on the middle Euphrates in the ninth millennium BC (silos?): 1 final Mureybetian phase at Mureybet, after M. van Loon; 2 final Mureybetian from Sheikh Hassan.

9000 BC we know that it covered more than 2 hectares, as at Jericho. The surface area of Jerf el Ahmar appears to be close to 1 hectare.

During the whole of Phase III at Mureybet the Mureybetian industry[21] forms a unified ensemble with quite typical elements. However, it does not stop evolving towards technical and aesthetic perfection. A fine new suite of weapons appears (Fig. 17), comprising both several flint or obsidian daggers and arrow-heads in greater numbers than before. Among the arrow-heads, the types with lateral notches progressively diminish in number in favour of leaf-shaped or tanged points rather earlier than is the case in the southern Levant and the Damascus oasis. Some of these latter prefigure the fine panoply of the eighth millennium, with their delicate manufacture by thin, flat retouch. Sickle blades, also growing in number, are long blades with narrowed base for hafting. However, there is also an important toolkit for working wood; besides some heavy adzes of local tradition, it now includes many scrapers. The flint scraper, the tool for all purposes since the Palaeolithic, now acquires a more specialised function that has been revealed by wear analysis. Often set in a sleeve like a hoe, it operated in the hands of the craftsman carpenter by means of a chopping blow.[22] The first polished axes made of greenstone also join these others in Phase IIIB. The bone industry for its part remains rich and varied. Finally, grinding equipment (querns and rubbers), until this stage not very prominent at Mureybet, now becomes abundant.

A third area of material culture is also witness to the technological advances of the Mureybetian. We have seen that baked clay was used from the first (in Phase IIIA) for the modelling of female figurines (Fig. 8). It is also used for very small receptacles, although we are still a millennium and a half ahead of the general use of pottery in the Near East (Fig. 18: 1–4).[23] We are not yet talking of pottery where these little vases are concerned: true pottery implies the effective addition of a mineral or vegetable tempering material to clay which helps to prevent bursting of the pot in the kiln. The problem is scarcely significant in these very small objects, which lack any temper. It follows that the action of fire in consolidating these modelled objects was well known and intentionally practised by the people of Mureybet from 9500 BC.

For the whole of Phase III only two burials were found within the area excavated at Mureybet. Both are secondary inhumations, which appear to involve only a single individual: a female skull and a group of long bones were buried very precisely under a small basin-shaped hearth in the interior of a house, while the rest of the same skeleton was interred outside the same house. The symbolic intention of domestic burial is quite self-evident. At Sheikh Hassan, as at Jericho, there are both primary burials and buried groups of skulls. In the domain of cult we have already noted the effective presence of the 'divine' duality of the Woman-and-Bull, introduced at Mureybet in the Khiamian period. However, not all the villages formulate this common symbolic system in the same manner. At Jerf el Ahmar, human representations remain rare, while a specific animal symbolism develops in the art, much more than at Mureybet, modelled in the round or engraved on stone, and associated with more abstract signs. The bull is present there (Fig. 19: 3b), but also a large raptor, quadrupeds (Fig. 19: 1a, 2a) and numerous snakes. A certain importance also

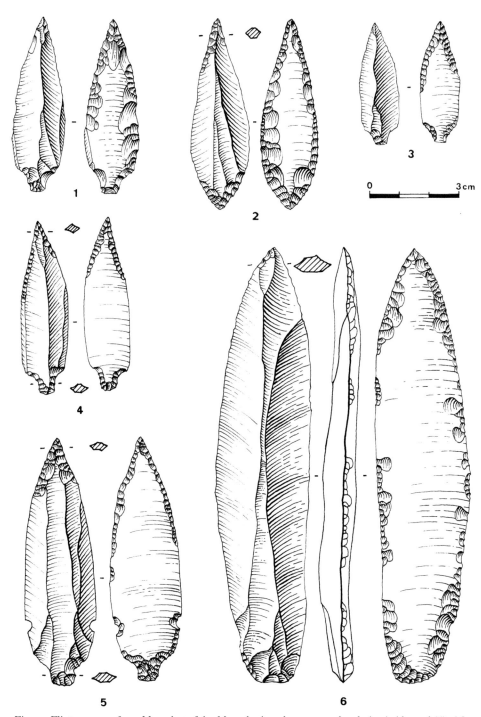

Fig. 17 Flint weapons from Mureybet of the Mureybetian phase: arrow-heads (1–5); 'dagger' (6). After M.-C. Cauvin.

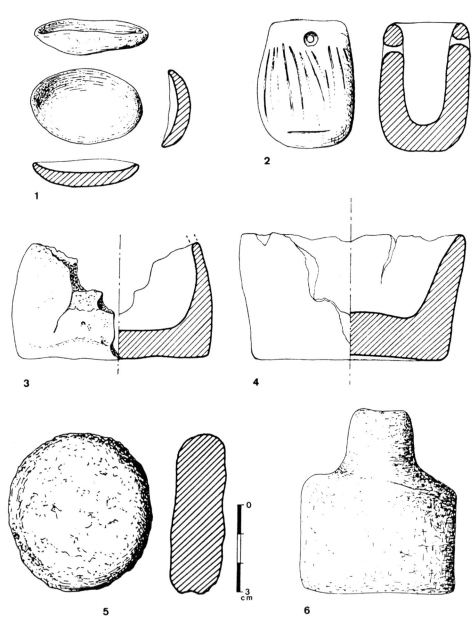

Fig. 18 Objects of lightly baked clay for Mureybetian date: small receptacles (1–4); disc (5); cylindrical object with 'handle' (pestle?) (6).

seems to be attributed to a nocturnal raptor, signalled only once at Mureybet where it exists in a quite strongly schematised representation on a little plaque (Fig. 19: 3a). Without going so far as recalling the owl of Athena, one thinks of the female statuettes of Tell Brak, much closer in time and space, in the Jezirah and dated to the Uruk period. Their form and immense eyes seem to play on the ambiguity between the goddess and the owl, the latter appearing from that time as the substitute for the former.[24] The exceptional and eloquent objects from Jerf el Ahmar, which are still

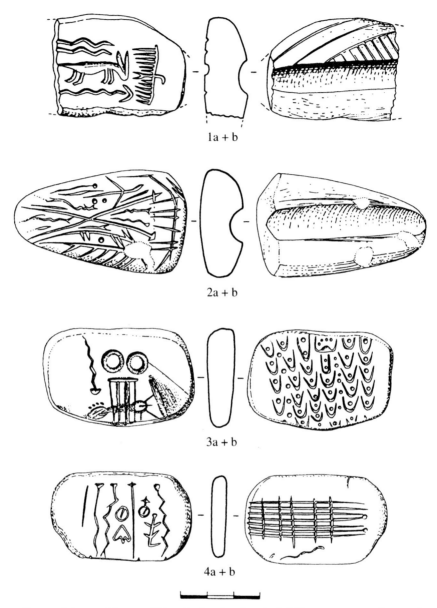

1a + b

2a + b

3a + b

4a + b

Fig. 19 Engraved signs and figures of Mureybetian date from Jerf el Ahmar: 1–2 grooved stones (1 raptor, horned quadruped, snake-like lines; 2 raptor (?), quadruped, snakes, etc.); 3–4 small double-sided plaques (3a small owl, large insect (ant?), serpent-shape; 3b field of pairs of horns surrounding a large, central pair of horns; 4a straight lines or snake-shapes, various other signs; 4b grid motif with snake). After D. Stordeur.

being studied, will lead us to important observations bearing as much on the religion of the Mureybetian period as on progress in graphical self-expression in prehistory, although we are chronologically only half-way between the first signs associated with Franco-Cantabrian animal art and the first writing of the urban period.

One cannot close this list of symbolic documents of the Mureybetian period without recalling the presence of artefacts which, without being completely removed from practical utility, bear witness to a particular enhanced value that goes beyond their role as artefacts by means of the aesthetic investment which is their main purpose. We cannot but be aware of the strong contrast that exists between the Mureybetian and the Sultanian of Palestine from the point of view of the quality of the finishing of their respective weapons, whereas they both ate the same hunted species. The armaments of the Mureybetian enjoyed a different prestige. We shall return to this subject when referring to the remarkable weapons of the PPNB culture which is derived from the Mureybetian. Here it is primarily a question of grooved stones and polished batons.

The grooved stone, a small portable object with a very extensive distribution in the Neolithic of the Near East, North Africa and beyond, has been interpreted by Ralph Solecki[25] on the basis of ethnographic observations as a tool for straightening arrow-shafts. It appears in the Levant in the Natufian, which seems natural if it is true that Natufian hunters already knew the bow.[26] Unlike the Natufian grooved stones, those of Mureybet (Fig. 20: 2–3, 6) are all, from the Khiamian period onwards, carefully decorated with linear motifs, often chevrons.[27] On the other hand, anomalies can be noted with regard to their supposed function, specifically, grooves of different depths and profiles, sometimes too narrow for their supposed use; one example in very soft chalk, without doubt a much too fragile material, where the chevrons are delicately cut in *champlevé* technique (Fig. 20: 6); and above all one example in a polished and decorated siliceous rock, which is manifestly broken (deliberately divided?) then repolished on the fracture, and thus, though still 'precious' in this final state, unable to serve because the groove would be too short (Fig. 20: 2). These objects will later become, as we shall see, indicators of Neolithic diffusion into Anatolia (Fig. 20: 5). The present author believes that it is already possible to attribute to them a symbolic (feminine?) value at least as important as their function as tools.

The batons of polished stone, common throughout the Mureybetian, exhibit a flagrant disproportion between the considerable time required for their manufacture and their debatable 'utility'. Their cross-section is often very specific (Fig. 20: 1) and inclines by contrast to their being recognised almost certainly as phallic symbols. As on the majority of Neolithic sites in the Levant, in addition to the grooved stones and the polished batons, there are at Mureybet a number of incised pebbles with various forms of decoration ('solar' motifs, incised pendants, etc.), which, like the personal ornaments and certain decorated plaques, obviously relate to the universe of 'signs', in the same category as the geometric signs of the caves of Périgord. Lacking a systematic and large-scale study, we cannot yet grasp coherently the subject of their discourse. This area of study evidently supposes other approaches beyond the merely technical.

Conclusion

These then are the three cultural groups in the Levant – the Sultanian, the Aswadian and the Mureybetian – among whom appeared the first signs of an agricultural economy, the nature of which we shall analyse in the following chapter. Here we have

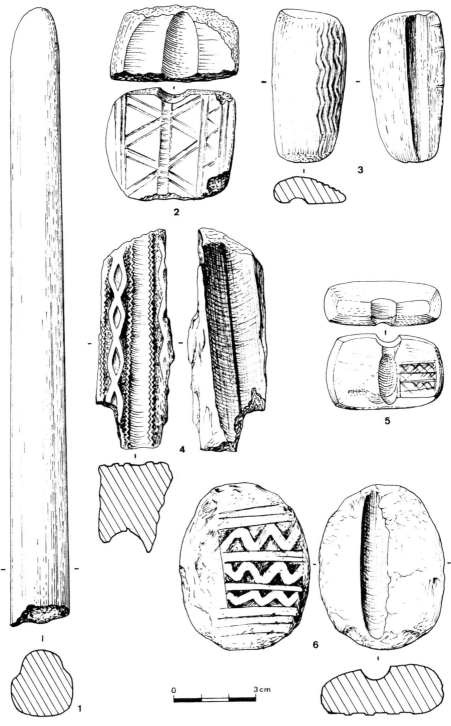

Fig. 20 Symbolic objects made in stone in the tradition of the middle Euphrates: polished baton (1 Mureybet III); decorated grooved stones (2, 3, 6 Mureybet III; 4 Sheikh Hassan; 5 Cafer Höyük PPNB).

seen the essential details concerning architecture, technology and ritual so far as they can be defined. These observations remain somewhat disparate. For simple economic reasons, excavations are concerned almost always with only a very restricted sector of any site. The chance discovery of finds, the conditions of their preservation, sometimes also the excavations methods used, all permit the better documentation of this or that sector of human life, but leave others in deep shadow. It must be chance that Kenyon found the tower at Jericho, as it was chance that we discovered at Mureybet a burnt house which retained the carbonised remains of pieces of carpentry and wooden vessels. The presence of certain traits on one site does not necessarily mean that their absence elsewhere is significant. Appraisal of the available information at least allows us to affirm that the first farming communities in the Levant emerged in the context of a cultural and social blossoming. Better than the Sultanian of Jericho, whose first phase remains poorly known, the example of Mureybet shows us that the agricultural economy was established not quite at the beginning but during the course of the cultural process of the Mureybetian, as if, in a certain way, farming grew out of it. A second trait common to the two cultural groups is that the second phase of the Sultanian and of the Mureybetian bears witness to a demographic explosion at the local level. It is demonstrated by the steep rise in the area of these two settlements. Thus one can see a correlation between the new economy, the growth in the size of villages and the more numerous population that this extension implies. But we have seen that this demographic phenomenon remains local: it is in no way part of a rise in population at the scale of the whole Levant, nor even of one of its sub-regions. We shall need to enquire further about the exact nature of this correlation.

5

The first farmers: strategies of subsistence

The agricultural economy found at the heart of the three cultural groups described, the Sultanian, the Aswadian and the Mureybetian, is not necessarily characteristic of all the sites which belong to these groups. The case of the village of Hatoula, situated in the Judaean hills, would be an example of a hunter-gatherer economy that continues into the full Sultanian period.[1] It is therefore not necessary to be Sultanian in order to subsist by agriculture. Our information on the first farming communities of the beginnings of the ninth millennium at present concerns only a precise and limited geographical zone. This is the fertile lands of the alluvial 'Levantine corridor', which reaches from the Jordan valley, past the lakes of the Damascus oasis to the middle Euphrates, and lies between the mountains and the semi-arid steppe. It is probable that the northern part of this corridor was in fact much more extensive and included part of south-east Anatolia, a region that is still poorly documented.

The archaeobotanical information recovered for the previous periods (Natufian and Khiamian) has shown that, as much on the Euphrates as in the hills bordering the Jordan valley, wild cereals were well represented among the indigenous vegetation. By contrast, they may have been lacking in the lower Jordan valley and in the Damascus oasis, where the site of Tell Aswad is situated, at the outer limit of their natural habitat zone. Wild cereals are known in the neighbouring Anti-Lebanon, but they seem to stretch less than 50 km to the west of Aswad. The farming settlements of the Aswadian and Sultanian will thus be found close to the natural habitat of wheat and barley (Fig. 1), but not firmly within it.[2]

Wild and domesticated species
How does evidence of agriculture show itself for prehistorians to see? As we have seen, the simple presence of tools such as sickles, querns and mortars is insufficient. Irrefutable proof resides, by contrast, in the 'domesticated species' among the carbonised plant remains recovered by modern excavation techniques. When species that have been native to an area are brought into cultivation, whether cereals or leguminous plants, morphological transformations that amount to the emergence of new species brought about by human intervention follow more or less rapidly in consequence. We shall see that various factors may have intervened to accelerate or retard these changes; and we shall consider if there could have been an intermediate state, called 'pre-domestic agriculture' (Gordon Hillman), where cultivation was practised but without perceptible results at the level of the morphology of the plants concerned. In this situation agriculture is difficult to identify, whereas its presence is of

fundamental interest to the prehistorian concerned to capture this change at its source in order to understand what caused it.

Every wild plant naturally has genetic characteristics that favour the dispersal of the seeds at maturity and their spontaneous self-sowing. Thus, for the cereals, which are plants where the seeds form in ears, the axis of the ear (or rachis), which holds the parts of the ear together, breaks up when the ear is ripe and divides itself spontaneously along natural articulations called 'nodes' or the 'abscission layer' (Fig. 21). By contrast, 'domesticated' wheat and barley earn their name because the nodes, like a human joint that is afflicted with arthritis, have become tough and rigid, even when the ear is dry. The crop in effect waits for the farmer to harvest it, but even then a vigorous beating is necessary to separate the parts of the ear from the straw. It is evident that the internodes, in this case violently damaged by threshing, do not have anything like the same appearance in section as a wild rachis which has broken of its own accord by the simple act of the retraction of the abscission layer. It is this difference that the botanist perceives when the carbonised plant remains pass under the microscope.

This characteristic of the toughness of the rachis arises quite spontaneously and randomly through mutations within the wild population, but those few plants with the mutation are practically unable to perpetuate themselves, precisely because of the handicap that this new characteristic represents for their spontaneous reproduction. On the other hand, when man gathers wild cereals for food, he will automatically tend, if he waits until they are ripe, to give a preferential advantage to these mutant forms for the very simple reason that their grains are still adhering to the ear, while the others are already falling to the ground. There is therefore an unconscious role for humans in natural selection for this 'domesticated' characteristic.[3] If he then sows from what he has harvested, this is the characteristic which from that moment will begin to dominate in his field, and in short order, as sowing is succeeded by harvest, we shall have a domesticated species in which the rachis will always be tough.

This theoretical schema for the domestication of cereals appears to imply that the process will be rapid. For a long time it was thought that a few generations of plants, that is at the most a few decades, would have been enough to effect the leap from one species to another, as soon as man began to plant them. That is why botanists have long considered the transformation of the rachis as the criterion both necessary and sufficient for detecting and dating the beginnings of the cultivation of cereals. Other changes, like the tendency of cultivated cereals and also the legumes to increase the size of their seeds, are slower and less progressive. These criteria are therefore rarely critical in the initial period which concerns us here.

The information first recovered at Mureybet and then at Netiv Hagdud has required us to rethink this schema somewhat in recent years, a schema inseparable from a particular model of harvesting which we shall see is not the only possible form. We shall begin here by describing the results from Tell Aswad which, in a traditional perspective, have seemed to pose the least problems for researchers.

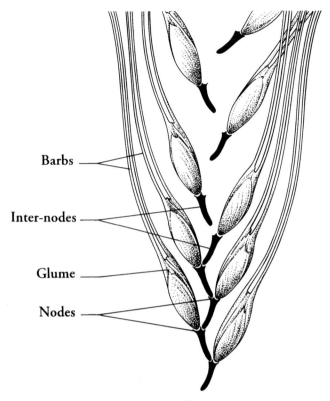

Barbs

Inter-nodes

Glume

Nodes

Fig. 21 Diagrammatic drawing of an ear of wild wheat.

The earliest cultivation in the oasis of Damascus

The oasis of Damascus itself, or 'Ghouta' as it is called in Syria, results from the utilisation of a mountain stream for the irrigation of the steppe on the eastern margin of the Anti-Lebanon, the Barada. The stream itself is totally exhausted by a prolific and complex network of canals that irrigate the cultivated fields. In this artificial form, the oasis is recent and scarcely goes back beyond modern times. In the Pleistocene period, the river still flowed out into a very extensive lake situated a little to the east of today's oasis. The level of this lake was constantly reducing, ending finally in the Holocene period in two small lakes. Around 9000 BC one of them, the lake of Ateibe, was fringed with marshes which provided the reeds used in the buildings of the Neolithic village of Aswad, which was built on its margin. Although the rainfall regime (today only 200 mm per annum) is theoretically too little for dry farming and, as we have seen, would not have permitted the spontaneous sprouting of wild cereals, the sedimentary soils, constituted by the lacustrine marls left behind by the retreat of the lake, and the alluvial clays brought by the Barada, moistened in addition by the proximity of the marshes, would have been very favourable to cultivation. The inhabitants of Aswad were the first to occupy this location. They arrived, perhaps from the neighbouring Anti-Lebanon, already equipped with seed for planting, for their practice of agriculture from the inception of the settlement is not in doubt.[4] Thus it was not in the oasis itself that they carried out their first experiments in farming.

According to Van Zeist, domesticated emmer wheat *(Triticum dicoccum)* is well attested among the floral remains at Aswad from the beginning, but there is no wild wheat. Barley is also represented, but the first case of 'tough rachis' of the domesticated type *(Hordeum distichum)* does not appear before the phase called IB, around 8300 BC. In the Aswadian period proper (Phase IA), the barley still exhibits a wild morphology *(Hordeum spontaneum)*. However, botanists admit that this barley may already have been cultivated in this form,[5] which supposes a long retardation in morphological transformation since its first cultivation. The legumes, peas and lentils, according to the botanists, were also very probably cultivated in spite of the absence of definitive traits of domestication, since their wild ancestors are not found in the oasis. Finally, to supplement their diet, some wild fruits, terebinth, capers and figs, were collected; meat resources were obtained only through hunting, and there is absolutely no question of animal domestication at this period.

We may therefore note that at Tell Aswad the presence of domesticated wheat has been inferred by Van Zeist from its morphological characteristics, and this has allowed the archaeobotanists to infer the beginning of cultivation generalised throughout a whole series of other species for which no particular critical characteristic is available, but which do not appear to be within their natural habitat in this particular biotope.[6]

The lower Jordan valley

When Jericho was being excavated, modern methods of flotation for the systematic recovery of plant macro-remains were not yet in use. This deprives us of irreplaceable information on the economy of the village. However, the excavators did miraculously chance to recover, through random sieving of a very few samples, four cereal grains, which are all of a domesticated morphology, emmer *(Triticum dicoccum)* and two-row barley *(Hordeum distichum)*.[7] That seemed sufficient to establish agriculture as a reality. Scarce examples of domesticated lentils *(Lens culinaris)* and chick-peas were also found; these latter were without a doubt cultivated too, for they did not grow naturally around Jericho.[8] It is impossible to be precise as to whether this cultivation is characteristic of the whole Sultanian period and exactly when within this period it may have first appeared.

Our principal documentation for the lower Jordan valley comes from another site which was also founded around 9000 BC, Netiv Hagdud. It is less prestigious than Jericho but has been more recently excavated. The information on agriculture is, alas, ambiguous. Remains of barley are abundant, but no more than 10% of the rachis are of the tough variety, that is 'domesticated',[9] the others remaining of the wild type. Three interpretations are possible, all with the same result. The first, envisaged by the botanist Mordechai Kislev, reverts to considering this weak percentage as insignificant. The second consists of saying that these villagers practised agriculture to a small extent but at the same time continued to harvest most of their barley in its natural environment. We might find it surprising that, knowing the prin-

ciples of this species' reproduction, people should have preferred going quite a distance into the surrounding hill country to gather their basic provisions in the wild
rather than practising cultivation where they lived. The third explanation, proposed
by Daniel Zohary, is to see here the process of domestication at its earliest stages,
with the morphological modifications in progress but not yet generalised. In this
view, all of the barley, whether domesticated or not, would thus have been cultivated.
In this account it is the speed with which the modifications were effected that
becomes the issue, since the Sultanian of Netiv Hagdud lasted for several centuries.
In any case, the sickles, querns and clay-built storage facilities which are abundant
on this site take on a real significance for indicating agriculture. But there is not yet
agreement among the botanists on the status of the cereals of Netiv Hagdud.

The middle Euphrates: economic evolution at Mureybet

Another example of early agriculture, also much debated, is that of Mureybet (Phase
IIIB). Here no evidence in favour of domestication can be found in the morphology
of the grains. Rather, thanks to palynological studies and experimental work, an
important bundle of cultural, economic, ecological and even directly botanical
assumptions have come together to confirm the presence of agriculture. Thus from
this apparent contradiction has come a fruitful methodological breakthrough and
some ideas on who were the first cultivators whom we have too often tended to
imagine on the model of ourselves.

First we should recall that Mureybet is distinguished from Aswad or from Netiv
Hagdud in that we have a case for believing that occupation was continuous from
the late Natufian. The Mureybetian is the cultural result of an *in situ* transformation
of Natufian and Khiamian hunter-gatherers (see chapter 4), while the Aswadian and
the Sultanians, equally culturally descended from the Khiamian, were new arrivals
at Aswad and Netiv Hagdud. Thus at present it is only at Mureybet that we can
observe, without having to leave the one settlement of the one surrounding country-
side, not only a continuous cultural evolution but also a no less progressive evolution from gathering to cultivation in the strategies of subsistence.

Installed on the very banks of the Euphrates, within reach of the gallery forest of
poplars and tamarisks which fringed the river and equally the steppe forest with scattered oaks and terebinth *(Pistacia)* that extended all around, the Natufians and then
the Khiamians for a long time held on to a very diversified hunting and gathering
strategy. Gazelles and equids of the steppe, and also some wild cattle, fallow deer
and wild boar from the riverine forest, plus many migratory water-fowl whose
passage was awaited, all were there for the taking, with a very important complement
being furnished by the river itself. These first villagers were very efficient fishermen:
fish and shell-fish represented an inexhaustible resource and it was fully exploited.
As far as vegetable protein is concerned, as we have seen, an intense crop of knot-
grass and astragalus was available to them, plus a very little einkorn wheat and wild
barley which could be harvested to complement this regime.

It is this combination of nutritional strategies that we see radically transformed
in the course of Mureybet Phase III. The new agriculture is only one particular

example of a very general change; in order to understand it, it would therefore make sense not to separate it from its context.

The first indication in favour of this new view of the beginning of cultivation comes from palynology,[10] which is believed to indicate the state of the floral environment through time. Pollen grains 'of cereal type' were present but very rare in the Natufian and the Khiamian, which appears to confirm the quite meagre crop of remains of these plants that were revealed by the study of the seeds. Only a little was gathered because there was only a little there. An abrupt augmentation of these pollens occurs around 9000 BC, during Phase III. Cereal pollen grains are relatively heavy, and, whatever the strength of the wind, they never fall far from the plant of origin. If their proportion abruptly increases at this site, it is because the plants themselves have been made to proliferate nearby, and such a localised proliferation can only be artificial.[11] This observation appears to support the argument for 'proto-agriculture', defined as human intervention 'favouring the development of wild species'.[12]

The study of carbonised seeds,[13] however, does not seem to have confirmed this diagnostic. Like the pollen, the seeds of cereals, barley and especially einkorn wheat *(Triticum boeoticum)* increase very greatly in number during the Mureybetian and this parallelism is in itself striking, but their morphology does nothing to indicate their domestication.[14] Moreover the botanists have not demonstrated for this period an appropriate expansion of the remains of unwanted weeds, which are usually associated with cultivated plants because they can take advantage of the working of the soil. For them the pollen grains 'of cereal type' are not considered a fully sufficient proof. They are in fact rather untypical and it cannot be excluded that they have been confused with those of other grasses that are not edible.[15] A simple, intensified harvesting of wild einkorn and barley, if it were far from the village because these species were not abundant in nature in its vicinity, could thus, at this stage in the research, account for the augmentation in the consumption of these species without confirming their bringing into cultivation.

This ambiguity in the palaeobotanical facts makes it desirable to turn to different methods of research in order to try to make things clear. In particular, if one proposes the cultivation of cereals despite the absence of traits of domestication in their morphology, is there a test that would assess the significance of the proposal?

The prime strategy of research has been the study of the micro-traces of wear on flint tools using very high magnifications. This method has been applied to the subject by Patricia Anderson, who has examined the lustred blades ('sickle-blades') of Mureybet in order to investigate the precise origin of their lustre. The second strategy has been experiments in simulation of the cultivation of wild cereals that have been carried out since 1985 at Jalès, in the south of France, with seeds collected in the Near East. Both of these approaches have produced important results.[16]

In the Natufian and Khiamian (Phases I and II), lustred blades were rare at Mureybet. Micro-wear studies have shown that they were mostly used for cutting cane and reeds, and that their usage was thus associated rather more with the work of artisans than of food-producers.[17] Those of the Mureybetian on the other hand are for the most part reaping tools: they served for cutting cereals which were not dry but still green, just before their full ripeness.[18] Germination tests carried out in the laboratory have shown that seeds that were gathered green and then dried in the settlement retain their capacity to reproduce and could thus have served as seed-corn.

When one knows the fragility of the ripe ears, harvesting wild cereals a little before maturity is a matter which causes no surprise as a simple approach to obtaining the best results. Fallen grains being lost grains, why should the reaper wait until that stage before taking them? But something must change in the theoretical schema of domestication that was put forward above, and which has weighed so much on the minds of archaeobotanists. Unconscious selection by humans for a tough rachis, self-evident for a harvest undertaken at full ripeness, is much less significant if the reaping is done while the plants are not fully ripe, when the grains will not yet have begun to disperse. Unlike domesticated varieties, it is not unusual for wild cereals to show different stages of ripeness from ear to ear within the same stand. People harvesting these stands would therefore always extract a cross-section that would be little different from a complete 'population' in the genetic sense of the term. Among the ears that were most advanced in their ripening, and only among these, some mutant individuals with a tough rachis would continue to be advantaged in the harvest over other, more fragile examples, but this selection exercises a considerably mitigated pressure rather less in favour of the domestication of the species. In other words, one could sow barley or wheat, harvest and sow again, that is, conduct oneself as a genuine farmer, for a long time before any perceptible effect on the level of the morphology of the plant would become manifest. 'Pre-domestic' cultivation becomes a genuine and theoretically acceptable outcome.

However one must not imagine these first agricultural activities as exactly similar to those of a more advanced agriculture. The familiar image of the farmer leaning on his plough or his hoe and covering the seed in the turned furrows does not seem to correspond to the first agricultural period. The wild cereals, as perhaps the most primitive domesticated forms, grow as well, or often even better, after a simple sowing on the surface of the soil, if need be after the clearing of the most bulky natural vegetation by burning or tearing it out. Finally, the last accepted idea that we must discard, annual sowing which is for us the requirement for the renewal of a field, seems superfluous in the 'pre-domestic' form of agriculture. When we take account of the variability of the times of ripening among wild plants and the inevitable 'loss' of grains from among the most ripe of them, even when the majority is harvested green, it follows that spontaneous reseeding by fallen grains would generally be sufficient to cause the stand of cereals to grow as densely as before in the following year. Thus deliberate sowing is needed only when one wishes to change the location of a field, or in the framework of a primitive practice of fallow, which is as good as saying that sowing of seeds must have been very intermittent. Neither does spontaneous regrowth exercise any evolutionary pressure in favour of selection for the domestication muta-tions, which further retards the process of domestication. Such are the important con-clusions of the experiments by Patricia Anderson and George Willcox at Jalès.

As far as methodology is concerned, it follows from these results that the morphological study of plant macro-fossils found on excavation can of itself prove the cultivation of cereals only inasmuch as morphologically domesticated species have already emerged. Cultivation cannot therefore be excluded in terms of the absence of morphological change. If there is therefore no direct proof of the beginnings of cultivation, on the other hand there can be circumstantial evidence[19] in its favour, resulting from the convergent facts of context, whether ecological, technical or cultural, which multidisciplinary research alone can at present bring to the fore.

We have thus seen that for Aswad, a site where the presence of agriculture is scarcely contested, it is the apparent domestication of a single species, emmer wheat, and the probable absence of local wild stock for three other species, that permits us without specific morphological proof to consider these latter as cultivated. At Mureybet the evidence is above all economic. In effect, in the Mureybetian period, it is the end of the subtle and eclectic economy of predation, where the species eaten more or less reflect the range of animal and vegetable species living around the village. This eclecticism was indispensable for assuring a regular food supply for sedentary hunter-gatherers who were not involved in production. By contrast, fishing in the Mureybetian, until then an essential contribution, almost disappears, and hunters ignore small game in order to specialise increasingly in the more profitable large animals. They hunted an equid (wild ass or *hemionus*) and above all wild cattle, the aurochs *(Bos primigenius)*, a species that was scarcely used in the preceding phases. Among the plants that were eaten, knot grass and astragalus both declined in relation to the spectacular rise of cereals. As we have shown,[20] this was initially a phenomenon of choice, which, far from confirming the idea of some sort of drying up of edible wild species (would the Euphrates have ceased to support fish?), saw the relinquishing of certain species in favour of others, and in the eventual investment of an increase in elaborate technology for their acquisition and their treatment.

As we shall see, the development of weaponry, which involves both quantity and quality as well as the choice of larger pieces as arrow-heads, could be explained by other reasons than the perfecting of hunting methods. But it must be added that, besides an increase in bravery, more organised and effective techniques of stalking the aurochs allowed people to make that species more than an occasional prey. Equally, the increase in grinding equipment and sickle-blades, now also much more numerous, more intensively used and more often devoted to the harvesting of cereals according to the evidence of micro-wear, suggests an analogous specialisation that is confirmed by the development of silos and also, in the micro-fauna, by a striking rise in the numbers of small commensal rodents which take up voluntary residence in human settlements.[21] But why speak of agriculture and not of a simple, specialised gathering of cereals, as the hunt had become at the same time with regard to the larger herbivores?

It is at this point that a third source of information comes in to reinforce our view, this time evidence of an ecological kind. The new hunting of aurochs does not indicate that their herds were frequenting the woodlands of the river valley in greater numbers than before. In the same way, the end of fishing is not a function of a harsh reduction in the populations of fish. All this is a matter of human choice, in a natural environment which we believe did not change significantly. On the other hand, wild cereals seem never to have been naturally abundant around Mureybet. Pollen and seeds were in accord in confirming this in the preceding phases. Even if the climatic amelioration of Phase III had augmented their natural presence a little, they could be given a central role in the food supply only on condition that people had intervened in their multiplication. That is why it is highly probable that an economy of production had been in progress in the Mureybetian period.

Thus there is a convergence of a great number of indications furnished by complementary archaeological disciplines, indications of which none on its own could prove anything; this convergence has allowed us to propose the presence of an important form of cultivation at Mureybet. As it is a matter of a form of agriculture without domestication in this case, we cannot depend on a single distinction in the morphology of the plant, which only becomes critical at a later stage. Finally, in 1990 this methodological step forward found confirmation in a quite unexpected fashion, when a batch of seeds from Mureybet III, already identified at Groningen as wild einkorn wheat, were submitted to a very novel method of determination using infrared spectrometry at the Institute of Archaeology in London. This analysis permits the differentiation of species and often of sub-species of cereals thanks to differences probably tied up with their respective lipid contents. In this sample there appeared, in addition to the expected einkorn, several grains of rye *(Secale cereale)* which were otherwise not identifiable, so close is the morphology of rye to that of einkorn, especially when carbonisation has obliterated the slight differential details.[22] We do not have an absolute botanical proof of cultivation here, for among the wild species of rye, only the form *Secale cereale vavilovi* is domesticable, becoming a domesticated plant under the name *Secale cereale cereale*. The relevant spectrographic analysis does not yet allow the distinction of these two forms of *Secale cereale*, which is to say that we cannot differentiate their status, wild from domesticated. However, recent botanical surveys in eastern Turkey[23] have shown that, quite differently from wild einkorn with its considerable faculty of adaptability which had allowed it to reach down to the latitude of Mureybet 12,000 years ago, *Secale cereale vavilovi* would have been much more particular in the matter of soil (it requires acid and volcanic soils) and altitude (it grows at more than 1,000 m). These characteristics do not at all correspond to the calcareous environment of the middle Euphrates. We have here a quite strong presumption in favour of *Secale cereale cereale*, that is to say, an argument for the bringing into cultivation of rye at Mureybet, using seed that could have been brought, for example, from Anatolia at the same time as obsidian.

We have seen that archaeobotany is, like archaeology, a developing science that is susceptible to modifying its views with time.[24] These most recent results not only confirm agricultural practice at Mureybet but also add rye, which it was thought was completely absent from this region, to the list of cultivated species for the Levant.[25]

Summary

From the study of the morphology of the seeds alone, it has seemed possible to conclude that, at the dawn of the ninth millennium, cultivation of wheat was already known in the Damascus region, and that of wheat and barley at Jericho. On the other hand it was difficult to accommodate the idea of a genuine 'farming economy' where exploitation was extended to the whole of a supplementary list of cultivated plants that were not necessarily 'domesticated' but which needed nothing to be done, except for human intervention in the form of gathering, in the particular ecological contexts where they were found.

To speak of a 'farming economy' implies that food-producing practices were already playing a major role in the survival system of the human population. That is an expression of the quantitative importance of the cultivated species that are archaeologically perceptible, whether or not they are domesticated. In other words, they were certainly not at the beginning of their farming experience. It is a matter of farming communities having completely crossed the threshold of economic neolithisation. If the progressive emergence of this new status is perceived neither in the Damascus oasis nor in the Jordan valley, that is because the occupants of those soils, as we saw, were newly arrived there. It has already been remarked[26] that the Natufian and Khiamian hunter-gatherers chose to plant their villages on the hills that dominate the valley, while their Sultanian successors descended into the alluvial plain. The first sporadic and limited bringing into cultivation of plants, which would have had little impact on the economy of these groups, could have taken place on very diverse terrains but necessarily in direct contact with cultivated wild species. Those, the cereals in particular, because of the low rainfall grow there naturally today only at altitudes significantly higher than the low-lying soils of the area around Damascus and the corridor of the Jordan valley. On the other hand, the promotion of these species to the rank of basic resources in an economy of production would also suppose the choice of the most propitious terrain for their artificial development. The deep soils of the alluvial plains would have been preferred to those of the neighbouring landscape, which was full of slopes and poor in humus. Thus, from the beginning of the farming economy, the choice of new resources entrained a no less evident choice of new habitats, with the exclusion of the cases, like Mureybet, where this favourable choice of settlement location was found to have been inherited from the pre-existing hunter-gatherers.

These geographical shifts of village communities, though the distances may have been short, could only have been motivated by the adoption of agriculture. In order to appreciate the quality of the soil, it is necessary to be a cultivator. This is as much as to say that at Aswad and Netiv Hagdud we are witnessing the 'invention' of agriculture. As with every act of creation and as with every genuine beginning, this invention is scarcely accessible to our present analytical tools. We see only the consequences, at a stage where the phenomenon, already well established, has substantially reshaped the mass of quantifiable information that we can get hold of.

It is still only a relatively short time since it was thought that the appearance of domesticated species at the beginning of the ninth millennium, still very irregular and sporadic, seemed both to define and to date this first emergence of farming practices, for their effect on the morphology of the plants was held to be almost immediate. Everything now suggests that these new species were the result of a secondary and much longer process, subject to the hazards of the techniques of sowing and reaping. They appeared against the older background of a farming economy that was 'pre-domestic', already established and economically efficient around 9000 BC, which was limited to a particular geographical zone, the 'Levantine corridor', and which itself implied a background of even earlier experience the first traces of which the archaeologist finds it difficult to locate. Even at Mureybet, where the transformation of the economy unrolled, so to speak, before our eyes, we can follow the stages in Phase III only in the form of a progressive amplification of the measurable changes. The human initiative which is at their source must have pre-existed and it is this that we must now try to define by analysing its causes.

6

Agriculture, population, society: an assessment

The transition to agriculture is not in its origins a response to a situation of penury: that has been the decisive contribution of the excavations at Mureybet. Up till now, however, prehistorians have scarcely been able to envisage any other explanation for this change than a disequilibrium in the food-supply between the human population and the wild resources. For Gordon Childe, the initial cause had to be climatic: the climate of the Near East having become more arid, not only people but also the domesticable plants and animals would have had to have taken refuge in zones that were spared the desiccation – oases and river valleys. Agriculture and herding would then have resulted from this necessary confinement within restricted and demographically saturated areas. Research has failed to confirm this climatic hypothesis. Then, in more recent models, it was population growth that became the unique key to the same biological disequilibrium and the new food-producing strategies that were devised to solve the problem. Thus, the 'marginal zone' theory[1] supposed a population surplus for the Levant among the first sedentary Natufian gatherers of cereals, and the expulsion of some of them towards the margins of the 'nuclear zone', where they would have invented agriculture in order to reconstitute the plant resources of their original habitat by artificial means.

We have seen that it requires a great deal to believe that all the Natufian villages would have had cereals as their basic food resource and in preference to others. The predatory strategies of survival of this period, flexible and versatile, could accommodate themselves to different environments, whether that might be in the interior or outside the zone of wild cereals. In the same way, the sedentism of the groups who were far from being the general rule was conditioned more by the global mass of the edible fauna and flora succeeding each other locally in the course of the year than by the precise nature of the exploitable species. More severe ecological conditions could have proved an obstacle to the installation of permanent villages, but they did not constitute a limiting factor in any way, either for the possibilities of survival of smaller and more mobile groups or for the extension of the Natufian culture to the arid zones.

Finally, at this stage in human evolution, a normal population growth would not seem to imply a sufficiently serious degree of competition for resources to justify the expulsion of a population surplus towards less clement areas. The distribution map of known villages in no way confirms this interpretation.

Not everything in the theory of marginal zones should be rejected, of course. Mureybet, which has absolutely no wild cereals in its neighbourhood nowadays, certainly had some at that time, demonstrating that the limit of the nuclear zone has gradually withdrawn to the north since the ninth millennium. Like Abu Hureyra, it must already have found itself at a latitude rather close to that of the absolute limit of the natural habitat of cereals. Mureybet therefore found itself at the periphery of the nuclear zone rather than at its heart. However, we know not to generalise this example throughout the northern Levant before we know the palaeoecological facts that are still lacking for all the Mureybetian sites located to date, whether further up the Euphrates, or to the west as far as the plain of Aleppo, or to the north-east as far as the upper Tigris basin.

On the other hand, in the central and southern Levant, the regions around Damascus and the lower Jordan valley were situated well outside the nuclear zone by reason of their lower altitude. The 'marginality' of these farming villages is confirmed in this case, but that does not make their agriculture a matter of invention. On the contrary these areas (see chapter 5) see a deliberate transfer of settlement sites to the most fertile soils in order to move to a genuine 'farming economy' a good deal earlier than we used to believe. In this perspective the supposed expulsion of superfluous gatherers becomes on the contrary the free choice of confirmed peasants. If it is found that for climatic reasons the wild cereals do not grow spontaneously in the Levant except in the hill country, then the alluvial plains would appear 'marginal' relative to the arc of the hill country, and the movement to the margins is evidence of a first short-distance migration of cultivators who had already undertaken experiments and were now interested in transforming their early efforts into a genuine economy of production. That is why Tell Aswad, Jericho and Netiv Hagdud do not give us any direct information on the 'origin' of agriculture.

Mureybet, a settlement that documents the transition, tells us more about three absolutely essential points: the absence of biological pressure in favour of new strategies, the social significance of local population growth, and the manifestly cultural origin of this new agriculture.

The absence of biological pressures
The transformation of subsistence strategies is total. It has been identified by both botanists and zoologists. Cultivation and specialised hunting developed in a context neither of impoverishment[2] nor of the exhaustion of the raw materials that were exploited up to that time, but through a new techno-economic device which concentrated on particular species chosen by man. What is astonishing is less the suite of plants and animals that provided the food resources than the list of those which were formerly used and are now virtually absent.

The nature of population growth
A correlation seems to exist between the increase in the surface area of settlements and in the population of Mureybet on the one hand, and the transformation of the food-producing strategy on the other. But we must not misunderstand the nature of this relationship,[3] nor must we install the old population–resources 'disequilibrium' at the village scale as the determining factor in the change. It is possible to imagine

that a purely local demographic pressure could have stimulated the population to revise their strategies in view of their productivity in the face of an increased demand for food. To kill a wild bull represents a much bigger yield of meat than the slaughter of a gazelle; the cultivation of cereals could be interpreted in the same way in a perspective of necessary increase in the food supply. This type of interpretation has evidently found favour till now with numerous researchers, inclined *a priori* to decipher all the elements of the past, even the most primitive, through the same rigid framework of economic interpretation. It has been shown through ethnographic documentation[4] that the numerical increase of an early human group is limited in general less by the capacity of its environment to provide food than by a quantitative threshold of a strictly sociological nature, whereby the social system ceases to function without a tension prejudicial to the cohesion of the group.

We have already seen (chapter 4) that what is suggested by the decrease in the number of settlements at the end of the tenth millennium, added to the sudden expansion of their surface areas, is a regrouping of sedentary populations as a social rather than a generally demographic factor. It is not simply coincidence that the extension of Jericho to an area of 2 hectares is accompanied by building activities of a new type: the communal architecture implies a co-operation in tasks with a collective purpose. The increase in the built-up area and in the population that occupied it seems to be inseparable from a new organisation of labour.

As at Mureybet, so also at Jericho, the agricultural economy implies a completely similar organisation of the activities of subsistence.[5] The contrast between the village of farmers and the village of hunter-gatherers has also been made clear by ethnographic research.[6] The dispersal of gathering activities and of the people who practise them over a territory that is at once extensive and diffuse, the small amount of energy the tasks require of them in a very limited working day, all this contrasts sharply with the spatial concentration as well as the collaborative labour required by work in the fields. This concentration is necessary at the time of sowing but even more at the time of harvest, since the effects of their cultivation serve gradually to harmonise the moment of ripeness of the plants of one species[7] and to cause the plants to hold their seeds for longer on the stem. Thus an organised mobilisation of labour for the harvest might be effected at a chosen time, as at present. Although there may not yet be any archaeological indication of an institutionalised social hierarchy (we have to wait until the fifth millennium for that), a change in the organisation of society whose exact nature it is still difficult to define is nevertheless required by the simple consideration of activities and their results.

This organisation being already an essential condition to make possible the cohabitation of a larger number of people, the increase in the population of the village could not in any way precede it, nor constitute in advance a biological pressure selecting for agriculture and other organised activities. Thus it is vain to search for a chronological sequence for these diverse phenomena. The new society must have experimented and installed its new structures throughout the transformations of its activities, whether they were concerned with food production or architecture. From that time on the farming economy seems a particular case of a more fundamental adaptation of human society to its own needs and to the tensions that run through it in the new modalities of a collective life. At this particular moment in our history, neither nature nor this or that social contradiction engendered by an increase in population could be looked upon as the determining factor in the Neolithic transformation, even if the food-producing efficiency of the new strategies was destined in time to favour biological expansion of the human population. The different factors continually impact on one another in an almost circular movement of reciprocal interactions, without anyone being able to identify exactly what set the wheel of change in motion at the end of the tenth millennium. For that we must go further back, which we shall now try to do.

The cultural origin of agriculture

From the point of view of simply natural requirements, the appearance of agriculture could seem to be an incongruity. Our overpopulated world certainly could not survive by hunting and gathering, but that was not the case 11,000 years ago. The rich landscapes of the Near East would have been able to accommodate the human population for a long time yet. The hunting and gathering way of life is elsewhere described as the 'economy of abundance' (Marshall Sahlins), where one can find not just an equilibrium between needs and resources, but even an excess of potential resources relative to basic needs. We should not imagine this equilibrium simply in quantifiable terms of the energy balance between the requirements of the human body in calories and the 'biomass' available in the environment and capable of furnishing them. We know perfectly well that, whatever the estimated food supply situation in this type of calculation, it is too easy to convince people that their needs are not satisfied and especially of their need to produce more, provided that their psychology can be sufficiently manipulated: today's advertising provides the evidence. Also from our own time, there is scarcely any common measure between the state of populations of the African Sahel, who suffer genuine biological malnutrition, and that of our own, sometimes critically disadvantaged, social strata, but where the experience of penury may be due as much to the contrast that is experienced between their way of life and what is defined as affluence by our own cultural consensus.

The importance of social norms of prosperity, where collective psychology is closely involved and which can vary in space and time for reasons which are not at all ecological, seems to be very much under-valued by current theories of the origins of agriculture. That a Natufian equilibrium existed in the Levant is incontestable, but we have searched in vain at the level of ecological and demographic estimates for what could have justified this break to the point of provoking as formidable a consequence as the production of subsistence. We must, then, admit that, beyond the number of gazelles and the number of hunters hunting them, there could be other reasons why the descendants of the Natufians might not have been satisfied with their ancestral system of survival, and these reasons may have been quite simply of a cultural nature.

Cultural readiness for the Neolithic Revolution is not a novel theme: Robert Braidwood, taking note of the delay of several millennia in the exploitation of cereals relative to the spontaneous emergence of their wild ancestors in the Near East, came to the conclusion that 'Culture was not ready.' Equally, this cultural preparation for agriculture has been attributed to the Natufian where sedentary village life and the technology of the future farmers was developed, but the new tools of the Natufian imply in no way that their usage was agricultural, but only that sedentism is an absolute precondition for agriculture, although cultivation will be seen to have been practised later in the context of semi-nomadism. This type of cultural development does not in fact reveal to us any dynamic impulse in favour of change. If they were not constrained, they must have 'wanted' to change. Such a wish could only come from the area of collective psychology, where our dissatisfactions emerge and transformations of culture which do not necessarily have economic reasons as their foundation are elaborated.

Our earlier analyses have led us to two conclusions: the first is that the economy of production, such as can be observed from 9000 BC, could only be explained by a process without detectable economic significance but necessarily situated earlier in time, namely, the agricultural 'initiative' as an inauguration of a new way of life for sedentary communities relative to their physical environment. We can locate that initiative only in the preceding period, somewhere in the course of the tenth millennium, that is, in the Khiamian or at the very beginning of the PPNA horizon. The second conclusion (chapter 3) is that this period was precisely the time when an ideological revolution occurred at the level of what Lévi-Strauss called the symbolic systems, a revolution which we have called the 'revolution of symbols'. The chronological order of these changes, a symbolic transformation preceding the agricultural economy, is a proven, stratigraphic fact. That is sufficient to dissuade us from making everything follow from a transformation in the infrastructure, as did Gordon Childe. What we are left with is the fact that the relationship that unites these two phenomena is not at first sight evident. We must now seek to shed light on that problem.

7

The Neolithic Revolution: a transformation of the mind

Our principal means of access to the collective psychology of ancient societies without writing remains their art, and the first change that we observed at the dawn of the Neolithic was concerned precisely with art. To pass from the art itself to the mental structures which it expressed is a difficult but pressing task. Recent developments in the historical disciplines should encourage us in this: we have moved on from the reductionist definition of creative acts of the human imagination as a secondary derivative of more concrete situations. On the contrary, as Jacques Le Goff has said: 'The imagination . . . is very often found at the root of historical motivations.'[1] It can of itself create the outcome and determine material facts. Georges Dumézil has familiarised us with the idea that the main social distinctions and the functions of governance among Indo-European societies reflected deeper mythic structures that were capable of directing and energising very diverse domains of social and cultural life. The idea of 'the feudal imagination', for example, has become established among historians, thanks to Georges Duby. In a more general way it is quite impossible to think of history as if the Annales school had not existed, or to be unaware of the scientific movement which over several decades has progressively challenged the positivist simplifications in the human sciences, drawing support from the study of collective representations. These derive from the same discourse with the image identified by psychoanalysis in the dream-life of the individual. This discourse, socialised and structured in the major symbolic systems which are at the root of social constructions, manifests itself clearly in religion and art.

What has that to do with prehistory? The prehistorians' 'materialism' arises from the fact that they most often have material facts to unravel and comment on. The 'technical thinking' of prehistoric people, that is the conceptual processes required for the fabrication and utilisation of their tools, has been made the object of intensive studies, especially in France, and correspondingly interest in their ideology and beliefs has remained summary. Archaeological information that would permit such an approach has for long remained very rare, indeed virtually non-existent. However, art had already existed before and during the Neolithic Revolution. Constrained by repeated refusals to search for the foundation of what is at the centre of the human agent himself, we should nevertheless not underestimate the importance of the first artistic documents to survive, nor refuse to push their analysis to the maximum.

The art of the hunter-gatherers
In the Levant, the art of the last Natufian hunter-gatherers has taught us little except that it was essentially zoomorphic. Franco-Cantabrian art in Western

Europe may be rather distant in space but immediately precedes Natufian art in time, since it came to an end around 12,000 BC, just as the Natufian commenced in the Near East. It is, however, much more expressive of what may have been the symbolic systems of the hunter-gatherers of the final Palaeolithic. Cave-wall art exists in addition to the portable art objects, where a profusion of animal images, long considered to be anarchic, in fact constitutes strictly composed unities.[2] Not only can the quantitative relationships of the species with one another be analysed with precision, but also the rules of their respective placing and their relationship with the geometric signs which accompany them. Thus André Leroi-Gourhan was able to show that this imagery was not at all a simple reflection of an empirical relationship with the animals they hunted: reindeer, the prey of choice for the Magdalenians, is represented very little, perhaps because of its excess of ordinariness, just as at Çatalhöyük and in the Near Eastern Neolithic in general after 7500 BC goats, sheep and pigs, the animals at that time domesticated and the basis of the meat component in the diet, were scarcely ever represented. To recapitulate Lévi-Strauss' expression, animals that are 'good to eat' are not necessarily 'good to think';[3] and it is with these systems of thought that we are concerned. The Palaeolithic system in particular expressed itself through a purely symbolic classification of the species into two complementary sets, one 'masculine' the other 'feminine', always arranged with reciprocal exclusiveness in the pictorial space. This basic partition into two, common to the whole of Franco-Cantabrian art, does not necessarily prevent a more differentiated or more 'tribal' usage of the animal symbolism, if it is true that Magdalenian groups or tribes could manifest more particular affinities with this or that species. In effect, species considered by André Leroi-Gourhan as interchangeable from the point of view of their common membership of a symbolic 'half' of the Universe, if one takes them one by one, appear reproduced to very variable degrees from one region to another, indeed from one cave sanctuary to another. This variability could refer to the distinction of territories occupied or used in transit by particular human groups. If the symbolic 'syntax' seems common to all, the 'vocabulary' is not, and its precise signification is anyway far from being clarified.

What matters to us here is not so much the particular numbers of images as that their spatial analysis suggests the form of hierarchical organisation that characterises Neolithic art. No animal personality is made prominent, as could easily have been done, dominating the others and capable of being taken as the figure of a supreme being. The animals of the Palaeolithic remain in general perceived and represented collectively. Even the most impressive of them, the mammoth, is shown at Rouffignac as a procession of mammoths and not as a 'Mammoth-god'. It is the same for those species that are most often represented, bison and wild horses.

In every human society, whether predatory or agropastoral, as Claude Lévi-Strauss has shown, the function of the symbolic is to render the world that surrounds us intelligible, and at the same time our place in that world. In particular there are ultimate situations which everyone encounters, such as suffering, death and the destructive anguish which these situations generate, to which every mythology must give a response in order to assure the internal equilibrium of societies, their psycho-affective cohesion and thereby their very survival.

The existence of such a system in the Upper Palaeolithic period seems evident but we lack the means of interpretation. We can hardly perceive how the Magdalenian hunter-gatherers, who could escape suffering and death no more than we ourselves can, mentally faced up to these, nor what 'wisdom' their mythic thinking had elaborated in response. In any case, in their underground sanctuaries which can only be places of initiation,[4] recourse to personified deities, albeit still in animal form, does not appear to play a part in the systems of explanation.

Can we object that hunter-gatherer societies with explicit divinities have indeed existed, since ethnographers of our own times have encountered them? The near-contemporary societies that they study unfortunately do not offer us any remedy. Even if they appear to be 'living fossils' (Jacques de Morgan) from the point of view of their economy, they may very often carry in their memory, whether in Africa or the Americas, something of the more or less conscious inheritance of societies that were much more evolved than them, even of the ancient states which once existed in the same geographical areas. We do not know at all well either the ideological effects of this inheritance or the conditions in which societies with a very primitive way of life can be ideologically contaminated by more elaborate neighbouring systems. We thus have no other solution when posing the problem of the origins of symbolic thinking in truly 'historical' terms than to turn to those documents which prehistory offers us, and which so rarely survive. This rarity of documentation must mean that the conclusions that derive from the following investigation will only deserve the value of a simple 'model'.

The divinity personified in the Neolithic

As opposed to the Franco-Cantabrian bestiary, the Woman and the Bull of the Neolithic appeared in the Levant as divinities whose emergence in the tenth millennium is followed by their diffusion throughout the ancient Near East. The Goddess, flanked by a male partner assimilated by the bull, will be the keystone of a whole religious system which is organised around her. The supreme beings will be able to change appearance in different regions of the world: the 'great Martian God' (Henri Lhote) of the Saharan area asserts itself as an enormous anthropomorphic silhouette, either female or asexual, dominating small human figures with their arms raised in the position of supplication (Fig. 22: 1), exactly like the 'spherical Ram'[5] of southern Oran with its similar entourage, the buffalo at Kef Mektouba (Fig. 22: 2) and many other examples.[6] The theme of the 'supplicant' introduces an entirely new relationship of subordination between god and man. These representations have in common that they all arise, in their respective areas, at the beginning of the Neolithic and then perpetuate themselves from that time on.

A significant development resulted, and it was of a psychological nature. We have characterised it[7] as a new distinction at the heart of the human imagination between an 'above' and a 'below', between an order of a divine force, personified and dominant, and that of an everyday humanity whose internal striving towards this perfect,

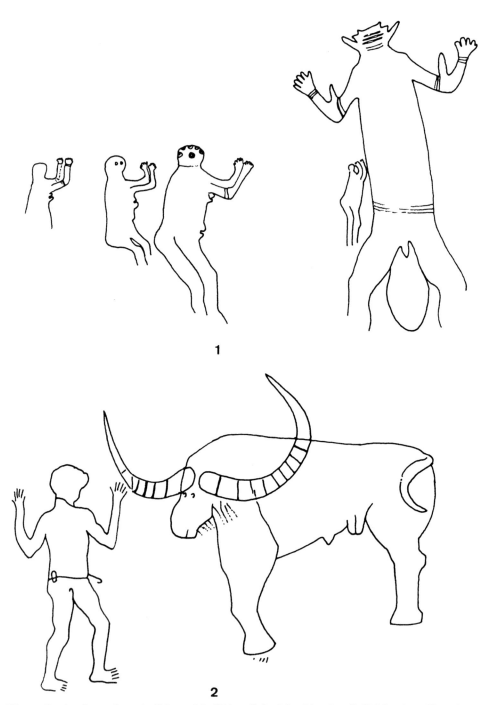

Fig. 22 Praying figures from the Saharan Neolithic: 1 Sefar (after Lhote); 2 Kef Mektouba at Kasr el Ahmar (after Frobenius).

transcendent being may be symbolised by the upraised arms of the supplicant. As universal Mother, the Goddess is well provided with explicitly 'royal' attributes, not least of which is her throne of Anatolian panthers. Travelling in imagination an inverse journey from that of the historical order, we can interpret it more readily as a throne when we think of the later thrones of the first oriental monarchies, pieces of furniture of course, but whose armrests will be sculpted in precisely the same form, with feline protomes. We know that at the time when the first states appear and when human society moves towards urbanisation and social stratification, the sovereign, both in Mesopotamia and in Egypt, will never be more than a representative of the divinity on earth and that he will therefore derive from the divinity the attributes that symbolise his function. It is thus significant that the very notion of sovereignty is first manifested in the artistic imagination of the Neolithic period, well before its social transposition which will cause it, so to speak, to come down to earth. It is still more important that the emergence of divine figures appears to have its introduction on the Euphrates as part of the process of neolithisation. That is not at all surprising since the literate, urban civilisations, which we too often see as the beginnings of History, were only continuing to intensify in a phase of rapid evolution a cycle of transformation that was inaugurated 12,000 years ago.

A dynamic drama
But how can we 'realise' the real relationship which could unite the revolution in symbolism with the production of subsistence materials which shortly followed it? May we attribute to this transformation in the structures of the imagination a dynamic sufficient to engender this series of changes? Or again, if we can be forgiven for resorting to a too summary linear causality, in what way were these changes another means of making manifest the transformation of imaginative constructs?

We shall see that from the Neolithic onwards suffering and death are well represented in the attributes of the oriental Goddess. These are lions or panthers, vultures and other animals that are dangerous for man, which form the immediate retinue of the Goddess and specify her powers to the exclusion of familiar and readily controlled species. The ambiguity of the symbol, where birth and death are joined, is readily decipherable for us who bear the 'terrible mother' in the deepest strata of our unconscious. As for divinity, however, the universal Mother-Goddess is seen on a transcendent plane where fears and conflicts are resolved, where the compliant panther becomes a seat, where the claw that tears and the raptor's beak are another, more hidden, aspect of the breast that nourishes, as if suffering from a certain point of view paradoxically irrigates human life. What is this discourse that is imposed by the power of its images, and that appears to be so close to that of the great historical religions that will follow? It is as if we were in some sort discovering their origin. And what new tension exists that man raises his arms towards heaven when invoking the divine being? He who 'prays' feels himself powerless and calls for help from above. A vertical topology is thus introduced in the very intimacy of the human mind, where the initial state of anguish can be transformed into a reassurance at the price of a truly experienced, uplifting mental effort in the form of an appeal to a divine authority external to man and elevated above him. This 'cult' is the other face of a misery that is experienced daily. The power of the god and human limitations are the two firm poles of this new drama which is established in the heart of man about 9500 BC.

We proposed above that there must have been other causes than simple malnutrition for the descendants of the Natufians to feel themselves dissatisfied with their traditional mode of life and to have wanted to modify it from top to bottom. What we can detect in the development of the imagination is the anthropological foundation of that dissatisfaction rather than its economic causes. The desire to change, the 'progress' which results and which will accelerate from this time on, everything that will characterise the later course of human history down to our own time, and which contrasts with the hundreds of millennia of previous slow evolution, can be traced back to this 'cultural revolution', where the idea that man can do things for himself brought into question his integration and role in nature and the cosmos.

This new chasm which was formed between god and man is dynamic in effect. It has no direct effect on the environment, but it must have completely modified the portrayal that the human spirit makes of itself, and, through some kind of release of the necessary energy to see them through, it must also have stimulated new initiatives, like the countervailing effect of an existential malaise never previously experienced. Till then spectators of the natural cycles of reproduction in the living world, Neolithic societies now took it on themselves to intervene as active producers. Technically speaking, this would have been possible well before, but neither the idea nor the desire ever came to them. It is precisely in this sense that Robert Braidwood's conclusion 'Culture was not ready' must be reinterpreted.

It is by no means irrelevant that the emergence of divinities took human form from the start. The Goddess is immediately depicted as a woman: this humanisation of art from the Khiamian period was the clearest and the most spectacular change noted. The supreme authority of that time, for all that it is distant in relation to man, is not totally alien to him. The fact that, through Her, humanity and nature emanate from a common source, since human infant and young animal are associated with her in Anatolia, can speak volumes on the novel metaphysical step of this period: not only is the Neolithic Goddess enrolled in the historical vanguard of the creationist theologies which follow, but in a certain manner man also recognises himself in all that surrounds him, since at the level of their symbolic genesis a personalised unifying principle reconciles empirical man and the natural world that he confronts.

Plate I
1 Natufian round house from Eynan-Mallaha, Israel.
2 and 3 House and sanctuary at Nevalı Çori, Turkey, PPNB.

4

5

Plate II
4 and 5 Polished stone vases of the PPNB at Cafer Höyük, Turkey.

6

7

Plate III
6 Limestone bas-relief with three human figures, PPNB, Nevalı Çori, Turkey.
7 An area at Khirokitia, Cyprus.

Plates IV and V
8–11 PPNB plaster statues from 'Ain Ghazal, Jordan.

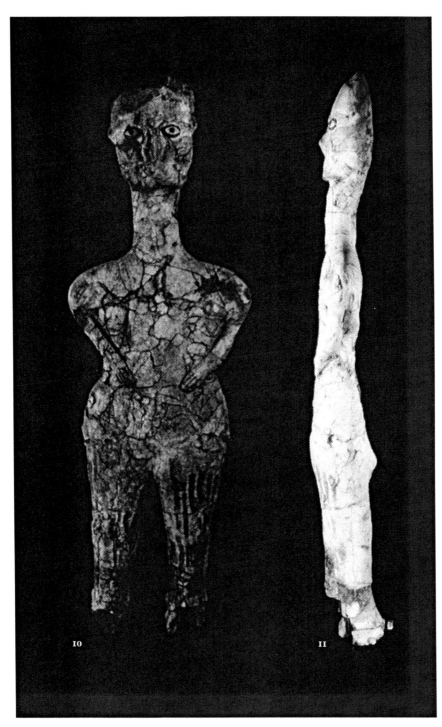

Plates IV and V
8–11.(*cont.*)

Plate VI
12 Skull with face modelled in plaster, PPNB, Jericho.

13

14

15

Plate VII
13 Skull coated with bitumen, PPNB, Nahal Hemar, Israel. 14 Stone mask from
Hebron. 15 Painted stone mask, PPNB, Nahal Hemar, Israel. Israel Museum,
Jerusalem. Photograph N. Slapak, with permission of O. Bar-Yosef. Rights reserved.

Plate VIII
16 Hare and hedgehog in polished stone, final PPNB, Bouqras, Syria.

PART II

The beginnings of the diffusion of the Neolithic

8

Geographical and chronological framework for the first stages of diffusion

In the revolution in symbols and the installation of a form of agriculture in the Levantine corridor, we have witnessed a process that establishes the foundations of our present humanity, but a process that is still very localised in space. At its beginning it does not even extend, as Gordon Childe and Robert Braidwood believed, throughout the hilly zones of the Middle East which were ecologically favourable for it.[1]

The first steps in the Neolithic, when neither herding nor the use of pottery had yet appeared, thus remains restricted to the Levant *sensu stricto*. When we then see the indications of subsistence production arising in the periphery of this zone of origin, with more or less marked chronological discrepancies in relation to that zone, it is *a priori* tempting to interpret them as the results of some sort of diffusion. However, the concept of diffusion cannot be a sufficient explanation if it is not simultaneously asked what cultural phenomena and what human behaviour lie beneath the term; failing that, not only in the Near East itself, but also across the whole of the Mediterranean and Europe, even Asia, all those regions that this process is supposed to have reached, the concept remains partly ineffective and the persistent scepticism on this subject is easily understood. It appears to us that these processes of diffusion were fully at work from the context of the ninth-millennium Levant, and that it is now possible to be precise concerning the modalities, sometimes even the motivations, that apply. Without wishing to treat here any of the longer-distance diffusions, the rehearsal of the evidence for the same phenomenon at the very point of departure of the process of neolithisation could help us to understand its significance in the more distant examples.

The phases of the PPNB
The PPNB (Pre-Pottery Neolithic B) owes its name, like the PPNA, to a phase in the stratigraphy of Jericho, where it was first defined. It is a culture that is strongly characterised by traits that remain constant and widely spread over the whole of the Levant and south-east Anatolia. While three distinct subcultures can be distinguished within the PPNA chronological horizon, here we find a real cultural unity for the whole of the Levant, whose principal significant traits concern techniques of chipping stone, stone tool typology and particularly the quantitative and aesthetic importance of weaponry, the extension almost everywhere of rectangular architecture, the subsistence economy, where herding appears and becomes general while cultivation becomes perfected, and finally a ritual practice known as the 'skull-cult'.

This aceramic culture lasts a long time. It begins around 8600 BC and its end is conventionally set around 7000 BC, when pottery comes into general use. For archaeologists pottery has a role of major importance since ceramic styles, which can be very diversified on a regional pattern, come to serve as the means of defining different cultures. The adoption of pottery, however, did not really have the importance that we have attributed to it: first, because the whole cultural context is not transformed at a single stroke as pottery comes into use, and second, because pottery on the one hand can appear at some sites from 7500 BC or just as easily on the other hand can show a long retardation until the last third of the sixth millennium (in the final PPNB of the desert zone).

A good deal more than a millennium is thus the long course of the PPNB's existence. It is usual to distinguish phases within this period, but all the regions of the Levant are not equally involved. The PPNB has its area of origin in one part of the Levant (Fig. 23) and then zones of progressive expansion all around that zone.

The early PPNB (8600–8200 BC) primarily concerns the parts of northern Syria previously occupied by the Mureybetian: it is from this last that the PPNB directly derives through an internal evolution. A first phase of expansion from here extends the Neolithic to south-east Anatolia.

The middle PPNB (8200–7500 BC) is the period of a second wave of cultural diffusion which still does not extend beyond the open forested steppe which in ecological terms defines the zone of dry farming. This new extension involves the southern Levant, while the multiple regional facies of the PPNB (in the middle Euphrates, the Taurus, the region around Damascus and Palestine) are distinguished as the general traits of the culture were superimposed on sites in particular different locales. This is the period when the herding of small ruminants began to appear in some sedentary village communities in the Levant.

Finally, the late PPNB (7500–7000 BC) displays a virtual explosion of the culture, and with it the expansion of neolithisation beyond the nuclear zone of the Levant which was the arena of its development. The Neolithic now extends as far as the temperate coastal zones of northern Syria that remained uninhabited during the PPNA, and the interior desert which had been almost abandoned by man after the Natufian (Fig. 45). Important economic changes, new forms of agriculture, the domestication of new species of animals and the appearance of nomadic pastoralism accompany this novel colonisation. From this point of view, the date of 7000 BC that has been assumed to mark the end of the PPNB[2] is of little significance, for the process of 'diaspora' extends without an evident break both before and after it. Our study will run further beyond the confines of the final PPNB in order to encompass the cultures with pottery which are its contemporaries during the first two-thirds of the sixth millennium BC (Fig. 50). The method to be followed will once again be to describe the information available, phase by phase, and then to attempt to weigh the diverse factors which are at the origin not only of the Near Eastern Neolithic revolution but also of its power of example and the worldwide future that awaits.

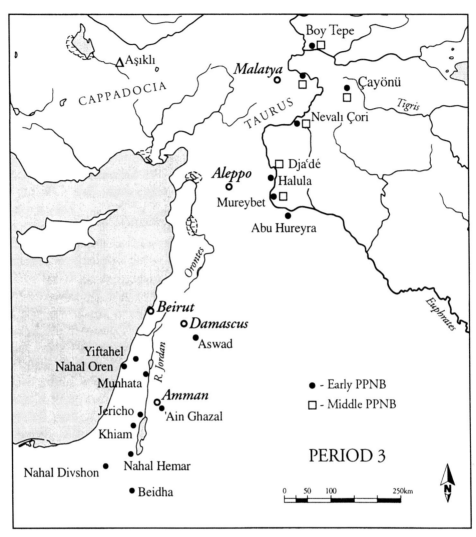

Fig. 23 Map of villages referred to in the text, belonging to the early and middle PPNB, 8700–7500 BC, 9600–8600 BP.

9

The birth of a culture in the northern Levant and the neolithisation of Anatolia

Before it was even known by this name, the PPNB was the first 'aceramic' Neolithic culture discovered in the Near East, and in the world. It was found in the 1930s in the southern Levant, thanks to the excavations of John Garstang at Jericho. This novel idea of a Neolithic without pottery, which is commonplace now, then provoked a great deal of surprise among European specialists in the Neolithic. Renewing the excavations after World War II, Kathleen Kenyon found that this aceramic Neolithic was not the first occupation of the site of Jericho, but that it overlay an even earlier Neolithic culture, the PPNA, which we have just described under the title of 'Sultanian'. No continuity was observed between the PPNA and the PPNB at Jericho. The round houses and the very poor weaponry of the former contrasted greatly with the rectangular houses with lime-plastered floors and the rich panoply of the latter. New funerary rites (the 'skull-cult') distinguished the PPNB at the same time as new cultivated species and the presence of herding. Kathleen Kenyon attributed all these innovations to newcomers arriving at the site,[1] and a little later Jean Perrot suggested that they may have come from Syria. We have thus for a long time defined the PPNB using one of its derived branches, since this culture was effectively born and matured in the northern Levant (Fig. 23).

On the margins of this real discontinuity between one phase and the next at Jericho we see that there also exist other cultural elements that reveal some gradual evolution within an indigenous substratum. It is precisely this juxtaposition of a local heritage with new traits which were in no way developed *in situ* that makes the Palestinian PPNB interesting for the problems that concern us.

The elaboration of the PPNB on the middle Euphrates

Things were very different on the Syrian middle Euphrates. We saw that pressure flaked products derived from 'naviform' cores already figured before 8800 BC, since the final Mureybetian; so did rectangular buildings, alongside persistent round house traditions, and a developed weaponry which, although it did not yet present any of the types characteristic of the PPNB, definitely prepares us for it. It so happens that the first phase of the PPNB, the early PPNB which occurs between about 8800 and 8200 BC, is the least well known in Syria. It has been investigated at Mureybet only in a very limited area, which happened not to include any buildings;[2] it is beginning to be better known thanks to the site of Dja'dé, now in the course of excavation.[3] There the first typically PPNB weaponry can be seen to make its appearance, with larger arrow-heads than previously, whose base and point are thinned by long,

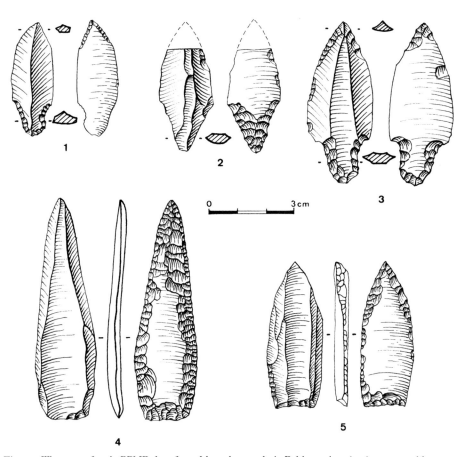

Fig. 24 Weapons of early PPNB date from Mureybet: archaic Byblos points (1–3); truncated base points (4–5).

flat, parallel removals known as 'lamellar retouch'. This retouch is used for points of several forms, in particular the 'Byblos points' (Fig. 24: 1–3), a new type which will endure for more than 2,000 years, and which is characterised by its retouch and its tang separated from the body of the piece by a double notch.[4]

Mureybetian features, such as the polished stone batons and the intensified and specialised hunting of wild cattle, do not persist beyond this phase, and some types of projectile point show that historical continuity is total, that is, that the emergence of the PPNB took place *in situ* and without a hiccough, by a simple, internal evolution from the final Mureybetian.

The following phase at Mureybet (Phase IVB), very quickly followed by the first occupation of Halula and the 'Aceramic A' Neolithic of Abu Hureyra,[5] reoccupied at this time after a long period of abandonment, belong to the middle PPNB. The houses are all rectangular. They are built of *pisé*, and at Abu Hureyra and Mureybet they comprise several oblong rooms, arranged transverse to the axis of the building.

The removal of large flint blades from 'naviform' cores was carried out by percussion. These blades form the base for making various tools, but above all for the

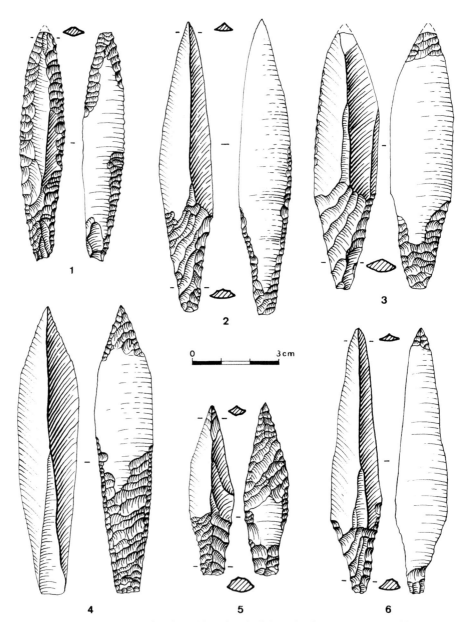

Fig. 25 Weapons of early PPNB date from Mureybet: leaf-shaped points (1–3); truncated base point (4); Byblos points (5–6).

characteristic weapons with flat, pressure flaked retouch, and elongated Byblos points, as well as other types that are equally finely made (Fig. 25). For their part axes and hoes made of polished greenstone completely supplant the hoes that were made of chipped flint in earlier periods.

Subsistence strategies are still imperfectly known. The hunting of equids, which was of great importance at Mureybet until the early PPNB, was interrupted, we do not know why, in the middle PPNB, and replaced by renewed hunting of gazelle.

Equally the hunting of gazelle prevailed in the middle PPNB of Abu Hureyra, but the very first indications of the herding of goats, which will become intensified in the late PPNB,[6] can be seen elsewhere, for example at Halula. At Abu Hureyra we also see the arrival of a form of einkorn of domesticated morphology; at the same time emmer, barley, lentils and beans were cultivated.[7] At Halula, emmer wheat is the principal domesticated cereal, while einkorn is absent. It deserves noting that emmer wheat never existed on the middle Euphrates in its wild form. It must therefore have come already domesticated from somewhere else (Anatolia?), perhaps thanks to some intensification of the exchanges that characterise the middle PPNB, which are also evidenced from the base of the stratigraphy of Halula by the first herding of goat, a species also absent from the region in its wild form (Helmer, pers. comm.).

Finally, these PPNB sites produce evidence of important ideological changes. Art is rare, but without doubt it is significant that at Mureybet there is only one figure, and that for the first time is male, taking the form of a pendant in polished red stone representing the head of a bearded man (Fig. 32: 4). Above all, the funerary rites were transformed: the PPNA tendency to inhume human skulls separately from the bodies was now amplified to form a veritable cult furniture. Skulls were in effect lined up on the floor of a house along a wall. Lumps of red clay were brought into the house and served as pedestals. They were thus exposed, set out so that they could be seen: this is something quite different from the secondary burials. At Abu Hureyra normal burials and others where the skeleton lacks a cranium lie side by side with deposits of skulls where no other bones are found. One cranium shows traces of paint.[8] This tendency to arrange human skulls like art objects is new. We shall see that it is much more spectacular in the southern Levant.

The important fact in the PPNB of the middle Euphrates is therefore its localised emergence. It is rooted in a tradition that goes back three millennia, to the Natufian, and constantly transforms itself step by step from that time. We shall find the PPNB from the Taurus to Sinai, but everywhere arising at different moments; each time it comprises discordant cultural traits relative to the local tradition. The Middle Euphrates, the only part of the Levant where the culture is indigenous, is thus its true cradle.

The penetration of Anatolia: the PPNB of the Taurus

For a long time south-east Anatolia remained a blank on the map of the Neolithic. Since 1964 only the aceramic site of Çayönü,[9] still being excavated in the basin of the upper Tigris, has been known. The construction of major dams on the upper Euphrates in Turkey and the surveys and salvage excavations that have resulted have very recently brought us knowledge of Cafer Höyük[10] and Boytepe[11] for the early and middle PPNB periods. Çayönü is therefore no longer alone, and on the basis of these three sites a particular cultural facies, the 'PPNB of the Taurus',[12] can be defined.[13] To these a fourth site, Nevalı Çori,[14] may be added. It is situated further south and at a lower altitude than the other three, at the northern limit of the rolling hills of the Syro-Turkish Jezirah (Fig. 23), and it exhibits traits intermediate between the PPNB of the middle Euphrates and that of the eastern Taurus.

As its name indicates, the PPNB of the Taurus combines original characteristics with dominant PPNB traits which would be quite at home on the middle Euphrates. These original characteristics may on the one hand quite simply reflect the different mountain environment, which provides for example a new material, obsidian; on the other hand, they may represent the persistence of a distinctive legacy of a local cultural substratum that is still poorly known.

Some aspects originate on the middle Euphrates, where we have seen them being steadily elaborated. These include first the typical PPNB armament[15] (Figs. 26 and 27) and the associated naviform cores which furnished the blades on which they were made, and second an architectural tradition of rectangular houses, whether with long, transversal rooms, or small, approximately square cells[16] (Fig. 28).

What is called the 'grill-plan' house in the early PPNB of Çayönü (Fig. 28: 1–2) is in fact a rectangular foundation level, composed of closely spaced parallel walls where the spaces between must have been filled with earth. The whole formed a raised platform on which the house proper (whose precise plan is lost to us) was built, probably of sun-baked mud brick.[17] Next at Çayönü, at the same time as the foundation of Cafer Höyük (Fig. 28: 4), we find a phase with tripartite houses, now called 'cobble-paved plan' by Özdoğan, with elongated oblong rooms, somewhat analogous to the 'pier-house' of the southern Levant (see below, pp. 98–100 and Fig. 34). Finally, in the middle PPNB both at Çayönü (Fig. 28: 6) and at Cafer Höyük there appears the so-called 'cell-plan' phase: these are buildings with small square or rectangular cells. In the excavations at Cafer Höyük (Fig. 28: 5) it became evident that these cells, reinforced with pilasters and some furnished with quadrant-shaped silos, served both as a foundation level and as storage space below a living floor that has disappeared. That living floor may very well have been of tripartite plan. Some of these plans in fact represent living spaces in the strict sense, but others are the foundations of buildings. Once we have noted the Anatolian tendency to separate living floors from complex sub-structures in various ways, the apparent variety of the architecture may be misleading.[18] Finally, Nevalı Çori presents a form intermediate between the grill-plan and the cell-plan: houses of cellular form had been erected on a stony platform which was cut by transverse 'channels' (Fig. 28: 3 and Pl. I: 2).

The large rectangular houses with a single room that are occasionally found alongside other designs are less characteristic, and we shall return to these. Finally, the use of plaster for floor surfaces is found sporadically, though it is far from being as general as in the PPNB of the southern Levant.

In spite of the particularly spectacular aspect that they take in eastern Anatolia, all these architectural traits can be traced to their roots in the traditions of the middle Euphrates in the early PPNB or a little earlier.[19] Other less immediately appreciated traits have similar significance. For example, the bone industry of Çayönü, as of Cafer Hoyük and Nevalı Çori, is simply an extension of the tradition of the middle Euphrates: it includes needles whose eye is made by means of longitudinal incisions on opposite sides of the shank[20] (Fig. 29). The needle with an eye is not a Levantine invention, for it existed in the European Magdalenian, but the particular process for making the eye that we have described has its origin before 9500 BC in the Khiamian

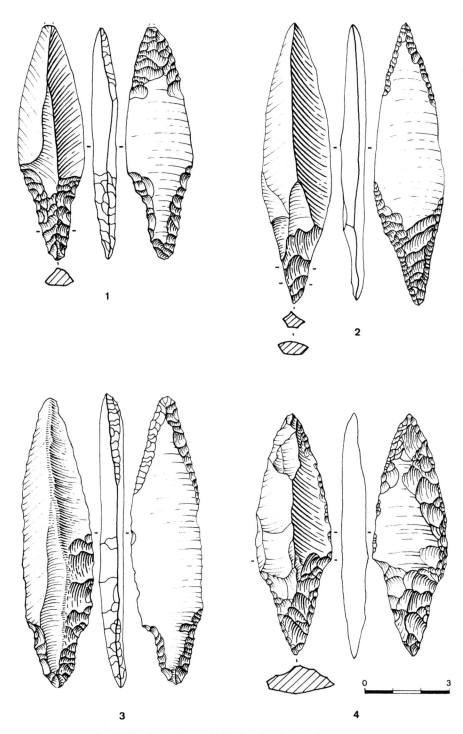

Fig. 26 Weapons from the PPNB of the Taurus: Cafer Höyük (after M.-C. Cauvin) (1–3); Çayönü (4) (after L. Braidwood).

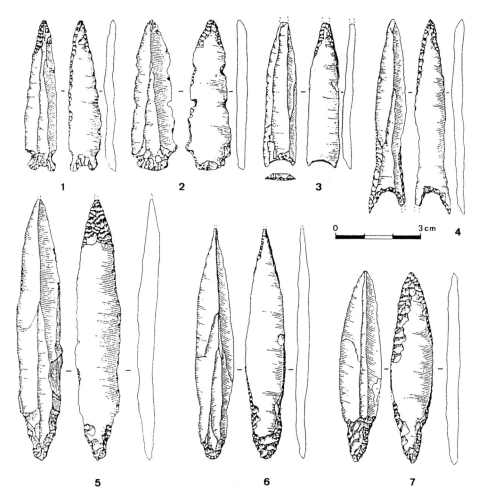

Fig. 27 Weapons from Nevalı Çori (Turkey) of PPNB date: points with a short tang, in the Mureybetian tradition (1–2); points with a concave truncated base (3–4); Byblos points (5–7). After K. Schmidt.

of Mureybet. We find it again in the PPNB of the Taurus around 8000, at Maghzaliyah in northern Iraq around 7500, and in central Anatolia (Çatalhöyük) later again, around 7000 BC. From there it can be followed westwards to the dawn of the Greek Neolithic (Argissa). Bone sleeves for axes and belt buckles of the same material are equally common in the middle Euphrates and in the Taurus. Finally, objects such as the grooved stones decorated with chevrons, often found in the Mureybetian, are also 'indicators of diffusion' well represented at Çayönü and at Cafer Höyük (Fig. 20: 5).

On the other hand other characteristics serve to individualise the PPNB of the Taurus. First there is obsidian, which was used extensively (for example for the distinctive 'Çayönü tools', Fig. 30). This brilliant, glassy volcanic stone occurs as a natural substance in both central (Cappadocia) and eastern Anatolia, in the Taurus mountains themselves (at Bingöl) and in the mountains bordering Lake Van (Fig.

Fig. 28 Architecture from the PPNB of the Taurus. Plans of houses: 1–2, 6 Çayönü; 3 Nevali Çori; 4–5 Cafer Höyük. Plans of sanctuaries; 7 Çayönü; 8 Nevali Çori. After M. Özdogan, H. Hauptmann, J. Cauvin and M. Molist.

33). Very small pieces of obsidian were imported from Cappadocia throughout the whole of the Levant from Natufian times. They are evidence of the early prestige of this material that had come from so far away, for its technological and economic role was non-existent.[21] But the PPNB of the Taurus is quite different, for obsidian was used as the basic raw material for its weapons and its tools. The village communities of this cultural group surely cannot have been in direct contact with the sources of

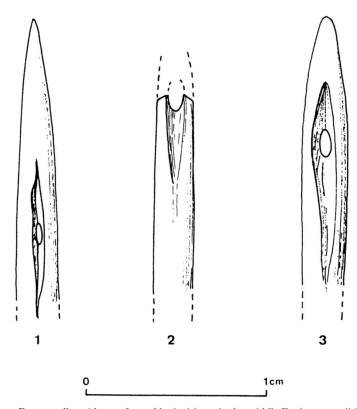

1   **2**   **3**

0 _____ 1cm

Fig. 29 Bone needles with eyes formed by incisions, in the middle Euphrates tradition:
1 Khiamian at Mureybet; 2 PPNB of the Taurus (Cafer Höyük); 3 Çayönü. (1–2 after
D. Stordeur, 3 after C. Redman.)

the raw material, however. Flint is often present in the immediate vicinity, and our
villagers made use of it. On the other hand obsidian could only be found more than
200 km from Cafer Höyük; however its inhabitants never shrank from such a journey
in order to provide themselves with the material, and in ever increasing quantities.
At the beginning of their history they brought 45% of the raw material from Bingöl
for their chipped stone industry, rising to 90% by the end. At Çayönü, where obsidian came from both Bingöl and also from Lake Van, the proportion relative to flint
is 5% at the beginning and 45% by the end of the occupation. At Boytepe, practically the totality of the toolkit was made of obsidian. Only Nevalı Çori further to the
south, whose architecture and armaments resembled the PPNB of the Taurus, is
different in the matter of obsidian, which always remained marginal relative to flint.

The PPNB encountered not only this new material when it reached Anatolia, but
also a mode of chipping stone that was uncommon in its homeland. Bipolar flaking
on naviform cores was not the only technique employed, for there was also another
technique in which blades were removed by pressure.[22] This involves leaning heavily
on a punch whose pointed tip is placed on the nucleus which is held immobile on
the ground (Fig. 31: 3).

This technique does not figure at all either in the PPNA or in the PPNB of the
Levant, and it therefore cannot originate there. By contrast it was known in the

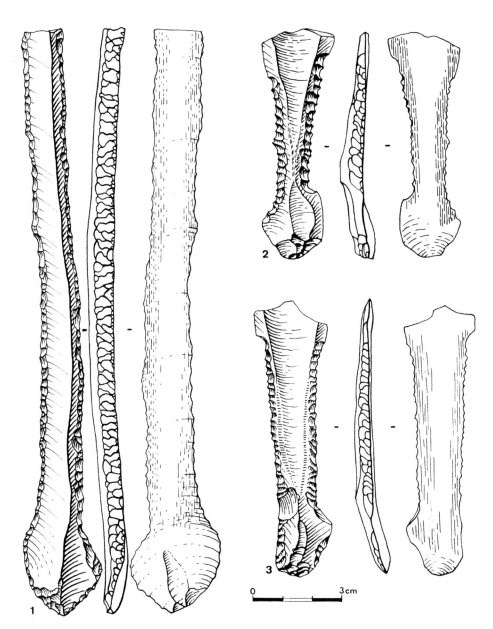

Fig. 30 Taurus PPNB 'Çayönü tools': 1 Çayönü (after L. Braidwood); 2–3 Cafer Höyük (after M.-C. Cauvin). These obsidian tools would have been used in the finishing of fine stone vessels and personal ornaments.

Zagros from around 9500 BC,[23] and it doubtless also existed in the eastern Taurus at this period, although poorly known to archaeology, as we have seen. This is also the situation for another craft, that of polishing marble (pl. II), which produced some very beautiful vases at Cafer Höyük and at many sites bracelets made by very elaborate techniques.[24] In this case, too, the antecedents are found not in the Levant, but in the Zagros, where marble had been worked since the Epipalaeolithic period.[25]

The important fact here, therefore, is that the PPNB of the Taurus appears from

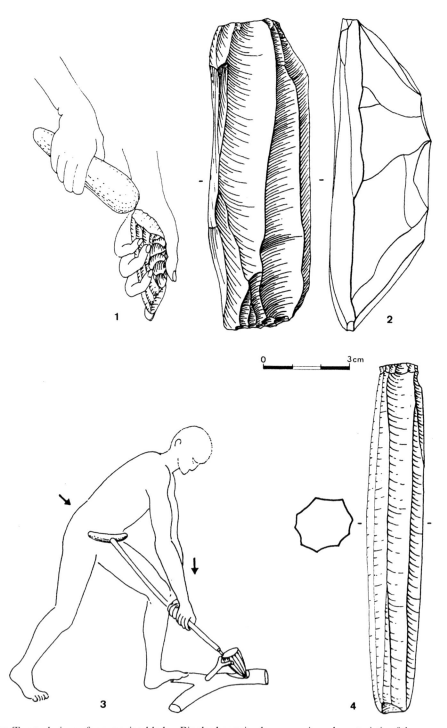

Fig. 31 Two techniques for removing blades. Bipolar knapping by percussion, characteristic of the PPNB in general; here (2): 'naviform' core of final PPNB date from Qdeir, Syria. Knapping by pressure as used for obsidian at the same period: (4) obsidian core (so-called 'bullet core') from Bouqras, Syria. After M.-C. Cauvin and J. Roodenberg.

its beginning as a mixed culture; according to a model that we shall refer to often, it demonstrates the acculturation of a local cultural background by a dominant, expansionist culture. This local cultural background is more than something derived from the new and different geographical and ecological environment to which the incoming culture must adapt; it consists of an indigenous cultural heritage that is in part subsumed into the new culture and in which the external elements integrate them to their own ways.

This neolithisation of south-east Anatolia naturally includes some economic aspects. From the grill-plan phase at Çayönü at first we find lentils and vetches predominant, but they are then gradually replaced by emmer wheat and einkorn whose morphology is still wild. These cereals only become 'domesticated' with the cell-plan phase,[26] that is, in the middle PPNB period, as on the middle Euphrates. At Cafer Höyük they seem to be domesticated from the basal level, that is, a little before the cell-plan phase.[27] As Van Zeist has suggested, it is probable that there existed a phase of pre-domestic agriculture in the early PPNB of the Taurus, as in northern Syria at the same period. Here too the production of subsistence is limited to cultivation; herding comes later, appearing only in the late PPNB.

Finally, knowing the general character of the process of neolithisation, it is not surprising that the symbolic elements were also present. Baked clay female figurines, some more or less realistic, others schematic, are numerous everywhere (Fig. 32: 1–3), and we may note at Cafer, Nevalı Çori and Göbekli Tepe some figurines that are explicitly male, though these are still rare (Fig. 32: 5). The presence at Nevalı Çori of a corpus of anthropomorphic statuary in stone at various scales, sometimes life-size,[28] is particularly interesting. There is also an extraordinary limestone bas-relief (pl. III) in which two anthropomorphic figures appear side by side with arms raised. In spite of the absence of any explicit indication of sex, the disparity in size suggests that for the first time this may be a genuine (divine?) couple. These two figures frame a third, smaller person, with short limbs and distended 'belly', too schematically rendered, it has to be said, to allow one to subscribe completely to its interpretation as a 'tortoise', as Harald Hauptmann has proposed.[29]

In the realm of animal symbolism, the shoulder-blades of cattle have been found in the interior of a house at Cafer Höyük with no connection with any residues of food preparation or cooking. These clearly recall those which accompany the bucrania of Mureybet.[30] Bulls are also very often represented among the clay figurines of Çayönü (Fig. 32: 6–7), together with other, less common, types of horned animals and dogs.[31] Nevalı Çori adds to this list representations of felines, snakes and raptors, both diurnal and nocturnal; snakes were present, as we have seen, from the Mureybetian period in Syria, in particular at Jerf el Ahmar. Together with the felines, the snakes form part of the iconographic repertory which a little later will accompany the Goddess of Çatalhöyük.

Finally, startling facts are now available concerning the PPNB 'skull-cult' in its Anatolian form thanks to recent finds at Çayönü.[32] More than seventy human skulls were found together in a unique building, inside small, chest-shaped cells, sealed by large flat slabs. This large building, a veritable 'house of the dead', was rectangular

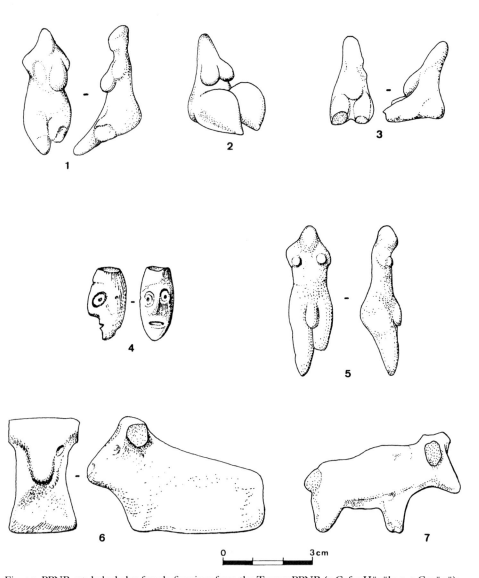

Fig. 32 PPNB art: baked clay female figurines from the Taurus PPNB (1 Cafer Höyük; 2–3 Çayönü); male figurine from Cafer Höyük (5). Bull figurines from Çayönü (6–7); stone pendant from Mureybet (Syria) in the form of a male head (4). After J. Cauvin (1, 4, 5) and V. Broman-Morales (2–3, 6–7).

in plan and in its earliest phase was exceptional in being extended by an apse (Fig. 28: 7). Besides the skulls it also contained various parts of four hundred individuals buried beneath its floor. The skulls belonged to men and women, and sometimes to children, but the majority were young adults. In the rectangular chamber of the building stelae were set vertical. One large flat stone (an altar?) has revealed on analysis traces of animal blood (large and small ruminants) and human blood.[33] At other periods in the history of Çayönü two other, large, rectangular single-roomed buildings[34] without doubt fulfilled the same role as sanctuary, if not of 'house of the dead'. They are remarkable for their dimensions and also for the care devoted to the preparation of their floors. The floor of one of them in particular recalls a mosaic, thanks to the effect of the contrast between lime plaster and coloured stones. A large slab decorated with a human head in relief also bears traces of human blood.[35] This particular sacrificial resonance, perhaps including human sacrifices, has not so far been reported in the Neolithic of the Levant.

Çayönü is not the only site in eastern Anatolia to have produced exceptional buildings, both in their plans and in their usage for cult practices. A genuine sanctuary also exists at Nevalı Çori (Pl. I; Fig. 28: 8). It is not a case here of a 'house of the dead': human skulls are found in the village, but inside an otherwise ordinary building. This sanctuary on the other hand exhibits in its earliest phase the same rounded end as the funerary house at Çayönü; its square room is likewise edged with large slabs, some placed flat covering little cells and others fitted flush with the internal wall face. As at Çayönü, the floor includes a large horizontal slab, while a schematically anthropomorphic sculptured stele is placed alongside it. There can be no doubt that this is a cult building.

Other sanctuaries are in the course of investigation by German archaeologists in the Urfa region.[36] One of them, at Göbekli Tepe, has produced representations of felines and also an ithyphallic human statuette in stone:[37] this emphatic virility is typical of the PPNB as one of its inspirational values.

Thus, thanks to these excavations, we encounter for the first time simultaneous evidence for public buildings and for the collective ceremonies of a religious character that took place in them. These must have served as a strong cement for the psychological cohesion of these sedentary human groups. If one accepts the stele from Nevalı Çori as evidence, it is also quite probable that they were addressing themselves to a personal divinity. This should not surprise us in view of what we know of the steady emergence of this particular form of the sacred since the tenth millennium.

The problem of the neolithisation of central Anatolia in the PPNB period
South-east Anatolia, then, became Neolithic well before 8200 BC. A process of acculturation by the early PPNB of the Levant, from the earliest stages of its elaboration on the middle Euphrates, is perhaps the origin of the phenomenon. It could even date back as far as the end of the Mureybetian period.

How far, then, did this wave of transformation reach? Did it also reach central Anatolia as it progressed westwards? The tell of Hacılar[38] some years ago produced traces in its basal levels of a village that is probably aceramic and which appears to go back to the first half of the eighth millennium and to present architectural affinities with the PPNB; however, its date is not fixed with any certainty. The village of Aşıklı in Cappadocia is at present producing more complete information that dates to the eighth millennium.[39] It consists of a very dense, all-covering fabric of agglutinated houses (Fig. 54: 1), each rectangular and with several rooms, the floors and sometimes the walls covered with lime plaster and painted red. The lithic assemblage is abundant. According to N. Balkan[40] it includes bipolar cores that are related to the 'naviform' type of the PPNB, but there are also tanged points made of obsidian that are different from the Byblos points, together with a toolkit of the same material and consisting above all of microliths, retouched blades and scrapers, perhaps representing an indigenous tradition. There is no trace of the pressure flaking that characterises eastern Anatolia. Only the animal figurines in lightly baked clay and in such poor condition that they are difficult to recognise and above all some belt buckles in bone present affinities with the contemporary cultures of the middle Euphrates and the eastern Taurus.

There is no herding of animals, and the game that is hunted is varied. Cultivation is without doubt present, but the cereals and peas that are capable of being cultivated so far seem to be rather rare. This is surprising in view of the considerable extent of the village (4 ha), and thus of its population, and its high degree of architectural elaboration. On the other hand, enormous quantities of hackberries have been recovered, which derive from gathering activities.

Funerary practice consists simply of burial within the settlement, without the particular rite of secondary removal of the head that is omnipresent in the PPNB.[41]

Two inferences follow from these early results. The first is that PPNB characteristics do not appear at Aşıklı, except in a very attenuated and minor fashion. One can confidently speak of influence from the Levant to explain the existence of rectangular houses and their techniques of construction, since they do not seem to derive from any local development from the evidence we have at present. However, the plans of the houses have nothing in common with the Levantine pier-house. Rather, they form the foundations of the tradition of agglutinative organisation of the village that is particular to Anatolia, such as we shall see later at Çatalhöyük. On the other hand, these PPNB influences in central Anatolia do not seem to come from southeast Anatolia, in terms either of the architectural plans or of the techniques of stone-working, since pressure flaking is absent. Perhaps they took the more direct route that had for a long time linked the Levant and Cappadocia for the 'obsidian trade'.

The second point to note, which needs further confirmation,[42] is the low level of subsistence production that is the weakness of economic neolithisation relative to the Levantine context. From the example of the Natufian, we know that villages of hunter-gatherers had existed before agriculture. Aşıklı may be witness to a persistence of this phenomenon into more recent periods, just like the villages of north Iraq that we shall touch on later. At any rate, Aşıklı seems to be rather atypical in relation to the process of diffusion that we are concerned with here.

Conclusions on Anatolian neolithisation
The diffusion of the Neolithic to Anatolia really concerns only the eastern Taurus and it has three singular aspects.

It is particularly early, indeed very close to the beginning of the PPNB and, at Çayönü, is perhaps even contemporary with the emergence of the PPNB from the final Mureybetian horizon.

It is inseparable from the economic neolithisation of a new territory, in that thanks to this process cultivation is introduced practically simultaneously with its emergence in the middle Euphrates. It acts as the vehicle for the original symbolic system of the Neolithic, in its double form of evocations of goddesses and of bulls, but now charged with new traits that are part of the general form of the system in the PPNB of the Levant. These are the beginnings of the humanisation of the male divinity and a 'cult of ancestors' that is given concrete expression in the deposits of skulls as distinct from the normal rite of burial. Through the richness of the cultic contexts that it reveals to us, Anatolia thereby inaugurates its role as the pre-eminent source of information on the domain of religion which it retains into the following period, with the already mentioned site of Çatalhöyük.

In any case, the contemporaneity of all these aspects – the organisation of living space and the techniques of manufacture as much as the mode of subsistence and the system of thought – suggests very strongly the contribution of a new population, at least in part. This population came from the middle Euphrates, an observation that seems to confirm another new development that concerns eastern Anatolian obsidian and its circulation in the opposite direction throughout the Levant, a phenomenon whose history should now be recalled.

The traffic in Anatolian obsidian in the tenth and ninth millennia
Obsidian, which was the basic raw material for tools and weapons in the PPNB of the Taurus, seems to us to be favoured in relation to other materials, such as flint, that are equally serviceable and much more accessible. Its rather fascinating physical aspect, generally brilliant and black, often also translucent and tinted with grey, green or red, may by itself account for this preference. In any case we have seen that only a particular prestige could explain how obsidian was diffused through the whole of the Levant from the eleventh millennium; it was distributed in the form of small blades and in such small quantities that the receiving communities could not have been interested in it for economic reasons as a raw material for manufacturing tools.[43] This primitive 'trade' strongly resembles that of native copper or turquoise, other prestigious materials that were diffused from Anatolia or Sinai, and also that of shells from the Mediterranean and the Red Sea (*dentalium*, basket shells, etc.), which from the Natufian period onwards deeply penetrated the whole of the continental Levant with a significance that was evidently more symbolic than utilitarian. Between 12,000 and 8800 BC, Levantine obsidian, which had already been found as far as the shores of the Dead Sea and the Jordan valley, came exclusively from the natural deposits of central Anatolia, that is from Cappadocia. Nothing is yet clear concerning the exact nature of the precocious diffusion of raw materials: the settlement of Aşıklı was yet to be founded, and Cappadocia has yielded no trace of human occupation contemporary with the Epipalaeolithic or the Levantine PPNA. No prehistoric sites appear to be stretched along the natural routes which this 'trade' must have taken from central Anatolia to northern Syria. Was central Anatolia uninhabited at this period, which could be explained by longer persistence of glacial winters and a rather later climatic recovery, as suggested by climatologists?[44] It would then be necessary to suppose that the villages of the Levant had despatched long-distance expeditions at the appropriate time of year direct to Cappadocia with the sole purpose of bringing back obsidian.[45] It is more probable that less easily detectable communities of hunter-gatherers, traces of whom have perhaps been concealed

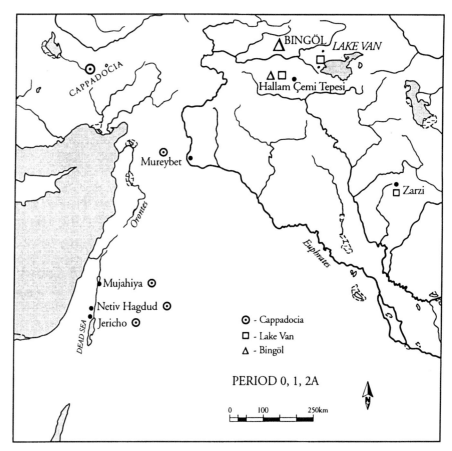

Fig. 33 The diffusion of obsidian in the Near East between 14,000 and 7000 BC. From 9000 BC eastern Anatolian obsidian (triangles and square symbols) take over the coastal zone of the Levant, previously supplied only from Cappadocia (circles). After M.-C. Cauvin and C. Chataigner (pers. comm.).

under the very heavy sedimentation which the valleys that descend from the Anatolian plateau have experienced, may have served as relays in a quite classic exchange system.

The novel feature is the role of south-eastern Anatolia as a new source of obsidian for the Levant from about 9000 BC. The sources in this region are at Bingöl, in the Taurus mountains, and near Lake Van, somewhat further east (Fig. 33). Physico-chemical analyses have shown that this eastern obsidian make its first appearance on the Syrian middle Euphrates, alongside the Cappadocian material that had traditionally been imported, from the end of the Mureybetian phase, that is, at exactly the time when the very first neolithisation of south-east Anatolia was taking place. As the Neolithic 'koine' was expanding into a new province, it appears that the new inhabitants of Anatolia maintained contacts with their old home country and inaugurated from this time a real flow of exchange with it.

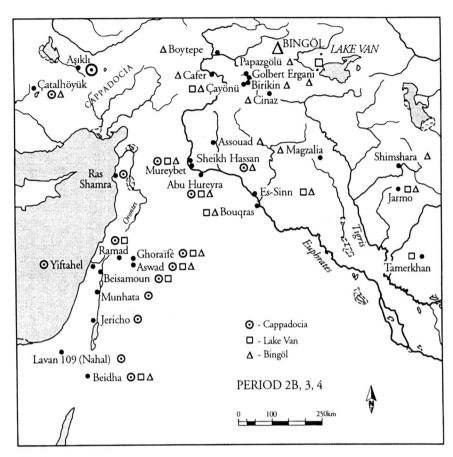

Fig. 33 *(cont.)*

10

Diffusion into the central and southern Levant

The diffusion of the PPNB into Anatolia in the early PPNB period, or possibly a little earlier, is one with the neolithisation of that region. That is not the case for the central Levant (the Damascus region) or the south (Palestine). There, whether at Aswad or in the Jordan valley, subsistence production was already present from 9000 BC. The diffusion in question here, coming later, is not a process of neolithisation because they were already Neolithic in economic terms: it was simply the expansion southwards of a northern culture which was exporting a different form of Neolithic culture, if one can use such a term.

This intrusive character is particularly obvious in the PPNB of the southern Levant, where the contrast between the new and the old architecture, the new and the old toolkits, is considerable. We shall take as examples numerous elements that bear on the exact nature of the PPNB expansion. The case of the region around Damascus, whose geographical position is intermediate between the northern and the southern Levant (Fig. 23), is less clear and the human phenomenon that lies below the arrival of the PPNB is more difficult to identify for lack of adequate evidence.

The middle PPNB of the Damascus region

As we have seen, the village of Aswad had been one of the earliest centres of the agricultural economy since 9000 BC. The site has been shown to be an agglomeration of semi-subterranean round houses, as was the norm for the PPNA horizon. At the end of the ninth millennium, this same village modified its culture and instead became PPNB.[1] However, in contrast with what is found elsewhere, the houses remain of the same type: they are still round holes in the ground with superstructures made of light materials. No rectangular architecture appears there and there are no plastered floors as in the southern Levant. Persistence in the composition of the chipped stone tool assemblage is also notable,[2] which implies persistence in a range of activities that are indicated by the relative proportions of different tools. There is a great abundance of sickle-blades, which were used both in what is properly called agriculture and for the cutting of reeds and rushes used in buildings.[3] There are infrequent scrapers and some exceptional chipped stone axes. In other words, the village community that evolved in some aspects also conserved its domestic habits and basic activities unchanged for generations. This phenomenon of 'cultural inertia' is common in sedentary communities across the ages and in diverse cultural contexts, as long as they can remain a viable self-reproducing community in biological terms.[4]

Where then are the changes? One of them concerns an agricultural detail: the range of cultivated plants is extended by a new variety of wheat, domesticated einkorn.[5] This species (*Triticum monococcum*) is derived from wild einkorn, which was, as we have seen, first harvested and then cultivated at Mureybet before finally becoming morphologically domesticated in the PPNB of Abu Hureyra. In its wild state, this species is entirely foreign to the central Levantine environment. The einkorn introduced at Tell Aswad can only have come from the north in an already domesticated form. However, the particular precociousness that is attributed to the farmers of the Damascus region in the matter of domestication of plants is not diminished in the PPNB period. Aswad is one of the only villages at present known where some species are found in domesticated form which will later spread elsewhere: these are six-row barley (*Hordeum vulgare*) and domesticated flax (*Linum usitatissimum*).

Otherwise, the most important change and the most directly cultural concerns the typology of the weaponry,[6] which we recall constitutes a 'sensitive sector' in which the transition to the PPNB is indicated in the strongest and most expressive fashion. The offensive weapons of Aswad not only become larger and more robust, but also present very different forms from those of the local tradition. Long retouch is used to fashion Byblos points, Amuq points and the oval points that are utterly typical of the PPNB. This type of retouch also serves to give a more developed appearance to some of the notched points of PPNA form which, without it, could easily be confused with earlier points. On the one hand one can detect in the weaponry a rather traditionalist aspect in relation to the northern Levant, where these notched points disappeared rather earlier, but on the other hand the clearest hall-mark of the 'modernity' of the PPNB. Perhaps the PPNB is only to be seen in this trait. There is no trace of the 'skull-cult' or baked clay female figurines, neither of which innovations appears at Aswad although they had existed elsewhere for a millennium.

The PPNB of the Damascus region, like that of Palestine, is a mixed culture, just as we have seen the PPNB of the Taurus to be. Nothing speaks for the PPNB better than the weaponry. Aside from the mode of removing flint blades which were now made from naviform cores, no cultural trait of the PPNB is found in this village which remains astonishingly conservative for a further long millennium.

The new contributions quite certainly came from northern Syria, but it is difficult to explain how. At this stage, the PPNB influence seems to have touched the region of Damascus only very lightly, and it certainly scarcely changed the local population base. This population did no more than arm themselves with the panoply which was *de rigeur* among the cultures of the time. There was thus a direct interaction with the PPNB context, but it was something entirely different from the Anatolian situation and from what we shall now see in the southern Levant.[7]

The middle PPNB of Palestine

Since prehistorians have been interested in Israel and Jordan for fifty years, the Palestinian facies of the PPNB has been known for longer, and the discoveries have multiplied in consequence. However no site is dated earlier than 8200 BC, and it is therefore only in its middle phase that the PPNB appears in the southern Levant. Its territorial range (Fig. 23) extends from the lake of Tiberias in the north to the Negev in the south, but without stretching as far as Sinai. What we find, as in Syria, are villages inhabited by sedentary farmers,[8] who are still at this stage strangers to the semi-arid zones of the Levant. Settlement in the hills of the Negev, which is now very arid, and in the Judaean desert seems to contradict this assertion, except that the reconstruction of the landscape by environmental scientists has repeatedly referred to permanent water and trees in those regions, where now there are only seasonal torrent-beds (dry wadis) and rocky terrain, and to wild cattle and fallow deer (a forest species) where now there are only gazelle. A slightly damper or cooler climate than today thus extended the western tip of the Fertile Crescent further to the south.

There are two ways to describe this culture. When one only knows the PPNB in the southern Levant, the totality of the observed traits contribute on an equal footing, so to speak, to its general definition. Alternatively, one can describe it as only a particular facies of the PPNB, what we have been calling the 'Palestinian facies'. The effort undertaken to date to make sense of this complex material and to distinguish the respective origins of its diverse elements with the objective of identifying the human factor in the origin and emergence of the PPNB culture in this part of the Levant leads to another kind of description. Just like its equivalents in the Taurus and Damascus regions, the Palestinian PPNB did not develop in an uninhabited landscape. Before the PPNB, a strong local cultural tradition occupied this landscape, that of the Sultanian Neolithic. This tradition left important traces: entire areas of its everyday way of life continued to exist, intact or evolving *in situ*. Among the diverse characteristics of the culture we are to examine, it will be prudent to differentiate between those which were novel and those which were traditional, between those which came from elsewhere and those which were indigenous. From a cultural as opposed to a chronological point of view, these conserved traits were not 'PPNB' to the same degree as the others.

Architecture

The irreducible trademark of the PPNB is multi-roomed rectangular architecture, with floors and walls plastered with lime plaster, for which we have no early warning signs in the southern Levant. When it arrives, it is present everywhere, from Galilee to the Dead Sea, from the Jordanian plateau to the Mediterranean coast.

It is rare to find complete plans. The single typical form is the 'pier-house',[9] a rectangular building with two or three oblong, intercommunicating rooms disposed perpendicular to the major axis of the building, with internal columns or posts to support the roof, and a hearth on the axis of the building (Fig. 34). This plan is not very different from the Anatolian tripartite plan, nor indeed from the Syrian form of Mureybet IV. It is thus part of the global character of the PPNB. It is only the axial hearth, which is not in the corner of the room as at Cafer Höyük, and the much more general use of lime plaster that form the 'nuances of dialect' that are special to the southern Levant.

Beidha,[10] the most southerly of our villages, situated to the south of the Dead Sea

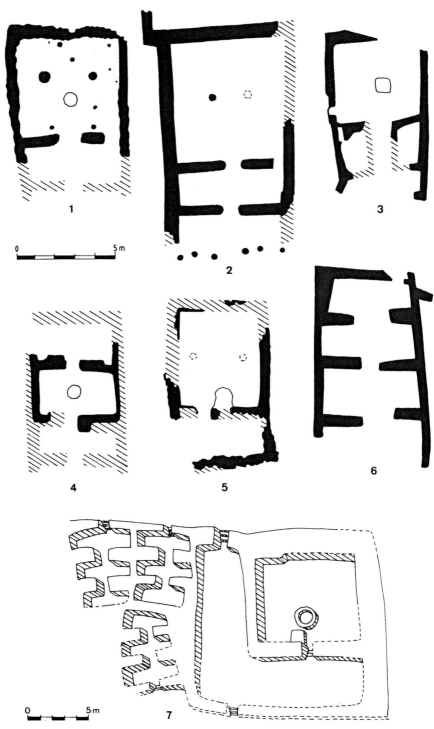

Fig. 34 PPNB architecture from the southern Levant. Pier-houses; 1–4 'Ain Ghazal; 2–3 Jericho; 5 Beisamoun; 6 Yiftahel. Houses and sanctuary (?); 7 Beidha. After B. Byrd and E. Banning (1–6) and D. Kirkbride (7).

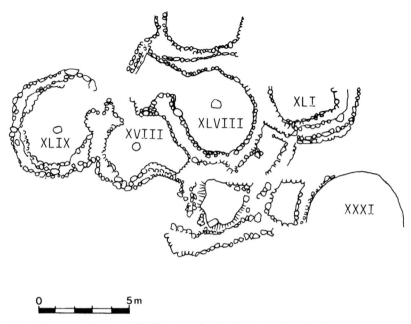

0   5 m

Fig. 35 Round houses of the basal PPNB level at Beidha (Jordan). After D. Kirkbride.

not far from Petra, is a particular case. Previously occupied by a Natufian group, it was reoccupied in the PPNB. In the beginning, each dwelling was formed of a group of round huts girdled by an enclosure wall (Fig. 35). The plan appears archaic, but the mark of the PPNB is seen both in the grouping of round structures, which forms the equivalent of the single multi-roomed house, and in the use of lime plaster on the floors. After this first phase, rectangular buildings make their appearance. They are quite original for the PPNB period, in that their floors are somewhat below ground level and each consists of a central corridor flanked on either side by three small cells opening off the corridor (Fig. 34: 7). Each of these buildings is in fact only the semi-basement of a dwelling-house which existed above; the semi-basement was used for workshops and storage, while the house above, according to B. Byrd and E. Banning, would have reproduced the tripartite plan of the pier-house, just as we have concluded for the cell-plan houses at Cafer Höyük. There also exists at Beidha a rather large, almost square, single-roomed building that is very different in plan from these standardised houses; it has a large circular hearth on the axis of the entrance and a flat limestone slab close by. All of these fittings were painted red, together with the base of the walls. An open courtyard adjoins to the south and east. There are further questions to be asked concerning the significance of this building, so different from the norms of domestic buildings of the PPNB at Beidha, and we shall return to it.

The economy: the appearance of herding

All the sites investigated are villages of farmers, apart from Nahal Divshon, a site in the Negev which was only a hunting station. Domesticated emmer was cultivated at

Jericho, Beidha, Nahal Oren and 'Ain Ghazal. Domesticated barley (two-row barley) accompanies it at Jericho and 'Ain Ghazal. At Beidha, by contrast, there is 'cultivated wild barley',[11] that is a form that has not yet reached the threshold of morphological domestication. We know that barley and emmer wheat were already under cultivation in the Levant from the Sultanian period. On the other hand, einkorn wheat, a northern cereal, did not exist. At Jericho domesticated einkorn joins the other species at the same time as the PPNB arrives, exactly as in Syria at Tell Aswad. The seed-corn may also have been brought ultimately from northern Syria.

Legumes play a major role in this agricultural regime. Indeed, they may have formed the major part of the crops, sometimes even the whole of the cultivated harvest. At 'Ain Ghazal peas and lentils were noted as being more abundant than cereals, and at Yiftahel only lentils and beans were cultivated.[12]

Finally, on the basis of detailed studies at Jericho and Beidha, it can be affirmed that the beginnings of the herding of goat occurred, as on the Euphrates, in the middle PPNB, at least in some of the villages of the southern Levant.[13] On what criteria? Some general information on animal domestication is necessary at this point. Human intervention through herding has modified the natural conditions of interbreeding by segregating animals from the general gene-pool of the wild flocks. Their feeding would also change. The exact consequences of these two types of disturbance are far from being completely clarified. As with the cultivation of plants, herding more or less quickly resulted in morphological changes that give concrete expression to the emergence of new, domesticated species. But here again, as with the beginnings of cultivation, the transitional phase may be difficult to discern: the activity of herding may have been already in progress for some time before the consequential morphological changes were sufficiently pronounced for today's specialist to perceive them. Another criterion has therefore been proposed (Pierre Ducos), which is the statistical analysis of the age profile of the animals killed, which can be determined on certain of the bone remains. This method is specially useful in determining what type of herding was practised and what kinds of products (meat, hides, wool, work, etc.) were expected.

If we take account of the fact that people intending to master animals would naturally select the least large and the least dangerous wild subjects, at least in the early stages the domesticated variety will tend to be smaller, and morphological changes will affect its defensive abilities. In the PPNB of Jericho there are indeed some twisted goat horns instead of the sabre-shaped horns that are found on the wild goat (*Capra aegagrus*), and these suggested the domestication of goat to Juliet Clutton-Brock. At Beidha, where wild goats were hunted in abundance in the Natufian period, it is the diminution in the size of the animals that is taken as evidence of the 'cultural control' that was established over them in the PPNB (H. Hecker).

The countries of the Levant, the middle Euphrates and the southern Levant, are thus the location of the emergence of the domestication of the goat. Anatolia remained ignorant of domestication until the herding of ovicaprids by the nomads of the Zagros further to the east. This ovicaprid domestication was thought for a long time to go back to the beginning of the ninth millennium, but it is now thought to be younger, in line with the redating of the stratigraphy of Ganj Dareh which had furnished the earliest evidence. Finally, and also contrary to what we had formerly believed, this first domestication of the goat seems to have been effected in a human environment which was entirely sedentary and not nomadic.

Tool-making techniques

The production of flint blades from naviform cores began in the southern Levant in the PPNB. Among the products of that industry the weaponry that first attracts our attention on account of its quantity and its quality is also to be found there (Fig. 36). Aside from the 'classic' arrow-heads common to the whole of the Levant, there exists a regional variant, the 'Jericho point'. It is only distinguished from the Byblos point, of which it is a local adaptation, by the sharp tips which flank the tang on either side (Fig. 36: 3–5). All these flint weapons are found on all sites, but we must now take into consideration that tanged points made of wood also served to arm arrows. One of the finest discoveries of the last decade has been the cave of Nahal Hemar in the Judaean desert,[14] a real 'treasure-store' of PPNB material culture, on which we must now revise our view on several counts. The exceptionally arid conditions which conserved the famous Dead Sea Scrolls in the same region have there preserved perishable materials that are very rarely encountered in prehistoric excavations. Generally recognised as over-provided with armaments when we take into account only the standard finds, the people of the PPNB now appear to us to be even more so when this exceptional chance discovery reveals to us what has disappeared elsewhere.

Sickle-blades are also of a new type, fashioned now on flint blades that are the products of a new flaking technique. In this regard, too, Nahal Hemar has produced the perishable complement: the handle of a curved sickle made of horn and with three flint blades set in a groove and fixed with lime plaster. In any case, these sickle-blades have nothing to do with the larger and thicker type which was in use in the Sultanian period.

It is not at all the same with the heavy stone toolkit intended, it is believed, for working wood: the Sultanian tradition of the bifacial *tranchet* axe of flint in fact continues in abundance. As for the other common chipped stone tools (scrapers, burins, etc.), as is frequently the case, they bear no distinctive cultural characteristics.

The tools made of bone conserve the principal types of the Sultanian with very little change. The *tranchet* axes in bone, which already characterised the PPNA in the southern Levant, are still present;[15] awls and flat knives for their part appear to be essential components in the toolkits for basketry and weaving. Thanks once again to Nahal Hemar, we have direct information on these crafts in the form of fragments of cord, of baskets and of linen fabric. Compared with the evidence coming from the rest of the Near East, and also of the Middle East, these traces, most often in the form of imprints registered on clay, allow us to identify a craft tradition that is special to the southern Levant. In contrast with that of the Zagros and the northern Levant, this does not include matting, but like them it practises spiral basketry and retains a certain exclusivity through its use of corded basketwork and basketry with superimposed layers.[16] These three techniques of basketry were present, we have seen, in the

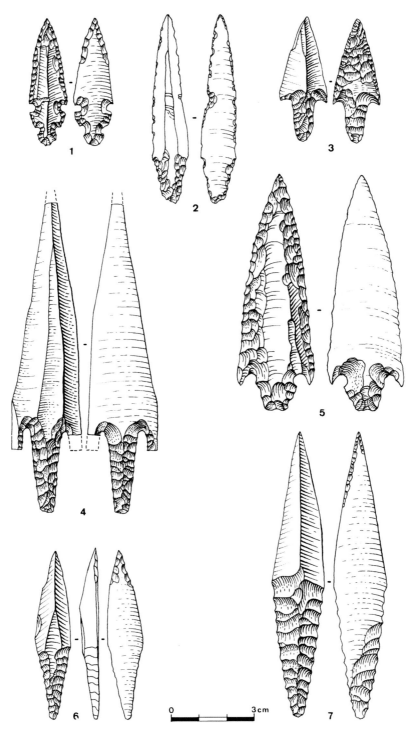

Fig. 36 Middle PPNB weapons from the southern Levant: 1 notched arrowhead; 2 'Byblos point'; 3–5 'Jericho points'; 6–7 'Amuq points'. (1 Beidha, after D. Kirkbride; 2–5 Jericho, after J. Crowfoot-Payne; 3–4, 7 Munhata, after J. Perrot.)

Sultanian of Jericho. There was therefore an indigenous craft tradition which seems to argue against any change with the arrival of the PPNB.

The anthropological perspective

In consequence, still keeping to the material culture, the contrast between PPNA and PPNB is very strong in the southern Levant, but less than the work at Jericho first seemed to indicate. Materials not then studied, such as basketry and the bone-working industry, now refute by their continuity the hypothesis of the replacement pure and simple of one culture by another.

What happened, then? Jericho is precisely the only excavation where an anthropological study undertaken phase by phase offers proof of what was otherwise suspected. In spite of the sometimes somewhat abstract manner in which we imagine relations between cultures in prehistory whereby one 'replaces' or 'influences' another without closer definition, it is doubtful whether a new culture of foreign origin could arrive in a place unless there were people to bring it. It is difficult to estimate the exact scale of this human support, which could range between total replacement of one population by another to much more restrained contacts ending up with mere borrowings of cultural traits. In the event, a new population of a type described as 'gracile Mediterranean', already present in the Mureybetians of northern Syria,[17] arrived at Jericho at the same time as some brachycephalic elements, together with the PPNB.[18] These new arrivals however did not replace the 'robust Mediterraneans' of the Sultanian culture, but added themselves to these to form a racially composite whole. The mixture of cultural traits is thereby explained in concrete terms. The PPNB acculturation is in this case the unambiguous result of an ethnic admixture which derives from the expansion of people coming from Syria; these overlay themselves on the indigenous population base, amalgamating with them rather than destroying them.

The analysis of the components of the PPNB in Palestine may be summarised as follows: the architecture and the weaponry, with a new technique of making blades in flint, bear the mark of the newcomers, as in Anatolia. At the same time they bring with them their northern cereal, einkorn. Elements of a more 'domestic' nature, bone-working and weaving of vegetable fibres, on the contrary represent local traditions continuing. Finally, other traits that are particular to the middle PPNB of Palestine, such as the Jericho points or the particularly intensive use of lime plaster, are so many 'nuances of dialect' added to techniques that have been brought from elsewhere.

The fact that the ethnic elements which arrived in the southern Levant introduced a new type of weapon and new methods of building houses suggests, if not an intrusion by force which would be difficult to establish, at least a vigorous process of acculturation that manifests itself in some relatively important, even prestigious, sectors. The flourishing of art and rituals which characterises the PPNB helps to confirm this impression, and we turn to these next.

11

The evidence of symbolism in the southern Levant

Wherever it extended, the PPNB brought with it the legacy of the religion of the PPNA in its specifically Mureybetian version; it consists of not only the female divinity, who appeared simultaneously throughout the Levantine corridor, but also a masculine principle represented in animal form, the Bull, whose presence had not previously been indicated in the southern Levant in either the Khiamian or the Sultanian period. The new religion seems to arrive precisely with the middle PPNB, at a later stage therefore than in Anatolia, where it had arrived rather earlier through the influences from northern Syria.

The figurines

Goddesses and bulls, plus the first anthropomorphic representations of males and some other animal species, show themselves above all in the form of figurines. In the southern Levant as elsewhere, these are objects of small dimensions, most often fashioned in clay, which is then, as one often reads in excavation reports, 'hardened in the fire', an ambiguous circumlocution for a form of baking that was sometimes fairly rudimentary. Furthermore, if the female figurines most often appear to conform to some stereotype that reinforces their symbolic function (the classic exaggeration, for example, of the breasts and/or the hips), the zoomorphic figurines are less given to this selective treatment of part of the body and their representation seems in general more neutral. In both categories, however, the modelling may be summary. Their small size is part of the reason for this, but above all it is a clear-cut and frequent choice to schematise in a style that is at odds with natural reality. This was true for the female figurines of the Mureybetian and the Sultanian, and all the more so for the simple, rod-like figures of the Aswadian where no features are recognisable. It was also true for the majority of the human and animal representations of the PPNB of the Taurus and that is also the case for the PPNB of Palestine. The same observation could be readily extended to many regions of the Middle East, the Mediterranean and the central European Neolithic.

For things that are drawn from the natural world, the word 'schematic' is often synonymous with 'careless' or 'gross'. These deprecatory terms may serve to exclude these object from any truly synthetic attempt at interpretation. If one follows Peter Ucko, author of an important work on prehistoric Near Eastern figurines,[1] a drawing together of the Neolithic female representations with the Near Eastern and Mediterranean Goddess should usually be set aside. Several different interpretations are proposed by him and those who follow him: that of 'dolls', that is simple toys for children to use, is curiously the most widespread, when their modelling is not attributed to the *a priori* clumsy fingers of the children themselves. However, these figurines appear in the Near East from the aceramic Neolithic period when the forming of portable objects in clay is not yet widespread. It would therefore seem dangerous to situate the first appearance of working in clay in the world of child's play, when we know that play has as its essential function to mimic the world of adults and to mirror their actions. Above all, we have already shown that in several parts of the Levant there existed more carefully produced representations, stylised of course, but quite beautiful and capable of attributing to the same persons a suite of quite explicit details that leave no doubt as to their meaning. Does a more summary way of making things eliminate this meaning? Would it be necessary, in our Christian tradition, to admit the religious value of a cross made of gold and studded with jewels from the treasury of a church and to refuse it for realisations of the same symbol in more modest so much more common wood? Is only the luxury object significant?

People who attribute less importance to the figurative prop than to the idea that it contains are happy with simplified and quasi-allusive evocations, the more so because they wish to multiply the idea and permeate the most varied circumstances of human life with it. That is very much the case with religious symbols. Contrary to what is claimed by P. Ucko and other researchers after him, the frequent rustic simplicity of their manufacture is not an argument against a special significance for the figurines; nor, as is equally often said, is the variety of archaeological context where they are found, whether funerary or domestic, an argument against their significance.

The clay figurines of the southern Levant offer us much more positive intimations. Female representations exist in the middle PPNB (Fig. 37: 1–2, 4): those of Jericho, Beidha, and Munhata remain of uncouth appearance although of quite different styles according to their place of origin. The female form is not schematised in the same manner; each site offers its own framework of aesthetic conventions, which scarcely supports the supposition that these are simply gratuitous playthings, as has been said. Among other, more summary pieces from 'Ain Ghazal, two figurines give clear evidence of an effort at decoration.

'Ain Ghazal is even more remarkable for its animal art, not that its very numerous zoomorphic figurines, almost all of clay, are of a more elaborate manufacture than elsewhere. On the contrary, about half of them are not identifiable, but the quarter that are absolutely certain represent cattle[2] (Fig. 38) and the same identification is probable for many others. However, the essential element among the species killed for food at 'Ain Ghazal consisted of goats, probably domesticated. These would have been the familiar animals that an art whose inspiration was purely imitative could not have failed to reproduce. The same discrepancy appears here as in Palaeolithic art, between the species represented and the species that were eaten. The aurochs was rarely hunted, as previously in the Khiamian of Mureybet, but it alone inspired almost all the identifiable animal art both at 'Ain Ghazal and at Jericho. That is not its only point of interest: at 'Ain Ghazal some bovine figurines, that are in other respects no better modelled than the rest, have flint blades stuck in the chest or head

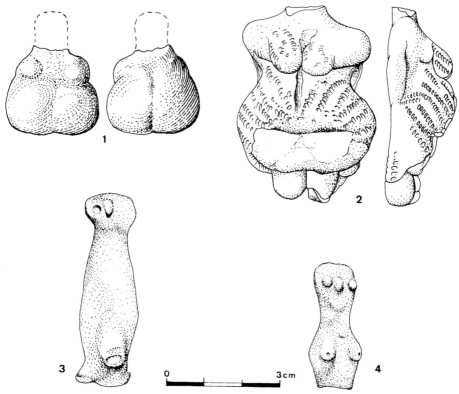

Fig. 37 Baked clay figurines from the southern Levant. Female figurines: 1 Beidha; 2 'Ain Ghazal; 4 Munhata. Male figurine: 3 Munhata. After D. Kirkbride (1), G. Rollefson (2), J. Perrot (3–4).

(Fig. 38: 3–4). Inserted into the still soft clay paste in the course of the making of the figurine, these blades are an integral part of the reality that is being portrayed: not just the animal by itself, but the animal assailed by man. It is difficult not to see in this, evoked by a different technique, the equivalent of the bull hunting scenes which will be painted only a little later on the walls of Çatalhöyük or the pottery of the Halaf culture. At least by allusion, the oriental 'contest with bulls' seems already to be present in the symbolism of the PPNB culture at the beginning of the eighth millennium.

If one allows this parallel with the rather later scenes of Çatalhöyük, it then becomes very plausible that the other horned animals which are rarely explicitly represented at some sites, whether ibex or rams, could be, like the ram or the deer at Çatalhöyük, simply substitutes for bulls.[3]

Female and bovine representations are not at all new as far as the PPNA of northern Syria is concerned. Indeed, it was through them that the 'religion' of the first Mureybetian cultivators was extended southwards in the eighth millennium. By contrast what is new is the symbolic use of the male body at almost exactly the same time as an analogous phenomenon is noted in Anatolia. Male figurines are at present known only from Munhata. There the 'canon' proper to that village reduces every human representation to a simple sausage shape of clay with a flattened base to make

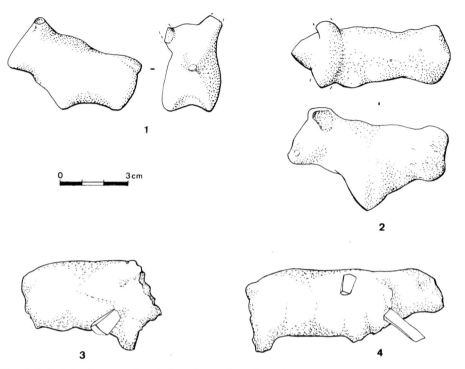

Fig. 38 Baked clay figurines of cattle from the southern Levantine PPNB: 1, 3–4 'Ain Ghazal (after G. Rollefson); 2 Jericho (after T. Holland). Numbers 3 and 4 are pierced by flint bladelets.

it stand upright, and a discoid head where the eyes are indicated by pellets of clay or incisions. But while the feminine version emphasises the breasts, the masculine version is plainly ithyphallic (Fig. 37: 3).

Finally, some small human heads of unidentifiable gender simply made in clay or bone are present at Munhata as at Nahal Hemar or Jericho (Fig. 39). There also, the facial features (nose and eyes) are fashioned in an apparently summary style, but the remarkable preservation of the bone objects at Nahal Hemar gives us the proof of the decorative intention of which they were the object. These heads are polychrome – black bitumen, green, red or white colours – and also encrustations in other materials for the eyes may serve to differentiate the features. Were there not these traces of minute applied details, which are a mark of how highly regarded these objects were, one would assuredly have spoken of carelessness in the same way as for the examples in clay from Munhata (Fig. 39: 4–5), which in terms of the modelling are practically identical to them.

The statues

It is important for the history of art that the first statuary, in the shape of representations of the human form in the round with dimensions rather more imposing than those of figurines, was born in the PPNB. It has already been mentioned that there are stone statues in Anatolia at Nevalı Çori. The statues of the southern Levant are not carved but modelled in plaster on an armature of reeds. Flattened before and

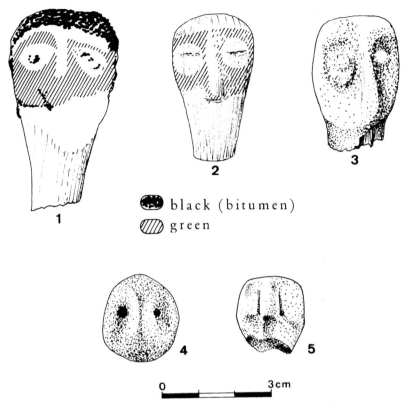

black (bitumen)

green

Fig. 39 South Levantine PPNB: 1–3 small human heads in bone from Nahal Hemar; 4–5 small baked clay heads from Munhata. After O. Bar-Yosef and J. Perrot.

behind, they were intended to be viewed from the front. Some, of which only fragments have been found, are at full scale, others are smaller but often more complete. The two sites of these discoveries are Jericho and 'Ain Ghazal. The single find that presents some aesthetic qualities, at least according to our contemporary criteria, was the first to be discovered. It is a remarkable human head, its eyes formed by shells, and it was found at Jericho by John Garstang[4] and interpreted as masculine because of the painted radiating lines that seem to portray a beard (Fig. 40: 1). The other fragments of bodies found by him, and then by Kathleen Kenyon (feet, shoulders, etc.) were very inexpressive, except that they seem to correspond to figures at three different scales. From these fragments, large, medium and small, John Garstang came to the somewhat precipitate conclusion that a 'holy trinity' was worshipped at Jericho.

The examples recently uncovered at 'Ain Ghazal by Gary Rollefson are very numerous (around thirty figures) and a detailed description is available.[5] All these 'statues' were found together as a cache in a pit (Fig 41); their condition of preservation was very fragmentary as a result of their vulnerability in the face of burrowing animals, necessitating reconstruction in the laboratory. They are not of full, natural scale; in fact two size categories may be distinguished. The first (Fig. 40: 2–3) measures about 35 cm in height and involves relatively squat forms, comprising only

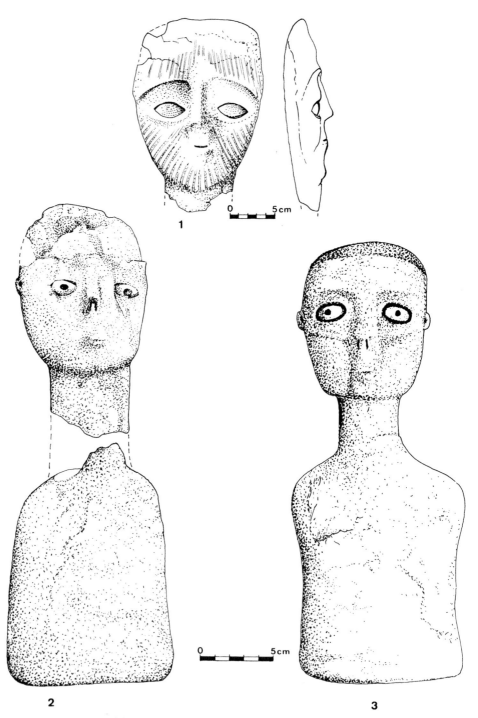

Fig. 40 Plaster statues of the middle PPNB in the southern Levant: 1 Jericho; 2–3 'Ain Ghazal. After J. Garstang and G. Rollefson.

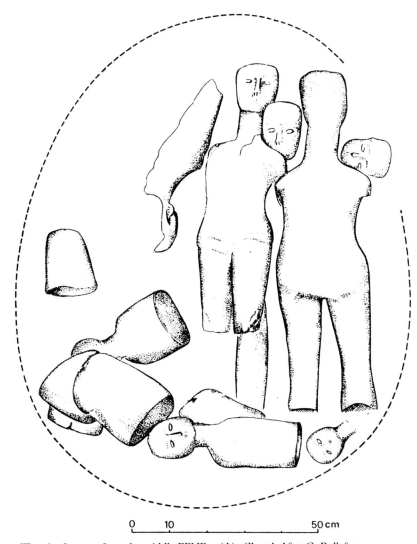

Fig. 41 The pit of statues from the middle PPNB at 'Ain Ghazal. After G. Rollefson.

a head and a body without limbs, but with a broad base to assure the stability of the object when stood upright. The second (about 90 cm tall) reproduces complete human silhouettes, rather elongated, with arms and legs whose small scale is quite out of proportion in relation to the rest of the body. The reeds of the armature form a projection at their base, apparently to allow them to be grasped, or possibly as a vertical anchoring. It certainly seems that these people wanted to represent human forms of both sexes, the female version being the only assured example, as one case of pendant breasts exists (Pl. IV). The absence of sexual distinctions could have been intended to make the representations either asexual, or, as is more probable, masculine by default, one might say (Pl. V). There is no further anatomical precision to assist us definitively on this point.

The general model is actually very summary and all the grossness that is remarked in the case of the clay figurines could equally be seen here, in spite of the change of scale. The contour of the eyes is outlined by a simple incised groove, the ears are unformed excrescences with a central depression; the nose is an upturned trumpet, the mouth marked only by a single incised line, and the rendering of the body is likewise quite 'maladroit', all these characteristics making these statues not very beautiful to our eyes. This reaction is not out of place since we know from the Jericho head that the sculptors of the PPNB could also produce work of talent.

However, as with the bone objects of Nahal Hemar, the rudeness of shape is compensated for by an intense decorative effort. These statues were painted or encrusted. Their bodies retain traces of orange bands on the legs or of black bitumen on the top of the head or at the joints on the limbs. The faces were also polychrome: the eyeball, through the selection of the purest lime plaster, is set off in sharp white from the rest of the face. The pupil of the eye is indicated by a black bitumen point, and the same material is also used to fill the groove around the eye, while a trace of green colouring made from a copper-based material (dioptase) is often superimposed on the lower limit of the eye. If one restores in imagination all the colour that is now almost completely effaced, the effect of these statues would have been striking. We should add that the bitumen which is frequently used is not only a colour but also an adhesive. If it covered the top of the head, might it not have been to fix some additional 'hair' made of vegetable fibre, as O. Bar-Yosef has tentatively suggested for the stone masks, as we shall see below?

In any case four conclusions emerge from these observations.

1 The PPNB statues are rarely the work of talented 'artists' in the sense in which we use the term; or, more precisely, the capability of plastic art to reflect individual characteristics did not have the importance that it later acquired.

2 they were however the object of considerable investments of craft skills which increases their value not only because of the generally rather sophisticated techniques of manufacture but also for the extent of their decoration. As far as one can tell from the little that survives, this decoration seems to respond to a precise code with no apparent room for improvisation.

3 the statues both at 'Ain Ghazal and at Jericho according to K. Kenyon were found laid flat in a pile in pits, in a situation that is consequently not a functional one, since they were initially conceived to be presented vertical and head on. We may therefore conclude that these statues 'functioned' only in intermittent and particular (ceremonial?) circumstances.

4 what do they represent? It is evident that they are not 'portraits' of particular individuals. On the other hand the representation of supernatural beings is very probable, even thought the hypothesis of J. Garstang (of a 'Holy Trinity') may not be demonstrable given the available evidence. Both at Jericho and at 'Ain Ghazal, one particular detail, feet that have not five but six toes, would seem to confirm this supernatural aspect. This anatomical trait, which today we know is the result of a genetic anomaly, has figured in pre-classical sacred art form the Middle East to the western Mediterranean (Malta), and even in Ireland in the legend of Cuchullain, as

a mark of transcendence. It characterises divinities or deified biblical heroes, for example the Giants, or Rephaim.[6]

The problem of their significance will be treated at the same time as that of the modelled skulls.

The modelled skulls

The 'skull-cult' is one of the most spectacular rites of the Palestinian PPNB. It was revealed in the first excavations of J. Garstang at Jericho and a great deal of ink has flowed on the subject since. We have learned that the cult is not limited to the southern Levant, but constitutes one of the characteristic traits of the PPNB in its entirety, including the late PPNB and some later cultures that derive from it. We have described its first manifestations on the middle Euphrates and in south-east Anatolia. It was still in existence in the sixth millennium in the skulls that are separated from the body to form a cult object on the Phoenician littoral (Byblos), in central Anatolia, and as far as the Halaf culture, since the painted pottery whose symbolic significance we have already described (chapter 3) includes an example in which a human skull was found.

It is still the case that it is only in the southern Levant that in addition to the simple partition of the skulls from the rest of the skeletons for separate conservation, the features of the face were also modelled, an 'artistic' act that is now added to the previous practice of decapitation. Skulls with modelled features have been found at Jericho[7] (Pl. VI), at Beisamoun,[8] at Kfar Ha Horesh and at 'Ain Ghazal.[9] In the late PPNB the practice extends beyond the southern Levant, and is found in the central Levant at Tell Ramad,[10] a site in the region of Damascus. In the Nahal Hemar PPNB there are also whole heads that are fitted together, cranium with mandible, but the facial features are not modelled. On the other hand the vaults of several crania are covered with a thin coating of asphalt on which there is a net-like pattern of rolled cords also of asphalt, forming something like a black bonnet,[11] which may also have been the base for fixing something else (Pl. VII). Elsewhere, at Beidha or at Yiftahel, the presence of headless skeletons shows the existence of analogous practices, even if the skulls themselves have not been found.

The interpretation of the skulls with modelled features is not easy,[12] usually for lack of satisfactory detail. First of all, on the level of the modelling itself: curiously, the material used as plaster has never been analysed, save at Jericho, where it has been shown to be lime, as for the statues. This plaster covers the face and the temples, and forms the features of the face. The mandible is rarely present, the upper jaw for its part having had the teeth deliberately removed *post mortem*. The eyes are rendered either by shells (cowries or bivalves) as at Jericho, or by a whiter plaster which makes them stand out. The general rendering of the face is sometimes considered as realistic and like the living person (K. Kenyon), sometimes on the contrary as very conventional and imprecise in its imitation of reality (Eugen Strouhal, Denise Ferembach). In fact, a similar contrast can be noted among the statues between rare achievements that denote some artistic talent (Pl. VIII) and the majority of others where there is a manifest disinterest from this point of view, at least at the level of the plastic modelling. Here again, painted decoration, which survives only in the form of faint traces, would have contributed markedly to the overall effect of the head. One piece from 'Ain Ghazal shows radial lines on the lower face that are of an identical appearance to those which adorn the head of the statue from Jericho.

The observations made on the headless buried skeletons from which the skulls had been removed concur with the skulls themselves in showing that this removal was done at an advanced stage in the process of natural excarnation, if not when the process was complete. Some years or some months after the burial, the tomb was reopened, then, in order to recover the head.[13]

Where were the skulls with facial modelling found? We have already seen one alternative, further to the north: either the skulls were found in their 'functional' place, situations in the interior of houses on clay supports, where they could be seen, or they were grouped as a deposit in carefully built receptacles. It is not always easy to discern what was the case for those of the southern and central Levant. There were probably skulls that were disposed of under the floors of houses, notably at Jericho, but the sequence of destructions and reconstructions of the houses has effectively confused the issue. On the other hand, the second option, the deliberate deposition, is well attested at Jericho and at Ramad, where a dozen skulls were grouped together in a construction of unbaked bricks and lime, three others being found in a pit. There also exists a third option, the modelled skull buried,[14] perhaps in consequence of some turning of affection against some of them that had for some reason proved 'useless': modelling of the features makes no sense at all for a skull that is buried.

And their meaning? On one side there are the skulls, and on the other side the graves with skeletons, often but not always headless. These are therefore the heads of certain of the community who have died and whose skulls have been recovered, conserved and treated. The idea that it is a particular form of veneration of the ancestors follows from this. However, not all the skeletons have lost their heads, which no doubt means to say that not all the dead could claim the dignity of ancestors. Aside from the fact that all the subjects are adult, the criteria for selection are not clearcut, even in the matter of sex. At Jericho, for example, ten out of thirteen skulls are male, while those from 'Ain Ghazal all belonged to men; on the other hand, the fortyfive skulls from Ramad are all female, as are those from Beisamoun. Local customs or beliefs may have played a role in this choice, alongside the particular histories of the dead, which meant that only a segment of the whole population had their skulls retained.

The same difficulties occur when it comes to defining the details of the cult: was it permanent (as in Buddhism today) or occasional? Based on the family or a wider collective? The indications we have are often contradictory. The skull set on a support within the house, as at Mureybet, suggests family veneration throughout the year in some sort of 'domestic sanctuary',[15] as is the case later at Çatalhöyük. On the other hand, the deposition of skulls, especially if it is done in a public building as at Çayönü, supposes an intermittent presentation doubtless connected with ceremonies. Moreover, it is rather improbable that the custom of taking an individual souvenir of the dead should endure for such a long time, as opposed to a general practice of veneration of the 'communal ancestors'. We shall see that the existence of collective sanctuaries in the southern Levant is very likely although not absolutely certain, but the deposits of skulls exist and those of Ramad confirm the significance of a temporary storage place. In fact, we find small, coarsely modelled clay statues packed in with the skulls, which have been interpreted as the anthropomorphic supports on which the skulls would have been grafted when they were exposed.[16] This interpretation remains possible, although the unique example that is complete, with its broad flat top surface, presents a problem. From these generally very badly preserved statues it is very hard to see how one should reconstruct the means by which the skulls with modelled features from Ramad could have been fitted together with them (Fig. 42), for these latter have extensions that form some sort of irregular 'neck' in lime plaster. On the other hand, we now know the statues of 'Ain Ghazal, which lack any complement based on skulls, although the method of their storage was similar. Whether the skulls and the 'statues' of Ramad are considered as complementary to one another or, as at 'Ain Ghazal, functionally distinct, the indications are in fact the same: there existed occasions with the character of a festival when this cult furniture was brought out, and could equally well have been carried or set up. The existence of masks helps to reinforce this presumption.

The masks
The existence of stone masks in the southern Levant has been known for a long time from chance finds in the area of Hebron (Pl. VII) that are in public and private collections.[17] In view of several aspects of stylistic resemblance to the sculptural art of the PPNB culture,[18] it is reasonable to attribute these to that culture.[19] This date has been strikingly confirmed by the recent discovery of an analogous, almost complete mask (pl. VII) and the mouth of a second in a well-dated context at Nahal Hemar.[20] On all these masks the eyes are circular holes and the nose a slight projection. In three examples out of five the half-open mouth has the teeth indicated by incisions in the stone.[21] The almost complete examples from Nahal Hemar retain in addition traces of red and green paint forming lines that radiate from the centre to the margins of the face, a motif that is once again rather close to that of the decoration on the Jericho statue.[22] These masks have a series of holes along their edges for fixing; in addition, at Nahal Hemar, there are traces of bitumen that may, according to O. Bar-Yosef, have served as an adhesive for some 'hair'.

These objects are of prime importance for our attempt to reconstruct the religious thinking of the PPNB. Although they are heavy to carry,[23] they appear to us to be inseparable from a ceremonial context that other indications would also suggest. They also seem to tip the balance in favour of ceremonies of a public character, since one could hardly imagine them used to cause fear in the family setting. Finally, if the mask were thought of as to be worn by an 'actor' who temporarily personifies some supernatural being, it is possible that we may be looking at the very, very ancient origin of the sacred theatre of the east Mediterranean world.

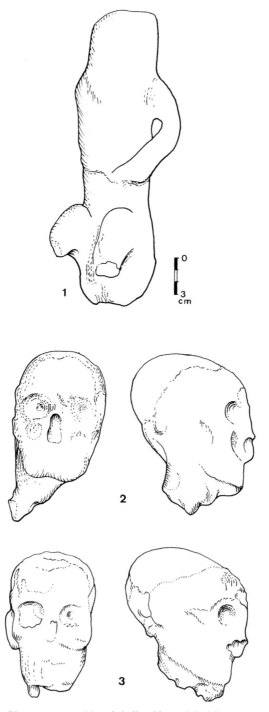

Fig. 42 Plaster statuette (1) and skulls with modelled features (2–3) from Ramad (Syria). After H. de Contenson.

Sanctuaries

If one thinks of ceremonies, one wants them to have a place suitable for their purpose. This is the function of 'sanctuaries' so long as one takes the word in its simplest meaning: that of a 'holy place' with a religious purpose. Granted this definition of the word, the Franco-Cantabrian painted caves were already sanctuaries, since one can scarcely define any other significance than symbolic for their pictorial adornment. We could not however define them as sanctuaries in the terms of another meaning of the term, 'a place sacred to a divinity',[24] since no 'god' can be identified as present. As the art of building develops with the Neolithic, we come upon a useful definition in the Petit Robert dictionary: 'sanctuary = building consecrated to religious ceremonies'. This does not imply that the building in question had been built for this purpose. In our own times, in our western civilisation, one can find suburban rooms dedicated to the observances of the church or the mosque, an everyday example of sacralisation through the use of a place that was built for some other purpose. For the archaeologist the problem is posed when, for example, a particular concentration of figurines in an ordinary house attracts his attention. On the other hand, this religious specialisation of a built space, whether acquired or intended from the start, does not in any way imply that it is a public edifice. Thus, in the seventh millennium the 'domestic sanctuaries' of Çatalhöyük, occupying one of the two rooms in each house, were repeated as many times as there were hearths, just as the altar of the ancestors delimits a sacred space of that order in any Buddhist household today.

We have long thought that public buildings could not exist before the Urban Revolution. For Gordon Childe the temple and the palace defined the city as urban. We can at present take them back to the transitional period when the premonitory signs of urbanism began to make themselves felt in the midst of the last prehistoric villages: that was in the appearance of the 'Ubaid culture' which existed between 6300 and 4600 BC in the Middle East. 'Temples' then begin to stand out sharply against the fabric of the village into which they have been implanted by reason of their plans and size, sometimes by their dimensions alone.[25] While we cannot be absolutely certain that these were religious buildings rather than places for secular gatherings (and admitting that this question has some significance at such an early date), they are in every case manifestly specialised buildings where some social function involving collective expression can be identified with enough certainty for us to say that they served as buildings for a special purpose.

At this point recent discoveries in the Anatolian PPNB put received ideas in question, for the sanctuaries of Çayönü and Nevalı Çori anticipate those of the Ubaid culture by more than a millennium. Consequently, the family sanctuaries of the sixth millennium at Çatalhöyük, while they remain quite exceptional for the richness of their decoration, do not constitute the evidence for any particular advance in the sociological sphere; indeed, rather to the contrary. Well before them, at Çayönü and Nevalı Çori we see buildings whose plans and dimensions are exceptional relative to the rest of the village, whereby they would be public buildings according to the criteria used for the Ubaid culture. Further, they furnish proof that they were places of cult and periodic sacrifice, for that seems to be the significance of the large, flat slabs on which blood had flowed.

No conclusion of this type has till now been supported for the Palestinian PPNB, but the Anatolian example invites us to look at the evidence again and with greater attention. It was in the Sultanian of Jericho that there had appeared a monument to a new feeling, the enormous tower of the PPNA period. It is possible that from its first construction it was regarded as sacred in some way, but we could never document that. The tower was still in existence in the PPNB, and the fact that its disused internal staircase was now crammed with human skeletons produces an effect of mortuary concentration that is quite comparable with that of the 'house of the dead' at Çayönü, although it cannot have been a place of assembly or cult. Kathleen Kenyon's suggestions of a religious interpretation for several other PPNB buildings are not totally convincing,[26] though she does describe one plan which is unusual, a building consisting of a large room with a small apse at either end, where the presence of some female and animal figurines reinforces the presumption of a religious use.

As we now know the Anatolian sanctuaries, the large building at Beidha, described above, is all the more astonishing since its dimensions are not the only features involved but also its large, square stone slab which recalls the 'altars' of the former.[27] A more hypothetical parallel can also be established between the apse with stone chest which lies on one side of the Anatolian monuments and the rather disconnected complex of curvilinear walls and chests made of stones, unique in the plan of Beidha at this period, which is adjacent to the courtyard of the large building and separates it from some perfectly standard corridor houses.[28] To tell the truth, the architectural correlation of this complex with the large building is by no means assured either on the published plans or in the author's text, which proposes a more prosaic interpretation for it as an enclosure for animals. However, Diana Kirkbride suggests that another complex situated further to the east[29] is a sanctuary; it is also curvilinear, with circular or larger oval cells containing large horizontal slabs and decorated stones, which make one think rather of the sanctuary at Nevalı Çori (pl. I). It seems very probable, therefore, that as in Anatolia we have here some buildings that are specialised for ceremonial usage, which accords with what we have inferred on other grounds, namely that ceremonial activity already existed in the southern Levant.

Several seventh-millennium Levantine villages, which are later but still Neolithic, and are also directly derived culturally from the PPNB, had rectangular buildings of a more simple form which are distinct from all the other houses in the village by reason of their having an apse at one end. In 1957 Maurice Dunand found one of these in the 'early Neolithic' of Byblos in the Lebanon, whose individuality is even more significant since the plan of this village is almost completely known. A concentration of female figurine made from pebbles as well as bovine frontals caused him to think of the building as a sanctuary.[30] An identical plan of the same date has recently been discovered at 'Ain Ghazal, where a similar inference has been made.[31] These buildings were evidently part of the legacy of the PPNB, where the existence of built sanctuaries can now scarcely be in doubt. It is curious to note that in this culture which was the first to introduce the rectangular plan for houses for people, the curved wall persists in order to distinguish religious building, an extraordinary convergence with the apses of our churches or the Islamic mihrab.

The PPNB cave of Nahal Hemar on the contrary, in spite of the remarkable concentration of cult furniture (skulls with modelled features, masks, figurines) and the diversity of material that it has harboured, recalls more a hiding place than a place for cult practices. Perhaps circumstances analogous to those which caused the deposition of the Essene manuscripts of Qumran in nearby caves had already occurred 8,000 years earlier? It is very improbable in any case that this material had been in use in the place where it was found.

The social significance of the sanctuaries
The discovery of public buildings consecrated to cult practices from the beginning of the eighth millennium, with all the wealth of evidence furnished in support by the Anatolian evidence, puts certain classical ideas in question. We should make these explicit in order to appreciate better the new developments that result.

Of course, neither the date nor the nature of urbanisation is in question. That process was set off in the fifth millennium by societies that were both internally differentiated and socially stratified. Mesopotamia rather than the Levant is considered as the primary theatre for this transformation, which translates itself into the archaeology as 'a real differentiation within the settlement founded in the advanced specialisation of some of the basic units'.[32] This differentiation, which from the fifth millennium may be followed by specialised crafts and skills which are the evidence for a degree of professionalisation of economic activities, is mirrored in a vertical hierarchy of functions which culminates with the emergence of the first Sumerian monarchies in the Early Bronze Age, relying on a religious and civil administration that was itself socially stratified.

It is from those considerations that there arises the importance attributed to the 'temples' of the Ubaid culture, which have for a long time seemed to represent the first transgression of the egalitarian structure which till that time could be seen in the homogeneous plans of the Neolithic villages. But after a phase of spontaneous sacralisation which caused them to call these 'temples', some archaeologists have thought it more objective to secularise them and to see in them some sort of communal house for assemblies and gatherings of a civil character.[33] We have already asked[34] if this opposition between religious and civil domains does not risk being a little artificial for the period under consideration. It is not the comparison proposed with the communal houses of the Mesopotamian villages, whose use was secular, that causes us trouble, since the historical dimension is precisely lacking in that comparison: how could we know if these architectural contrasts were expressing the same thing 7,000 years ago as today? Even if we pull the problem into the contemporary world, what are we going to think, in default of less fragmentary objective proofs, of the churches in our villages, or the town hall or the covered market? Is it not the ideology or the personal preferences of the archaeologist, or those of the current period that will finally dictate his choice? There is no shelter from this kind of problem when the facts themselves are mute, and history is written in the light of the present.

Indeed this is what makes the PPNB buildings and artefacts whose usage is so clear to us, especially those from Anatolia, so singular and valuable. Thanks to them, we now know that the first public buildings in history go back to the beginning of the eighth millennium and that they were indeed sanctuaries. Their great sacrificial slabs, besides, could come to the support of the hypothesis that the similar slabs in the later 'temples' of the Ubaid were also altars. These temples, whatever else one may say of them, would not then have usurped their title to the term. But in the other direction nothing proves that the PPNB sanctuaries are an index of precocious social stratification nor that any specialist 'clergy' served in them, as is too often claimed for buildings of a religious character.[35] The fact that the religious dimension is expressed through a collective architecture and that a specific built space is consecrated to a religious purpose implies nothing more than the existence of occasional gatherings in which the whole village community participated. Without doubt a 'ceremony' was generally conducted by some particularly qualified person, but that does not suppose any other social distinction than that which results from individual abilities. The most primitive societies always find in their midst some inspired individuals (shamans or sorcerers) whose function simply results from a spontaneous recognition among their fellows of a 'natural' superiority that applies in certain defined circumstances, in the same way that the war leader in certain palaeo-Indian tribes only remained chief as long as the war continued. No more than for the sanctuaries in Palaeolithic caves does the specialisation of the place imply some regular and institutionalised specialisation of one element within the society, nor any 'power' other than that which results from the occasional exploitation of personal competences, which must always have existed. We should not therefore attribute to the PPNB sanctuaries more than they speak for, nor because of them push back the date of the process of urbanisation. The concept of an egalitarian structure for Neolithic societies does not seem to us, therefore, to be threatened in the least.

What remains is that the PPNB sanctuaries prefigure very well in their own way the temples of the Ubaid culture and those of the urban period which follows. It is in the PPNB period that the members of a community gathered for the first time to build and use buildings that were beyond the everyday, and this usage was not utilitarian but related to symbolic activities. This is a turning point in history which once again we see as derived from an impulse of the religious imagination. But just as, for its period, the throne of the Goddess at Çatalhöyük does not refer us to some sort of terrestrial monarchy, so the sanctuary does not reflect some form of effective social stratification, which in fact must wait for three or four millennia.

12

The dynamics of a dominant culture

It was perhaps several centuries after farming villages had been disseminated over a vast area in the Levant that farming first reached the eastern Taurus. We have in fact watched two diffusion phenomena that start from one of the original hearths of the Levantine Neolithic, centred on the middle Euphrates in northern Mesopotamia. These move in opposite directions, one towards the north and north-west, the other towards the south.

The northward diffusion into Anatolia represents the first historical case of 'secondary neolithisation': for the first time, the model of the Neolithic way of life, including subsistence production, took over a region in which it was not native. This expansion is linked to that of a well-defined culture, the evolved, complex Mureybetian in the last stage of its early PPNB form, and there is scope for thinking that there was a real increment of population who came to join a basis of indigenous hunter-gatherers. This indigenous population was apparently not at all numerous, but it remains hypothetical for us rather than well documented in archaeological actuality.

Some centuries later, a second wave of expansion arrived in the southern Levant. As we have seen, it is beyond doubt that it involved yet another colonisation with a genuine ethnic component. But this colonisation is not expressed in economic terms: the middle PPNB carried to the southern farmers, whose existence is already confirmed, almost nothing in the economic domain apart from a new cultivated cereal species. As for herding, the first stages were more or less simultaneous on the middle Euphrates and in Palestine, which in this regard as with others received nothing from the north. Thus there is no element of 'neolithisation' in this example, even though it represents a territorial expansion of the PPNB culture.

So what was the reason for this expansion? An explanation that is favoured among processualists would call on some regional population pressure pushing some part of the population towards the peripheral zones. It seems scarcely to have merited discussion that settlement in Syrian upper Mesopotamia seems to have been fairly sparse. Even allowing for sites that are unknown to us, virtually nothing before 8000 BC suggests the necessity of leaving home in order to spread out. The expansionary force of the PPNB must rather relate to an internal dynamism within the culture itself. Even if it may have brought farming to Anatolia, its southward diffusion expressly demonstrates to us that it was not essential.[1]

We shall attempt to comprehend the nature of this dynamism by reviewing the cultural traits – not restricting ourselves to a mere description, but seeking beyond that the complex structural unity which gave those traits their sense and efficacy and which above all can give some account of the fact that, from its beginning, the PPNB was a conquering culture.

Material culture and symbols

'Symbolic archaeology' or 'contextual archaeology', initiated by the ethnoarchaeologist Ian Hodder,[2] has to some degree prepared the way for us: Hodder in effect maintains that in human societies utilitarian objects have a meaning that goes beyond their simple technical value and that material culture in its entirety constitutes a system of signification which is very well adapted for the simultaneous explanation of the global functioning of society, its adaptations to concrete circumstances and its eventual changes. However, the case studies that he first pulled together[3] most often refer to living societies of a type that is certainly archaic but much more evolved than those which concern us here. It is always a matter of putting some particular aspect of material culture, for example shapes and decoration of pots, house-plans, furnishings or funerary arrangements, into relationship with some aspect of social stratification (power, institutionalised division of labour, dominant groups, etc.). It is the same for the rare archaeological examples that are developed: all refer to the late Neolithic or the Bronze or Iron Ages, that is, to societies that were already stratified or on the way to becoming so. The 'symbolism' under discussion has no other purpose than precisely to permit us to detect social distinctions and hierarchies.[4] Such a process has scarcely any meaning for our early Neolithic villagers, with their homogeneous and egalitarian social systems, but one may still ask if material culture could not symbolise something other than a type of social organisation that did not yet exist.

The 'symbolic system' in the sense that this term is given by structuralists is an altogether different matter. The expression refers to the mental structures themselves which, quite unconsciously, rigorously organise people's mythologies, their rituals and kinship systems. The fundamental intuition of Claude Lévi-Strauss was in effect that a single mental system governed the different levels of reality and makes them 'homologous' one with another. Unfortunately, for lack of information, this kind of study can be applied not to archaic but only to living societies where oral enquiries can be made, or to extinct societies which have consigned their mythology to writing. This is almost to say that the prehistorian should scarcely be concerned, because the distance between the detailed, indeed prolix, recitations of myths reported by Lévi-Strauss and the simple symbolic 'images' that we see in prehistory is enormous; at best, we can suggest some fundamental, structural relativities between these symbols on the basis of spatial analysis. We should recall, however, with Jean-Pierre Vernant,[5] that structuralism was strongly influenced at source by linguistic models. That is the reason why the image remains subordinated to the myth, as the word to the phrase, and the image makes sense only in relation to the myth. In this perspective, we could scarcely get anywhere with our Neolithic females and bulls, since we are missing the thousand complex twists and turns in which the oral tradition of these societies must have engaged in their mythological discourse.

However, Jean-Pierre Vernant, following the work of Creuzer and Ernst Cassirer, shows that the symbolic image precedes the myth. The image makes it immediate and visible and, before all other forms of discourse, reveals in a concrete form available to the senses 'the presence of that which, while divine, escapes the limitations of the concrete, the sensible, the finite'.[6] Moreover this 'divine' is itself felt as a power more than as an idea. We may conclude that in such matters as these there is exchange with elements of the human unconscious that are more dynamic than simple, cold organisational principles of the imagination and reality. We should also understand that the unconscious mental structures which, according to Lévi-Strauss, characterise 'the savage mind' may have left an impression of a certain intellectual thought, and that we could be reproached with not having taken proper account either of the effort of material adaptation of society to its environment or of its transformation through the course of time.[7]

Moreover we are dealing here with major and revolutionary processes in the relationship of humans with their environment. The little that we can perceive of the 'Revolution in symbols' around 10,000 BC had the advantage of direct influence on a new environmental practice, that is, bearing at once on real life and its maintenance. In other words, the symbol was of itself a power capable of generating a more tangible change: the appearance of the farming economy.

In our opinion, it is possible to undertake a similar study of the PPNB that depends simultaneously on the two sides that are too often isolated from one another in the analysis of prehistoric cultures: that is, on the one hand culture's non-utilitarian component, art and ritual, which is more directly revealing of the way the collective psychology functions, and on the other hand material culture, the economic strategies and artefacts, whose most significant elements have been shown to correspond with the other non-material components. Consequently we should seek to appreciate not only how the PPNB represents a new stage in the elaboration of the Neolithic mentality but also how this change was at the origin of specific behaviour patterns and their spread.

The religion of the bull
We could call the PPNB people the 'people of the bull', so clearly has the importance of this animal in their world of imagination become to us. We have seen that this choice was rooted in the cultural tradition of upper Mesopotamia, beginning with the Khiamian of the middle Euphrates. In the whole of the Levant in the Natufian period, and in the southern Levant until the arrival of the PPNB, herds of wild cattle were an element in the landscape, but while they seem rather to have been avoided by the hunter these beasts excited much more than indifference in the area of cultural production. This is the demonstration of the observation that an animal species can be integrated into the bestiary of symbolism of a culture only in so far as, in some manner, the culture recognises something of itself in the animal and projects on to it some subliminal dimension of its collective psychology.

The idea that the image of the wild bull signifies a brute force, instinctive and violent, is spontaneous in us and is without doubt universal. However, it is worth

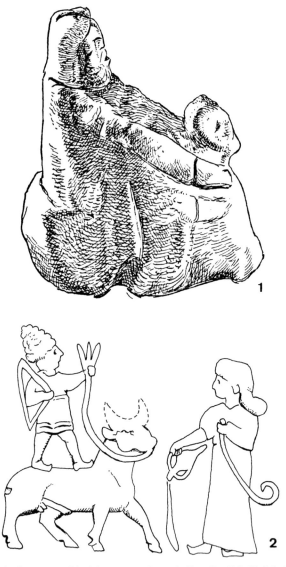

Fig. 43 Anthropomorphic deity mounted on a bull: 1 Çatalhöyük, Neolithic, seventh millennium BC, Turkey (after J. Mellaart), height 107 mm; 2 Hittite god of the storm (after J. Garstang).

confirming the point by means of reference to iconographic and documentary sources provided by the later urban civilisations of the Bronze Age in the same cultural region. The image of the bull is in effect perpetuated generally, most often associated with a masculine, anthropomorphic god of whom the bull is the attribute or the animal form. Through this image the god at once symbolises the generic force of the storm and the qualities of the warrior. Before the storm, humans can do absolutely nothing: they can only submit to this 'cosmic' form of unleashed violence, or shelter from it. Only one god, whether he was Phoenician Baal, Hittite Hadad (Fig. 43: 2), or earlier perhaps the Neolithic male God of Çatalhöyük (Fig. 43: 1), could ride the storm-clouds and the celestial Bull, in exactly the same way that the Goddess alone could dominate the panther. But in man brute violence, once mastered ('humanised'), could be converted into an organised power of confrontation. Through the image of Baal of Ugarit who was master of the Bull or could himself become the Bull, and who was represented as warrior-hero and civilising force,[8] by braving the wild bull-animal man could learn to seek the opportunity to prove his mastery over it, his courage and his effectiveness in combat. It is thus not surprising that, from Çatalhöyük, through Minoan Crete to Iberia, the confrontation between man and bull should be unfolded as a solemn and ritual act, whose still vivid reverberations are preserved in the brilliant costume of the matador of today.[9]

A clear-cut evolution can be perceived, therefore, in the relationship of the prehistoric people of the Levant with the bull. The first bucrania of the Khiamian of Mureybet remained buried within the thickness of the walls of buildings, not visible therefore to their occupants. Perhaps they only metaphorically wanted to ensure the resistance of the building to all forms of destruction by appealing to this new symbolism for an initial consecration. The time had not yet come for direct confrontation with the animal. Then the Mureybetians were the first – indeed the only people of their time – to hunt wild cattle regularly. But besides the persistence and multiplication of the bovine symbol and its early diffusion into Anatolia and the southern Levant, the PPNB now adds two original thematic elements: the appearance in religious art of man himself, that is to say a human male, and the first explicit allusion (at 'Ain Ghazal) to the bull-fighting act.

Consequently the instinctive force is in part drawn from its animal straitjacket when it finds a 'man' to confront it. What the imagination embraces in the category of the 'virile', whether generic or combative force, ceases to be lived in the spontaneity of instinct, since only he who can control instinct can truly and precisely be a man, and since, despite their common impetuosity, the hero is something quite different from the brute. It may be that this dialectic of 'virility', taking the form of a dominant self-confidence, emerged in the Mediterranean consciousness around 8000 BC; and in that dialectic the real internal dynamism of the PPNB culture that underlies the more visible manifestations perhaps lived on at the level of the predominant mythical images. It is these visible manifestations that we must now tackle.

The love-affair with weapons

Every point of flint or obsidian, cursorily retouched or even unretouched, could arm an arrow-shaft or a weapon in the hand. Particularly when blade techniques made their appearance, with methods of preparing the core so that the products were long, parallel-sided and light, with sharp edges and often spontaneously pointed at the tip, a minimum of retouch was sufficient to prepare the base for fixing into its haft or, if necessary, to sharpen the point. As we saw, the Khiamians throughout the Levant and their Sultanian successors in the southern Levant chose to truncate the base of their points and facilitate the binding of a ligature by the simple creation of two lateral opposed notches. This is what we call the 'Khiam point' (Fig. 5: 1–2; Fig. 12: 1–2). Another solution, known since the European Upper Palaeolithic, consisted of chipping a tang for fixing the weapon in its hafting. In the Levant, a combination of the two methods resulted in a particular type of arrow-head known as the 'Helwan point'; this point appeared at the end of the Khiamian period, and had both tang and notches. In the simple forms that have been described,[10] all these finishing touches required little more of the prehistoric manufacturer than a few seconds work, as contemporary experimenters have shown. In all the regional facies of the PPNB we have noted a new and common pursuit of style in weaponry. They used a new type of retouch in the Levant; the retouch was long and shallow, at this stage it was confined to weapons and it goes well beyond what would be needed by a simple search for efficiency. Even if this weaponry was utilised in part for hunting, its seems unreasonable to deduce from its abundance and even more from its quality that there was some intensification in that activity, since this is exactly the time when the beginnings of herding begin to modify the relationship between human communities and the animal kingdom into a more peaceful mode. This technical domain has become quite simply a matter of prestige, requiring additional craft investment and an otherwise inexplicable aesthetic quest. Rather than a new 'need', we thus perceive in the origin of this new technique a new mental attitude which values weaponry and which also had its origin in the Mureybetian where it was first found. This is to say that it is closely associated in time with the 'religion of the Bull' from its origins and down to the appearance of the warrior gear that surrounds the male divinities of the Bronze Age.

Indeed, we might wonder whether the PPNB expansion was in fact achieved through 'force of arms'. The appearance of warfare in the Neolithic as the logical consequence of the new need to defend property is postulated by prehistorians rather than demonstrated on the basis of the available information. One arrow-head retrieved here or there stuck in a human vertebra is perhaps not as adequate a proof as has been claimed. In this regard the dominant culture brought by the newly arrived people seems to have reached a 'marriage' with the former inhabitants rather than their brutal elimination. And if the newcomers imposed their new customs in many areas of life, there is nevertheless no indication that they constituted any sort of elite in the sociological sense of the term, as was the case in conquered territories in much later times. We may therefore confidently speak of expansion, even if the PPNB now had as its major symbol, alongside the Goddess proper to the whole of the Neolithic, a virile male figure whose principal significance, somewhat later, explicitly concerned war. We stay with the homology demonstrated by Claude Lévi-Strauss as we discover an analogous arrangement in the particular values attributed to a certain category of artefacts. This weaponry indeed has a 'symbolic' value, as Ian Hodder would say. However, at this stage, it is the collective psychology of the culture that is in part revealed as a result, rather than new social structures.

The tamer of goats

In the early and middle PPNB, while hunters indeed confronted the bull in more than symbolic fashion, the frequency varying with the environment of the site, they had yet not domesticated it. It is only in the late phase of the same culture, in the late PPNB, that domestication of wild cattle became effective in some areas. The cause of the lateness was probably the evident difficulty of the enterprise. The grazing species that was first to be domesticated, the goat, is of a more easy-going manner. The sheep followed closely after.

Thus, while the wild ram is sometimes represented among the PPNB figurines, the goat is apparently not. No specific 'mental preparation' would here seem to prefigure its herding. It was only much later, in the Mesopotamian Chalcolithic and Bronze Ages, that the goat would appear in sculpture and on seals, accompanying some divine person like the bull or the feline. We might therefore be tempted to retain the descriptive sequence long ago proposed by certain zooarchaeologists: in the course of a preliminary phase of specialised hunting which had already made the goat an economically dominant species in the meat food supply of human groups, they see the hunters progressively familiarising themselves with the wild herd on which they depended, making themselves accepted to the point that they could approach the animals more and more easily and being able to choose the animals to be killed according to their age and sex, and finally reaching a more and more rational strategy of management of the herd. At the end of this long apprenticeship in reciprocity between people and animals, people would find themselves at the head of the herd that was 'domesticated' in terms of its dependence on humans. Then they would arrive at the point where they would control the movements of the herd, and, later, control the breeding itself. This is why specialised, selective hunting might be called by some a form of 'proto-herding', because it seems to establish the necessary, if not the sufficient, conditions for the transition.

Note that this schema is descriptive but it explains nothing. Above all, it does not describe every case. In effect it postulates that the domestication of a species is established where that species already occupied a fundamental place in the subsistence economy. Such a process may have taken place at Beidha, where goats are considered domesticated from the middle PPNB, while the early Natufians, long before the PPNB, had already been engaged in intensive hunting of goats for simply ecological reasons.[11] But this is not always the case: at Abu Hureyra, a site that is very important for us since it is perhaps the oldest where goats were herded, goats were domesticated from the beginning of the middle PPNB period, thus at least by 8200 BC, but they still represent only 6% of the faunal remains of food animals, that is to say, no more significant than the wild sheep of the Natufian of the same site 2,000 years earlier. It was only somewhat later that goats reached 70% of the fauna.[12] Domestication therefore does not appear to be linked in this instance to a preliminary context of specialised hunting. As Daniel Helmer has recently shown,[13] all that seems to happen is that the domesticated animal does no more than replace with a similar quantity of meat what was previously provided by its wild equivalent, whether that wild species was hunted intensively or not.

How is it that we have not seen that there is an analogy between the beginnings of herding and the beginnings of cultivation and these same preconceived ideas have been allowed to engender in both areas the same errors of interpretation? We must not confuse the origins of herding with those of an economy founded on it, any more than the development of cultivation with the beginning of farming economies. If, as Brian Hesse has said, herding was essentially at the base of a modification of 'the cultural interface between people and animals',[14] we can recognise that we must once again look for the causes on the cultural side and not in the economic logic of progressively greater control of a food resource in which they were already specialised.

In his remarkable work, *L'homme et les animaux domestiques*, Jean-Pierre Digard has been able to show, mainly on the basis of ethnoarchaeological observations but also through an analogy with our own conclusions on the beginnings of cultivation, that the motivations of obtaining food-stuffs were the least probable in the appearance of animal domestication. Animal domestication was above all a response to the human desire for domination over the animal kingdom: 'The stupefying zeal for domestication in man', he says, 'is not explained by anything other than through the quest for domestication for its own sake and for the image that it gives of a power over life and living things'.[15] Recent information now available for the PPNB exactly confirms that view: it is no coincidence that the earliest known domestication saw the light of day when Neolithic culture was concerned with 'virility', and at exactly the time when the symbolic motif of human confrontation with animals emerged. We are quite a long way from the rather thin reasoning that is most often cited today – that of stabilising meat supplies.

The rectangular house
Besides the cult of the Bull and the symbolic promotion of weaponry, there is a third strand of evidence for the development and diffusion of the PPNB culture that began to appear in the final Mureybetian phase: rectangular buildings. There are doubtless reasons of pure technical convenience to explain why the first human houses were round. What Olivier Aurenche calls 'the original house'[16] was at the start a simple pit, and it was usual for it to be round. The circular (or oval) semi-subterranean house is thus the first type of construction to appear in the Levant, in the Kebaran and the Natufian. In the same way, long after rectangular buildings had become widespread, as the nomadic pastoralist groups of the seventh millennium returned to a sedentary life, they once again reproduced the primitive design of the circular pit, which from then on appears as the solution of first resort for any culture that does not have, or has lost, experience in the art of building.[17]

It has therefore been thought legitimate to advance the idea that the circular plan connotes very straightforwardly nomadic or semi-nomadic communities, and indeed those at the very beginning of becoming sedentary, while the rectangular plan characterises farming villages that are fully sedentary.[18] This model is of debatable historical value in the Levant, since the large farming villages of the PPNA period all conserved the round house tradition. They retained it precisely because the rectangular house had not yet emerged in the cultures of the Neolithic. This emergence is a historical process in which the Levantine PPNB is the first diffusing agency, and we must give some account of the process.

It has been emphasised that the rectangular house for its part allows additions to be made in the form of extra rooms, while the round house from the start has a defined area for living and, from the perspective of adding extensions, presents an impasse.[19] Thence comes the second model proposed by Kent Flannery, where the rectangular house is linked to a new type of family structure that brings together under the one roof the parents, their children and in time their children's offspring, while each round Natufian 'hut', on the basis of ethnographic examples taken from African or American compounds, would have been occupied by only one or at the most two persons in a polygynous family structure.

In that regard we may remark that if the nuclear family was already in existence, for example in the Sultanian of Jericho, from the evidence we have it could not manifest itself through the medium of rectangular architecture for the simple reason that such buildings had not yet been invented. To attribute this invention to the pressure of accommodating a given family structure can be no better than very hypothetical. Admitting the incontestable advantages of this form of building to provide shelter for such a group, it is a much more delicate matter to weigh up the different factors which may in reality have been in operation at its emergence. In our opinion these are of three kinds, and it will help to describe them separately.

The first is simply technical. The construction of rectangular buildings supposes that people knew how to make a free-standing rectangular wall-plan stand up, and also how to fit two walls together at right angles. Learning about vertical walls came about in the first instance from the internal division of round houses. They experimented notably with new ways of using a framework of wood which was intended both to ensure the cohesion of walls made of *pisé* and to consolidate the angles by means of interlacing the wood.[20] Then it was only in the final stage of the Mureybetian period, at Mureybet itself and at Sheikh Hassan, that there appeared the first buildings defined by four walls at right angles.[21] It is a matter of technical progress: we have seen in other examples that this progress follows a more or less regular and constant course without reference to other changes. Here too, the new architectural form makes things possible, but it cannot by itself explain its appearance, any more than the querns and sickles that preceded the adoption of cultivation directly engendered it.

The second factor, the principle of the internal division of living space, seems to be linked to a social pressure. We have seen that the principle can be put into practice without having to wait for rectangular architecture. That indeed may be simply a response to the impasse already mentioned, that of the inconvenience of the circular form when it comes to increasing the number of rooms. However, the example of the first houses at PPNB Beidha shows that round cells could be juxtaposed with some shared walls and set around a court (Fig. 35) in order to obtain the same result. It is particularly difficult to understand why there exist at a somewhat later date villages where the rectangular houses have only one room, for example in the later PPNB at Ramad in the Damascus region, and in the 'Early Neolithic' of Byblos on the coast.[22] These single-roomed houses characterise certain geographical regions. Olivier Aurenche certainly views it as a matter of cultural choice by their populations.[23] In any case, these show that the multi-roomed design and the rectangular plan are not necessarily linked. Finally, one would like to understand why, independently of any technical aptitude, certain cultures of the seventh or sixth millennium deliberately retained round plans, whether in Cyprus, or in the Halaf culture of north Mesopotamia. Builders were fully competent[24] and there is no reason to postulate a return to archaic family structures.

It is therefore necessary to envisage a third factor which does not always exclude the other two but which must be able to account for formal choices at the cultural level that are manifestly independent of the other factors. As we shall see, that is important for elucidating the surprising regressions to forms of house that are apparently outmoded, and it is also important when the transition from circular to rectangular houses is proclaimed as a 'world first' for the PPNB of the Levant.

Geometric forms have a deep significance in the human mind, and we should not forget that fact, even though other considerations, whether technical, ecological or sociological, are also pertinent. From the Natufian, and throughout the Neolithic period, these forms are present not only in personal adornment, where beads are among the first human products to be given geometric forms,[25] but also in small objects, which are frequently found in excavations and often thought enigmatic. These spheres, cylinders, discs, cones or parallelipeds, sometimes in semiprecious materials and often enhanced with incised signs or more complex geometric motifs (Fig. 44), for the present lend themselves poorly to any precise interpretation. However they are the evidence for a very precocious vocabulary of fundamental shapes that prehistoric people had not elaborated for utilitarian reasons, at least at this first stage.[26] This 'language' of geometric shapes certainly in part intersects with certain symmetries observable in nature (stars, flowers, shells, constellations), but we find it from the start at a high level of abstraction, independent of all figurative intent. And above all, contrary to what is usually supposed, this geometry does not appear to be derived from the practical activities of people in their everyday environment, such as for example methods of surveying or measurement. From this point of view, the thinking of the Pythagoreans, on the cosmological significance of geometrical forms such as the circle and the square perhaps represents an intellectual framework that is at least as ancient as their derivation of theoretical knowledge of geometry from practical experience.[27]

On the question of the plans of houses, this direct symbolism of geometric shapes is even more in danger of passing unappreciated as it joins with other factors to produce a final outcome in the form of a building that is at once very utilitarian and also planned under constraints of other kinds, whether technical or social. However, as Mircéa Eliade has said: 'the cosmic symbolism of the house is attested in numerous primitive societies. In a more or less clear manner, the house is considered as an *imago mundi*. Since one finds examples at all levels of culture, it is difficult to see why the first Neolithic people of the Levant would have been an exception, the more so as it is in this region that the cosmic symbolism of architecture will later see the more rapid development'.[28]

From this perspective, what could the transition in house plans from the circle to the rectangle mean? No direct source exists to aid our interpretative directions, guiding us on the two principles which have inspired this book: one is that Neolithic

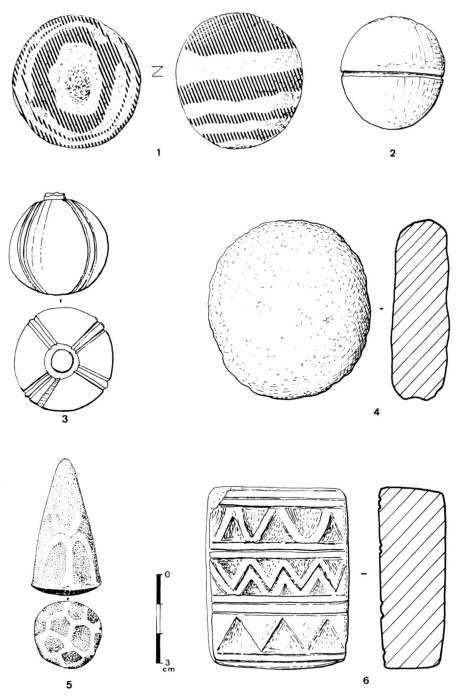

Fig. 44 Geometrical objects of Neolithic date: 1 sphere in red, banded stone (PPNB at Cafer Höyük); 2 limestone sphere divided into two halves by an incised line (Mureybetian period at Mureybet); 3 limestone sphere with omphalos and divided into four zones (Byblos, seventh millennium BC); 4 baked clay disc (Mureybetian period at Mureybet); 5 fossil coral in the shape of a cone (PPNB at Cafer Höyük); 6 paralleliped of chalk decorated in chevrons (Mureybetian at Sheikh Hassan). After J. Cauvin (1–2, 4–6) and M. Dunand (3).

thought was not foreign to our own, since, in a certain manner, ours is historically based on that source through the play of cultural transmissions in the Mediterranean basin; the other supposes that, although the imagination has a history and it is one of our goals to analyse its evolution and developments in the Neolithic, the symbolic vocabulary also has recurrent aspects that today's historians of religion find again and again almost everywhere as if they constituted 'specific innate constituents' (Gilbert Durand). Thanks to them, we can free ourselves without too much danger from the cultural area to which we have confined ourselves up to this point for our comparisons. In the universal language of simple forms, the circle (or the sphere) signifies both that which transcends man and remains beyond his reach (the sun, the cosmic totality, 'God'), and also that which, at its own sub-lunar level, relates to germination, to the maternal,[29] to the intimate. On the contrary, the rectangle, examples of which are rare in our everyday observations of nature, requires human initiative for its existence: the stone is not cubic or rectangular unless so fashioned. The square and the rectangle denote then the manifest, the concrete, that which has been realised. We also know that at the level of the still very elemental imagination, the curve is feminine while the straight line and the angular are masculine. In these respects also, as Mircéa Eliade has said, there is no reason to think that the people of the Neolithic were any exception.

Consequently, to half bury oneself in the ground in a circular pit may seem primitive, and later perhaps rather regressive, not only from a technical point of view, but also at the level of the symbolic function itself. On the contrary, the 'square house', generally built on the surface, is witness to a different mental attitude, where the progress of technical knowledge encounters the initiative that utilises it, an attitude which imposes an entirely new, artificial, preconceived form on a basic need for shelter.

One can see that in the Natufian house people used stones or wood merely to consolidate a pre-existing wall formed from the Earth itself where the house was dug into it, and then finally roofed the construction. The emergence of the house into the open air and its transition to a rectangular plan thus realise a technical and at the same time a mental linking. We must not forget that when rectangular architecture appeared at the end of the Mureybetian period, it had never before in any way existed in the world, but then it very rapidly became the archetype of the human house.[30] In that way sedentary people left the hole of their origins and the circular matrix of their first homes. This fact can only be understood as the emergence of an affirmation of conscious and culturally expressed self to which other documents appear to bear witness. We shall therefore consider the rectangular house as a trait 'homologous' with its predecessors, in the structuralist sense of the term.

An expansionist culture

Thus a more coherent portrait of the PPNB culture is little by little delineated. Four dominant traits absolutely characterise it, leaving aside the local and more variable characteristics: these are a start in the process of developing symbols of virility, the emergence of animal domestication which would become general in the late PPNB, an elaborate weaponry, and the origination and diffusion of rectangular architecture. All these facts are usually presented as if they were independent of one another: however, they appear to us to be interrelated, as if from within, by a unique network of meanings. The PPNB imagination, immediately perceptible at the level of art and rituals, seems to play the role of a 'formal causality', in the sense used in Greek philosophy, in relation to domains that were *a priori* more commonplace: the house, the panoply of weapons, and the techniques of subsistence.

Our second conclusion is that, in the neolithisation of the Levant, there was a new mental transformation that was prepared in the course of the preceding phase by the Mureybetian culture of Syrian Upper Mesopotamia and by it alone. This transformation had nothing to do with the birth of agriculture. That, the first 'humanising' process in the world, had already accompanied a raising of the human figure into art – but it was a female figure. This invention was made, we could say, under the aegis of the Goddess and could well have been, both concretely and symbolically, a female affair.[31] Without renouncing this religious matriarchy[32] in which the Goddess remains the supreme authority, the PPNB culture goes through an episode of deep concern with virility which prefigures what will be the promotion into mythology of gods and heroes in combat, at the same time in the Bronze Age when metal weapons would be developed. The symbolic attributes of this concern began to fall into place in the eighth millennium. From this observation one could suppose that animal domestication, as a function of the emotional dimensions that it sets in motion, must have been at its origin a male initiative. It is also this masculine aspect that must have given to the PPNB culture its 'conquering' nature, of which its rapid diffusion is evidence. The wild bull is not a symbol of equilibrium or of tranquil settled life. This symbol is suffused with the values of expansionism, when the human male is assimilated into ritual and raises blind impetuosity and instinct to respectability through the confrontation in the battle with the bull.

As the corollary of this, we have seen the human form itself, male and female, proliferate in art and ritual. Statues, figurines and skulls with modelled features form as it were an abundant counter-society, where it is difficult but perhaps superfluous, in particular for the statues, to establish if they are divinities or heroic ancestors. Even the conserved skulls which very probably mark out ancestors selected from among the dead (we do not know on what criteria) display the same global phenomenon as the art itself, the omnipresence of the human face in the religious environment. This is something very new and different from the simple funerary piety that had long existed, but which now buried in the grave with the dead person a memory that could soon be reclaimed from oblivion. This is the remaking of a presence, no doubt periodically and with ceremony. We have emphasised elsewhere[33] how, as the divinity himself was revealed more and more with these human traits, this intensified cult that the people of the PPNB reserved for their own kind supposes a strong and new confidence in the value of that humanity and a cementing of the social and ideological bonds among its members of a kind that had never previously been achieved. In Hegelian terms, one might speak of the arrival of a 'self-awareness', not yet individual but collective, and yet 'alienated' by being projected on to the figures.

That specialised sanctuaries appeared at this moment is not at all surprising in this connection. We should however recall that in the aceramic Neolithic it is not necessary to imagine any priestly body or warrior caste, or even organised chiefdoms which would have left perceptible traces, whether in the organisation of the houses or in some hierarchy of individual burials. One may simply postulate an increased degree of co-operation that would assure both the construction of collective buildings and their ceremonial use. The necessary authority to bring these matters to a successful conclusion could be provided either by a council of elders, the family relatives, or some other 'natural' group in the body social, for which ethnology offers a whole range of possible models.

This embryonic organisation would in any case need to suffice for the execution not only of 'festivals' but also of collective departures and an expansion towards new territories, whether they were already inhabited by others or not. This expansion we have noted from the first stage of the PPNB through which we have now travelled. We believe that we have detected in the mental frameworks of the culture the energising ingredient that must have motivated it. We shall now see that these colonising advances before 7500 BC only prefigure a much more vast exodus which will be the mark of the later PPNB.

PART III

The great exodus

13

The problem of diffusion in the Neolithic

The Neolithic Revolution, born in the Levant, is now about to export itself. The thesis of local neolithisation by processes developing autonomously all over the world was originally proposed in reaction to what had been called, not without some impatience, 'le mirage oriental' (the illusion that all things derive from the Near East). But this thesis has lost more and more ground, at least in so far as Europe, the Middle East and perhaps also North Africa are concerned. It falters when it confronts the extraordinarily rich range of plant and animal species that were already domesticated in the Levant between 9500 and 7000 BC. Some species only existed there in the wild, while others with much wider distributions were domesticated earlier there than anywhere else and were diffused in their domesticated form at the same time as the cereals. We may recall that before 7500 BC Neolithic communities in the Levant were already cultivating wheat, barley and rye among the cereals, peas, lentils, beans, vetches and chickpeas among the legumes, and flax for textiles. The botanist Daniel Zohary reasons on genetic grounds that this whole list of plants was domesticated within a very short space of time and within a very restricted zone.[1] But we have also seen that the 'domesticating zeal' of which Jean-Pierre Digard speaks,[2] and which has here been attributed to palaeo-psychological origins, counts for more than the potential of the domesticable species which people had at their disposal. The same holds good for the animal kingdom, where the dog was man's earliest companion in the European Upper Palaeolithic, while the horse appears to have been controlled only a little later in the plains of Ukraine.[3] On the other hand, our principal meat-providing mammals, goat, sheep, cattle and pig, were domesticated in the same civilising stride, in the same area and at the same time. These are the species that are found in the four corners of the Old World from the beginning of the Neolithic.

The contribution of molecular biology

To this diffusion of domesticated species is added the genetic make-up of today's European populations. Together they demonstrate the human migrations that carried the crops and herds.[4] It appears that the Near East played a considerable role in the peopling of Europe, if we may judge from a process whose effects on the genetic composition of contemporary populations are attenuated in proportion to the distance from the point of departure. It is evident that this 'colonisation' did not happen in an empty landscape and that the exogenous human component was blended with pre-existing populations in progressively decreasing numbers from the

Balkans to Scandinavia. The initiators of this analysis, Albert Ammerman and L. L. Cavalli-Sforza, believe that only the Neolithic diffusion has assumed a sufficient degree of generality to explain the phenomenon. We also owe to them the 'wave of advance' theory, where it has been calculated that this expansion progressed westwards at an average speed of 1 kilometre per year.

The contribution of linguistics

A third scientific discipline, historical linguistics, claims to be able to identify the Neolithic colonisation issuing from the Near East as the diffusing agent for Indo-European languages in Europe and Asia.[5] As proposed by Gordon Childe and then by Maria Gimbutas, the classic theory of the expansion of the Indo-European languages towards western Europe and Asia sets the process in the first millennium BC, originating in a heartland in the Russian steppes of the Don and the Volga basins. This diffusion would thus have furthered the dissemination of pastoral economies, metallurgy, the horse and wheeled vehicles. Thomas Gamkrelidze and V. Ivanov have laid out the evidence against this view: 'Proto-Indo-European', whose reconstruction has been achieved through a comparative study of modern Indo-European languages, contains on the one hand a majority of words relating to agrarian activities (both tools and species), and on the other hand words that denote plants and landscapes in mountainous country, very different from those of the steppes proposed by Maria Gimbutas. For them therefore it is Anatolia that is defined as the source from which this linguistic diffusion spread, together with the neolithisation of Europe as its economic vector.

In 1987 Colin Renfrew presented a sensational synthesis of these very different theoretical advances by setting the results of molecular biology and linguistics in the context of recent archaeological discoveries. In his view the neolithisation of Europe can be understood as a genuine colonisation that started in the seventh millennium from a source in Anatolia and involved the arrival in Europe of new population elements.[6] He considers these as the carriers of the Indo-European proto-languages, moving forward in accordance with a 'wave of advance' model. More recently,[7] he has extended his theory beyond this family of languages by referring to the so-called 'Nostratic'[8] hypothesis proposed by Russian linguists. At one level, comparative methodology has allowed the definition of families of languages (for example, the 'Indo-European' family) in terms of affinities of vocabulary, morphology of words and phonology, all the languages of a family being derived from a hypothetical common ancestor. Now it is further proposed that certain of the families themselves present affinities that allow them to be grouped in their turn into 'macro-families' that equally point back to a common source. Therefore a 'Nostratic' proto-language was the origin of the Indo-European, Hamito-Semitic, Elamite-Dravidian, Uralic and Altaic families, that is of the great majority of the languages spoken in Europe, Asia and North Africa. Colin Renfrew links this conclusion with a 'four-lobed' theory of the first Near Eastern Neolithic peoples,[9] which were, according to him, the Levant, Anatolia, the Zagros and perhaps Turkmenia. Based on an original community of 'Nostratic' language, each of these four lobes may have given rise to one of the four directions of simultaneous agropastoral expansion and linguistic differentiation: Anatolia gave rise to the westward direction (the Balkans and Europe) with Proto-Indo-European, the Levant to the south (Arabia and Africa) with Proto-Semitic, the Zagros towards the east with the Elamo-Dravidian languages, and finally Turkmenia towards central Asia with the dialects of the Uralic and Altaic families. It goes without saying that this very attractive theory may very well relate to reality, but, at the present stage of archaeological and linguistic research, it is Renfrew's opinion that it is not possible to consider it as anything more than a speculative hypothesis, only the European direction seeming for the present to be sufficiently supported.

The archaeological difficulties

One could readily deduce from the preceding chapters that from the viewpoint of a Near Eastern prehistorian the 'four-lobed' concept of initial neolithisation proposed by Colin Renfrew is less and less acceptable in those precise terms. It divides Robert Braidwood's 'nuclear zone' redefined from a palaeo-botanical perspective by Daniel Zohary and Maria Hopf[10] into four parts; and it requires that the whole mountainous region of the Near and Middle East bordering the Fertile Crescent where the wild ancestors of the domesticated cereals were available should be considered as the global and synchronous zone within which cultivation and herding first emerged. We have seen that presence alone is not enough, and that there was no neolithisation in the other 'lobes' simultaneous with that of the Levant. Were these perhaps the receiving zones of a first phase of diffusion out of the 'Levantine corridor'? That is now shown to be the probable case for Anatolia, at least to the satisfaction of the present author although it is still debated by others. However, in the matter of diffusion towards the Balkans, Anatolia remains the necessary route, and that is much less debatable.

The principal archaeological difficulties are of a different order.[11] The linguist demands that the archaeologist should furnish hard historical evidence to put a human face on the diffusion of languages. That their speakers travelled across vast distances is in effect the indispensable precondition for these long-distance transmissions. We have seen that the presence of animals and plants brought from the Near East into the whole of Neolithic Europe was the most irrefutable indication of such a movement. But the exact nature of the human migrations is much less clear. In fact, only the fifth-millennium Neolithic movement known as the Danubian or Linearbandkeramik (LBK), whose characteristic houses and pottery with incised linear decoration extended from the plains of Hungary to the Paris basin, always recognisable despite many progressive transformations en route, constitutes the textbook example. In that culture we can effectively watch the actual advance of a sedentary population of mixed farmers as each new generation constructs a new village 20 km further on,[12] practically all the way to the Atlantic coasts. As they made their way onward, they scarcely mixed with other peoples and their cultural characteristics remain identifiable from one end to the other of this long journey spread over many centuries.

There are other less straightforward cases. First among them, in the Balkans there is the problem of an entirely new Neolithic culture which arose in sharp contrast with the traditions of the local hunter-gatherers, but whose own origin remains culturally unidentified. Only the domesticated species together with the geographical position of the region plead in favour of a Near Eastern origin. For certain authors, it is sufficient to invoke the transmission of ideas without the need for the people themselves to move, or at the very most to suppose trade to explain the influences that were received from the Near East and overlaid on a foundation of indigenous culture. Even in the example of the Danubian movement, whose route from the plains of Hungary to France can be readily charted, this process is less easy to discern for the first part of the 'journey', between Anatolia and central Europe. The Linear Pottery culture (LBK) seems to derive by successive transformations from the early Neolithic of northern Greece.[13] But that culture appeared fully developed in Thessaly, and represents a complete rupture with the indigenous Mesolithic. Considering the domesticated species present and the allochthonous character of this new culture, the fact remains that there is no precise reference point, in terms of either its architecture or its portable material culture, that one could consider with any conviction as marking contacts with its Near Eastern origin.[14]

A second group of cases raises even more difficult problems. These are the cultures that are used by several authors[15] to contradict or modify Colin Renfrew's hypothesis, where neolithisation was effected without a rupture and with evident cultural continuity with the indigenous hunter-gatherers. This is notably the case at Franchthi in the Argolid[16] in Greece, and also with a large number of European Neolithic cultures where pottery and the subsistence strategy of farming are imposed on manufacturing traditions that are completely local, especially in the chipped stone traditions. These authors speak of influences and, for the domesticated species, of exchanges involving seed and breeding animals,[17] evidence which in every case seems incompatible with the migration hypothesis and even more so with the linguistic transformations that population movement alone can explain.

A spectrum of solutions has been proposed ranging from the simple acceptance of Colin Renfrew's model to the radical denial of diffusionism, at least in the form of population movement. That of Marek and Kamil Zvelebil seems one of the more reasonable: it admits a restricted phase of initial colonisation in the period 7000–5500 BC, limited to the Balkans, the Danubian movement and Mediterranean south-east Europe. The continuation of this diffusion would then have unfolded in several steps, including a later diffusion proper to the Bronze Age and completely in conformity with the classic model of Maria Gimbutas.[18]

A number of theoretical problems still exist, however. On the one hand the modalities of Neolithic diffusion, as we have seen, remain rather obscure. It is necessary to choose, case by case, between a hypothesis which supposes that as soon as they crossed the Sea of Marmara emigrating people lost their cultural memories of their place of origin, and an alternative hypothesis of indigenous populations acculturated by one knows not what process. In regard to the latter, the 'transfer of ideas' model lacks concreteness and the evidence of 'trade' in the early Neolithic seems too slight to provide a complete explanation. It is certain that the motivations behind Neolithic diffusion, whatever form that diffusion is thought to have taken, are not self-evident. We have had it thoroughly explained to us[19] that the new economy, which was much more productive than hunting and gathering, must have caused a rise in population inseparable from an expansionist attitude, or that for the same reasons of productivity the local hunter-gatherers could not but adopt with enthusiasm this model of exploitation that was superior to their own. But our earlier analysis of the conditions under which the productive mode of subsistence emerged in the Levant has made us distrustful of this kind of argument. In Europe it does not seem that the first farmers, constrained by various ecological and technical handicaps, would have enjoyed such a clear superiority over the hunter-gatherers; nor have the economic viability or the population density of the indigenous hunter-gatherers been properly appreciated.[20] In the matter of European neolithisation, therefore, it seems that one might reach a conclusion quite analogous to that which we adopted for the Natufian of the Levant: the Mesolithic people did not initially have to change their economic system because of any insufficiency in what they were accustomed to practise.

The orientalist point of view

The process of Neolithic diffusion from the Near East is thus right at the heart of a vigorous, multidisciplinary debate. Not only is the origin of the farming cultures of Europe and elsewhere in dispute, but also the origins of our genetic heritage and the languages that we speak. If it is true that these transformations came from the Near East, it means that the Near Eastern prehistorian, working at the point of departure of this process of diffusion, is well placed to investigate its causes and the forms it takes.

We have already seen that diffusion phenomena appear within the Levant itself as part of these first experiences of agriculture from the end of the ninth millennium. The expansion of early and middle PPNB around 8000 BC allows us to glimpse a complex ensemble of possibilities and typical situations. In the PPNA cultures and in the PPNB of the middle Euphrates there was indigenous neolithisation. In the PPNB of the Taurus there was colonisation that brought the Neolithic way of life to a pre-existing cultural entity. In the PPNB of Palestine we see the cultural colonisation of a pre-existing Neolithic without any economic component. The PPNB in the Damascus region represents marginal acculturation without any population component. Finally, there is perhaps somewhat of a neolithisation with a rather restricted cultural component and without genuine economic transformation in the Aşıklı culture in central Anatolia, a phenomenon whose elements can fairly be said to be poorly known.

We have shown that this series of different cases of diffusion in the Levant does not exclude a search for a unified explanation. Rather, the task has been simplified by the fact that a single expanding culture, the PPNB, is found to be involved in all the cases of diffusion. Moreover, all of this took place still within the interior of the nuclear zone, in the ecological sense that natural historians give to that phrase.

What we are calling the 'great exodus', between 7500 and 6300 BC, at the time of the later PPNB and the pottery Neolithic cultures that derive from it, represents an intensification of the earlier movement of expansion and its spreading beyond its initial ecological zone, although they remained close to its boundaries. In the conquest of these new territories, which include both semi-arid landscapes and an island situation (Cyprus), we can see reproduced in even greater number the situations typical of secondary neolithisation, including those where it is very difficult to recognise through comparative studies the cultural origin of the immigrants, however obviously they may be defined as immigrants for other reasons. We are now in a position to benefit from an intense international harvest of facts that have at last brought us the possibility of synthesis. And we hope that this analysis will contribute to the clarification of certain continuing mysteries of Neolithic diffusion.

We must now return to a more factual description. We shall then attempt to make sense of it.

14

The completion of the Neolithic process in the 'Levantine nucleus'

We shall treat the twelve centuries between 7500 and 6300 BC as a single block, although two distinct sub-periods can be differentiated[1] if one takes account of the very widespread use of pottery on sites across the Near and Middle East from 7000 BC. However, this last date does not represent a fundamental cultural break in the Levant: the architecture and the tool manufacturing traditions of the PPNB continue without interruption. There is increasing regional diversification as new types of portable equipment are invented, of which pottery is one.

By 'Levantine nucleus' we mean the Syro-Palestinian zone where the sedentary agropastoralist communities appeared and where they progressively consolidated from the tenth to the eighth millennium. We would include within that zone the extension of the steppe country of the Jezirah into modern Turkey as far as the first foothills of the eastern Taurus.[2]

The total number of villages increases, both those known as excavated sites or those simply located by survey. This would seem to indicate a general population increase, especially since some villages attain dimensions previously unparalleled. And for the first time a considerable disparity between the north and the south of the Levant begins to appear.

At the end of the tenth millennium the farming economy had begun to take off simultaneously throughout the whole sedimentary corridor, from the Euphrates to the Jordan. Then, in the early PPNB, northern Syria seems to have become a pivotal centre, the point of departure of a cultural diffusion which passed southwards beyond the Dead Sea. But the Palestinian middle PPNB had no reason to envy the Jezirah or eastern Anatolia in terms of material or ideological creations. As we have already seen, the beginnings of animal domestication were the result of initiatives that were more or less simultaneous in both provinces of the Levant. Step by step the situation now began to change. The sedentary settlements of the south little by little began to be abandoned, which does not necessarily signify that the region was depopulated; by contrast, the north saw an increase in the number of settlements. It is in this regard that we can speak of a 'completion' of the process of neolithisation: as far as the last missing elements of a Neolithic culture in the most traditional and most complete sense of the term are concerned, pottery and certain domesticated species not previously encountered began to figure in its inventory.

We should also note that the first diffusion of a sedentary Neolithic culture beyond the Levantine nucleus began to take place from 7500 BC, emanating from its northern half. From now on this area will no longer exclusively benefit from the technical and economic innovations that we shall examine. However, the innovation of nomadic pastoralism (which will be mentioned here but discussed more fully in chapter 17) constitutes an important agent of diffusion that involves the whole of the Levant. By this means we see the extension of the Neolithic to the extensive semi-arid zone that borders the whole area.

The intention to treat separately the initial area of neolithisation must not exclude the other regions of the Levant that are by this time Neolithic. Indeed, they provide much richer evidence in certain domains. This treatment is justified by the resolutely diffusionist perspective that the facts impose on us, even if the 'centre' soon declines in importance in relation to the new blossoming on the margins.

The southern and central Levant in the late PPNB period: spatial reorganisation

The map of settlements is transformed (Fig. 45). We have elsewhere described this rather spectacular reorganisation of settlement sites as 'house-moving fever', which is a vivid contrast with a no less evident basic cultural continuity. The Jordan valley, where Jericho ceased to be occupied, was entirely empty for more than a millennium, while further south, where Basta succeeded Beidha, several villages continued at altitude. Everything seems to point to the majority of the sedentary farmers concentrating deliberately in the higher and better-watered regions, such as the mountains of Judaea and the Negev, upper Galilee, and the upper part of the Jordan valley. Further east, 'Ain Ghazal remained in occupation on the Jordanian plateau.

In the central Levant, Ghoraïfé replaced Aswad in the Damascus oasis. Then Ramad appeared during the last centuries of the eighth millennium, 20 km away from the oasis. The locations change, but the regional population appears to be stable.

Architecture
At the excavated sites of Ramad,[3] Abou Gosh[4] or Basta,[5] the houses perpetuate the rectangular plan with walls of stone and floors of plaster typical of the Palestinian PPNB, except for the central Levant, where, as we have seen, the houses are most often mono-cellular. In the far south, the village of Basta reveals houses with several rooms where the plaster floors are based on a platform built of stone and cut by parallel channels covered with slabs. This mirrors a construction technique already observed in eastern Anatolia at Nevalı Çori. It is doubtless designed to create a sanitising void below the house.[6] Within the PPNB cultural family we see the same completely original technical solution reappearing, but apparently shifted forward by several centuries and some 800 km distance.

However, at Ghoraïfé and in the basal level of Ramad, as well as at small sites like Tell Eli, on the lake of Tiberias, or Tell Farah in Samaria, we know of examples of huts in round pits. It may be a case of populations with a fully sedentary tradition but who adopt rectangular building plans later than others. That is without doubt the case at Ghoraïfé and in basal Ramad, according to what we have seen of the architectural archaism in the Damascus region in the middle PPNB. It could also be an

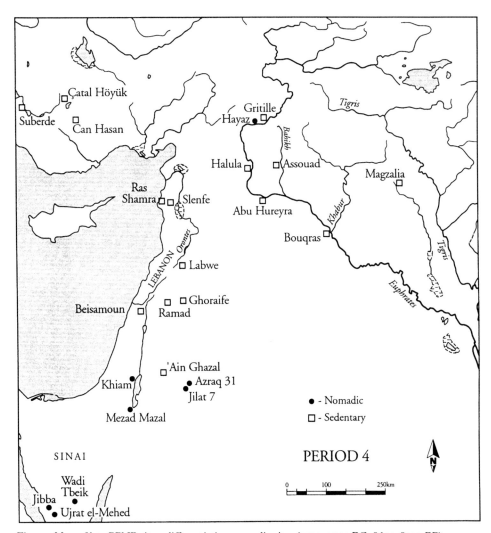

Fig. 45 Map of late PPNB sites, differentiating nomadic sites (7500–7000 BC, 8600–8000 BP).

example of groups who were formerly nomads returning to sedentism, following a model that is demonstrated elsewhere in which they revive primitive methods in the art of building.[7] The same is true in the southern Levant, where this type of site is witness to the parallel existence of mobile populations whom we intercept, if one may put it like that, at the very moment when this mobility is interrupted, whether for good or merely temporarily. We shall return to this aspect of the settlement of Palestine.

Industries

Whatever the type of house, the chipped stone toolkit remained the same. Relative to earlier times, the taste for weapons again grew. Pressure flaking, which was limited to the tang or the point of weapons, now began to cover the whole surface. The effect

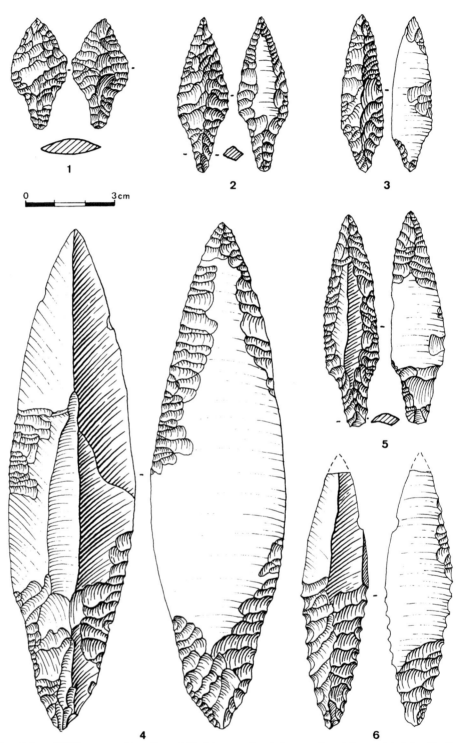

Fig. 46 Late PPNB weapons from Ramad (Syria): arrow-heads (1–3, 5, 6) and dagger (4). After M.-C. Cauvin.

is above all aesthetic (Fig. 46). Among the arrow-heads, the 'Amuq point', which was present in the middle PPNB in the central Levant from the area of Damascus (Aswad) to northern Palestine (Munhata), is now found throughout the whole of the Levant. At Ramad there are points with notches which continue to distinguish the Damascus area in the tradition of the Aswadian and the middle PPNB of Aswad II.

Another modification concerns the heavy tools: chipped axes in flint which have a square or semi-circular blade produced by centripetal removals (Fig. 47: 4) and are often polished, replace the *tranchet* bifaces of the middle PPNB of which only a few specimens survive. These axes were made from the area of Damascus as far south as the Dead Sea, where seasonal groups went to knap them at the place where the natural deposits of flint are found.[8] However, the greater part of the stone toolkit scarcely changed, and the bone and textile industries remained entirely the same.

An important technical innovation characterises the end of the late PPNB which is witness to an increasing mastery of pyrotechnology. People began to make vessels in lime plaster, the so-called *vaisselle blanche*, which prefigures and prepares the way for the appearance of pottery.[9]

Ideology
Finally, the continuity with what preceded in the symbolic domain was total: we have already described the cult of the ancestors of this period at Ramad.[10] We should however note the new method of treating female figurines. At Ramad around 7000 BC a new stylistic trait appeared: an elongated neck and an occipital elongation stretching the skull up and backwards (Fig. 48: 2–3). The idea that underlies these deformations is not clear. These traits will be found in numerous other later cultures of the Levant and the Middle East[11] in slightly different forms and not always associated with each other. In some examples only the occipital elongation is indicated, but as an elaborate head-dress in the form of a chignon or some high-piled coiffure.

There is an iconographic variant which emphasises the eyes of the figurine. At Ramad two pellets of clay, elongated and incised, were used in a technique known as the 'snake's eye', a trait which is taken up sporadically in several other later cultures throughout the Levant and Middle East.[12] From Anatolia to Iran we may note other traits in the form of painting or inlays of shell, obsidian or bitumen. The important point is not the technique but the theme that it expresses, the insistence on the 'gaze', a probable allusion to the fascinating aspect of the Goddess.

For their part representations of animals are not uncommon. They are most often simply fashioned in clay and are rarely identifiable as to species. An interesting creation from Ramad is made of bone: the indented profile probably represents a goat's head (Fig. 48: 1), a species that we scarcely find in the Neolithic bestiary.

The later PPNB in the southern facies of the culture undergoes no decline, whether cultural or economic. On the contrary, the traditional cultivation of barley, einkorn, emmer wheat and legumes is enriched by the addition at Ramad of new species (naked wheat, flax). In several villages (Basta, Ramad)[13] sheep were herded as well as goats.

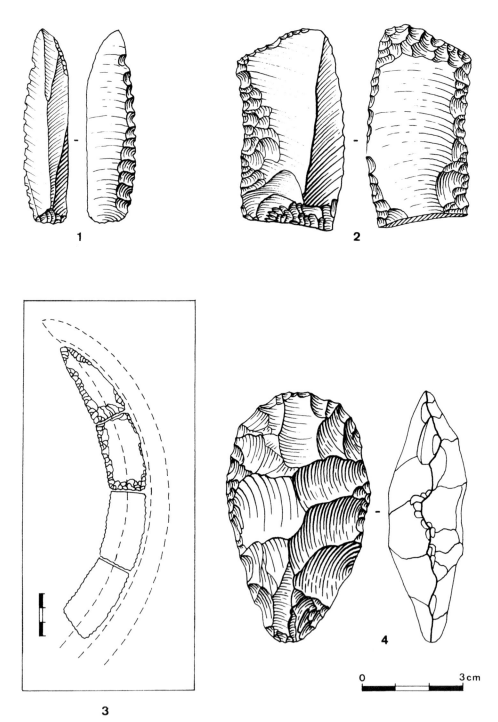

Fig. 47 Late PPNB tools from Ramad (Syria): 1–2 sickle elements; 3 reconstructed mounting for sickle blades; 4 chipped flint axe. After M.-C. Cauvin.

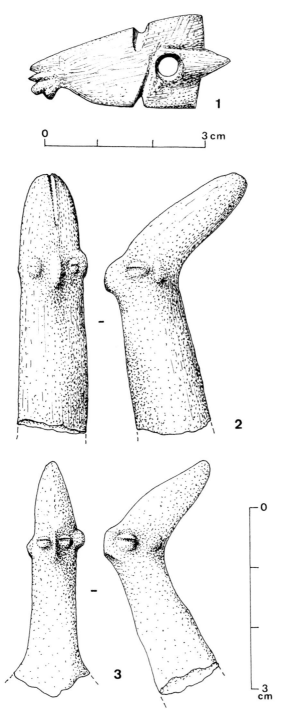

Fig. 48 Late PPNB art from Ramad (Syria): 1 head of a caprine (?) in bone; 2–3 heads of female figurines in baked clay. After H. de Contenson.

The exodus
Explicit evidence of the pottery Neolithic phase that must have succeeded the PPNB
has been found neither in the southern Levant nor in the region of Damascus. In
other words, in those areas there is no trace of *in situ* evolution of the PPNB towards
the cultures that come after 7000 BC and which derive from it. The only apparent
exception is the final phase at Ramad, where a monochrome burnished pottery,
similar to that of the Amuq, has indeed been recovered. However, it was found in a
context that was entirely at odds with the preceding stratum, in huts in circular pits
which had been dug through the lime plaster floors of the late PPNB. This break in
architectural tradition is without doubt evidence of the arrival of nomadic groups
bringing pottery from north-west Syria.[14]

In the southern Levant there are almost no sedentary villages during the second half
of the eighth millennium.[15] On the other hand, surface scatters are abundant. They
are poorly dated for lack of excavation, but some at least can be attributed to this
period. The extensive dunes of the coast of Israel are well known for the scatters of
small arrow-heads entirely covered with retouch, probably left by mobile groups
belonging to the whole seventh millennium and beyond. Jean Perrot has called this
interruption in sedentary life 'the Palestinian hiatus', and has speculated that a climatic
desiccation, even if it were very slight, might have been sufficient to make these already
relatively arid regions incapable of sustaining agriculture.[16] But there is still almost no
direct evidence of such a climatic deterioration anywhere in the Levant. On the other
hand, around 7000 BC the same exodus of sedentary communities also affected the
central Levant and the higher and wetter zones of the southern Levant, which were
distinctly more hospitable. If the persistent occupation of 'Ain Ghazal is excepted,
together with the atypical reoccupation of Ramad by nomads, then the whole southern half of the Levant seems to have become devoid of sedentary settlements.

What became of the inhabitants? We can understand that a change in the way of
life such as a transition from sedentary life to nomadism would be sufficient to
remove them for the most part from the reach of our archaeological investigations,
since nomads at most times scarcely leave any identifiable trace in our excavations.
They may also have gone to found villages elsewhere. Indeed, it is when we leave the
Levantine nucleus in order to examine the marginal areas that we shall find them,
and we shall then try to explain their departure.

The late PPNB, then, was indeed both a consequence of and an end to the agricultural cultures of the southern and central Levant. Some villages would reappear
from about 6300 BC,[17] and later again towns would grow up. But for several millennia this land ceased to be a world focus of social and economic evolution; for a long
time it would receive only repercussions of developments elsewhere.

The northern Levant in the late PPNB period: an expansion
The impression given by the northern Levant is quite different, that is, for those parts
that we would include in the Levantine nucleus, the middle Euphrates and the Syro-
Turkish Jezirah (or upper Mesopotamia) as far as the piedmont of the eastern
Taurus.

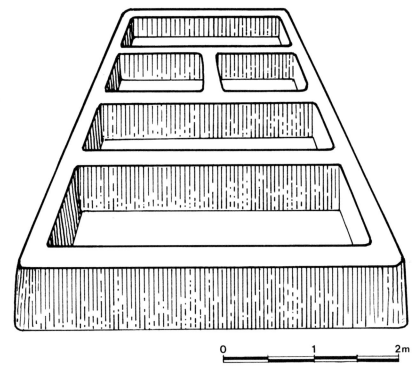

0   1   2m

Fig. 49 Late PPNB house from Abu Hureyra (Syria). After A. Moore.

In these regions, the major expansion of the PPNB seems clearly situated in this period, seen primarily in the number of sites (Fig. 45), although we are far from knowing all of them. Besides Abu Hureyra and Halula on the Euphrates, whose occupation was not interrupted, villages are found on its tributary, the Balikh (Tell Assouad[18]). New occupations are also found in the hills of the northern Jezirah, in Turkey (Gritille, Hayaz[19]), while sites such as Nevalı Çori and, further east, Çayönü probably persist into this period. Much less well surveyed than the southern Levant, and mostly in a very selective manner prompted by the building of major dams on the Euphrates, these regions certainly have many more discoveries in store.

Architecture

The development of some of these settlements in terms of population and architecture is impressive. This is when Abu Hureyra attained its greatest size and a new complexity.[20] Its area was almost 12 hectares, thus attaining a new threshold since the maximum extent of the villages of the PPNA and middle PPNB period did not exceed 3 hectares. The houses were densely packed: only a few courtyards and some narrow passages separated the houses. These, built of sun-dried mud bricks and furnished with plaster floors, comprised five rooms (Fig. 49) or more, with frequent internal doorways between them. They have been proposed as the first known example, destined to be developed widely throughout the whole Mesopotamian region, of the 'multi-cellular complex plan' defined by Olivier Aurenche on the basis of this provision for internal circulation.[21]

Industries

The weaponry, as in all the Levant, consists of types similar to those of the middle PPNB, but the finish is often superior. However, as distinct from the southern and central Levant, there were no chipped stone axes made of flint in the northern Levant. Instead, following the tradition of the Euphrates since the Mureybetian period, they fashioned all their axes on greenstone and polished them all over. Important items of personal adornment exist in the same material or even in obsidian and rare, imported, marine shells.

Vessels at Abu Hureyra were of limestone or polished gypsum plaster. *Vaisselle blanche* is not found except in the form of containers of large dimensions made of gypsum plaster, which no doubt served for storage. Baked clay was known, but was reserved for a few animal figurines. By contrast, a more manageable *vaisselle blanche* is well in evidence further north,[22] as well as limestone plaster floors. The PPNB of Tell Assouad in particular contains an abundance of true pottery, which is the earliest known, if the radiocarbon dates that have been obtained are to be believed.[23] It has simple shapes but an advanced technical quality.[24] The surfaces are burnished and light in colour. This pottery, occurring earlier than 7000 BC, makes the label 'PPNB' (Pre-Pottery Neolithic B) deceptive in this instance. It seems to be at the beginning not only of the ceramic tradition which will follow in this region, but also of the darker ceramics with comparable forms and technique of manufacture that were described long ago on the north Syrian littoral as 'DFBW' (dark-faced burnished ware)[25] or the pottery of the Amuq A phase, of which we shall speak later.

Subsistence economy

Cereals were cultivated at Abu Hureyra, and among them a naked wheat (*Triticum aestivum/durum*) which was a new domesticated species spreading through the Levant in the late PPNB.[26] Goats and sheep were herded everywhere, and much more intensively than the first domesticated goats of Abu Hureyra in the middle PPNB. Above all, domesticated cattle (at Hayaz and Halula) and, scarcely later, pigs (at Kumar Tepe) make their first appearance.[27] We may note that these animals were also herded both west and east of our nuclear zone, in lands that were newly colonised by the Neolithic diffusion. These recent discoveries make obsolete the hypothesis of the first domestication of cattle in the Balkans that was envisaged ten years ago. Cattle and pigs were indeed part of the Levantine Neolithic conquest, at the very moment when it began to take off.

Simultaneously in the fields of architecture, pottery and domestication, important material changes were initiated in the Jezirah in the late PPNB. This culture, in this region, was not the end-product but the means of transition to something else. We also know, thanks to recent surveys[28] and excavations that are still in progress,[29] that the regions bordering the middle Euphrates and the northern Jezirah at the beginning of the seventh millennium generated an important culture with burnished pottery related to that of Tell Assouad.[30] Finally, we know that this culture in its turn generated another, around 6000 BC: this was the celebrated Halaf culture which expanded all over the Levant and Middle East, from the Mediterranean to the Gulf. Our Levantine nucleus does not cease for quite a while, in its northern half, to be the source of creativity for the sedentary Neolithic communities. But from late PPNB times, without artificial distinctions one cannot separate it from the new neighbouring territories which it was in the process of annexing. It is this diffusionist, indeed expansionist, thrust that is from now on our principal subject of interest and investigation.

The arrival of farmers on the Mediterranean littoral and in Cyprus

We now turn to a new land where the Neolithic had not yet appeared. This is the coastal strip of the northern Levant, from Beirut in Lebanon to the area of Antakya. This region is separated from the Syrian interior by a double chain of mountains, the Lebanon and the Anti-Lebanon, and further north the Jebel Ansarieh. From 7000 BC we shall find that this coastal zone extends along the Cilician coast of the Anatolian peninsula.

Here we find a distinctly Mediterranean climate, where the mean annual rainfall exceeds 600 mm, and where wild cereals do not grow spontaneously. The maritime façade of the Levant is much better watered by the rains brought on the west winds than the country on the other side of the mountains, accentuating the climatic contrast between the two sides of this natural rampart. The coastal plain is generally narrow, but it sometimes pushes back towards the interior like the fingers of a glove, starting from the estuaries of two significant water-courses. One is the Nahr el-Kebir (the Eleutheros of the ancients), which separates the Lebanon range from the Jebel Ansarieh by means of the 'Homs gap', the other the Orontes, whose valley breaks through the Jebel Ansarieh and separates it from the more northerly range of the Amanus mountains. The Orontes traverses a sedimentary and marshy plain a little before its mouth, around the Amuq lake. This will be of great importance from the seventh millennium, as is also the case for the high plain on its upper course where its source is situated, the Beqaa, which forms a north–south valley between the Lebanon and Anti-Lebanon mountains.

This coastal region, especially its Lebanese portion, which is the best known through survey, was occupied by Epipalaeolithic hunter-gatherers until Khiamian times,[1] but, despite intensive surveys carried out since the beginning of the century, nothing seems to have followed. It is the same in the Beqaa: the Natufian has been noted but nothing follows until the end of the eighth millennium.

The reoccupation of the littoral in the late PPNB

The reoccupation of the coastal regions began about 7500 BC, thus in the late PPNB (Fig. 45). This is a demonstrable but little appreciated fact: there is only one excavated site in Syria where this aceramic Neolithic has been reached, at Ras Shamra, level Vc, in a sounding of only 37 m^2 area. Another restricted exposure exists at Labwe in the Beqaa valley. For the rest, we are dealing with unexcavated sites.

In addition to naviform cores the sites of the Lebanese coastal plain[2] (Fig. 45) produce numerous sickle-blades, flint axes with polished cutting edges, and a weaponry composed of Byblos points. There is also a great variety of notched points of elaborate forms, which we have already seen to be characteristic of the Neolithic tradition in the Damascus region. At Labwe,[3] the same industry is found associated with buildings with lime-plastered floors and *vaisselle blanche* like that of Ramad. There can be no doubt that this Lebanese Neolithic has come from the Syrian hinterland that lies to the east of the Anti-Lebanon.

Much further north, on the Syrian coast near Latakieh, we at present know only that the famous Bronze Age city site of Ugarit (Ras Shamra) was founded around 7500 BC, in the late PPNB, by people with a mixed farming economy who came there to establish the first village. The excavation of this earliest level[4] is very restricted, and we know little of the houses except that they were rectangular, with the bases of the walls built of stone. The chipped stone industry appears a little different from that of the Lebanon. Again there are naviform cores, sickle-blades and Byblos points of the finest craftsmanship, but the industry lacks the notched points and the flint tools for working wood; instead there are polished greenstone axes and adzes, as on the Euphrates. Also lacking are the lime plaster vessels, which only appear later at Ras Shamra. From the beginning, they cultivated cereals and herded sheep and goats. The herding of cattle and pigs began in the course of this aceramic phase,[5] at very much the same period as in the Taurus, at Hayaz (see above). If we add to this a type of stone ornament which seems to have a very close affinity with that of Abu Hureyra,[6] we may judge the assemblage to be more closely related to the PPNB of the middle Euphrates than to that of the central Levant. But the documentation remains rather weak to confirm this origin with any confidence, especially since the vast region which separates the Euphrates valley from the north Syrian coast is still very poorly known and could yet furnish intermediate milestones in this transfer form east to west.

The first Pottery Neolithic cultures of the Phoenician coast

Pottery appeared on the coast around 7000 BC, when human occupation was becoming more dense (Fig. 50). From the outset it attained excellent technical standards. This was by no means a new invention. As we have seen, baked clay already existed from the middle of the tenth millennium BC with the first female figurines and also the very small pots of the Mureybetian period. The firing of these containers was cursory, however, and the absence of temper at this stage forbade the firing of larger vessels. Throughout the aceramic Neolithic in the Levant, by contrast, the addition of straw to clay to temper its plasticity and assure its cohesion in the drying process was standard practice in the preparation of clay for *pisé* building (Mureybet) or sun-dried mud brick (Cafer Höyük). When the first usable pottery appeared in the Jezirah at the end of the eighth millennium,[7] the paste contained mineral or vegetable temper; the shapes, as we saw, remained simple, but the firing and the surface treatment by burnishing were already excellent.

The pottery of the Phoenician coast could be derived from this source. Following the definition of R. Braidwood[8] for the Amuq plain, it is generally all put together under the label of dark faced burnished ware (DFBW), but the name is actually

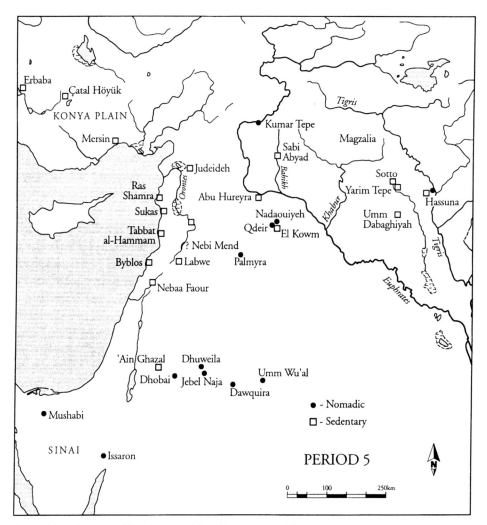

Fig. 50 Map of final PPNB and pottery Neolithic sites in the Near East (7000–6300 BC, 8000–7600 BP), differentiating nomadic sites.

inadequate when we move south to Byblos where the pottery is not dark in colour but rather light.

In fact, if there is one aspect where each region, sometimes of quite small extent, emphasises its own stylistic originality, it is the pottery. Everywhere the pottery is burnished directly on the fabric, without the addition of a slip, and decorated with incisions and impressions, but not yet any paint. What changes from site to site is sometimes the general colour but usually the decoration. Several groups may be distinguished.

The true DFBW, that of the Amuq (Tell Judaideh), is black or dark in colour. Whether or not it is burnished, it is decorated with incisions or impressions, either punctiform or made with a finger-nail, or indeed with applied clay (in cordons). Its distribution reaches north to Mersin[9] on the Cilician plain and south to Ras Shamra (level Vb).

A second group is found south of the Homs gap, from its seaward mouth[10] as far as the northern Beqaa[11] at its eastern end. This pottery is equally dark but is characterised by impressions of fine or plaited cord.

Finally, the pottery of 'early Neolithic' Byblos on the Lebanese coast is pale buff in colour. The majority of the impressions are made with a cardium shell,[12] in a curious convergence with another pottery called 'cardial impressed' that is found in the Mediterranean basin at the beginning of the Neolithic (in Liguria, Provence and eastern Spain).

The pottery thus contributes to the diversified aspect of these coastal cultures, which have perfected the PPNB legacy in these recently colonised zones. From this point of view, the weaponry of Byblos (Figs. 51 and 52) attains unequalled perfection.[13] The architecture, recovered over a large area, is uniquely formed of rectangular houses with walls of stone, each building consisting of a single room with a lime plastered floor, exactly in the tradition of Ramad.

Ideological evolution in the seventh millennium

Byblos, where the 'Early Neolithic' lasts throughout the seventh millennium, gives us excellent information both on the ideological roots of this period in its PPNB past and on the new transformations of the ideology that were in progress. The apsidal house form that is unique to Byblos has already been mentioned for its distinctive plan, together with the presence of anthropomorphic statuettes and the shoulder blades of bulls,[14] which mark it out as a traditional sanctuary in a symbolic context that is familiar to us. A particular concentration of burials around it appears to accentuate the sacredness of the place, although it is certainly not a 'cemetery' in the normal sense. The rest of the burials are generally spread throughout the whole village. But the burials are all single and, in contrast to the PPNB burials, the skull is never removed. In this region the 'skull-cult' has thus run its course.[15] On the other hand, there are inequalities in the funerary treatment.[16] Some graves are surrounded by stones, but the rest are simply in the soil.[17] Only the former, a small minority, have pottery and items of personal adornment as grave goods. These burials framed with stones are also furnished with the finest 'daggers' of flint (Fig. 52). One also has a chipped and polished axe (Fig. 53) of the same type as the general run of flint axes, but made on a rare imported material (a fine-grained basalt) and with a quality of manufacture superior to the rest, which causes us to interpret is as a weapon.[18]

We have seen that 'symbolic archaeology' of the kind that was first conceived by Ian Hodder has as its prime objective to reveal social inequalities in funerary rites, like the research of Jean-Daniel Forest[19] in the Middle East for the data from the sixth millennium and later. Nothing at the level of the village plan of Byblos indicates any social differentiation: with the exception of the 'sanctuary', the settlement is very homogeneous. But we may ask whether some sort of elite is evidenced among the dead. In the PPNB we know that not all the dead were made the object of *post mortem* decapitation, nor of modelling or separate conservation of the skull. We have

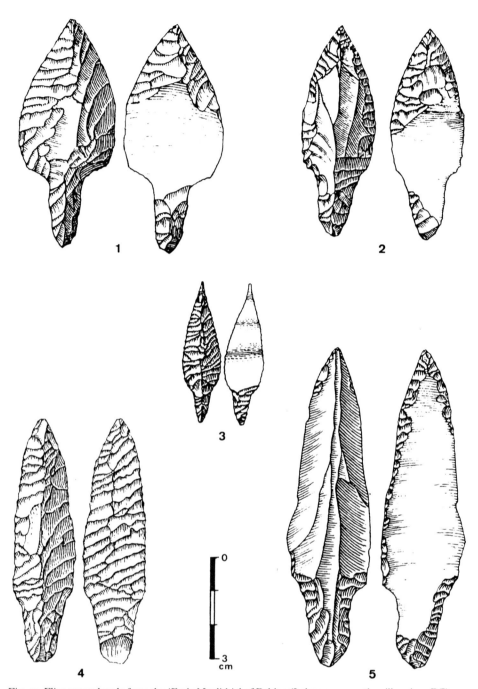

Fig. 51 Flint arrow-heads from the 'Early Neolithic' of Byblos (Lebanon, seventh millennium BC).

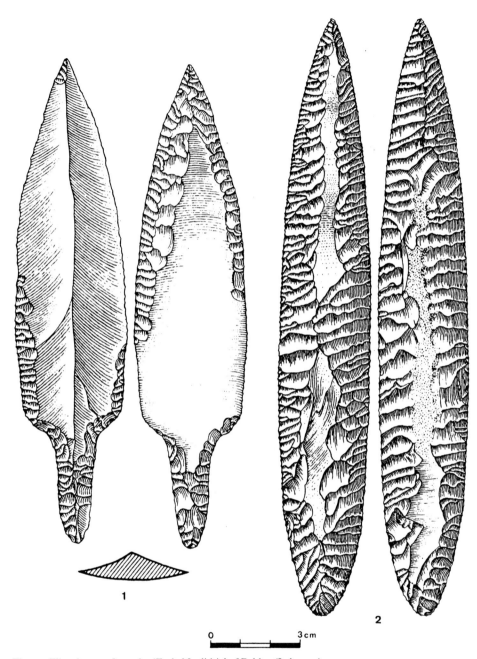

Fig. 52 Flint daggers from the 'Early Neolithic' of Byblos (Lebanon).

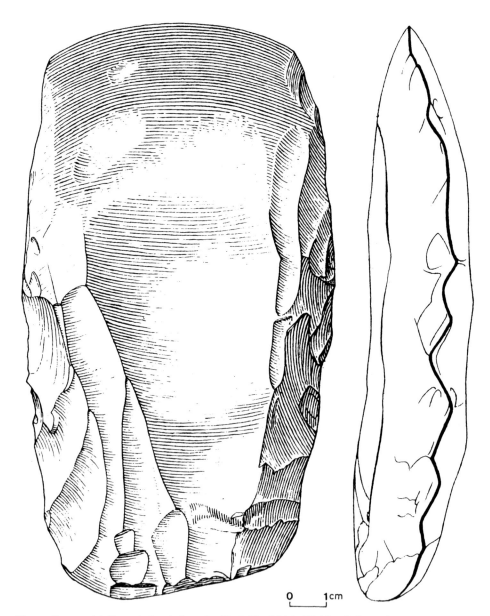

Fig. 53 Ceremonial (?) axe in basalt from the 'Early Neolithic' of Byblos (Lebanon).

to conclude that there was some selection, even if the singularities which occasioned this choice are more or less lost in the final anonymity of the skull deposits. At Byblos, on the contrary, these singularities are expressed in the individual tomb in terms of the offerings and the prestige equipment. However, we cannot say that we are looking at a 'social organisation' where the superiority of privileged lineages is perpetuated[20] or where a 'social class' is defined rather than a completely personal prestige acquired in the course of life. At the very most we may note that any social differences are at present better demonstrated in the funerary practice. They do not acquire any more strictly 'sociological' significance until the early stages of urbanisation.

A migration of sedentary people

The first settlement in the coastal zone seems therefore to perpetuate sedentary village traditions elaborated in inland Syria and rapidly extended to this new territory in the late PPNB. There is no break except the geographical gap, and no local development can account for them: everything comes from elsewhere and it is therefore a diffusion phenomenon involving migration that we see here.

The cases of Ras Shamra and of Labwe, which are the oldest of these settlements, are important. They show that from their arrival the newcomers not only cultivate their fields and herd their flocks but they also know perfectly well how to build. They have not lost their knowledge of architecture, as is often the case for Neolithic pastoral nomads. Although sedentary in origin, pastoral nomads may forget this skill in the course of generations of mobility. Even better, the details of material culture of this western late PPNB allow us to detect quite precisely its place of origin in each case. The Lebanese Neolithic cannot come from anywhere else but the region of Damascus, having jumped the Anti-Lebanon and then, for the settlements of the coast, the Lebanon chain also. That of Ras Shamra includes more northerly elements that we shall understand better when we know more about the very considerable territory that separates the coast from the middle Euphrates.

This case of diffusion may be related closely to the 'Danubian' type of diffusion, as defined in Europe. These are sedentary farmers who on their arrival are exactly as they were at their departure, conserving the full range of cultural traits that characterise life in villages. In a case of this type the implied element of mobility does not seem to have gone beyond the duration of the journey from one settlement to another.

Central Anatolia

It is not possible to interpret the dense Neolithic peopling of central Anatolia after 7500 BC in the same manner. It probably results from a more complex process. It was at this time that the villages of Can Hasan[21] and Çatalhöyük[22] were founded on the Konya plain, and further west the village of Suberde,[23] and a great number of probably contemporary sites that have not been excavated. We have already noted that the Cappadocian site of Aşıklı was in existence in the preceding period, corresponding to the middle PPNB of the Levant and eastern Anatolia, and that it also poses us a problem. Several cultural traits with PPNB affinities are found in the chipped stone industry side by side with indigenous characteristics, and these are difficult to interpret given our poor present knowledge. The rectangular houses with plastered floors at Aşıklı would be quite at home in the context of the Levant at that period. However, their general disposition in a very tightly packed village fabric (Fig. 54: 1), with almost no space separating the houses, directly prefigures the remarkable 'agglutinative plan'[24] of the Çatalhöyük culture. This lay-out at Çatalhöyük

itself (Fig. 54: 2) and at Can Hasan III clearly represents an original Anatolian creation, bearing no relation to any other site, and one that still persists in some modern
Turkish villages. Circulation from one house to another was not at ground level but
across the roofs. Access to the village, like the entry to each house, therefore neces-
sitated the use of ladders. This settlement plan is perhaps an adaptation to the
climate of the Anatolian plateau, which is much colder in winter than the Levant.

These two villages of the end of the eighth millennium are fully agricultural in the
sense of cultivation of crops; but their practice of herding is still ambiguous,[25]
perhaps continuing the slow take-up of animal domestication that has already been
observed in the PPNB of the Taurus in SE Turkey. On the other hand, aurochs were
certainly hunted, as was the case with their Mureybetian predecessors on the middle
Euphrates. Çatalhöyük continued in existence through most of the course of the
seventh millennium (until about 6400 BC), and developed the herding of ovicaprids, but the status of the cattle, always important in quantitative terms, has been the
subject of contradictory opinions. Perhaps that indicates that the aurochs was in the
process of domestication.

The obsidian industry comprised an abundant weaponry based on oval or tanged
points covered with flat pressure flaking that seems to be very much in the evolutionary line of the PPNB arrow-heads. At Çatalhöyük they were accompanied by
magnificent daggers, in both obsidian and flint. For both symbolic and practical
reasons, these prestige armaments may be readily correlated with the importance of
the wild cattle and with the presence of a masculine anthropomorphic God (Fig. 43:
1), as in the PPNB.

We shall not rehearse the considerable interest of the seventh millennium
Çatalhöyük culture, principally in the area of religion, for the richness of its documentation has already been called on more than once as guidance in interpreting
even older information. Çatalhöyük is a huge agglomeration that is very tightly
squeezed together by the density of its agglutinative houses extending over 12 hectares. One in every two rooms, moreover, is a domestic sanctuary that is not only
equipped with frescoes and sculpted figures, but also devoted to the burial of the
dead who were placed under the clay benches, while skulls severed from the body
served, as in the Levant, as cult furniture. The spectacular importance of this religious atmosphere goes hand in hand with the elaborate quality of very diverse crafts,
such as work in bone, wood, leather and native copper. Together with Bouqras and
Tell Assouad, Çatalhöyük is one of the rare sites in the Near East where we have
found particularly early pottery, in the basal levels that are earlier than 7000 BC. As
in northern Syria and on the Phoenician coast, it is a monochrome burnished
pottery, but here it is light in colour, as at Byblos, and compared to the Levant its
forms are completely original.

Finally, we may distinguish three elements in this culture. First, the rustic urbanism which continues that of Aşıklı is indigenous to central Anatolia, where it was
born in a somewhat enigmatic context with only very attenuated PPNB influences.
Second, all the ideology, now in a fully refined expression, derives from a foundation common to the whole of the Near East, having been originated, as we saw, in

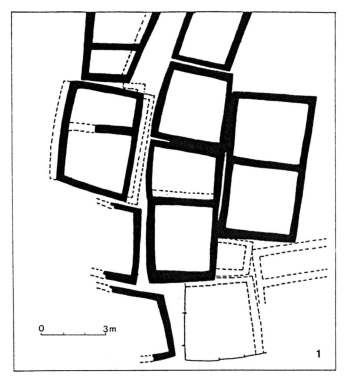

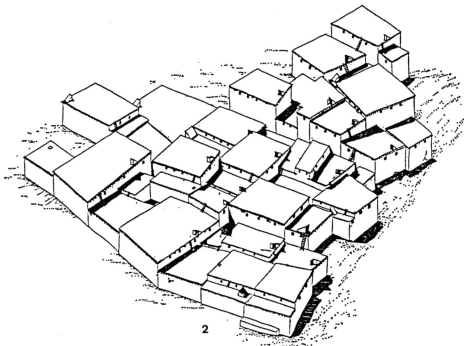

Fig. 54 Examples of agglutinative architecture from central Anatolia: 1 Aşıklı (about 8000 BC);
2 Çatalhöyük (reconstruction, seventh millennium BC). After U. Esin and J. Mellaart.

the Khiamian period on the middle Euphrates and then borne in several directions by the PPNB migrants. It was within this same movement, which is much more perceptible at Çatalhöyük than at Aşıklı, that the customs of *post mortem* decapitation and the weaponry of obsidian and flint originated.[26] The third element is a technical maturity and particular inventions that were brought about there. Their quality is responsible for the celebrity of the discovery, as is the marked originality of the assemblage. We can recognise the emergence of a novel culture, blending and recomposing into a very individual system influences that came from elsewhere.

For the period in which we are interested here, there was clearly a diffusion phenomenon, but it is difficult to be precise about its form and even its exact origin. This is in part because of the complexity of the results and in part because of the lack of intermediate pointers between central and eastern Anatolia, and indeed between central Anatolia and western Syria. We shall encounter a more secure factual base concerning colonisation when we turn to the island of Cyprus.

The overseas exodus: Cyprus

Is it merely coincidence that, while the Syro-Cilician coastland only 100 kilometres away was being repopulated, the island of Cyprus experienced its first significant human occupation? It was quite easy to cross the stretch of sea that separated the island from the coast of the mainland, from where it is visible in clear weather. The skill of navigation had been known for a long time, and Anatolian obsidian is always present in the first villages of Cyprus, showing that relations with the mainland posed no more and no less of a practical problem than the circulation of materials on land. It is thus not at all strange that Neolithic populations having reached the Phoenician coast in their westward push should then embark to occupy the land seen in the distance. However, the neolithisation of Cyprus holds its share of mystery.

On the one hand, we cannot immediately recognise in the first Neolithic villages all the cultural traits of the PPNB of coastal Syria, which may be supposed to be their place of origin. On the other hand, the peopling of the island, which was uninhabited in the Palaeolithic, seems to have taken place in several stages. It was contemporary with the aceramic Neolithic of the Levant, but the first 'Neolithic' immigrants themselves were not necessarily Neolithic in the socio-economic sense. Finally, the chronology of these inputs itself poses some problems.

The first stage appears very fugitive: around 9000 BC a very small group of people, provided with a rough and ready toolkit of flint, occupied a rock-shelter at Akrotiri *Aetokremnos*.[27] This occupation appears to be associated with the remains of dwarf hippopotamus and dwarf elephant, that is, with the indigenous wild fauna that was a distinctive feature of the Mediterranean islands which had been cut off from the mainland in remote geological times. This occupation was thus contemporary with the Levantine PPNA, but without any Neolithic input of any sort, or any cultural reference in the toolkit, which is very crude and general-purpose. There may have been other occupations of the island of the same kind, but, as has been said for the first peopling of Corsica, we may ask if these were not shipwrecks rather than colonisations. In any case, it is impossible to see whence they came.

The second stage has very recently come to light in the excavations by Jean Guilaine now in progress on the site of Shillourokambos, on the south coast near Limassol.[28] At Shillourokambos there was a dense occupation in the open air covering several hectares. The site's oldest phase is dated around 7600–7500 BC, or possibly a little earlier,[29] which makes it approximately contemporary with the end of the middle PPNB in the Levant. No houses have been found so far, but there are very large, more or less curvilinear enclosures that are indicated by trenches set with posts and interrupted only by 'gateways'. These suggest strong palisades of posts with their bases firmly set in the ground. The space within these enclosures is sometimes subdivided by other trenches or lines of posts that suggest partitions made of light materials. These spaces presumably served for the penning of flocks, but perhaps there were also huts of slight construction for human use: some fragments of white (lime?) plaster were recovered, some of them coloured with ochre, and these may have covered their floors or walls.

The chipped stone industry consisted for the most part of tools made on flakes, which are of little use for cultural parallels. There is also a small component of bipolar reduction for making blades from elongated cores that is comparable to the 'naviform' cores of the Levantine PPNB. Some blades are elements of sickles bearing 'oblique' silica gloss characteristic of mounting at an angle, a trait known in the late PPNB, not on the coast but at Halula in the middle Euphrates region or Tell Assouad in the Jezirah.[30] There are also blades with convex backs that give them the form of large segments of a kind that is present on the same sites in north Syria. Finally, the rare arrow-heads are made in a precisely PPNB tradition, and there are also a few blades of Cappadocian obsidian.

The fauna recovered is no less surprising. Sheep and goats were herded and pigs were also kept, but there are also remains of fallow deer and cattle. The cattle, which soon disappeared from Cyprus until the Bronze Age, can only have been introduced to the island in domesticated form, according to J. Guilaine.

The third stage, starting around 7000 BC, is none other than the brilliant Khirokitia culture, well known thanks to the excavations first of P. Dikaios, and then of Alain Le Brun at Khirokitia itself,[31] and known also at another dozen sites (Fig. 55). In the upper levels of Shillourokambos we see this culture developing to some degree. The first round houses with thick walls appear,[32] a form which characterises the later culture. The chipped stone industry loses its few PPNB 'reference points'. And at the same time the cattle that were imported at the beginning of the occupation disappear.

The villages of the Khirokitia culture were fully agropastoral: they cultivated wheat, barley and lentils; they herded sheep, goat and pigs, not forgetting the domestication of dogs and cats. Fallow deer were also present, as at Shillourokambos. Perhaps this animal had also been brought from the mainland and was the object of a short-lived attempt at domestication, or at least of the 'controlled management' of a wild species that is easily tameable. These villages have in common that they are agglomerations of houses built on the surface. The houses are circular (Pl. III) rather than the rectangular structures that characterise the majority of contemporary

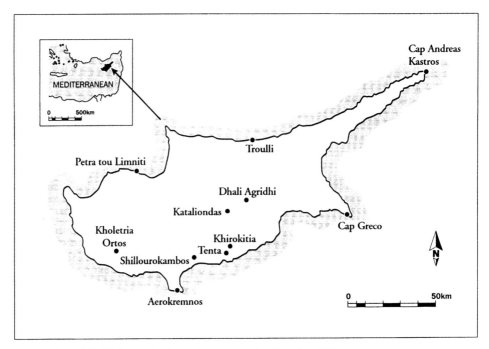

Fig. 55 Map of Neolithic sites in Cyprus in the seventh millennium BC.

sedentary people in the Levant. However they are in no way primitive. The houses may be arranged in small clusters around a courtyard, the normal family house having become more complex than a simple circular cell. The techniques of construction and the interior arrangements appear particularly elaborate. Curiously the circular walls of the houses, variously composed of juxtaposed rings of sun-dried mud brick, *pisé* or stones, are extraordinarily thick, attaining a metre on occasions at Khirokitia. Thus the diameter of the habitable internal area may be reduced to two-thirds, or even a half of the total diameter of the building.

We may further note the choice of defensive sites for these villages, on a rocky spur on an islet (Petra tou Limniti) or in a natural amphitheatre (Cap Andreas *Castros*). Where the natural defences were not felt to be enough, a wall was constructed to ensure the isolation of the inhabited space. This is the case at Kalavassos *Tenta* and above all at Khirokitia, which is virtually a defended ridge. The first wall, which was 3.5–4 m thick, was rebuilt further out when the village expanded. The entrance to the village has been found (Pl. III): it consisted of a dog's leg passage arranged in a sort of mud brick buttress set against the encircling wall, a complex arrangement making access difficult and defence easy. The question that comes to mind is who were the inhabitants guarding against?

The chipped stone industry is surprising for its rustic and poorly differentiated nature. It does not include bipolar reduction to produce blades, nor the flat retouch seen at mainland sites and at Shillourokambos. There are no arrow-heads at all, a generic type which elsewhere constitutes the principal objective of these two manufacturing techniques. The essential tools are made on flakes of flint used in their raw state, often as sickles, and there are the backed flakes, burins, and ill-formed scrapers and borers that are present in any prehistoric industry.[33] The bone industry[34] is well made but unremarkable.

On the other hand, while this island Neolithic exhibits the same lateness in the appearance of pottery as the final PPNB Levantine sites, there exists in the ground stone vessels a sector that is highly elaborated in terms of both its technical virtuosity and its aesthetic quality. This highly original industry consists of fine and sophisticated vases, some round and others rectangular in shape, sometimes provided with pouring lips or pierced lugs for suspension and sometimes also decorated. This industry has no stylistic affinity with the products of those other great specialists in stone vases who were, as we have seen, the new inhabitants of the semi-arid zone in Syria at the same period.

What can we learn from the information on religion? As at Byblos, the funerary rites consist of simple single burials in pits, but while the villages of the Levant buried their dead, some infants excepted, outside the houses, the burials at Khirokitia are all kept inside the houses. This practice, which had existed in the Natufian period and which now persisted only in Anatolia, has the quality of drawing tighter the symbolic bonds between the community of the dead and that of the living.[35] Artistic representations are almost entirely anthropomorphic. There are simple, schematically represented silhouettes of a kind that is quite classic in the Levant, in one instance with arms raised in a painted fresco at Kalavassos *Tenta*. There are also statuettes (or heads) of a very particular style that is very schematic and without indication of sex (Fig. 56). The absence of explicitly female or male depictions is certainly noteworthy.

The problems and lessons of Cyprus

Until recently the enigma of Cyprus resided in the apparently sudden and dense arrival of the village culture of Khirokitia as the first peopling of the island, as it was believed by most.[36] These Neolithic colonists could only have come from the Near Eastern mainland, but absolutely nothing related them in any way to the cultural tradition of the Levantine PPNB.

Now Shillourokambos has appeared, older by more than half a millennium. Where are we now with the enigma? This example is for the present peculiar to Cyprus: the arrival of the first Neolithic colonists is thus not only older but also less grand in scale than one might have thought. It is not however necessary to postulate a new wave of colonists for the 'third stage' of the occupation of the island. The Khirokitia culture grew up *in situ* through internal evolution from aceramic Shillourokambos, within the framework of a normal demographic expansion.

As for the origin of the earlier population, it is now more clear-cut. As we have seen, some PPNB elements are present in the initial toolkit, but they later fade out completely. One can no more see the rectangular houses of the mainland PPNB at Shillourokambos than at Khirokitia. The new arrivals appear at first more concerned to shelter their animals than to accommodate people. These were herdsmen who must have brought from the mainland at least the essential breeding stock for their

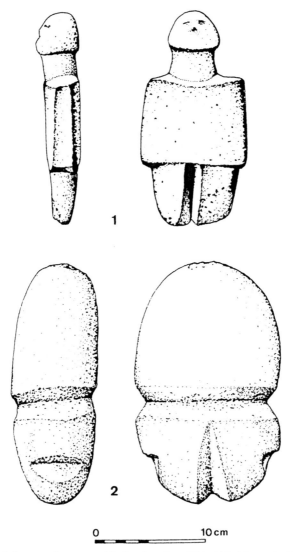

1

2

0   10 cm

Fig. 56 Stone anthropomorphic figurines from Khirokitia (Cyprus). After A. Le Brun.

livestock, implying relatively large-scale means of navigation: cattle, even when young, are more unwieldy than other species.

When finally the first built houses appeared, they were of an archaic circular type, taking the form of a model that has been found in the Levant when pastoral nomads become sedentary (see chapter 14). But while these newly sedentary people in general soon rediscovered the usual rectangular house-plans of the PPNB villages, Cyprus waited for the Bronze Age before such a plan was adopted. We should also not forget that the recognisable PPNB elements of the aceramic Neolithic of Cyprus appear to us to relate not to the nearby Phoenician coastlands, but to a more easterly and northerly variant of the late PPNB, that of the middle Euphrates. It is conceivable that Neolithic people facing the difficulties of an exodus might have taken to the sea in order to reach an island that could be seen in the distance. One cannot exclude the hypothesis that this was a sort of 'sea-borne nomadism', carrying with it characteristics that one senses were originally from the interior of Syria rather than from the sedentary settlements of the coast.[37]

There remains a chronological problem: on the mainland neither the occupation of the Phoenician coast nor the herding of cattle and pigs seems at present to be earlier than the late or final PPNB.[38] However, since there were no wild ancestors on the island, the Cypriot ungulates could not have been domesticated there. If the occupation of the island was indeed related to the migratory phenomenon discussed earlier, and if the imported cattle were indeed domesticated at that time, in the present state of our knowledge it is very difficult to situate all that on the mainland before the late PPNB, that is, earlier than 7500 BC. One might therefore be tempted to reject some of the ^{14}C dates from Shillourokambos as too old, at least until further discoveries on the Asiatic littoral can show both the movement westwards and the domestication of cattle and pigs to be several centuries older. And that is perfectly possible.

Aside from these uncertainties, the neolithisation of Cyprus is of very great interest for the understanding of the mechanisms of Neolithic diffusion. Its originality from the start is perhaps less surprising than has been said. The scarcity, indeed the total absence, of stylistic references at the level of artefacts that would signal the area of origin of the migrant population has embarrassed researchers so often that some theoretical lacuna in the way that the problem has been posed might be suspected. The simple achievement of introducing techniques as fundamental as the obtaining of subsistence into a novel environment, or, in the present case, the art of grinding and polishing stone, are not negligible cultural inputs, even if one has to wait to find more formal and precise characteristics that are more readily identified.

We are still unaware of the reasons which caused a human group that was transferring itself into a completely novel situation to reorganise more or less completely the stylistic repertory of the things that they made, indeed to invent some techniques and to 'forget' others. But this renewal is not less clearly observed elsewhere: we shall see it when dealing with the expansion of the Neolithic towards the east. With overland journeys, one may suspect it was the effect of nomadic pastoralism, which was emerging at this period and which had the effect of making people forget over several generations of mobility a good part of the sophisticated components of the comforts of their abandoned sedentary life. When they returned to sedentism, these groups reactivated their latent technical knowledge in order to make things that were entirely new.[39] We have seen that this was not the case in the Levant for the foundation of Ras Shamra or Byblos, for which there is no need to postulate episodes of nomadism. But it is possible that the first Neolithic inhabitants of Cyprus may have suffered the phenomenon of cultural loss of that kind if their mainland origin was not sedentary.[40]

It remains to explain the very particular architectural history of the Cypriot Neolithic. When buildings in stone appear at Shillourokambos, they are round houses, which is not surprising if our hypothesis is adopted. This is a type of house that remained unaltered over several millennia through a long period of sedentary life, and a type that does not reproduce the developments that are general in the Levantine mainland. However, the villages of the Khirokitia culture are not at all 'primitive' in the socio-economic sense, nor are their builders inexpert. Alain Le Brun is happy to describe these anomalies in terms of the psychology of the people, attributing them to something specific and of a non-material nature concerning island environments.[41] When one compares them, other traits that are no less aberrant in their respective domains appear to relate to the same psychology. The 'obsession with massive structures' that Le Brun has emphasised, with house walls that are much thicker their normal function requires, and the multiplication of walls and of defensive systems, are examples. To them may be added the concern to bring together the dead and the living within the protective cell of the 'primeval' house, a preoccupation elsewhere in the Levant long forgotten. All these traits point to withdrawal and to the closing of human communities in the face of dangers whose nature it is difficult for us appreciate.[42]

Even if one supposes that communities of Cyprus, which were quite numerous by the Khirokitia period, were unstable and inclined to attack one another, the absence of any kind of weapons in their chipped stone industry would still be surprising. The contrast with the contemporary rich panoplies of weapons from the mainland is extraordinary. We should note however that other kinds of threat may have existed, or may have been felt to exist.

Closer than we are to the times that we are concerned with, the Homeric world considered islands besieged by the sea on all sides as magical places full of risks. It is of no consequence whether the Cyclops, the Lestrygons or Calypso the magician did or did not exist: the sailors described in the Odyssey believed in them and for them they existed. Human technology can show itself to be as industrious in the cause of self-protection from 'mythical' perils, against which arrow-heads are of not much use, as against a rival village of malevolent sailors. John Evans has already remarked the tendency of insular or maritime cultures of proto-historic times to shut themselves up in massive constructions and to strive towards a sort of 'megalithism', whether in the matter of the living or for the dead. One thinks of the Maltese temples of the Bronze Age, of the cyclopean walls of Mycenae, of the statue-menhirs of Corsica, or even of the colossal statues of Easter Island in the middle of the Pacific Ocean. Certain anomalies, especially when they are grouped together in significant bundles, bear witness to a collective psychology, to appropriate options and their eventual excesses. This is also a matter of history, as historians have long known.

16

The sedentary peoples push east: the eastern Jezirah and the Syrian desert

The westward advance of the Neolithic was not stopped by the sea. We saw that it could also take ship and give rise to genuine maritime colonisation movements in the Mediterranean. To the east, on the other hand, is the whole of continental Asia, of which the Levant is only the Mediterranean façade. We are concerned not only with the northern arc of the upper Mesopotamian plains and the Zagros piedmont in NE Iraq, areas that are as favourable for dry agriculture[1] as the Levantine nucleus, but also with the semi-arid steppe whose aridity increases as one moves south. This aridity constitutes a major obstacle to sedentary life, except where river water and springs in oases have created local ecological niches that favour the cultivator in return for the little he needs to know in order to use them.

In the present state of our knowledge, we may suggest that these two environmental zones, the one relatively well watered, the other arid, were simultaneously the objects of a diffusion of the Neolithic economy of production from west to east. Our information on this diffusion concerns the period on which we are at present focused (7500–6300 BC).

The climatic difference between the two regions correlates with different adaptive behaviour. We shall find sedentary people but also pastoral nomads. However, at least in the wetter zone, this diffusion did not take place in a landscape empty of other people. To the best of our ability, we shall need to identify both the source of this population contribution and the manner in which it was received. Here for the first time we shall be dealing with an eastward extension of the Neolithic economy exclusively in its sedentary village-community form.

The eastern Jezirah: an autonomous cultural tradition

Upper Mesopotamia, known in Arabic as the Jezirah, extends on either side of the modern Syro-Iraqi frontier, which also conventionally separates the Near from the Middle East. We saw that the Syrian part, at least west of the river Khabur, was fully included both in the Levantine cultural tradition and in the primary nucleus of neolithisation. Nothing of this kind exists further to the east, where the Sinjar region (Fig. 57) is beginning to be rather better known because of recent excavations and requires us to start by going back in time. There, a cultural tradition quite different from the Levant had existed, whose distant source is doubtless to be sought in the eastern Upper Palaeolithic, the so-called Zarzian, already known in the Zagros. More recent sites, of the twelfth to the ninth millennia BC, have for some time

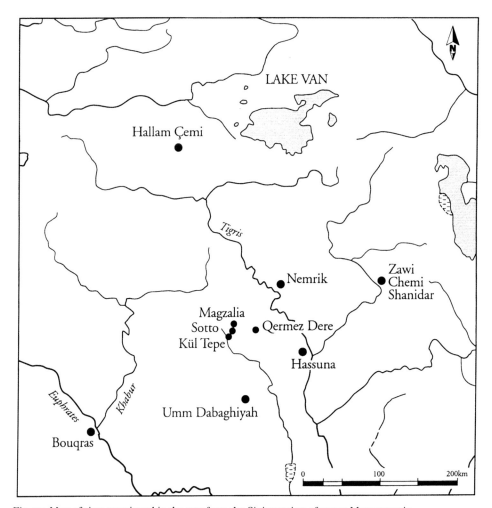

Fig. 57 Map of sites mentioned in the text from the Sinjar region of upper Mesopotamia.

allowed us to glimpse the Epi-palaeolithic successor to the Zarzian culture in the western Zagros[2] or the region of the upper Tigris.[3]

At Qermez Dere[4] and Nemrik,[5] the high plains around the Jebel Sinjar are now beginning to reveal more clearly a similar Epi-palaeolithic tradition that evolved between 9500 and 7600 BC with only minor changes. The tradition is contemporary with the Natufian of the Levant but different, and it continues over the whole duration of the PPNA and the early and middle PPNB in the Levant.

As in the Levant, there are sedentary hunter-gatherers already living in villages from the eleventh millennium. However, they display an architectural competence quite superior to that of the Natufians. The original house-form, half underground in a circular depression, includes not only wooden posts but also two or four massive internal columns,[6] each consisting of an orthostat of stone enveloped in clay and covered with plaster. The pillars may be schematically modelled in anthropomorphic form (at Qermez Dere). These posts and pillars supported a flat mud roof. The floors and walls were covered with a lime plaster that was often refurbished. The use of this material thus appears earlier than in the Levant.[7] The lamellar pressure flaking of flint and the polishing and grinding of stone[8] are equally early.

It seems that for the two millennia and more that this cultural tradition lasted its transformations remain amazingly simple. Around 9500 BC the 'Qermezian' industry was enriched with arrow-heads of the El Khiam type, a manifest Syrian influence but in a context that is quite different from the Khiamian. Then, in the final 'Nemrikian' phase, lozenge-shaped, quite distinctive points appear, called 'Nemrik points'. The basic chipped stone industry otherwise remains very stable.

Above all, there does not seem to be any trace of an agricultural or pastoral economy during the whole of this sequence,[9] a broad spectrum hunting and gathering economy remaining the rule. Gazelle in particular were hunted, and also hare, fox, some cattle, equids, ovicaprids and wild pig. Wheat, barley, lentils, peas and vetches formed part of the indigenous wild flora and were harvested, but without trace of domestication. There is no artificial preponderance of cereals over the other species that might suggest a pre-domestication agriculture, as is the case in the Neolithic on the middle Euphrates. In short, the revision of the definition of the Neolithic proposed by Trevor Watkins should be resisted. He places the production of subsistence as secondary and promotes to first place the elaborate architecture and the 'ideology of the home' of which the Sinjar sites are early evidence.[10] We conclude that these sites are not Neolithic, even if they are sedentary.

There is also a very expressive tradition of symbolism, but no goddess and no bull here, however. In their place, a symbolism of birds was developed.[11] The beautiful representations of raptors in polished stone from Nemrik (Fig. 58) echo the astonishing deposit of raptor bones at Zawi Chemi Shanidar,[12] almost all of them wingbones. Solecki derives from this the hypothesis of a ritual usage of wings (or of wing-feathers) of raptors as ornaments for clothing or head-dresses. Several other animals are also modelled in clay or engraved on the stone vases: wild boar, lion and snake at Nemrik, and, much earlier, a carnivore (fox?) at Hallan Çemi. Finally, about fifteen skulls of wild goat were associated with the deposit of bird-bones at Zawi Chemi Shanidar. This selection from the skeleton allows us to catch a glimpse of some symbolic intention, as with the birds. Given the present state of our information, wild cattle, although present and occasionally hunted, seem scarcely to have interested the artists.[13]

Is it simply chance that the cultures from beyond the Khabur seem to lack both agriculture and herding on the one hand, and the particular ideology that accompanies them in the west? The absence of the divine figures of the Levant would scarcely constitute evidence for this if there were not art, but there is, and its principal themes, so far at any rate, seem quite distinct.

The neolithisation of the eastern Jezirah
One fact is certain: after 7500 BC, when cultivator-herders finally appear in Iraqi upper Mesopotamia, we once more return to a land of knowledge. As much in the

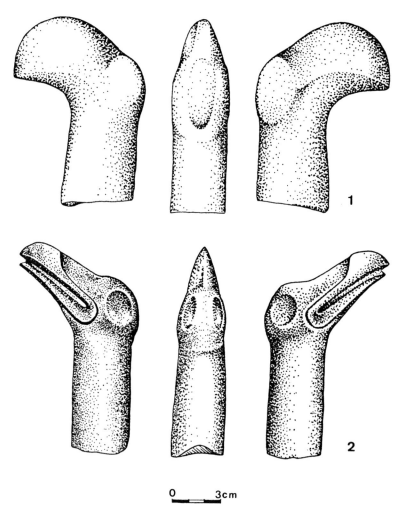

Fig. 58 Heads of raptors in stone from Nemrik (Sinjar, Iraq). After S. Kozłowski.

area of technology as in the area of ideology, we can detect the cultural relationship with the PPNB, transformed but still very clearly seen. In other words, in these regions, which till now have not belonged to the western cultural movement, this ideology is now diffused together with the economy of production. As with the 'colonisation' of the coastlands, it is sometimes possible to determine which facies of the PPNB was involved. That is, we can identify a quite precise geographical origin for these inputs.

A key site is Maghzaliyeh, on the southern slopes of the Jebel Sinjar.[14] What we see here is the PPNB in its Taurus facies, of the kind that we have seen at Cafer Höyük or Çayönü. It has come back down from the hill-country which we saw it reach in the early PPNB. The weaponry, with its Byblos points that are the general mark of the PPNB (Fig. 59: 2–4), is typical. Traits that are specific to the Taurus facies are also recognisable at Maghzaliyeh: although we are 300 km from the

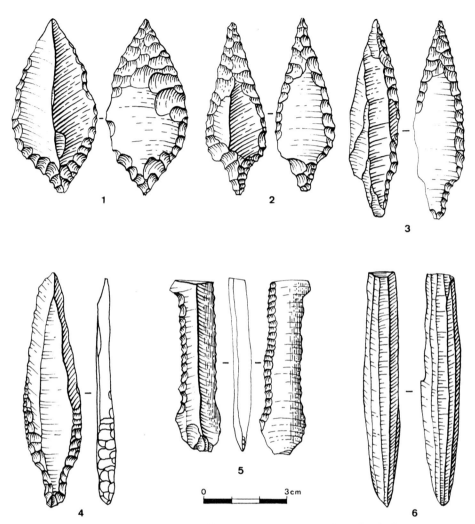

Fig. 59 Chipped stone from Maghzaliyeh (Sinjar, late PPNB): 2–4 Byblos points in flint; 5 'Çayönü tool' in obsidian; 6 obsidian core of 'bullet core' type. After R. Munchaev, N. Merpert and N. Bader.

sources, obsidian is predominant[15] and the manner of its pressure flaking (Fig. 59: 6), the making of 'Çayönü tools' (Fig. 59: 5), which were the particular invention of the PPNB of the Taurus, and the marble bracelets all point to the Taurus connection.[16]

In the bone industry we also find needles with eyes made by incision, newly arrived in eastern Anatolia from the Syrian middle Euphrates. They occur further east and south and at lower altitude, although they have entirely disappeared from their area of origin. In the architecture, rectangular at last, we can recognise both the plan with long, transversal rooms, constructed as in the Taurus on a stone platform, and plans with small cells. But here it is not the early or middle PPNB as at Cafer Höyük but a well-dated late PPNB. Although the villages of Cafer Höyük and Çayönü housed cultivators who were still ignorant of herding, at Maghzaliyeh they not only cultivated cereals but also herded goats and sheep.[17] On the other hand, while the village might still be aceramic, the presence of white ware in gypsum plaster is one of the rare common traits shared across the whole Jezirah and the Syrian desert. In this regard the people of Maghzaliyeh owe nothing to a source in the mountains of south-east Anatolia.

The neolithisation of the Sinjar region is thus brought about in the late PPNB as a movement not simply west to east from the neighbouring western Jezirah but also from eastern Anatolia. It is as if this fundamentally Levantine culture had reached the eastern Jezirah only after a detour through its northern, mountain branch, and considerably moderated in the tenth millennium by its contacts with the local Mesolithic tradition.

In the same Sinjar region, very close to Maghzaliyeh and immediately succeeding it in time, a pair of sites, Sotto and Kültepe, next appear. They belong at the beginning of the Iraqi Hassuna culture period and date after 7000 BC.[18] To these we should add the village of Umm Dabaghiyah that was established further south, deep in the semi-arid zone.[19] This group of sites constitutes the cultures known as the Umm Dabaghiyah-Sotto (or proto-Hassuna) culture, in which pottery is now present, as it is across almost all the Near East. As one might expect, this pottery is original from the outset, painted red or with a few painted lines below the rim.

The rest of the decoration consists of clay applied in relief (Fig. 64). In contrast with the coastal forms, there is no impressed decoration, nor, at this initial stage, any decoration by incision. For the rest, the Anatolian affinities of Maghzaliyeh are as if rubbed out. It is now the PPNB tradition that is relevant, but the analogues seem stronger with the late PPNB of the western Jezirah and with the sedentary villages of the 'final PPNB' of the Syrian desert.[20] There is a series of traits that seem to relate to the villages of northern and eastern Syria: the significant use of gypsum plaster in the buildings, some Byblos points in the weaponry,[21] the absence of pressure flaked debitage (except for the obsidian blades, which are much less common than at Maghzaliyeh, and which are products that arrive ready made in the Sinjar, and show no sign of being manufactured *in situ*); also, the herding of cattle and pigs that have joined the sheep and goats at Sotto.[22] We shall soon unfold the elaboration of these traits in the late PPNB of Bouqras, deep in the semi-arid zone. It is very likely that the Umm Dabaghiyah-Sotto culture is the result of the encounter of a 'Maghzaliyian' base with new and important inputs arriving directly from the west.[23] The mixture of these different elements and their more precise interpretation require deeper study of the material.

Sedentary villages of the Syrian desert

Since the end of the Natufian period the arid lands where less than 200 mm of rain fall each year had been all but abandoned. Having adapted very well to the dry environment during the Epi-palaeolithic, the peoples of the Levant quit the region at the end of the Natufian and drew back into the moister open forest steppe where the wild cereals grew. There they developed both cultivation and herding. It is only from the late PPNB that a centrifugal movement caused them to occupy the coastlands

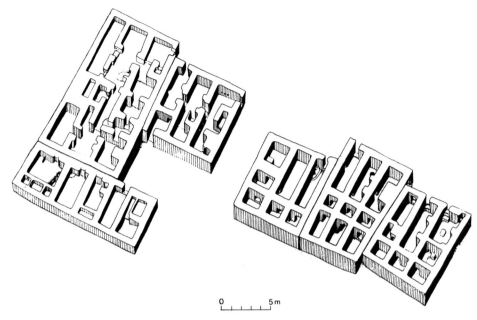

0 ⌊_⌊_⌊_⌊_⌊ 5 m

Fig. 60 Late PPNB houses from Bouqras (Syria): isometric view. After J. Akkermans *et al.*

and reoccupy the western Jezirah. The impulse continued and pushed the sedentary agriculturalists to conquer the semi-desert steppe once more, or at least the oases and river valleys where, despite the climate, water remains available.

Two sites are particularly significant. One, Bouqras, was established on the right bank of the Euphrates in the late PPNB. The other, El Kowm, occupies a basin with artesian springs in the region of Palmyra. It belongs to the final PPNB, that is to say the latest phase of this culture which persisted in ignoring ceramics long after the majority of settlements in the Near and Middle East had integrated the craft into their everyday equipment (Fig. 50).

Bouqras

At the latitude of Bouqras, green vegetation exists only in the narrow flood-plain that borders the river on both banks. The steppe in that region receives less than 150 mm of annual rainfall, and has never supported trees. The prehistoric village,[24] perched on an escarpment above the flood-plain, extends over almost 3 hectares. Its architecture is dense and elaborate. The houses are close together, their walls almost contiguous. The various 'quarters' are centred on 'squares', or separated from one another by streets, an evident progress in village urbanism. The houses (Fig. 60) have multiple rooms that may either be rectangular or take the form of small square cells that communicate with each other by means of low doorways, as at Abu Hureyra at the same period. However, in contrast with Abu Hureyra, the long rooms, like the lines of cells, seem to be oriented on the long axis of the house rather than the transverse, a trait which is found a little later at El Kowm. The use of gypsum plaster for the floors and walls is intense and new layers are continually added. The internal wall surfaces may be painted red, and sometimes also have decorations in high relief or figurative frescoes.

Plaster is also used to make considerable amounts of *vaisselle blanche*, but Bouqras, along with Tell Assouad, is one of the rare sites in the Near East to exhibit a little pottery even before 7000 BC.[25] The forms are simple, most often rounded but sometimes also carinated as a little later at Umm Dabaghiyah and Sotto. As on those sites, there are some examples of a general red wash or even of linear painted decoration in the same colour. It seems that we may be at the origin of the tradition of painted pottery which will soon characterise not only the Iraqi Umm Dabaghiyah-Sotto culture, but also the generality of Neolithic ceramics of the Middle East. Consequently, this 'oriental' ceramic tradition, which is clearly different from the monochrome tradition of the western Jezirah and the Mediterranean littoral, would seem to have appeared like that of the Levant in the full flow of the PPNB. Thus the Khabur seems to mark the frontier between these two styles of inventiveness in the domain of ceramics.

There can be no doubt that this all takes place against a PPNB background in its middle Euphrates facies. The architectural plans are in the lineage of those of Mureybet IV and Abu Hureyra, although much more complex. The chipped stone industry[26] exhibits naviform cores, as well as the whole gamut of projectile points typical of the PPNB. And there are wood-working tools (axes, adzes, chisels) of polished greenstone, appropriate to the northern facies. Relations with Anatolia, which were doubtless mostly commercial, can be seen in the relatively important deliveries of obsidian, including some cores known as 'bullet cores' (*en balle de fusil*), from which the blades were extracted by pressure rather than percussion. Among the finished tools, there are some 'Çayönü tools',[27] which are one of the principal exports from the Taurus region after 7500 BC, and are found throughout the whole Zagros region.[28]

Another remarkable creation of the local craftsmen working in stone at Bouqras, especially at the end of the life of the settlement, is the great number of polished stone vases made of calcite, marble, gypsum (alabaster) or hard stones. At first there are simple little cups (Fig. 61: 1–2), then more closed and four-footed forms (Fig, 61: 3–5); these pieces were made at the site and are remarkable for their technical quality and their miniaturisation. Jacobus Roodenberg remarks that they require stone drills for the process of hollowing them; the interiors were not simply chipped out. Vases in polished stone are present but rare at most of the Neolithic sites of the Levant; they are more numerous in the 'Qermezian' Epi-palaeolithic, in the PPNB of the Taurus and especially in Cyprus, but in different types. Those of Bouqras, marked out by their abundance, their delicate finish and their forms, do not extend beyond a limited geographical range, comprising the Jezirah and the Syrian steppe desert.[29]

The inhabitants of Bouqras cultivated the soil in the flood-plain of the Euphrates. Several species of domesticated cereals have been identified,[30] as well as lentils and peas, although this diverse agriculture does not seem to have played a very important role in the economy of the village. These sedentary villagers were above all herdsmen. Indeed they were pioneers in this regard, since, as early as at Ras Shamra,

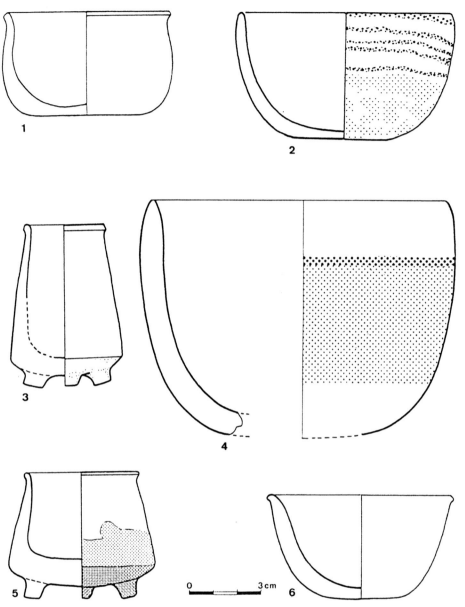

Fig. 61 Polished stone vessels from the late and final PPNB periods in semi-arid Syria: 1–3, 5 Bouqras; 4 Qdeir; 6 El Kowm 2. After J. Roodenberg and D. Stordeur (4 and 6).

they added to the predominant herds of goats and sheep some domesticated cattle and doubtless also some pigs.[31] Finally, hunting also remained important.

The banks of the river offered a relatively favourable eco-niche. The life of the village and the material culture of its inhabitants were in no way inhibited by the arid environment – indeed, rather the contrary: the culture of Bouqras is shown to particular perfection in the tripartite plan of the houses, the household equipment and the subsistence strategies.

El Kowm

El Kowm lies in the semi-desert steppe between the Euphrates and Palmyra, but here the eco-niche is provided not only by a river but also some thirty artesian springs which have created an oasis.[32] This abundance of water at a latitude where it is rare has attracted humans all through prehistory, from the Lower Palaeolithic to the Natufian. After an abandonment around 11,000 BC, reoccupation occurred around 7000 BC. An important sedentary village of 3 hectares was built on either side of a spring. In time these became two neighbouring Neolithic tells, El Kowm 1 and El Kowm 2, which form a single village community. El Kowm 1 has only been sounded,[33] and most of our information comes from El Kowm 2, which was excavated by Danielle Stordeur.[34]

El Kowm was occupied during the first half of the seventh millennium, coinciding with the last phase of Bouqras. The absence of pottery, a paradoxical phenomenon at this period that we shall also find in the desert zone of the southern Levant, causes us to attribute this site to the final PPNB. But this absence of pottery is in no way a sign of cultural backwardness. As at Bouqras, the material culture is fully developed; indeed in certain respects it was ahead of its time. This is above all true of the architecture. The mastery of the builders is first expressed in the planning and preparation of the spaces to be constructed. Extensive platforms were first constructed on which were set not one but several houses. Then there is an intense utilisation and differentiation of plaster, made easier in an environment full of gypsum. Plaster not only covered the floors and the mud brick walls, but also served for the manufacture of huge amounts of *vaisselle blanche*[35] and many kinds of domestic installation – rectangular fixed basins or storage compartments that were covered with a removable slab with a pierced lug handle. Finally, there are the architectural plans themselves and their novel and complex fittings. On the one hand there are houses with small, more or less rectangular, inter-communicating rooms, where for the first time in the Near East we see domestic arrangements for running water – channels in the plaster to carry water across a room or a threshold, holes for drainage passing through walls and even genuine closed water channels passing under the plaster of floors.[36] On the other hand there is a large rectangular building formed of a long, T-shaped room, whose long axis is flanked on both sides by smaller cells (Fig. 62). At some time it was added to, when a sort of replica of the earlier plan was built, but with a long room that was L-shaped (or half-T-shaped) with cells this time on only one side. Each of the long axial rooms exhibits the same complex assemblage of three juxtaposed structures – a built oven, a hearth in a recess in the wall and a small circular hearth on the floor. The exact function of this distinctive type of building is not yet clear, but Danielle Stordeur has drawn attention to the entirely novel character of its plan.[37] Up to this time, the long rooms or the files of cells had been organised transversely in relation to the long axis of the rectangle, following the original conception of the PPNB pier-house. Maghzaliyeh has revealed more complex plans but of the same basic inspiration. At El Kowm, and perhaps also at Bouqras, the tripartite idea exists, but it is longitudinal. This will be echoed in the buildings of the Mesopotamian Ubaid culture of the sixth millennium BC,[38] too far away

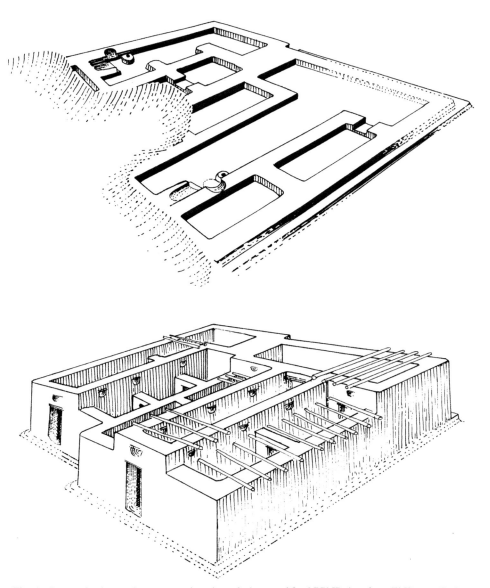

Fig. 62 Isometric view and reconstruction view of a house of final PPNB date from El Kowm (Syrian desert). After D. Stordeur.

therefore in both space and time to allow us at present to propose some distant relationship. The Ubaid architectural plans are in any case completely transformed relative to the standards of the PPNB, although the construction methods remain reasonably close to those of Bouqras.

Other cultural elements are also transformed, but they nonetheless retain clear traces of their origin. The PPNB chipped stone industry devolved here in the sense of typological impoverishment and aesthetic degeneration:[39] Byblos points are present but rare and their manufacture is less careful. The great majority of tools are burins on blades or flakes and some scrapers, making this a rather untypical assemblage of mediocre appearance. The bone industry gives the same impression.[40] Let us once more affirm that a chipped stone or bone industry may not be at all 'beautiful', but it can still respond effectively to the tasks that are demanded of it. For a prehistorian accustomed to the Levant, the chipped stone tools of the Middle Eastern Neolithic therefore appear to be of a distressing banality, as are those to the west, from Cyprus or from Greece. That does not prevent them from fulfilling their basic functions of cutting, piercing, scraping and so on perfectly well. We must dissociate the efficacy of a tool from its aesthetic qualities. These latter reveal an investment that is more cultural than utilitarian, of which the customary weapons of the PPNB have given us a good example, as also the splendid bifacial points of the Solutrean culture of Europe at an earlier date. 'Impoverishment' is thus the sign of a relative lack of feeling for the formal quality of the object: it is not incompatible with a real stability in technical knowledge, nor even with progress in this field.[41]

By contrast, a sector of material culture that was highly valued at El Kowm is that of cups and small vases in high-quality marble (Fig. 61: 6), but these were not the product of local craftsmen. They are comparable with those of Bouqras, and they may prove to have arrived by way of exchange.

The techniques of food production had been perfected. Four different species of cultivated wheat and two of barley were grown. Considering the aridity of the climate and the difficulty of assuring regular harvests except in years that were unusually wet, a primitive form of irrigation using the springs is quite probable.[42] Finally, while they kept sheep and some goats, and perhaps also some cattle,[43] hunting, particularly of gazelles, continued to play a role in the food-quest that was more important than in the contemporary villages in less arid environments. This higher profile role of meat in the diet, as at Bouqras, is perhaps an insurance against the annual hazards of the harvests.

In conclusion, this settlement out in the desert does not look like a poor village, any more than Bouqras. They did not use pottery only because they had developed more than anyone else techniques using plaster. The apparent ordinariness of their toolkit relates more to an aesthetic disengagement than to technical inability: in that regard, El Kowm heralds a general trend in the Middle East. The strategies of subsistence reinvest all the knowledge acquired in the Neolithic of the Levant while diversifying it still further. Finally, the architecture surprises us with its innovations, especially the facilities for channelling water in the house. Are these, as Arnold Toynbee might have said, a sort of riposte from their culture, a defiance of the dry climate that this sedentary community in the desert faced as a challenge rather than allowing it to grind them down?

The ideology of the desert people
The impression of a cultural blossoming is amplified when we consider the symbolic domain, whether at Bouqras or, further east and a little later, at Umm Dabaghiyah or Sotto. Artistic expression exhibits a richness and a rare quality. First, the classic themes, if one may call them that, of the Levantine Neolithic are expressed at

Bouqras as elsewhere by means of female and animal figurines (in which there is a predominance of bovine figures), plus simple small human heads in baked clay. There is also an elaborate craft in carved bone. There are pins with schematically carved heads in human or animal form, and two amazing objects made from tubes of bone decorated with incisions (Fig. 63). One ends with one terminal, the other with two terminals, which the excavators interpret as the head and raised arms of an anthropomorphic figure in the act of prayer, but which one could equally read, in our view, as the fore-parts of a bull.[44] At Umm Dabaghiyah or Sotto the theme of the Goddess is manifested in reliefs on pots (Fig. 64: 3). At El Kowm, a schematic male figure with raised arms is incised on a plaster vessel (Fig. 65: 2). It seems that an analogous representation may also have existed, though half destroyed when found, on a mural painting at Umm Dabaghiyah.[45]

The desert villages also display fresco art. This type of art was perhaps less exceptional in the Levantine Neolithic than might be thought, our imperfect knowledge of it depending on the state of preservation of the walls. For its exceptional value in terms of information on matters of religious art Çatalhöyük no doubt owes its reputation to the remarkable preservation of its architecture. However, we have seen that traces of geometric frescoes had already existed two or three millennia earlier in the round houses of the Mureybetian. Elsewhere, the custom of colour-washing the walls and floors with ochre is sporadically found in the Levantine PPNB, from Beidha to Abu Hureyra, especially when the priming coat of lime or plaster is well enough preserved to retain the traces we need. Ochre washes are found at Bouqras, too, but this site also has a wall relief made of plaster that is painted in red representing a human head, with the two eyes marked by inlaid fragments of obsidian.[46] Further, a fresco with an animal subject – cranes – was found there, while a mural painting at Umm Dabaghiyah portrays onagers[47] (Fig. 65:1). People were not content simply to colour their walls; they decorated them with figurative motifs. Their zoomorphic art concerns animals of the steppe, which are apparently preferred to the cattle, sheep and goats that were most frequently represented earlier in the Neolithic.

This particular repertory of beasts is also the subject of sculptures in polished stone, completed to a fine standard of finish (Fig. 66). Technical mastery of this material was already found on vases. There are equids, hares and a hedgehog at Bouqras (Pl. VIII), a small rodent and a gazelle (?) at El Kowm. Somewhat further north, at the boundary of the two climatic zones, several objects from Abu Hureyra dating to the late PPNB show the same inspiration through the schematic representations of gazelles.

The preserved frescoes are still too rare and the stone animal sculptures, like many of the portable objects, are wanting in the contextual relations that might shed light on their precise integration in the system of thought and allow us to capture this system of imagination. We may observe not only that the symbolic exemplars of the Levantine Neolithic, the Woman and the Bull, are indeed present, but also that a new sensitivity integrates into the art various animals that are absent or more unobtrusive elsewhere. One can just as easily see in this a novel attention given to the

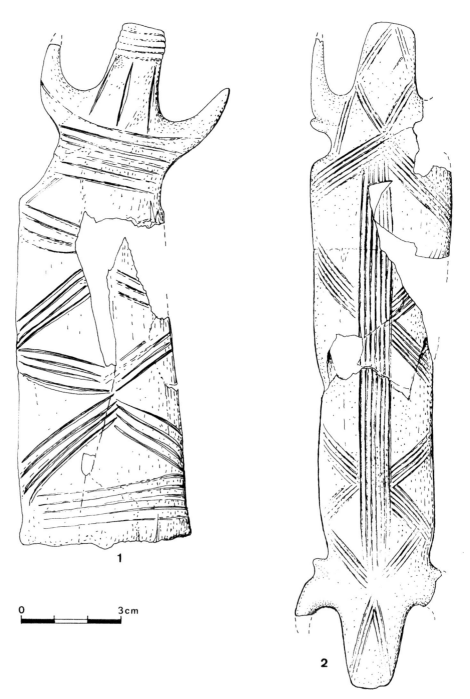

Fig. 63 Bull representations in bone from Bouqras (late PPNB, Syria). After J. Akkermans *et al.*

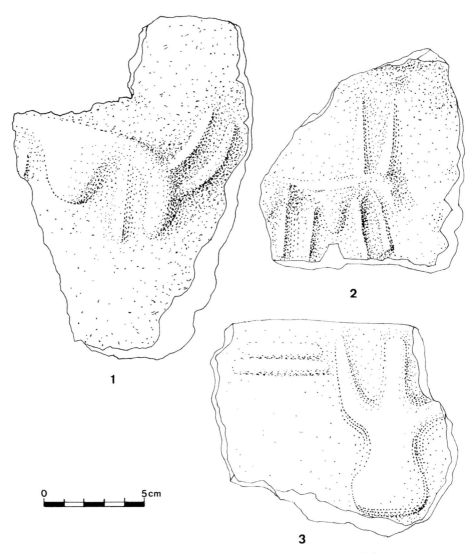

Fig. 64 Relief decoration on pottery from northern Iraq (seventh millennium BC): 1–2 Umm Dabaghiyah (after D. Kirkbride); 3 Sotto (after N. Bader).

swift-moving species of the steppe and a certain mythology relating to them which is, at the technical level, an influence from the Nemrikian tradition from beyond the Khabur. There too, as we saw, they were very fond of working in polished stone.

Conclusions

The process of neolithisation of the villages of the eastern Jezirah and that of semi-arid Syria are not then fundamentally different. In the two cases, starting around 7500 BC, we see an eastward extension of sedentary cultivators initially issuing from the middle Euphrates. If we have treated them separately, it is because the pasts of the two regions were not the same. In the eastern Jezirah, an autonomous tradition

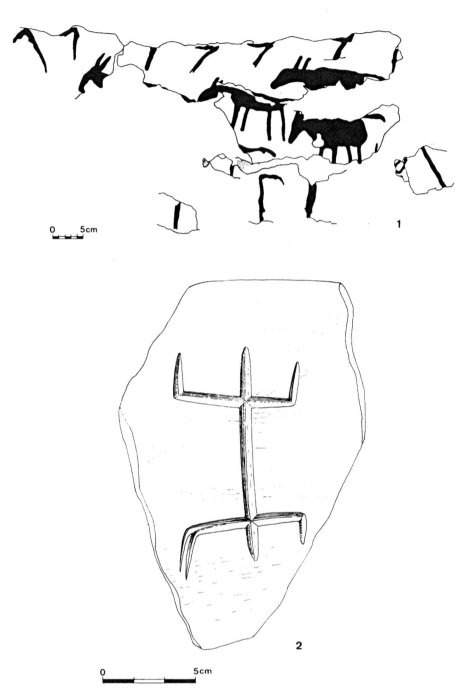

0 5cm

1

0 5cm

2

Fig. 65 Art of the seventh millennium BC in the arid zone: 1 painted fresco with equids (Umm Dabaghiyah, Iraq); 2 schematic male representation on a plaster vessel (El Kowm, Syria). After D. Kirkbride and D. Stordeur.

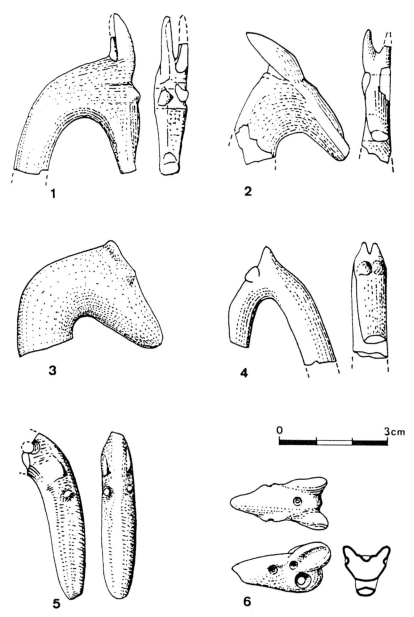

Fig. 66 Animals in polished stone from the semi-arid zone in Syria: 1–2, 4 late PPNB from Bouqras; 3 Abu Hureyra; 5–6 final PPNB from El Kowm. After J. Akkermans *et al.*, A. Moore and D. Stordeur.

unified the region between the Jebel Sinjar and the Zagros. The remarkable cultural development before 7500, however, was apparently not accompanied by any process of neolithisation of the economy. The absence of a true Neolithic earlier than Maghzaliyeh can no longer be attributed to a lacuna in our knowledge. For its part, the Syrian desert was empty before the sedentary cultivators arrived.

The phenomenon of diffusion is thus clear in both cases. The complete rupture, cultural and economic, between the sites of the Nemrikian tradition and that of Maghzaliyeh, although they are very close in space, speaks of the arrival of a completely foreign population. Further south, it was the new occupation of an unpopulated wilderness. These transfers of population, carrying with them an elaborate architecture, are phenomena of confirmed sedentary people transferring their villages into new territories. In that regard, they do not differ from the new inhabitants of the Levantine littoral. Again as in the coastal region, if they are put on the map, they demonstrate a phenomenon with its own orientation (this time towards the south-east), but quite complex and finely shaded when the points of departure are more precisely envisaged. The founders of Maghzaliyeh came from the Taurus, those of Bouqras, culturally close to Abu Hureyra, can only have come down the Euphrates. In the following period, the sites with pottery in the Sinjar region in part inherited the legacy of Maghzaliyeh,[48] but a new input coming directly from the west also appears probable. In these villages in turn a cultural phylogeny was founded that was particular to the Middle East. Still further east, it would comprise the cultures of Samarra and Ubaid. This more easterly expansion, which is only poorly defined because it has never been studied as such, lies beyond the present field of study. For the present purpose it is more important to complete our survey of the mechanisms of diffusion of sedentary peoples by another no less important means, that of pastoral nomadism.

17

Pastoral nomadism

Without exception we attribute a nomadic way of life to the small-scale communities of palaeolithic hunter-gatherers. In the Levantine Epi-Palaeolithic, when small sedentary village communities came into existence, this mobile way of life persisted in the semi-arid zones where hunting played a more important role than gathering. On the other hand, we have scarcely any trace of nomadism when first agriculture and then herding were developed in the context of the villages.

The nomadism with which we shall be dealing here was different and was in no way an archaism. It was a deliberate option for certain communities who had become producers of subsistence, but who valued mobility in their way of life. Pastoral nomadism is a phenomenon of people who, like today's Bedouin, have lived in permanent villages in a previous phase of their history and who, at some time, have changed. Their subsistence production, on the other hand, is not necessarily limited to herding. Agriculture may be practised in a form different from that of the sedentary people. We shall describe well-attested cases of a mixed economy, although in a nomadic context.

All cultivation, however, implies staying in one place long enough for the growth cycle to reach completion with the harvest. Certain authors (Khazanov 1984, for example) prefer to speak of 'semi-nomadism' in this case, reserving the term 'pastoral nomadism' for the more specialised examples of 'pure' pastoralism. Here we use a more general definition of pastoral nomadism that takes account of the dual criteria of the predominant, but not exclusive, importance of herding and the absence of permanent settlement for all the community.[1]

It is true to say that the study of Neolithic nomads has hardly begun. Such a study is difficult, for a nomadic community, by definition, leaves few traces. Nomadic people build scarcely any solid structures and, after their temporary stops, they usually leave behind them only a few dropped objects and the ashes of their fires, which are quickly dispersed by the wind. In the Levant as elsewhere, we have only felt certain of the existence of pastoral nomads when texts allude to them, which is not before the Bronze Age and writing. Thus, the Mari archives make reference to royal campaigns to protect the kingdom from them. In central Asia, an ideal landscape for pastoral nomads, recent syntheses which describe and explain this way of life go back no further than the Bronze Age,[2] even if A. M. Khazanov believes in a more ancient origin.

Some Neolithic communities of the Near East may have been thought to be nomadic. Fifty years ago, Gordon Childe mentioned pastoralism, but it was in the course of a purely theoretical approach based on belief in a mistaken idea. That idea was the then widespread view that herding had been first invented by nomads who were the direct descendants of the mobile hunter-gatherers of the Palaeolithic. We now know that herding in reality began in the context of sedentary villages, and that pastoral nomadism is a relatively recent phenomenon, certainly much later than the beginnings of the production of subsistence. The more recent occasional allusions to nomadism in the Neolithic are intended to justify the poverty of certain remains (a small surface scatter, for example, that never formed into a tell, or a sounding that failed to produce evidence of walls) rather than to describe or explain the phenomena themselves. This argument 'by default' is insufficient. From the late PPNB, when herding became generalised among the villages, sheep and goats evidently did not live permanently in one place, any more than did their shepherds. Their daily grazing, indeed their seasonal transhumance from one pasturage to another, would leave only a few pieces of chipped flint on the surface. And that does not make them nomadic societies.

In recent years our information has become more precise. Through the study of contemporary nomads by means of ethno-archaeology, which can help us to understand better the behaviour of other people at other times,[3] information has been garnered and its interpretation improved. The most eloquent information concerning the semi-arid zone in the southern Levant comes from Sinai and from the Black Desert in Jordan, and for the northern Levant from the region of Palmyra, in particular from the El Kowm depression (Fig. 50). In all these examples, particular ecological conditions must have existed that caused even transitory occupations to leave sufficient remains to support real archaeological study. The arid zones here play their trump card – sand-storms. Aeolian deposits resulting from sand-storms can very quickly seal the ashes of hearths and the cooking remains that the nomad leaves behind him, or whatever is protected from the wind by some obstacle, thereby causing the formation of an archaeological deposit. Two quite different scenarios are significant. In stony landscapes, nomads are not content simply to erect their tents or their light shelters, as we can see from contemporary examples;[4] a low curving dry-stone wall is frequently built to protect them from the wind (Fig. 67: 1). After their departure the whole set of these more or less contiguous stone circles may come to form something like a phantom-hamlet looking like a honeycomb. This is soon invested by aeolian sands, fixing any residues, which become more expressive in the course of the nomads' cyclical movements, as the same place is generally reoccupied many times. That seems to have been the case for prehistoric nomadic occupations in the southern Levant. A second scenario is represented by the Syrian oasis of El Kowm, where such stone structures do not exist. There, the two factors that interact are the very considerable aeolian deposition and the presence around the artesian springs of low vegetation that holds the sand to form hillocks around the springs, a kind of entirely natural eminence which may be several metres in height.[5] Within these hillocks, the surfaces that are produced by the most fugitive human occupations are found preserved intact and neatly stratified, including organic remains that allow analysis of the nomads' way of life. From the bones and carbonised plant

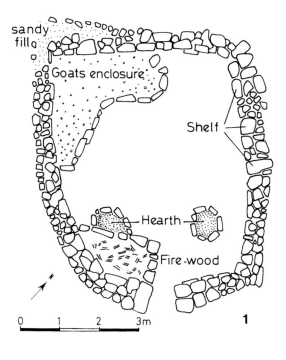

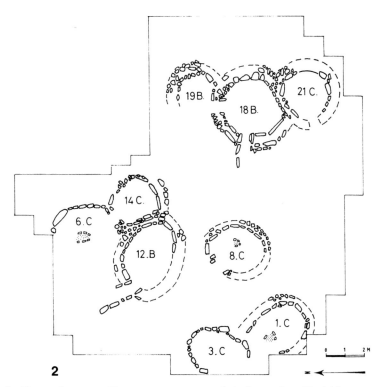

Fig. 67 Tent enclosure used by contemporary nomads in the southern Sinai (1); stone structures used by Neolithic nomads from the Wadi Tbeik (2). After O. Bar-Yosef.

remains it is possible to obtain indications concerning hunting or herding, gathering or cultivation.

We should not forget that one of the virtues of a mobile way of life is that it permits the exploitation of different types of environment by turns. A stay for cultivation would thus concern only one of the points on the annual round. Hunting stations in an area rich in game would not necessarily exclude the practice of herding in parallel, which might not leave any visible trace at that place. Thus the first excavations in the Neolithic 'round structures' of the Black Desert in Jordan[6] suggested a PPNB in full economic regression, because only wild fauna were found. Recent research has produced a clearer picture, but only in so far as a single mobile human group may be the originator of several rather different sites. Since they do not carry out the same tasks at all their sites, there remains a good deal of work to be done and information to be assembled in order to achieve a genuinely synthetic understanding of the complete cycle of these groups. In conclusion, while the existence of nomadic communities in the semi-arid zone of the Levant from 7500 BC is now a certainty, it is still not possible to affirm that pastoral nomadism was the way of life throughout.

Nomadism in the semi-arid zone of the southern Levant

We have seen that the considerable decline of the Jordan valley in terms of sedentary sites after 7500 BC may signify that a part of the population had tipped over into a nomadic way of life. The available information was too poor, however, to measure the true extent of the phenomenon. Sites are far more numerous in the semi-arid periphery of this zone, which formerly was almost empty. A form of exodus to that region is incontestable.

Sinai has produced a score of sites, known most often from simple surface collections but sometimes from excavations, some in the north, in the Jebel Maghara, others in the south, in the mountains or on the coast of the Gulf of Suez. Culturally, these sites belong some to the late and some to the final PPNB. The diverse assemblages of this culture occur everywhere, including true Jericho points of the southern Levantine form. In addition the final PPNB sites include 'desert burins', a type that is exclusive to the semi-arid regions at this period. It is the predominance of these burins that marks out the so-called 'burin sites' of Syria and Jordan.[7]

In southern Sinai,[8] Ofer Bar-Yosef has proposed a seasonal alternation of occupation between the mountains (Wadi Tbeik, Ujrat el Mehed) and the littoral, similar to that which is practised by the Bedouin of today; the latter build curving structures of stone, which are the same as those found in the Neolithic (Fig. 67), around the footings of their tents to protect themselves from wind and cold. It should be emphasised that there are traces of agriculture (cereals) at Ujrat el Mehed,[9] while the fauna everywhere includes an abundance of ibex (*Capra ibex*) suggesting hunting and nothing else. Bar-Yosef reminds us that the bones of ibex are distinguished from those of goat only with great difficulty[10] and he concludes that pastoralism cannot be completely excluded.

In northern Sinai the Neolithic sites of Jebel Maghara, especially in the region of

Mushabi,[11] appear to belong to the final PPNB. These are unexcavated sites known only from surface collections, and thus we lack detailed information on the subsistence economy. But in the far east of Sinai, on the edge of the Araba depression, at a lower altitude, the late PPNB site of Nahal Issaron[12] has recently been excavated; it has produced a honeycomb of circular structures which contain bones of domesticated goat. The site appears likely to have been a pastoralists' camping-place.

Neolithic nomadism in the Sinai seems then to have been well established, but its general economic structure is still not clear. Subsistence production existed, agricultural at Ujrat el Mehed, pastoral at Nahal Issaron. Do hunting stations reflect a complete return by certain groups to predatory subsistence strategies, or only temporary and localised episodes in a more diverse annual cycle? The writer leans towards the second hypothesis while being unable at present to exclude the former.

The Black Desert and the Azraq oasis

In eastern Jordan there are two complementary environments comprising the basaltic expanses of the Black Desert and the oasis of Azraq. PPNB sites in both environments exhibit the same round stone structures as those of Sinai and are likewise dated between 7500 and 6300 BC. As in Sinai, this is a Palestinian facies of the PPNB with Jericho points, and its geographical origin is thus clear enough. At the beginning of the seventh millennium, these industries mostly comprised great numbers of 'desert burins', which sometimes out-number all the rest.[13] These burins of course signify a preferred activity related to these camp-sites, but that activity is unfortunately not yet identified. The problems and the conclusion are the same as for the Sinai sites: pastoral nomadism existed with domesticated ovicaprids. An exclusively wild fauna (gazelles) has been recovered at two sites, while in the oasis traces of agriculture are found.[14] The combination of these diverse elements poses a problem, because the sites excavated or sounded are still very scarce in relation to the mass of sites surveyed. The same suggestions and reservations as for the Sinai are offered.

The El Kowm oasis and the region of Palmyra

The steppe that separates the coastal region of the central and northern Levant from the middle Euphrates has been a transit territory for Bedouin tribes almost as far back as written history can reach. Camel nomads were already crossing the region in the classical period, perhaps also in the Bronze Age,[15] with the oasis-city of Palmyra serving as a caravan halt. As for the smaller oases (Sukhneh, Taibeh, El Kowm) that mark out the itinerary from Palmyra to modern Raqqa on the middle Euphrates, they seem at all periods to have served as temporary camps for sheep-herding 'lesser' nomads (i.e. not camel nomads). They could cover vast distances, from the coast to the Taurus, but they made the shorter transition between the flat, steppe country and the greener and more wooded high ground of the mountain ridges which cross the steppe from south-west to north-east (Jebel Mqaibara, Jebel Bishri).

That this nomadism in fact goes back to the Neolithic is a recent discovery.[16]

Thanks to the 'hillocks with springs' and to the many camp-sites that have been surveyed in and around the El Kowm oasis, a particular facies of the final PPNB can be
isolated, the nomadic facies called the Qdeir PPNB. It is different from the neighbouring but sedentary facies of El Kowm, and different again from the nomadic
PPNB of the southern Levant. It is evident that it neither shared the same origin nor
followed the same trajectory.

The eponymous site of this facies, the hillock of Qdeir 1, has layer upon layer of
stratified nomadic camp-sites without buildings. Minutely careful excavation has
permitted the definition of occupation areas with light structures juxtaposed with
areas for working flint.[17] These people were herders, specialising in sheep with a few
goats and some cattle.[18] They were great hunters, too, pursuing gazelle and several
other steppe species, but they also cultivated cereals during their stays, as the rare
carbonised grains and the characteristic gloss on their sickle-blades attest.[19]

They are otherwise characterised by a particularly intensive craft activity, the
knapping of flint from raw material whose sources are found less than 2 km from the
camp-site. They made the complete range of tools necessary for their everyday life
(borers, scrapers, sickle-blades, etc.) in small numbers; but they also made in much
greater numbers the famous 'desert burins' (Fig. 68: 6), which we have already
encountered from Sinai to the Black Desert.[20] Moreover the intense manufacture of
flint blades from bipolar, naviform or related cores (cf. Fig. 30: 2)[21] seems to have
had the making of weapons as its principal objective,[22] namely the PPNB arrow-
heads whose interest here is twofold. On the one hand their varied typology (Fig. 68:
1–4) does not include Jericho points of the southern Levantine form, thereby signal-
ling a different and more northerly origin for this nomadic movement. On the other
hand, their sophisticated manufacture retains a cohesion with the whole of the previous PPNB. At this date, the beginning of the seventh millennium, only the cultures
of the coastlands with pottery (Byblos, Amuq, etc.) seem to have maintained the
quality of their weapons to this degree. In this sense, however close in space they
might be, Qdeir 1 is at the opposite pole from the sedentary final PPNB of El Kowm
1, where weaponry and aggressive ideology seem to have become extinct somewhat
earlier.

The numerous camp-sites found in the interior of the oasis and on the hills round
about all belong to the cultural facies of Qdeir,[23] but by contrast the relative proportions of the different tools are very varied. In the absence of excavations,[24] these variations are the best indication of specialised activities at each site. Besides two other
base-camps similar to Qdeir 1, which exhibit a similarly complete range of subsistence and craft activities, there are other kinds of sites: hunting-stations where arrow-
heads predominate to a great degree; 'burin sites' where, on the contrary, points are
lacking; and workshops situated at the sources of flint for the primary preparation of
the raw material, producing only cores.[25] It may be that several groups of nomads
used to circulate within this region, each of them producing several stations of
different types.[26]

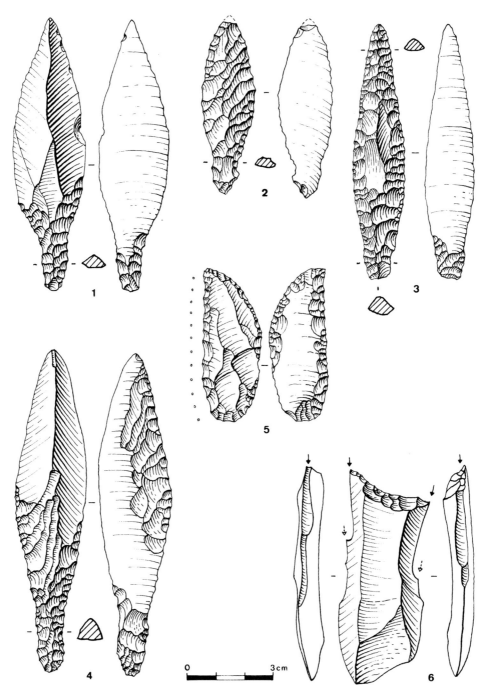

Fig. 68 Weapons and tools from the nomadic final PPNB of Qdeir (Syria): 1–4 arrow-heads; 5 sickle-blade; 6 'desert burin'. After O. Aurenche and M.-C. Cauvin.

Why pastoral nomadism?

The conditions of the desert are, we know, very special. In that environment techniques of survival that are proper to more temperate regions are soon found to have limitations. Even when there is water locally – as is the case with oases – it remains risky to cultivate without irrigation. The much later civilisations of lower Mesopotamia had recourse to irrigation, and perhaps the sedentary Neolithic people of El Kowm prefigured them in this regard. But why leave the fertile fields and rich pastures of the 'Levantine nucleus' in order to confront arid areas for which they were not prepared and where everything was so much more difficult?

It is true that pastoral nomadism, especially when it relies on the herding of sheep – a very sociable species whose movements are more easily controllable than those of the goat – offers some compensation for this difficulty, rather as irrigation does for sedentary people. The steppe that we are concerned with receives between 50 and 200 mm of rain per year, and is not absolute desert. It is green in spring and can then feed the flocks; otherwise, people could profit from the new mobility of their livestock and play on an alternation of highlands–lowlands, as in Sinai, or even make summer incursions into the neighbouring temperate regions.

In any case, whether in sub-Saharan Africa, the Near East or Central Asia, it is above all nomads who inhabit the desert regions, because they are better adapted to confront the dry climate. From there it is an easy step to consider that nomadism was everywhere 'invented' with this objective. Indeed, that view has often been expressed, while the additional effort required by this novel adaptation has appeared capable of justification only because of a constraining necessity. That is why O. Lattimore explained the origin of Asiatic nomadism in terms of the expulsion of certain human groups towards the margin of the fertile areas, whether this expulsion had demographic causes, or, for more recent times, political reasons.[27] The argument from demographic pressure has also been applied in the Middle East to explain the appearance in the seventh millennium of the Mesopotamian Samarra culture and of its irrigation agriculture in previously uninhabited semi-arid zones.[28] For the Levant the same model has been followed to account for both irrigation agriculture and pastoral nomadism.

These explanations depend on a simple logic which has as its basis propositions that appear to be so self-evident that they have never even been discussed. These initial general-purpose axioms held by a scientific community which acquired them on the benches of their undergraduate lecture theatres as part of the discipline itself are what Thomas Kühn[29] calls 'paradigms' used for long periods to form the impassable horizon of all research. That agriculture and herding could only be invented when hunting and gathering were not sufficient to feed people was, as we have seen, one of these pseudo-facts. That human groups could only leave a land flowing with milk and honey to confront the desert because others had expelled them is another of them. The appeal to demographic pressure has the effect of reducing the phenomenon of territorial expansion to the simple proliferation of a species and resultant competitive behaviour of the kind that animal ethologists describe. Such behaviour doubtless exists by virtue of the biological roots of man in the animal kingdom, and the notion of *Lebensraum* is sadly familiar to us. That, however, does not make demographic pressure a panacea that is useful for all circumstances.

In the present case, to cast doubt on the idea of demographic saturation of the Neolithic Levant, as we have done several times, is insufficient. It is incontestable that the overall population of the Levantine nucleus grew strongly after 7500 BC, and it is not well understood at what particular moment in social and ideological systems that were different from our own the increasing numbers of human communities would have been felt by everyone to be uncomfortable. The archaeological facts themselves reveal the anomalies that discredit this fashionable explanation, facts which are actually more varied than the simple hypothesis of demographic pressure would suppose.

It appears very debatable that pastoral nomadism, as perhaps also with irrigation for that matter, first saw the light of day in the arid zones. The very great rarity in the temperate regions of sites that could be attributed to nomads contributes to the archaeological difficulty of supporting this idea with evidence. However, without recalling our ideas about Cyprus, we have already mentioned[30] the late PPNB site of Hayaz in the Turkish foothills of the Taurus, full in the Levantine nucleus. The excavator was surprised[31] not to have encountered any built structures, despite the extent of the excavation. However, the remains of workshop areas for chipping flint were abundant, as at Qdeir 1, plus all the indications of intensive herding. Hayaz looked to be in this respect a pioneer community, because, in addition to its sheep and goats, it is one of the oldest sites to have produced evidence of domesticated cattle.[32] In the region of Damascus we have also seen nomads digging their pits in the PPNB tell of Ramad. These we know had previously frequented not only the desert but also the littoral, since they brought their characteristic pottery with them.

These examples and several others already cited for Palestine suggest rather strongly that Neolithic nomadism did not have the arid zones for its initial, exclusive setting. We cannot therefore hold that its originality derives solely from the necessity of accommodating to environment. Nomadism certainly permitted people to extend their presence to territories otherwise inaccessible to subsistence producers, but the potential mobility of pastoralism existed from the beginning in all sorts of natural environments. And that shows that not every nomad was an exile, and that ecological imperatives have not played as decisive a role as is said to be the case in the birth of this way of life.

In our own times, Bedouins or Gypsies are very far from attributing to themselves an inferior status to that of the sedentary people who live beside them, even if these latter often fear and reject them. This rejection is completely reciprocal: poorer in terms of material goods than the villager or city-dweller whose enervating comforts he scorns, the nomad values his freedom of movement and prides himself greatly on his mastery of space, eminently positive values that should be understood as the matters of choice.

Even if it is impossible to reconstruct the ideology of the first nomads, two important consequences follow from the preceding analysis. On the one hand the sedentary–nomadic dichotomy did not reflect a sharp distinction in the Neolithic between cultivators and herders. Purely pastoral nomadism could very well have been a later specialisation. On the other hand mobility itself, which could allow them to alternate between modes over time, was valued more than the resources exploited. The ecological distinction that we introduce between arid lands and other regions has a restrictive force only for sedentary people who are obliged to live within a defined territory. Only a short time ago, Bedouins erected their tents at the gates of Beirut and only returned to the steppe in the rainy season. The nomad is therefore characterised less by his occupation of a particular climatic zone than by the possibility of coming and going from one area to another in step with the rhythms of the seasons. For this reason we accord to the nomad an eminent historic role in the exchanges that relied on their movements between village communities, as also in the progressive formation of stable territorial units which in the fourth millennium became the first states of the urban era.[33]

Less constrained to one specific environment than sedentary people, the nomad has the ability to explore new territories. For those phenomena of diffusion from the Levantine nucleus towards the neighbouring lands which concern us here, this form of nomadism that we have just described, based on a mixed economy of pastoralism but also cultivation, has surely played an important role.[34] Similarly, from 7000 BC, pastoral nomadism began to spread the Neolithic economy and religion on a grander scale, towards the Balkans, the Middle East and probably also North Africa. We have learned that the 'conquest of the desert' is only one among several possible directions of exploration. We may now ask what type of initiative, natural or cultural, could have been responsible for starting all these departures.

18

Hypotheses for the spread of the Neolithic

The period from 8000 to 6300 BC, but especially from 7500 BC, was fundamental for the neolithisation of the regions peripheral to the Levant, and far beyond. To the east, the neolithisation of the central Zagros seems to have taken place from 7500, at the same time, then, as that of the Sinjar. In the eastern Zagros and the Deh Luran plain which borders the Zagros the available information is hardly older than that. The first aceramic Neolithic there may go back to 7800 BC,[1] possibly like that of Pakistan,[2] even further east. In the opposite direction, the Balkans and the Mediterranean, and to the north Transcaucasia and Turkmenistan, became Neolithic in the seventh millennium.[3]

All these processes are later than the Neolithic Revolution in the Levant. Perhaps it is premature to explain them all in terms of diffusion, but the chronology is not at all against such a view. The objections that might be based on the very different cultural individualities lose much of their force in the face of what the Levant itself and its immediate periphery have taught us. It would be a most delicate problem to discern the precise nature of this diffusion in each case; we have already seen diffusion take very varied forms. It would also be necessary to take account of the fact that a great number of sedentary sites in the Middle East (Hassuna, Ganj Dareh, Tepe Guran, Abdul Hussein, etc.) started with a phase without built structures, universally taken to signify the arrival of nomads.

If we are to retain the idea of an 'exodus' for the area under review, it requires as a corollary a setting in motion of social groups whose true size has to be estimated case by case, the colonisation of virgin lands being only a quite rare and atypical case. According to the evidence these departures may have been effected by successive waves staged over more than a millennium. Nevertheless, when seen from a sufficient distance, the overall picture represents a single coherent phenomenon. We know that it is not unique of its kind in human history[4] and also that the different kinds of investigation of other disciplines, such as historical linguistics and population genetics, are also led to envisage migration over very long distances. Of course there is no such thing as a departure without a cause. We should now recapitulate the possible hypotheses for its explanation.

The climatic hypothesis

For a long time this was the only explanation: climatic desiccation, though slight, around 7500 BC may thus have put an end to agriculture in the southern Levant for some time, at least at lower altitudes. This would provide the reason for the increasing occupation of the mountainous margins. However, climatological studies give no precise information on this subject.[5] The relative depopulation of the central Levant from 7000 BC cannot be explained in this way. Finally, the occupation of new territories by colonists from northern Syria and from the eastern Taurus, areas which remained inhabited and actually escaped this kind of climatic constraint, is incapable of being explained in such terms. This is especially so when it is a question of the colonisation of semi-arid regions that are less desirable in terms of climate. One could imagine that the cultivators of the upper Jezirah might seek out the better-watered soils of the littoral, but not that they would have braved the desert at a time of desiccation. Most of the exodus phenomena are explained in terms of this very partial hypothesis.

The demographic hypothesis
The explanation of Neolithic diffusion in terms of population pressure within its area of origin remains dominant today. We saw that it was well and truly under way in the northern Levant around 7500 BC, but only in the northern Levant: there was a considerable growth of sedentary population, seen both in the increasing density of the distribution of villages and in the increasing dimensions of some of them. Even researchers like Colin Renfrew, who accept that Neolithic migrations of great size reached the Atlantic coastlands, have proposed no other explanation for the departure from the Near East than excess of population. Besides the difficulty of assessing at what threshold this increase would have reached saturation and signalled an exodus (and it seems that they remained far below that point), one might ask[6] what obliged the demographic excess to pour out to such great distances. The migrations of ethnic groups constitutes a cyclical event that is often repeated in history, but Islamic orientalists, for example, hardly claim that the arrival of the Arabs in Spain should be attributed to over-population in Arabia. That would be to ignore the essential element, the dynamic for conquest that possessed Islam.

The tectonic hypothesis
We rarely think about this hypothesis, but it merits consideration. Western Asia is one of the regions of the world that is most troubled by tectonic movements. A major fault line runs from the Red Sea to Anatolia, along which the Arabian plate is moving north-west relative to the African plate. Earthquakes are therefore very frequent events in the history of the region. They are all too localised, however, to allow us the hope of founding on them a sort of earthquake chronology of general application, as some have curiously sought to do when faced with the destruction levels in the cities of the Bronze Age.[7] It would seem *a fortiori* simplistic to search in the past, even at a regional scale, for traces of some grand catastrophe that was sufficiently generalised to have provoked a stampede of survivors.

Historical seismology, however, is a fast-developing science.[8] It tells us that there may have existed periods in the past when the Earth was more earthquake prone than others, to the point perhaps of creating a climate of insecurity that would favour major departures. The detection of the effects of earthquakes is unfortunately less easy in Neolithic villages than in the urban examples of later times, with their more spectacular and typical destruction levels. Notwithstanding more detailed research in the future, at present nothing exists on this subject in the archaeological literature for the Neolithic Levant.

We should recall, however, some scattered facts suggested by other disciplines in the natural sciences, in particular by oceanography. After the last glacial maximum, the general sea-level continued to rise, sometimes quite quickly, to reach present levels around 7000 BC. To this marine transgression may be attributed the fact that the Arabo-Persian Gulf, which had been totally dry through the course of the preceding recession, was at that time filled with water which at one stage penetrated Mesopotamia even further north than today's shore-line.[9] As we have seen, the relative slowness with which the plains of the Middle East attained climatic conditions as favourable to agriculture as those in the Levant is also attributed to this process.[10]

Throughout the world, the several stages in this rise in sea-levels are also marked in the study of corals which, though they can only form close to the surface, are found today at great depths.[11] Closer to home, we can link to sea-level change a series of events, some gradual others brutally sudden, which must have affected communications across the narrows between the Black Sea and the Mediterranean. The Black Sea was once an inland sea of fresh water fed by waters from melting glaciers, while the Mediterranean lay below it and in receipt of its excess.[12] Further west, in Thessaly, it seems clear that the first Neolithic inhabitants were installed on a plain that had relatively recently been the bed of a shallow lake whose waters would have escaped towards the sea in consequence of a seismic event. Fieldwork by geomorphologists concurs well with ancient Greek myths in this regard.[13] Finally, there have been relatively recent episodes of intense volcanic activity in Anatolia, of which some could concern our period. But the vulcanologists' work on dating them is still in progress.

All that scarcely answers our question since we lack precise information concerning the Levant, and in particular the Jordan valley, which we know was very prone to tectonic shocks. Elsewhere, the apparent absence of human occupation between 7500 and 6300 BC in the region of Malatya in the western Taurus, a region also subject to frequent earthquakes, and the contemporary migration into the Sinjar region could very well be in some measure attributed to those earthquakes. However, at present there is no direct evidence.

We keep this type of hypothesis in mind and wait for more detailed information because of the existence in the traditions and legends of the Near East and the eastern Mediterranean of a form of catastrophism. In this view of the world, important turning points in human culture were associated with natural destruction events (for example, the floods of Noah or Deucalion). This is difficult material for the historian to handle; it is dangerously appealing to the imagination and because of this it feeds a specialised literature of very debatable worth. But that is not a sufficient reason to dismiss it entirely, as we shall show.

Can we appeal to mythology?

André and Denise Capart[14] had the idea of bringing together information furnished by earth sciences and the prehistoric archaeology of the Neolithic in the Levant with the foundation myths at the basis of our Judaeo-Christian culture, for instance the story of Noah's flood in the book of Genesis.

Such approaches have been much abused in the service of enterprises that are ideologically oriented to literal acceptance of the Bible. However, they should not to be avoided *a priori* because we know so little of them, or in order to avoid the mixing of different styles of discipline, whether by the anthropologist or by the historian of thought. Perhaps historians in general should give some thought to the idea that certain 'myths of origin' that are found integrated into the sacred foundation texts of urban civilisations may be the vehicle for very ancient, prehistoric information. Those ideas may have been transmitted by oral means over many centuries before writing and much massaged and transformed by the human imagination in oral transmission. They may also have been reformed later by moral and metaphysical attempts to integrate them into what is called 'wisdom literature'.

Here one thinks of the problems encountered by historians of Greece as they try to work their way into the dark age of the Greek world. Or of their efforts to draw historical material from the Homeric epics in relation to the archaeology of the Troad. Or again of their attempts to extricate something from the flood of legends that surround the real personality of Minos, Cretan king of the Bronze Age, taking into account the discoveries at Knossos and other Minoan sites.

The book of Genesis, the foundation myth of our civilisation, has surprised the writer.[15] There is a homology between the process which recent research suggests for the beginnings of subsistence production and the biblical scenario. On the one hand, we have seen that a psychological-cultural process seems to have anticipated the new mode of exploitation of the environment. On the other hand, an event that is equally psychological in its essence, the Fall of Man, engenders consequences that one could think recount everything that the study of artistic representations of the Neolithic has suggested to us. Scarcely veiled in the symbolic language, one reads first of a feeling of human finiteness ('nudity') in response to a distancing from the 'divine', which is now perceived as inaccessible. This brings about the end of a certain easy quest for subsistence[16] in the Garden of Eden, and thus the beginning of labour 'by the sweat of the brow'. This sequence outlines precisely the first beginnings of cultivation (Cain), then of herding (Abel, the younger brother). With all these traits that expressly characterise the Neolithic Revolution, it is difficult not to think that this is what the stories are about. And why should we be surprised, when the book of Genesis and the beginnings of farming shared a cradle in the same region of the world?

Genesis was certainly not composed in the Neolithic, but it is known to bring together more ancient texts that were collected around 900 BC in which there must have figured the most ancient memories of those dark ages that the people of the Levant could put into writing. One can also compare the story of the Fall with the myth of Prometheus, the hero who, in Greek tradition, brought fire, farming and technology to men. That was a crime that was again followed by punishment, attesting the same guilty memory that people in the Near East had retained of their gradual gaining of control over nature. The robust materialism of our scientific data should not condemn us to indifference to the way that people in antiquity perceived and related these same events that we are dealing with.

Can we now draw anything from these ancient narratives about the phenomenon of Neolithic diffusion? The biblical story of the Flood, and also its Babylonian prototype recounted in the Epic of Gilgamesh, have already been compared with the thick strata of sterile alluvium that separate the Ubaid culture levels from those of the Uruk culture at several sites in lower Mesopotamia.[17] At various localities enormous inundations can be archaeologically dated to the middle of the fifth millennium BC. These must have severely interrupted human life on the banks of the Euphrates and may have inspired the flood stories in consequence. This flood, as we can see, is not Neolithic, but belongs rather to the Chalcolithic, pre-urban period; besides, it was limited to southern Mesopotamia.

The Caparts' interpretation is different. The Noah story, in part because of its allusion to Anatolia (Mount Ararat) which makes it a not exclusively Mesopotamian affair, is compared with Diodorus Siculus' accounts of various floods in the eastern Mediterranean, especially the biggest of them, 'Deucalion's flood', as recounted by the ancient beliefs of the inhabitants of the island of Samothrace. Diodorus relates that they had had a great flood caused by 'the rupture of the earth . . . which formed the Hellespont. The Euxine, that is the Black Sea, was then only a lake, but so swollen by the waters of its crashing waves that it overflowed, turned its waters into the Hellespont, and drowned a large part of Asia [Minor]'.[18] In the mind of Diodorus, an earthquake may have been the cause of this event.

All this constitutes nothing extraordinary in itself. Oceanographers have observed the signs of the 'overflowing' of the Black Sea; glaciologists are clear that the melting of the polar ice-cap was responsible for the gradual rise of sea-levels and the swelling of rivers coming from the north (the Don and the Dnieper); finally, geologists are accustomed to seeing periodic earthquakes in the eastern Mediterranean and the Levant. What we lack, however, are the sources of archaeological information that would allow us to disentangle from their legendary amplification and dramatisation the true amplitude of the natural phenomena and their historical and cultural consequences. We also lack any precise chronological data concerning these phenomena.[19] The comparison of legends and history focuses our attention on stories that have found their definitive form in an atmosphere very different from our own. Objective results from scientific thought are still very much in the process of early development, and information never stops growing, sometimes changing, at the hazard of new discoveries. From our perspective, the convergence can be troubling: recourse to myths has weak heuristic validity, as it is only when we already know the history that we can occasionally recover information from it. Hypotheses prematurely founded on the interpretation of legend are therefore dangerous for archaeologists;[20] historians of religions on the other hand may be able to draw on the objective ingredients contained within certain mythical stories and the processes of their formation in this comparison of interesting information.

It therefore seems that we should not *a priori* reject as too romantic the idea of a causal role for natural catastrophes in some of the interruptions of sedentary life in the Levant; nor should we accept them for lack of certainty as to their origins. Natural catastrophes could not in any case have been the sufficient and decisive 'cause', given the geographic spread of the zone of the migrations, their duration over a millennium or many, many generations, and given the migratory movements, and the very distant lands which they ultimately reached.

The psycho-cultural hypothesis
There were, then, not too many inhabitants, constraining some amongst them to depart, nor was there a generalised flight from some great disaster. On the other hand, it is as important to be able to explain the colonisation of those unpopulated regions, islands and deserts, as to explain the radical transformation of indigenous populations who remained where they were and whose way of life had been well integrated with their natural environment. Finally, we should not accept 'multi-factorial' explanations, where archaeologists of moderate view rehearse an inventory of different factors that may have played a part, without excluding or favouring any of them. Such pluralities of factors of course apply in any situation, but we need to take account of the evident coherence of the whole and of its expansion over time.

In the matter of diffusion to the east, the case of north Mesopotamia (Sinjar) seems to us to be rather clear-cut: the major role of the Levantine PPNB is undeniably seen there. Further east, the less well detailed information from Iran has long allowed the belief that it was an indigenous neolithisation, until, that is, the chronology first adopted was questioned. The hypothesis of an indigenous neolithisation seemed to find encouragement in the presence in the region today of the relevant plant species (cereals) and the domesticable animals. However, for climatic reasons already discussed,[21] a doubt still hovers over the exact date of the arrival in the Middle East of this assemblage of plants and animals. And we of course know that the simple presence of a domesticable species has never constituted a sufficient incentive to control it.

To the west, on the other hand, from Anatolia to the coasts of Atlantic Europe, this doubt has never existed: wild cereals and ovicaprids were simply absent. The species arrived domesticated, necessarily brought by people, in spite of the cultural variability of the contexts where they are found. They arrived at the same time as a disruption in basic techniques, including the production of subsistence, and the beginnings of architecture, of pottery, of polished stone and, often, of new methods for fashioning things from flint and bone. At the same time a new symbolism appeared that can be defined as the religion of the Neolithic. All these elements form a whole, at once ideological and technical, rather like the putting into practice of the ideology that we saw dawn in the first half of the tenth millennium in the Levant. If we give pride of place to the economic data alone, let us repeat that it is our own 'mythology' that we allow to persist. Such a view is not the outcome of a scientific process of evaluation: at best such an evaluation would leave us in doubt on this point.

This Neolithic ideology, then, is found far to the east of the Levant as well as to the west, and even further to the north. Bull and female figurines in effect represent the same central preoccupation in the Neolithic, whether in Iran,[22] on either side of the Caspian Sea, in Transcaucasia[23] or in Turkmenistan.[24] Their appearance everywhere coincides with the appearance of cultivation and herding, repeating what we have observed in the Sinjar. We have also seen that this symbolism that first arose in the Levant as the opening stage in the change to the new economy created the necessary mental frameworks whereby people could transform their world. In its more developed form it related the divine and the human planes, and it bore within itself all the existential malaises, the impatience, the material progress and the future accelerations of historical times to come.

This psychological aspect of the process of neolithisation was a powerful force from its inception, at once a new mode of cognition and a source of energy. It surely must have played as important a role in the diffusion of the Neolithic. The example of south-eastern Anatolia from the beginning of the ninth millennium has shown us that the new Neolithic farming way of life very quickly revealed itself to be expansionist. *A fortiori*, for these people only a little later to confront the desert and throw themselves into sea voyages when nothing required them to do so supposes hardiness and a spirit of adventure, for the danger and risk lay before them and none behind. There is scarcely a historic example where such great collective movements of expansion have not drawn their justification and even more so their energy from an accompanying bubbling and boiling in the cultural sphere. At least in their first stages, there is often what amounts to a state of messianic self-confidence. We recognise that this explanation has been deduced logically from an insufficiency of other causes and by analogy with more recent situations. It should rather be demonstrated by the facts of the period (though the lack of texts is crippling here). However, it seems to us equally to be the only account that can justify the amazingly positive welcome that the Mesolithic populations reserved for the new arrivals. Doubtless the first colonists from the east would have been joined in their march forward by the addition of newly neolithised ethnic groups. Indeed they may have been crossbreeds, like the North African Berbers who assisted the Arabs in the Islamisation of Spain in the ninth century of our own era. There is no reason to think that the hunter-gatherers of Europe or Asia found themselves in such a state of economic crisis that the agropastoral model would be imposed straightaway, as has been claimed, simply because it was a more productive economy than their own. This last assertion is at the root of the understandable scepticism of authors such as Robin Dennell[25] about diffusion itself. Neolithic superiority in the matter of providing for their needs was at this stage not at all evident.

Just imagine, by contrast, what was the effect on hunter-gatherers from time immemorial of the arrival of human groups, even rather scattered groups, driving before them docile goats and sheep, where the exotic nature of the species would add to their surprise at the mastery of the herdsmen. We should ask ourselves if this strange power would not have had a much more considerable impact than the simple perspective of a controlled reproduction of their subsistence resources. Recourse to irrational explanations is not at all incongruous here: it is a matter of other ways of subjugating people than by force of arms or economic wealth. The native peoples of the Americas yielded nothing in these two regards to the conquering Spaniards of the fifteenth century. Yet they nevertheless bowed before them without a fight, because this invasion seemed to match their myths and their expectation of the supernatural. Nothing prevents us from envisaging analogous phenomena in the Neolithic, since so many other explanations fall short. Such an explanation would also help us to understand why a new religion might everywhere have accompanied the new economy, the one being the secret of the other. Perhaps also it might explain how Indo-European languages might be diffused at that time, a whole family of languages whose expansion cannot be conceived outside the context of some powerful cultural prestige.

Conclusion

Throughout this work we have retained the word 'Neolithic' in the sense that has been traditional since Gordon Childe: that is where the determining criterion is the production of subsistence. From that began the rise in the capability of humanity of which our modernity is the fruit. We have rejected an economic causality as an explanation for its emergence, since the change was in the first instance cultural. But we have not rejected the fact that the most important manifestation of this cultural innovation was the mastery and transformation of nature. Neolithic man is therefore 'Neolithic' in the sense that he is the first human producer and there was no other before him.

The 'wild' and the 'domestic'

Some authors have accepted in principle the priority of the symbolic over the economic, as we proposed in 1978, and have dismissed, as we have done, the primacy of external factors such as climate or demography in the evolution of producer societies. However, these authors[1] have recently sought the psychological foundations of neolithisation in different directions from our own. The have made a play on the word 'domestication', which contains the root meaning of *domus*, the house, in its etymology. And they have advanced the idea that the control of other species is essentially no more than an expression of a natural tendency inherent in man to push back the frontiers of the 'wild' while extending those of the 'domestic'. The model and point of departure for this is the idea of 'home', 'one's own place' in the sedentary village in so far as that is the first portion of space over which he has extended his empire. That is why the sites of northern Iraq where cultivation was still absent can still be considered as Neolithic simply because of their architectural advancement.

This reading of history is interesting, but, for our present purpose, it does not suffice. In this case there is in effect no need for the 'revolution of symbols'. The first villages could be taken back to the Palaeolithic in central Europe or to the Natufian in the Levant, and all the rest would follow without any new ideology. The control of plants and animals is nothing but a metaphorical means of extending the house in this view.

And yet the rupture in symbolism does exist at the beginning of the Neolithic. Reduced to its psychological motivations, the ideology of the home contains no dynamic. Indeed, it connotes a dimension of intimacy and withdrawal rather than of expansion and annexation of the world. We have searched for the reason why advanced villagers from outside our Levantine region did not develop subsistence production for themselves. And we have found the answer in the identification of a completely new ideology, the advent of divinities who, by opening up the sphere of the intimate self, awakened in the people of the Levant the necessary energy for a new type of expansiveness. That is why regions peripheral to the Levant did not become 'Neolithic', any more than Europe, until the new ideology reached them from elsewhere, along with the new methods of acquiring subsistence.

The pre-eminence of the symbolic
This development of imagination was thus decisive. It was evolved within Khiamian societies that were neither more extended nor more complex than those of the Natufian villages that preceded them. There is nothing to indicate a social tension that might, following a Marxist analysis, have generated some sort of competition for available resources. There was no poverty of environment resources, no indication at this stage that individuals or minorities within these societies had acquired the ability to monopolise the products of gathering or hunting so as to make paupers of the rest.[2] It is only several centuries later that some of the social and economic consequences begin to become visible to us in the larger villages of the PPNA horizon. In these villages we found a genuinely agricultural economy, although the 'invention' of cultivation as a new practice, strongly charged with meaning but without immediate impact on diet, may well have begun earlier, indeed more or less contemporary with the religious revolution itself. Thus cultivation manifests in practice what we also see in the art. It is unnecessary to seek a strict relationship of causality between the two phenomena: rather there was a 'correspondence' between two sides, the internal and external aspects of one and the same transformation. The quantitative revolution in the economy of production and its effects on society can claim the rank of chronological 'consequences' derived from this initial change, which was at once ideological and practical.[3] A similar relationship must have existed between the first, remarkably simple herding, and the psychological changes that are part of the PPNB culture.

Finally, Neolithic diffusion beyond the Levant presupposes a deep psycho-cultural initiative that is not reducible to natural or economic disasters striking at their homelands. We cannot exclude the possibility of some catastrophic events, and these may have contributed to the drawing together of communities around their cultural values at particular moments. In that sense events may have encouraged people to embark on a sort of exodus that is indistinguishable from the spirit of the crusade. The diffusion of the Neolithic is not just a circumstantial response to some sort of crisis. It is a phenomenon of long duration, on a scale of several millennia, whose amazing diversity only appears coherent by reference to the 'symbolic system' which governs it.

Cognitive changes and social dynamics
In all these instances, it seems that 'religion', far from being purely irrational, first developed a sort of 'transcendental logic' at a non-utilitarian level, a logic that was then applied to the real world, imprinting on it new significances in a novel and

different system of relations. This cognitive aspect of the Revolution of Symbols is fundamental. By means of this system man had generated a general theory of a self-regulating world, which extended to the role that he had given himself in it. These new understandings are above all reflected in the major changes that were worked out in its system of representation, and are readily perceptible in art and ritual.

At this point in history, this system of representations evidently had nothing to do with a conceptual and discursive mode of thought. We can recognise that the 'symbolic forms' (in the terms of Ernst Cassirer) that are then codified and socialised through mythology and religion relate to an intuitive and immediate intelligence. It is an intelligence that nonetheless has its own internal logic and above all its own ability to regulate certain aspects of fundamental human behaviour. Thus, in the PPNB of the Levant we have noted the simultaneous emergence of rectangular architecture, herding and prestige weaponry, and at the same time an evident cultural expansionism. These clearly express the same structure of coherent thought as that which made its symbols explicitly virile and expressed that theme most overtly in figurines and statues.

Neolithic people would not have commented on or rationalised this profound unity as we do, precisely because the symbols were too saturated with meaning and too intellectually overwhelming to need assistance from formal intellectual analysis.[4] We alone, with our inevitable distance, find it interesting to try to make this structural rigour explicit. For them it was perceived and lived in concrete form at all levels. If 'logo-analysis' (to use the terminology of Michel Serres) allows our contemporary intellects to draw the formal relations that are accessible to pure reason from the raw symbolism,[5] it is still a matter of 'religion'. The explanatory aspect is important but it is by no means everything, since it also embraces what we have learned to distinguish as relevant from the emotional and moral sphere. We have therefore always insisted on the 'energising' value of the new images and their effect in determining the other changes.

According to the thinking inherited from Rousseau and Hegel, religion may be represented as an 'alienation' of the human subject by virtue of the way that the divine personalities are projected as supernatural by the human consciousness. This alienation would be nothing like the desolate dispossession of self, the hell of misery and the fantasy refuge in illusion, the 'opium of the people' and the 'sigh of the creature overcome by hardship', to quote the powerful images proposed by Marx in a celebrated text.[6] Applying that model to prehistory means mistaking the cause for the effect. The sentiment of 'misery', or more precisely of human finiteness, that accompanies the religious thought that appears in the Neolithic seems to have made new mental constructs manifest rather than engendering them. As the internal expansion of consciousness that we have described, alienation reshaped human cognition. In addition, like two electrodes that are held apart to cause heat and light by means of the current that continues to flow between them, this differentiation made the human mind clearer and more effective in its increasing influence on external reality. It also stimulated the development of the human capacity for the organisation of his environment and society. At the same time a passionate desire to break down the old equilibria was born. In this we can recognise at a larger scale that 'cultural heat' that according to Edgar Morin characterises the 'cultural broth' where inventions are born and jostle with each other, indeed the 'mystical state' in which inventiveness itself is found, according to Albert Einstein.

Having appeared in the area of the collective psyche where man is one, where thought, intention and action are still not abstracted and dissociated, the Revolution of Symbols thereby also becomes a revolution in action. In our modern world perhaps only the results of psychoanalysis can help us to understand, very imperfectly and in terms of the individual, the links which can exist between symbolic thought, the heights and the depths of psychic energy, and the actual actions and behaviour that follow in consequence. These appear 'irrational' when the source is not fully conscious and can be explained only through the effort of analysis. In the realm of collective psychology, at least in their early phase of elaboration, religions seem to move in the same zone of indistinctness. At this stage, while they may have a very dynamic unity, they remain more or less opaque to reason. Even so, we cannot deny their effective historic role at the source of great turning points in civilisation.

Prehistory and the end of materialism
This manner of seeing things is not new. It has been making its gradual way in the West for more than a century, since the return of 'symbolism' in poetry, art and psychology began to bring the naïve materialism of science and its reductive positivism little by little into question and opened the way for less restrictive conceptions. Epistemologists like Karl Popper and Ludwig Wittgenstein have put us on our guard against this 'ideology' of scientific truth. Nietzsche had already called it 'the rational myth of the West', where no account is taken of the underlying beliefs which are at its root and are much less rational than is claimed.[7] Prehistorians should not neglect these warnings: they are deeply integrated in the procedures of the so-called 'hard' physico-chemical and biological sciences that have learned to limit and relativise their objectives and their results. We can agree with Henri Atlan[8] that there are several possible approaches towards knowledge. At one extreme is an approach that is linked to scientific practice, which can and must adopt an inevitable methodological reductionism. It should not create illusions for itself, however, on its chances of attaining a total and ultimate reality. At the other extreme is a different approach that appeals to only a few; it is more immediate and cumulative, and operates through the mediation of art or mysticism. We can also ask if it is not possible by means of a 'human science' like archaeology to settle on the facts that are observed, following the positive and critical method common to all scientific disciplines, but retaining a non-materialist theory of human evolution in a perspective freed from all reductionism.

In *German Ideology*, Marx and Engels established the foundations of historical materialism. They could very accurately expose prehistory as the domain *par excellence* where 'historical speculation naturally takes over . . . because it believes itself to be impregnable to "hard facts", and also because it gives full rein to its speculative instincts'.[9] Historical materialism, as we know, 'does not explain practice in terms of theory. It explains the formation of ideas according to material practice'.[10] We should not underestimate the dialectical complexity of Marx, in whose writing retroaction of ideas on the material infrastructure is often emphasised. The fact remains that he (and many others after him) could denounce as 'idealist' anyone who seemed to doubt the decisive role of material changes only because it was a matter of a paradigm particular to the scientific views of his time.

We would be well advised to keep in mind that we should not expect to resolve problems of our evolution in terms of a 'pure' philosophy, inadequately held in check by objective observations. Scientific epistemology having evolved as it has, and the discipline of prehistory having run its course too, it is intriguing to note that it was the 'hard facts' of stratigraphy which contributed to making the materialist position untenable in this area. The hard facts of stratigraphy inverted the chronological order of the 'causes' and 'effects' in an important chapter of human history that is steadily becoming better understood.

Postscript

Since the first French edition of this book in 1994 and the revisions for the second edition that appeared in 1997, research in the field has moved on in the Near East, as well as analyses in the laboratory and theoretical discussions.[1] Several important new publications have appeared, and these have been integrated into the general bibliography of this English edition.

Nothing seems to us of such significance as to require modification of the basic ideas of this book, but there is relevant new information that confirms some of the hypotheses, and sometimes also requires that they be adjusted somewhat.

The natural environment

An important special issue of the journal *Paléorient*[2] was devoted to 'Palaeo-environments and their relations with human societies in the Near East and Middle East from 20,000 BP to 6000 BP'. It extends geographically and chronologically beyond the framework of this book. For the southern Levant, Syria and Anatolia, the special issue includes useful syntheses and discussions concerning climatic change in relation to the history of human settlement in these regions. Of particular note are the general syntheses of Sanlaville[3] and Watkins.[4]

As for the beginning of the Neolithic, in consequence of the radiocarbon dates from Abu Hureyra and the analysis of the wood charcoals from the same site by V. Roitel, in the northern Levant it is now possible to locate with greater precision the climatic episode of desiccation that coincided with the later and final Natufian and the Khiamian (see chapter 1). On the one hand, the 'Younger Dryas' phase of desiccation, when wild cereals disappeared at this latitude, became significant only around 10,600 BC, a rather more precise date than the 11,000 BC that has been generally quoted before. On the other hand, the impact was relatively moderate: in the steppe around Abu Hureyra trees such as the almond and the terebinth (*Pistacia*), which are not present today, persisted through this phase, although in reduced numbers. Now less than ever is it possible to consider that this climatic phase, reputedly hostile but in fact rather similar to today's conditions, played an important causal role in triggering the Neolithic Revolution. Rather it seems to have driven the human population out of those territories that were becoming desert at this time, as they have remained to this day: thus, for example, the region of El Kowm in Syria (see chapter 16) and Sinai in the southern Levant.[5]

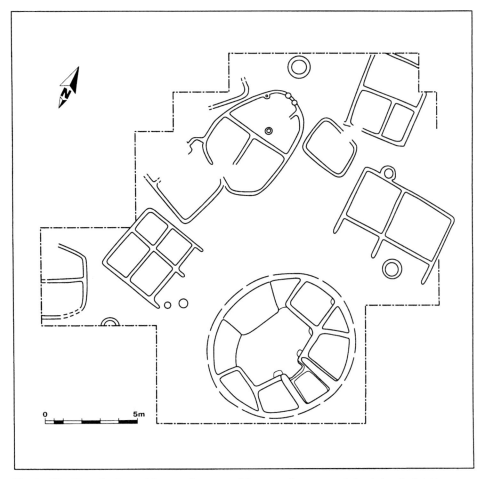

Fig. 69 The Mureybetian architecture from one of the strata (west mound, level 2) at Jerf el Ahmar. The large round house with internal divisions was totally below ground level. It seems to have been at once a place of storage and the nodal centre of social and perhaps religious organisation for the rest of the houses built on the surface around it. After D. Stordeur, in press.

The first agricultural economies of the PPNA

PPNA (Sultanian) sites remain rare in the southern Levant, but the excavations at Netiv Hagdud have now been extensively reported.[6] In the northern Levant, the excavations of the Mureybetian site of Jerf el Ahmar have continued and have been the subject of several recent publications.[7] This period of transition between circular and rectangular architecture is very much better illustrated here than anywhere else (Fig. 69): there are simple round cells that are sometimes agglutinated in twos and threes to form a single 'house', large round houses with internal dividing walls similar to House XLVII at Mureybet (see Fig. 15), rectangular houses with rounded corners, and finally genuinely rectangular buildings, some internally subdivided and others not, some with antae that form a courtyard in front, all together next to each other in the same stratum. In addition the rear walls of buildings along a series of terraces that scale the slopes of the site were bonded into the construction of the terraces themselves: thus a preconceived planning of the settlement is attested and collective building operations were at work simultaneously on several houses, confirming the highly co-operative character of the architectural work of the community, as we have already seen at Jericho (see chapter 4, p. 36).

The analysis of the plant remains from Jerf el Ahmar that is still in progress[8] seems to confirm the presence of pre-domestic agriculture in the Mureybetian, but here it is focused on barley and not on einkorn or rye. Barley was better suited to the particular environment of this settlement, which has very uneven terrain and poor soil. Further, as far as hunting is concerned, the strong representation of wild cattle that was observed for the same period at Mureybet is not found at Jerf el Ahmar, where aurochs is present but where the hunters concentrated much more on equids and gazelle. All of this requires a slight adjustment to our previous conclusions on the subsistence strategy of the Mureybetian. In the PPNA in the earliest cultivation as in the practice of hunting it seems that the choice of species that were exploited was still very variable from one site to another, dependent to a high degree on the particular environment of each site. Agriculture and herding will become more homogeneous only in the middle PPNB. The PPNA, then, is a period of intense originality in which architectural solutions and subsistence strategies of amazing diversity coexisted.

The problem of the extension of the Mureybetian in eastern Anatolia: new information
We envisaged (chapter 9) the possibility that the Mureybetian might have already reached the Taurus highlands in south-east Anatolia at the end of the PPNA, that is, around 8500 BC. This hypothesis now seems to be confirmed in consequence of the deep sounding carried out by Schmidt at Göbekli, where an apparently Mureybetian industry has been found.[9] At Çayönü itself a study of the chipped stone industry of the earliest, round house phase by I. Caneva[10] has brought to light several Mureybetian affinities within an assemblage that is in general rather simple. Much more than is the case for the 'PPNB of the Taurus' that follows this period, it seems that there is a juxtaposition of elements derived from the middle Euphrates with a substratum of local origin. However, we still do not have confirmation that this Anatolian 'Mureybetian' had already become 'Neolithic' in the sense that we mean this term, that is, in terms of the practice of cultivation.

Trevor Watkins has rightly emphasised that from the tenth millennium and even earlier there exist sedentary village communities in the Near and Middle East beyond the 'Levantine corridor':[11] he cites as examples Qermez Dere and M'lefaat in northern Iraq and Hallan Çemi in south-east Turkey. Some of the 'blanks' on the map may be effectively attributed to the incompleteness of our research; after all, in the Levant itself the existence of the Natufian of the Euphrates region has only quite recently been recognised.

For us, the ultimate criterion of the 'Neolithic' for the villages of the beginning of the ninth millennium remains the effective presence of subsistence production. We have already explained our difference of view from that of Watkins in this matter, a divergence which is simply a matter of a different definition of terms.[12] The notion that there could exist important 'Neolithic' villages that still lived only by hunting and gathering has recently been taken up for even more recent periods in Anatolia.[13] Mehmet Özdoğan considers that there is no true agriculture at Çayönü before the cell-plan phase, around 8000 BC, that is to say before the middle PPNB, when domestic cereals are found in abundance. According to his reasoning, in view of the considerable quantities of 'wild pulses' recovered from this period, the extraordinary settlement of Çayönü was therefore founded on a hunting and gathering economy throughout the grill-plan phase, at the end of the ninth millennium. The importance of pulses at Cafer Höyük, where morphologically domesticated cereals are also present from the beginning, seems to point to a generally diagnostic feature whereby agriculture played a very secondary role, even when it existed. All of this does not prevent Özdoğan from considering the grill-plan phase at Çayönü as genuinely 'Neolithic' in accordance with the necessary 'revision of the concept' that is in the same sense as that of Watkins' definition of the term.

For the Taurus sites, our disagreement relates entirely to a question of archaeo-botanical methodology. Just as Van Zeist has done for the grill-plan phase of Çayönü,[14] D. de Moulins has concluded that the pulses of the basal phase of Cafer[15] were probably cultivated, even though there is no morphological evidence. The idea of 'pre-domestic agriculture' has not yet been taken into account by the prehistorians working in Anatolia. Further advance in this area will only come from new methods of palaeobotanical analysis such as those initiated by Hillman and Willcox; these are based on the study of the suites of weeds that are associated with the dominant crop species. It is the suites of weeds that have led to the confirmation that the Mureybetian and the early PPNB of the Middle Euphrates were already practising cultivation of cereals, even before conventional 'domestication' (see chapter 5). In eastern Anatolia cultivation seems to us to have begun with peas, lentils and vetches rather than with cereals. This cultivation could have begun in the round house phase of Çayönü and the basal phase of Göbekli (presumably PPNA), but that remains simply hypothetical without proper botanical evidence, for lack of appropriate methods of analysis.[16]

In the Levantine world, we have shown that the emergence of subsistence production was rooted in a mental transformation whose first traces can be found in the Khiamian. But we did not exclude the possibility that the first experiments with cultivation in the Khiamian are still so unobtrusive and likely to be present at one site but absent at another that till now we have missed them. Hence our decision in this book to consider the Khiamian as the first stage in the process of neolithisation. However, being itself a process, each step within it is a process, and even the first step does not emerge *ex nihilo* but has its origins in the phenomena that precede it. That is why in an earlier publication[17] we considered it possible to identify this first step in the process of neolithisation in the sedentary, pre-agricultural villages of the Epi-palaeolithic. These villages had already formed a psycho-social milieu that was favourable to the emergence of a new ideology through their rooting communities to a particular place and gathering people into larger groups than ever before. This point of view is thus not far from that of Watkins. But on the simple lexical question we continue to mean the word 'Neolithic' to indicate a state and not a process, and to restrict it to those communities that have adopted a productive economy. That includes those which will once again become mobile in the eighth millennium BC, allowing us to speak of 'Neolithic nomadism'.

If this precocious adoption of agriculture is confirmed for eastern Anatolia, that region could be considered along with the Levantine corridor as being part of the 'nuclear zone' (as Braidwood conceived it) where agriculture first began. This triggering of agriculture would then coincide with the expansion of the Mureybetian and the early PPNB to the Taurus. It will then be difficult not to see in it a secondary neolithisation effect in parallel with the diffusion of this southern cultural complex which, we should remember, was originally formed in the north Levant[18] and which is intrusive in south-eastern Anatolia.

The early and middle PPNB
Since 1996 sites of the PPNB period have continued to be discovered in every part of the Levant and eastern Anatolia. The specially remarkable development of Anatolia at the end of the ninth and the beginning of the eighth millennium BC is further confirmed. The discoveries at Çatalhöyük, Cafer Höyük and Nevalı Çori are in the process of being spectacularly complemented by the excavations now in progress at Göbekli.[19]

In central Anatolia there has been some doubt about the role of agriculture at Aşıklı (see chapter 15). More systematic palaeobotanical analyses[20] have put an end to that ambiguity. Cultivated cereals are present in abundance and great variety: domestic einkorn and emmer, naked wheat and two row hulled barley, as well as cultivated pulses (bitter vetch, lentils and some peas). Hackberries are found in large deposits here and there on the site. Herding appears to be absent, confirming its relative lateness in Anatolia by contrast with the Levant. Thanks to the cultivation, Aşıklı would appear therefore to be fully Neolithic, which is in line with its size and the considerable architectural elaboration of the village. Doubts continue to exist, however, as to the exact origin of its very original lithic industry, for which there does not till now seem to exist any precedent in that region. In spite of certain technical affinities (naviform cores in particular), the industry remains quite distinct from that of the Levantine PPNB.

If no important discovery has recently emerged to change our understanding of the PPNB in the southern Levant, the salvage excavations on the Euphrates have produced the same effect in northern Syria as in Anatolia: they continue to reveal exciting and unsuspected new aspects.

The early PPNB village of Dja'dé[21] seems, on the basis of its architecture, to represent a regression by comparison with the Mureybetian. There are small rectangular houses with spaces between them, and among them, traces of more flimsy structures either placed directly on the surface of the ground or set above the ground on a substructure built in a 'grill'-plan. The chipped stone is intermediate between the Mureybetian and the middle PPNB, and it confirms the progressive elaboration of the tools that characterise the PPNB of northern Syria. Pre-domestic agriculture is likewise confirmed, and barley is the dominant crop.[22]

But it is Tell Halula that has produced the most informative finds[23] from an occupation that continues from the middle PPNB, around 8000 BC, into the sixth millennium, at which time it reached 7 hectares in extent. The houses of the middle PPNB are completely rectangular and multi-roomed, and they conform to a highly standardised plan. Walls and floors are covered with lime plaster. In addition, there are several structures with grill plans which recall those of the oldest levels at Djaʿdé. They probably supported platforms for drying some materials. Finally, there are circular silos constructed in *pisé* both inside and outside the houses.

Most importantly, there are important data concerning the agriculture:[24] now we have domesticated cereals (barley, emmer and naked wheat) present from the beginning of the occupation, and also flax. We know that the local wild wheat of the middle Euphrates valley, whether gathered wild or cultivated, was einkorn. Emmer could only have arrived here already domesticated. Similarly, the domesticated goat is present at Halula from 8000 BC: the domesticated sheep appears only a little later and domesticated cattle at the end of the middle PPNB around 7700 BC. But there was no wild goat present in northern Syria. It must have arrived there from elsewhere already domesticated, at Halula as at Abu Hureyra. Biologists suggest a more northerly location for these various domestications, probably in the hills of the northern Jezirah or the outlying foothills of the eastern Taurus.[25] Thus it is possible that the zone of original domestication of several species is situated in those parts of southeast Turkey that are still very little explored.

All of this strengthens our impression that around 8000 BC the relative autonomy of the village communities came to an end. In the ninth millennium these villages had the space to undertake quite diverse experiments, each in its own way even within a single region where settlements were quite close to one another. *A fortiori* one could witness the emergence of three quite distinct regional cultures, the Sultanian, the Aswadian and the Mureybetian. Indeed, it is for that reason that the term PPNA has gradually come to have more of a chronological than a cultural significance. In complete contrast, in the middle PPNB there emerges a tendency towards simplification and a degree of cultural reunification. This is evident equally in the domesticated species that were exploited in cultivation and herding as in the architectural and technological domains. In spite of some incontestable regional individualities, the PPNB can genuinely be considered as a single Levantine culture, apart from central Anatolia once again.

New information on the symbolic aspects of the early and middle PPNB of Anatolia

Göbekli Tepe is quite remarkable in this regard. Not only has the monumental character of sacred art in Anatolia been confirmed by the recent finds, but as the excavation continues[26] T-shaped pillars of stone 3 metres tall have been found (Fig. 70).

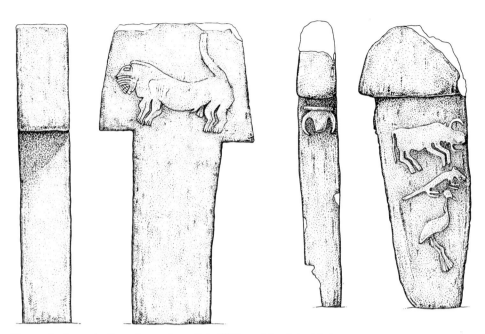

Fig. 70 Sculptured pillars of stone from Göbekli Tepe. After Schmidt, in press.

They bear relief sculptures, representations of animals which further enrich the icon-ographic repertory that had been in part inherited from the Mureybetian. There are bulls, a lion and a canid, but also a bird, some species of large wader; this kind of bird is an image that has not been encountered in the Near East at this period. Little by little the symbolic vocabulary is filled in, in addition to the representations that are generally dominant, the bull and the human form. Work in progress will attempt to penetrate their significance as far as possible.

The neolithisation of Cyprus

In the 1997 edition the recent discovery of Shillourokambos allowed us to take back the date of the neolithisation of Cyprus by several centuries and relate it to the Near East. We situated it at the time of the 'Great Exodus' around 7500 BC, setting aside as rather too high some of the radiocarbon dates that the site had produced which were earlier than that. The reason for doing so was that domesticated cattle were part of this colonisation movement, and no examples of such an early date were known from the mainland. Now the recent discoveries at Halula that have just been described change the facts of the situation. Domesticated cattle appear there in the middle PPNB, around 7700 BC, earlier than anywhere else. The indications that we had from elsewhere that the colonisation was effected from northern Syria are now considerably strengthened, and it is very probable that the first occupation of Cyprus was more or less contemporary with the early levels of Halula, that is practically con-temporary with the extension of the PPNB into the southern Levant.

We should add that a communication by Carole McCartney at the third Workshop on Neolithic Chipped Stone Industries, which took place in Venice in November 1998, showed that the Cypriot site of Tenta exhibits, like Shillourokambos, lustred pieces backed in a convex curve and arrow-heads with PPNB affinities, both of which are also present at Halula. The number of 'primary' Neolithic sites in Cyprus at the beginning of the eighth millennium is thereby increased to two.

The arrival of the late PPNB in central Anatolia

We have seen that the village of Aşıklı in Cappadocia, which dates to a time that corresponds to the middle PPNB, could not be related to that culture. On the other hand, at the end of the eighth millennium, the first inhabitants of Çatalhöyük seem to have been strongly influenced by the PPNB tradition. Recent survey work in Cappadocia has now brought to light sites that belong in the intermediate period. They show that the date of the arrival of the PPNB in central Anatolia was in its late phase, that is, just after the time of Aşıklı. This is most clearly seen at the settlement of Musular Mevkii, which is now being investigated by M. Özbaşaran.[27] On the contrary, in eastern Anatolia there is no pressure flaked debitage, although the tools and the typology of the arrow-heads imitate in obsidian the flint industry of the late PPNB of the Levant. That would seem to confirm a direct influence from the western Levant around 7500 BC which did not come via central Anatolia.

New information on the trade in obsidian

Important progress has been made on the prehistoric exchange of obsidian. We can now link the archaeological sites in the Near East where obsidian has been found with greater precision with the Anatolian sites which produced the material.[28] The surveys of the volcanic sources in Cappadocia have been coupled with systematic physico-chemical analyses of the materials. New sources of obsidian have been found whose distinctive chemical composition corresponds with sources that have not previously been identified. In addition several prehistoric workshops for preparing obsidian have been found associated with obsidian sources. One of them clearly provided artefacts for the nearby village of Aşıklı, while another (Kaletepe) has techniques of manufacture with naviform cores that are closely similar to those of the sites of the end of the ninth millennium on the Syrian middle Euphrates. This relationship is confirmed by the analyses, which show that this workshop was the source of the material found on the Syrian sites.

Conclusion

These then are the principal components that research since 1996 has brought to bear on this crucial period of the aceramic Neolithic of the Near East. These new results can be seen to offer a greater depth of factual support; they do not, so far as we can see, require modification of the theoretical content of the book. They correct certain chronological inferences, particularly as concerns the initial neolithisation of Cyprus, and they adjust or add to the strength of some of our other conclusions. The role played by the PPNA period in the northern Levant in the ninth millennium, in the 'dawn of civilisation', seems to become more and more fundamental. Many of the criteria by which Gordon Childe characterised the 'Urban Revolution' in the fourth millennium (for example, major collective building works, and probably also the presence of some social authority with 'power' whose precise nature still remains to be defined) can be seen to have their deepest roots in the period of the earliest agriculture. When one takes into consideration the data from Jerf el Ahmar, these first 'pictograms' on little stone tablets may be seen to prefigure that other 'urban' invention of writing that emerged much later, in the Uruk period.

The PPNB of the Levant and eastern Anatolia would seem to confirm this first creative flowering, amplifying the data and extending its geographical range. At this period there is some degree of 'hardening' into a greater socio-economic and ideological uniformity, although of course there continues to be a degree of local variation. The standardisation of the houses at Halula is in sharp contrast with the superabundance of architectural types at Jerf el Ahmar. Socio-religious authority affirms itself with greater force in the monumental constructions which continue to be found in south-east Anatolia. Certainly one of the most interesting tasks for the future will be to attempt to define the precise nature of this power and the ideological content that sustains it. It is apparently very different from the exclusively administrative and economic authority that the word 'power' usually evokes today.

Finally, it should be clear by now that we do not seek to make matters 'religious' the cause of everything in man's world. The word 'religion' in this context refers simply to a way of thinking about and comprehending the natural world that is essentially mythic and imaginative (in the sense that it operates in terms of images). No other mode of thought existed before the appearance of Greek 'rationality'! The Neolithic Revolution is the clear demonstration of the fact that man could not completely transform the way he exploited his natural environment, his own settlements as much as his means of subsistence, without showing at the same time a different conception of the world and of himself in that world. Even if changes within the human mind may have made themselves perceptible to the archaeologist earlier in the domain of beliefs and ideas than in the domain of physical techniques and methods, that should not be taken to imply a *chronological* primacy of one phenomenon over another. These are simply two faces, interior and exterior, of a single revolution. How these ideas have been expressed in this book is a reaction against a pervasive and narrowly economic view that is progressively and dramatically invading every other domain. It has simply seemed important to us to insist in this book on an interior aspect of these events that is too often overlooked.

NOTES

Introduction

1 Binford and Binford 1968.
2 Even when such questioning is the result of an accumulation of facts that existing theories are not capable of explaining. *Cf.* Gardin 1993: 155.

Chapter 1 Natural environment and human cultures

1 See the recently published article by Rossignol-Strick (1995), the collective work edited by Bar-Yosef and Kra (1994) and finally the climatological synthesis by Sanlaville (1996).
2 Rognon 1982.
3 *Ibid.*
4 The existence of deposits like Ein Gev, in the Jordan valley, and Nahr el Homr, in the Middle Euphrates, suggests that the apparent void in the settlement record of the interior zone could be a lacuna in our knowledge.
5 Thus Nadaouyieh 2, in the Syrian oasis of El Kowm (Cauvin, M.-C. and Coqueugniot 1989).

Chapter 2 The first pre-agricultural villages

1 See Bar-Yosef and Valla 1991.
2 For Mount Carmel see Garrod and Bate 1937; for Eynan-Mallaha, see Perrot 1966a; Valla 1984; Stordeur 1988; Perrot *et al.* 1988.
3 Perrot *et al.* 1988; Belfer-Cohen 1990.
4 Maréchall 1991.
5 Garrod 1937; Perrot 1966a.
6 Stordeur 1988: 111. See also the Natufian colloquium volume: Bar-Yosef and Valla 1991.
7 Valla 1988; Byrd 1989; Cauvin, M.-C. 1991a. The Harifian culture, limited in extent to the Negev and Sinai, seems to be a regional aspect of the Natufian that was particularly adapted to an arid environment and dated from 10,500 to 10,000 BC, overlapping the final Natufian (cf. Mureybet Ia) and the early Khiamian (cf. Mureybet Ib) of the Levant. See Goring-Morris 1991b.
8 See Cauvin, M.-C. 1991a.
9 See the contributions of Büller and Anderson-Gerfaud in Cauvin, M.-C. 1983.
10 Bouchud 1987; Pichon 1991.
11 Moore and Hillman 1992.
12 Van Zeist and Bakker-Heeres 1984.
13 Anderson-Gerfaud 1983; Anderson 1991; Anderson and Valla 1994.
14 Cauvin, M.-C. 1979b.
15 Coqueugniot 1983.
16 Perrot *et al.* 1988; Barthélémy de Saizieu 1989.

Chapter 3 The revolution in symbols

1 Cauvin, J. 1977.
2 Bar-Yosef 1990.
3 Lechevallier and Ronan 1990. The site of Abu Madi in Sinai could be a form of Khiamian that is later by several centuries, to judge by its radiocarbon dates.
4 Aurenche 1981.
5 Cauvin, J. 1987.
6 Leroi-Gourhan 1965.
7 Cauvin, J. 1978: 134.
8 Hodder 1982.
9 Cauvin, J. 1972a.
10 Five human representations have been proposed for the Natufian period: a schematic stat-uette from 'Ain Sakhri representing a scene of sexual intercourse, a small schematic head from El Wad, and a small upper torso without head or limbs from Eynan-Mallaha. Two incised objects from Eynan-Mallaha have passed elsewhere as human heads, but are very debatable (see Cauvin, J. 1972a: 24 and Fig. 5, and our inventory of Natufian art found to date, *ibid.*: 125–6). Nothing new has been added to this series since then, except a dubious object with a long ridge from Nahal Oren, where one interpretation, which has it as a poorly defined animal head (canid?), is opposed to another that is scarcely more convinc-ing, as a human head (cf. Noy 1991: Fig. 5: 1).
11 Cf. also the curious animal repertory of Mureybetian date from Jerf el Ahmar (see below, p. 00 and Fig. 19).
12 Cauvin, J. 1977.
13 Mellaart 1967.
14 Melllaart 1967 and Cauvin, J. 1987.
15 These naturalistic bucrania are found in the Tigris basin at Ginnig (Campbell and Baird 1991) and in the seventh millennium in the Syrian Jezirah at Tell Assouad (Mallowan 1946).
16 Hijara 1978.
17 From the time of the middle PPNB, that is from 8200 BC, this animal incarnation is dupli-cated in some instances by anthropomorphic male representations. On certain figurines from Çatalhöyük itself, he appears as a bearded man astride a bull. See below, p. 000 and Fig. 43.
18 The only 'supreme duality' that one can perceive at Çatalhöyük is limited to a doubling up of the Goddess herself: she appears on some relief sculptures under the form of Siamese twins, where only one of the two juxtaposed females is giving birth.

Chapter 4 The first farmers: the socio-cultural content

1 Kenyon 1957, 1981.
2 Bar-Yosef 1986.
3 Bar-Yosef 1990; Bar-Yosef and Gopher 1997.
4 Noy *et al.* 1980.
5 Lechevallier and Ronen 1994.
6 Noy *et al.* 1973.
7 Stordeur 1989a.
8 Aurenche *et al.* 1981; Hours *et al.* 1996.
9 Cauvin, J. 1978.
10 Contenson *et al.* 1979; 1995.
11 Cauvin, M.-C. 1995.
12 Van Zeist and Bakker-Heeres 1982. For micro-wear studies, see Anderson in Contenson

1995. The morphological 'domestication' of cereals is contested by Kislev (1992): it is surely a matter of 'predomestic agriculture' as in the Mureybetian (see above).

13 Van Loon 1968.

14 Cauvin, J. 1977, 1978.

15 Cauvin, J. 1980.

16 McClellan *et al.* in preparation; Stordeur and Jammous 1995; Stordeur *et al.* 1996; Stordeur 1998b, in press (1), (2).

17 Cauvin, J. 1977: 38; Aurenche 1980.

18 These traces of painting were analysed by X-ray diffraction analysis by J.-P. Rioux (Laboratoire de recherche des musées de France, Louvre). They appear to be simply the application of charcoal, red ochre and chalk with no detectable trace of a binding agent.

19 Molist 1989

20 Van Loon 1968. This type of structure has also been found at Sheikh Hassan (Cauvin, J. 1980) and at Jerf el Ahmar (McClellan *et al.* in preparation; Stordeur *et al.* 1996; Stordeur 1998b, in press (1), (2)).

21 Cauvin, M.-C. and Stordeur 1978

22 Coqueugniot 1983.

23 Cauvin, J. 1974.

24 The bird that 'sees in the night', a trait that is underlined by the insistence that is attributed to the representation of the eyes, the barn owl (or the brown owl) could have been a symbol of psychic powers or the powers of divination since the Neolithic. In relation to this ambiguity of the Eye-Goddess (Crawford 1957) at Tell Brak, note the increasing insistence in Neolithic imagery on the eyes of female goddesses (see below, p. 000).

25 Solecki and Solecki 1970.

26 Valla 1987.

27 The same applies to those from Sheikh Hassan (Fig. 20: 4) and Jerf el Ahmar. At the latter site, two grooved stones also bear the schematic animal decorations already described (Fig. 19: 1-2). The geometric decoration of grooved stones also exists in the Sultanian of the southern Levant (see Bar-Yosef and Gopher 1997).

Chapter 5 The first farmers: strategies of subsistence

1 Lechevallier and Ronan 1990.

2 For all that, it deserves underlining that the ecological limit of their extension has not changed since the Neolithic. This recession seems probable at present to some environmentalists (e.g. Willcox 1996).

3 For more detail, see Zohary 1992 and Hillman *et al.* 1989.

4 Van Zeist and Bakker-Heeres 1982.

5 *Ibid.*: 237.

6 This last argument, as has been seen (above, note 2), is not as strong as was thought: if the PPNA period was more moist than the present (cf. Sanlaville 1996), the distribution of the species today could be misleading. Nevertheless, if wild wheat had been present then in the Damascus oasis, traces would have been found in the botanical samples of the Aswadian. The existence of agriculture therefore remains quite probable.

7 Hopf 1983. The same uncertainty exists as for Aswad and all the southern Levant over the validity of these determinations which were carried out at Jericho on too small a sample (Kislev 1992).

8 Zohary 1992, but see above, note 2.

9 Kislev 1992: 89.

10 Leroi-Gourhan 1974.

11 This increase in the quantity of cereals comes about in the context of a somewhat more

moist phase at the end of the tenth millennium BC which saw a global increment in the percentage of grasses, but a much weaker increase in the cereals (Leroi-Gourhan 1974).

12 Leroi-Gourhan 1974: 445.

13 Van Zeist and Bakker-Heeres 1984b.

14 It is true that in the absence of any glumes in the carbonised samples which have been analysed, the study must be undertaken on the 'bare' grains, whose form and dimensions, according to some botanists, at this stage have yet to acquire a genuinely diagnostic value. On the other hand, the presence of abundant imprints of glumes in the *pisé* of the buildings of this period, which has very recently detected by G. Willcox (pers. comm.), shows that the chaff from the dehusking of this hulled (einkorn) wheat had been often traditionally used in the preparation of clay for building.

15 Van Zeist and Woldring 1980.

16 Anderson *et al.* 1991; Willcox 1992. The important role played by Gordon Hillman in this research should be stressed: having long ago foreseen that 'domestication' and 'agriculture' may not coincide exactly, he has greatly encouraged and assisted the experiments at Jalès with his advice.

17 Anderson-Gerfaud 1983. That does not mean that in the zones where wild cereals were naturally dense, similar lustred blades could have served for reaping them: see for example the Natufian of Hayonim, close to Mount Carmel (Anderson and Valla 1994).

18 Anderson *et al.* 1991

19 Zohary 1992; Cauvin, J. 1992a.

20 Cauvin, J. 1978: 75.

21 Helmer (pers. comm.).

22 McLaren *et al.* 1990.

23 Survey work by D. Zohary, G. Hillman and P. Anderson (pers. comm. P. Anderson).

24 George Willcox is presently experimenting in the middle Euphrates valley with the study of weeds in order to gain evidence concerning pre-domestic agriculture by means of palaeobotany. The central question requires the determination of the existence of some 'working of the soil' (which would not necessarily involve turning the soil) whose purpose would be to clear the fields of the most bulky steppe plants before sowing the crop. This selection would have the effect of favouring the presence within the cultivated crop of annual 'weeds' (self-propagating and adventitious colonisers) as against perennial plants. In this manner a pre-domestication agriculture may be demonstrated for the early PPNB of Dja'dé and probably (the study is still in progress) also for the Mureybetian of Jerf el Ahmar (Willcox 1996).

25 I express my gratitude to P. Anderson for having furnished me with this unpublished information which is necessary for this discussion of the role of rye.

26 Zohary (pers. comm.); Bar-Yosef 1990.

Chapter 6 Agriculture, population, society

1 Binford and Binford 1968.

2 Note that the same applies for more modern economic revolutions: neither the first financial capitalism of the sixteenth century in Venice, Amsterdam and London, nor the earliest form of industrial capitalism, founded on the working of copper and textiles, that appeared at the same time in Belgium, took off in a context of impoverishment (cf. Lefort 1978: 113).

3 Cauvin, J. and Cauvin, M.-C. 1984.

4 Flanner 1972: 48.

5 Cauvin, J. 1978.

6 Sahlins 1972.

7 Anderson *et al.* 1991.

Chapter 7 The Neolithic Revolution

1 Le Goff *et al.* 1986: 15. [Translator's note: the French term 'l'imaginaire', as used by some of the Annales historians and the author of this book, is difficult to translate, and it is a word that is important for Cauvin's case. In English 'imagination' has become associated with a facility to create (fictional) ideas in the mind: what is intended here, however, is the ability to form images in the mind or create mental models.]
2 Leroi-Gourhan 1965.
3 Lévi-Strauss 1989.
4 Vialou 1987.
5 According to some (e.g. Muzzolini 1991), this 'ram' could be a bull.
6 See Antoniewicz 1968. Somewhat later, on Mesopotamian seals of the fifth millennium, the oriental Goddess will be seen surrounded by human figures with arms raised.
7 Cf. Cauvin, J. 1987.

Chapter 8 A geographical and chronological framework

1 Until 1986, based on the excavations of Philip Smith at Ganj Dareh, it was thought that the Iranian Zagros had also been an autonomous and precocious centre of neolithisation, contemporary with the PPNA of the Levant. But the radiocarbon dates have been revised and this has reduced the age of the sequence (Hole 1987; Stordeur 1994). Its rectangular architecture in any case has much closer affinities with the much later PPNB of the Levant than with the PPNA. Agriculture in the eastern Zagros is therefore not earlier than the eighth millennium BC. Was it locally developed or derived from that of the Levant? That is another matter; but it is clear that it is later than that of the Levant. The western Zagros (Iraqi Kurdistan) has for its part produced settlements like Karim Shahir or M'lefaat, contemporary with the Levantine PPNA, but no trace of subsistence production has yet been identified there (Howe 1983), and the first farming villages of Kurdistan, such as Jarmo, are also of the eighth millennium BC. More recently, new excavations at Qermez Dere (Watkins *et al.* 1990) and Nemrik (Kozłowski 1990a, 1990b), villages situated in the Sinjar hills and the Tigris valley respectively, at the foot of the western Zagros mountains, have brought us evidence of an independent cultural tradition that runs in chronological parallel, from 12,000 BC, with the Natufian, the Khiamian and the PPNA and PPNB cultures of the Levant, but lacking cultivation before 8000 BC, in spite of a sedentary life and highly elaborated circular buildings from its beginning (cf. chapter 6).
2 8000 BP, or 6000 bc according to the traditional ^{14}C chronology, which corresponds to about 6900 BC.

Chapter 9 The birth of a culture

1 Kenyon 1957; 1979.
2 This is the phase called IVA at Mureybet.
3 Coqueugniot 1994.
4 As its name indicates, the 'Byblos point' was first identified at Byblos, a much later site on the coast of Lebanon. As with natural historians, the norms of nomenclature among prehistorians do not designate according to the historical origin of a type, but by the site of its first identification.
5 Moore *et al.* 1975. For Halula, see Molist 1996.
6 Legge, cited by Helmer 1992, see below. For Halula, see Helmer in Molist 1996.
7 Hillman in Moore *et al.* 1975. It is now necessary to add rye to that list, as had been suspected by Hillman: cf. McLaren *et al.* 1990.
8 Molleson *et al.* 1992.

9 Çambel and Braidwood 1980; Braidwood and Braidwood 1982; Özdoğan and Özdoğan 1990; Özdoğan 1995.

10 Cauvin, J. and Aurenche 1982; Cauvin, J. 1989; Molist and Cauvin, J. 1991.

11 Balkan 1990.

12 According to its inhabitants and Turkish geographers the region is the eastern part of the Taurus. It is better known in western atlases as the Anti-Taurus.

13 Cauvin, J. 1988.

14 Hauptmann 1988.

15 The weapons from Cafer Höyük and Çayönü are mostly Byblos points (Fig. 26: 1–3, 4). The weapons from Nevalı Çori (Fig. 27) comprise both this type and points with a concave base or a short tang, closer to the earlier Mureybetian tradition.

16 Aurenche 1982a.

17 The grill-plan principle is also known in the early PPNB of the middle Euphrates. At Dja'dé several grill-plan structures, much smaller than those of Çayönü but a little older (around 9200 BP, i.e. 8500 BC), also served as foundation structures quite distinct from superstructures that were doubtless built of lighter materials. Cf. Coqueugniot 1994.

18 Cf. Aurenche and Calley 1988.

19 One might have hoped to identify better the local populations of the Taurus region who would have 'received' the PPNB by means of the presence at the base of the Çayönü stratigraphy of a phase earlier than the grill-plan houses, with round houses. It was formerly interpreted as manifesting an archaic architectural tradition already encountered in the Zagros (Cf. Aurenche and Calley 1988: 8; Cauvin, J. 1975: 73). This preliminary phase has not yet been more than summarily described in print by the excavators. According to the material that was shown to us in 1994 and 1996 by M. and A. Özdoğan in Istanbul, there would also seem to be Mureybetian elements present in the round house phase. If these affinities are confirmed by the study of the Çayönü material by I. Caneva that is now in progress, it could push back by several centuries, as far as the Mureybetian phase itself, the 'ascent' of southern influences into the eastern Taurus region. That would render the neolithisation of Anatolia practically contemporary with the beginnings of an agricultural economy in northern Syria, that is, in the first part of the ninth millennium BC. (For further information on this point, see the Postscript at the end of this volume.)

20 Stordeur 1988.

21 Cauvin, M.-C. 1991b.

22 For Cafer Höyük see Calley 1985. Blade cores characteristic of this mode of flaking exist both at Cafer and at Çayönü, for flint as well as obsidian.

23 Inizan 1990.

24 Maréchal 1985. Experiments have allowed P. Anderson and C. Maréchal to identify the obsidian tool which must have been used for decorating the stone. It is a thick blade with abrupt lamellar retouch, showing specific striations associated with its use on the lower surface. These tools are known as 'Çayönü tools' (Fig. 30).

25 For example, at Karim Shahir (Howe 1983) and at Zawi Chemi Shanidar (Solecki 1981); these sites, also referred to as 'Proto-neolithic', are contemporary with the PPNA of the Levant, although they do not show evidence of the practice of agriculture.

26 Van Zeist and de Roller 1994; Özdoğan 1995.

27 Moulins 1994.

28 Hauptmann 1993.

29 Hauptmann 1993: 67. Almost identical representations have been found in central Anatolia in relief decoration on pottery at Kösk Höyük, belonging to the end of the sixth millennium BC (Silistreli 1989: Fig. 12). They are part of a context of goddesses, bucrania, silhouettes of bovids and other horned animals. They are not easy to interpret in that context either.

30 In the sixth millennium the similar presence of bovine shoulder-blades in an apsidal house

of the early Neolithic of Byblos may be noted. The building is interpreted as a sanctuary by Dunand (1973: 25).

31 Broman Morales 1990.

32 Özbek 1988; Özdoğan and Özdoğan 1990. The human remains are now being studied by F. Le Mort.

33 Cf. Özbek 1988. Note that the possibility of genuinely distinguishing between animal blood and human blood is not unanimously accepted by biochemists.

34 Schirmer 1990.

35 See Aurenche and Calley 1988: 17.

36 Schmidt 1995.

37 *Ibid.* Fig. 1: c.

38 Mellaart 1970.

39 Esin 1991.

40 Balkan-Atli 1991.

41 At the base of the Hacılar stratigraphy severed human skulls were found, borne on supports of pebbles. Their affinity with the PPNB is evident, but their true age is uncertain.

42 The need for confirmation arises from the surprise at the results, rather than the conditions of recovery and the identification of the floral remains carried out by H. Woldring (Gröningen) according to entirely reliable procedures.

43 Cauvin, M.-C. 1991b.

44 Cf. Balkan-Atli 1994.

45 This would be supported by certain chipping workshops for obsidian that have been found in Cappadocia in close contact with the natural sources. It would be possible to analyse the *chaînes opératoires* (sequences of manufacture), which also have their cultural significance. If in certain workshops they could be shown to have reduced obsidian for the supply of the aceramic villages of the region like Aşıklı, there are also those pieces that consist of elongated naviform cores and the characteristic dexterity of the Syro-Palestinian PPNB. The blades extracted from these cores have almost all left the workshops: they are found dispersed on numerous sites in the Levant where the chemical analysis of the material has permitted the establishment of the exact source (Cf. Cauvin, M.-C. 1996). Cauvin, M.-C. 1991b: 172.

Chapter 10 *Diffusion into the central and southern Levant*

1 For Phase II at this site, see Contenson *et al.* 1979.

2 Cauvin, M.-C. in Contenson *et al.* 1979 and in Contenson 1995.

3 Anderson in Contenson 1992.

4 Stordeur 1988: 115.

5 Van Zeist and Bakker-Heeres 1982.

6 Cauvin, M.-C. 1995.

7 A brief phase intermediate between the Aswadian and the PPNB, dated to the end of the ninth millennium BC, produced some evidence of a northern influence from the early PPNB, but the excavation, which was of limited extent, gives little information on this subject.

8 The principal sites are Munhata (Perrot 1966b) and Jericho (Kenyon 1957, 1981) in the Jordan valley, 'Ain Ghazal (summary and bibliography in Rollefson 1989) on the Jordanian plateau, Beisamoun (Lechevallier 1978) and Yiftahel (Garfinkel 1987) in Galilee, Nahal Oren (Noy *et al.* 1973) on the coast, Nahal Divshon (Servello 1976) in the Negev, and Beidha (Kirkbride 1966, 1968) to the south of the Dead Sea.

9 Byrd and Banning 1988.

10 Kirkbride 1966.

11 Helbaek 1966. There is also a little domesticated emmer wheat to add to the case.

12 Garfinkel 1987.
13 Helmer 1992.
14 Bar-Yosef 1985.
15 Stordeur 1983.
16 Stordeur 1989a.
17 Özbek 1976.
18 Strouhal 1973.

Chapter 11 The evidence of symbolism

 1 Ucko 1968.
 2 Twenty-five of them are grouped in a single cache. Rollefson 1983.
 3 For the interpretation of the ram as a symbolic substitute for the bull, see Forest 1993: 5.
 4 Garstang and Garstang 1940.
 5 Walker-Tubb 1985.
 6 Barnett 1986–7.
 7 Kenyon 1957: 60–72; Strouhal 1973.
 8 Lechevallier 1978. The site of Beisamoun is not well dated, and may also belong to the late PPNB.
 9 Rollefson 1983. For Kfar Ha Horesh, see Goring-Morris *et al.* 1994.
10 Ferembach 1970.
11 Bar-Yosef 1985.
12 See Cauvin, J. 1972a and 1978
13 On one skull from 'Ain Ghazal, traces of incisions on the surface of the cranium allow us to infer deliberate removal of the flesh quite soon after death.
14 Thus at Beisamoun and 'Ain Ghazal. The case of Kfar Ha Horesh is more complex: the skull seems to have been in a rectangular basin of lime plaster, itself covered with a lime plaster 'floor'. But the plastered skull is unique in being found with human bones and the skeleton of a gazelle (Goring-Morris *et al.* 1994: 84). Elsewhere on the site, a (foundation?) deposit seems to be associated with a human skull that is not modelled and the cranium of an aurochs (*ibid*: 83).
15 We have no proof, however, that the unique building encountered in the course of the sounding in the PPNB levels at Mureybet had been a simple house and not a 'collective sanctuary', as there certainly existed at this period.
16 Contenson 1967; Cauvin, J. 1972a.
17 One is in the Israel Museum at Jerusalem (pl. IX), the other is part of the Dayan collection. Another, found at Er Ram to the north of Jerusalem, is at the Palestine Exploration Fund in London. For a complete inventory, see Bienert 1990.
18 And also with a bone pendant from Jericho which seems to be a miniature mask (Kenyon 1957: XIXc).
19 Perrot 1978.
20 Bar-Yosef 1985: 14.
21 Only the mask from Er Ram has neither the eyes nor the mouth perforated: it seems to be unfinished.
22 That therefore makes three occasions that we have found the same decoration of the face on apparently very heterogeneous objects: on a stature from Jericho, on a skull with modelled features from 'Ain Ghazal and on the present mask from Nahal Hemar.
23 They could also have been made in lighter by perishable materials.
24 Aurenche 1977.
25 Aurenche 1981, 1982b; Cauvin, J. in. Lichardus *et al.* 1985; Huot 1990; Margueron 1991.
26 Kenyon 1957: 59; Cauvin, J. 1972a: 47. Given the area excavated, the houses uncovered at

Jericho are not numerous and those whose plan is completely known are extremely rare. How then can we know if they are exceptional?

27 Kirkbride 1966; in the light of the new Anatolian information, O. Aurenche has envisaged a reinterpretation of this building as a sanctuary (Aurenche and Calley 1988: 18).

28 In the hypothetical case that these chests contained human skulls, as at Çayönü, we should not be surprised to have found them empty. In spite of the presence of headless burials, no skulls were found at Beidha, even though a large area was excavated. D. Kirkbride thinks that they were taken away by the inhabitants when they finally abandoned the settlement.

29 Kirkbride 1968: 95

30 Dunand 1973: 25.

31 Rollefson *et al.* 1992: Fig. 7.

32 Margueron 1991, 2: 18.

33 Aurenche 1981.

34 Cauvin, J. 1972a: 204.

35 For example, Mellaart 1967, for Çatalhöyük.

Chapter 12 The dynamics of a dominant culture

1 This also eliminates a second type of explanation in the present case, which, throughout the length of the Neolithic diffusion across Europe, finds the principal reason for this expansion in the economic efficiency of the new mode of subsistence (cf. Renfrew 1987).

2 Hodder 1982.

3 Hodder 1982, 1989.

4 This was already the traditional position of American anthropology, cf. Binford 1972: 208–43. In France this method was applied to the study of Near Eastern Chalcolithic cultures of the Ubaid period: cf. Forest 1983.

5 Vernant 1990.

6 *Ibid.*: 20.

7 Hodder 1982: 8–9.

8 Caquot *et al.* 1974.

9 Cauvin, J. 1996.

10 And not the more evolved notched points of which examples exist in the Mureybetian and Aswadian as well as in the PPNB itself (see above).

11 We should always remember that the intervening period, between 11,000 and 8000 BC, seems not to be represented at Beidha.

12 Legge in Moore *et al.* 1975, and more importantly a paper given at the colloquium on the Natufian at Valbonne in 1989 (cited by Helmer 1992: 147). Now also see Legge 1996.

13 Helmer 1992.

14 Hesse 1984.

15 Digard 1990: 215.

16 Aurenche 1981: 185.

17 Cauvin, J. 1978: 61; see chapter 17 below.

18 Flannery 1972: 39.

19 *Ibid.*: 30; Aurenche 1981: 188 and 1980: 52.

20 Aurenche 1981: 87.

21 We may observe that at this same period Jerf el Ahmar begins to show buildings that are more or less rectangular, but the corners are rounded, thus avoiding to some extent 'the problem of the right angle' (Stordeur 1997). It is only at the end of the occupation that houses appear that have a genuinely right-angled plan.

22 Dunand 1973.

23 Aurenche 1981: 192.

24 There were sometimes rectangular antechambers in front of the circular 'tholoi' of the Halaf culture. Cf. Aurenche 1981.

25 Maréchal 1991. These objects, where the geometric shape is sought for its own sake and is not dictated by utilitarian considerations, should certainly be distinguished from the 'geometric microliths' that appear in the Levant together with the 'trapezes' of the Kebaran Geometric. The shape of these latter is simply the outcome of a technical rationale that systematically applied to flint blades simple and long-known actions (preparation by truncation and by backing) in order to produce homogeneous elements intended to be inserted in composite mountings (Cauvin J. 1983: 263).

26 Schmandt-Besserat (1978), struck by the frequency of objects of this kind in baked clay in both the urban and pre-urban periods, has proposed that they were *calculi*, that is instruments of accounting (cf. also Le Brun 1985). While it is very plausible for the time when a market economy was developing, this interpretation accords less well with the relative scarcity of these objects at earlier dates, where they appear to be primarily products of the human mind, like the geometric forms that recur more and more frequently in items of personal adornment. Cf. Chevallier and Gheerbrandt 1982; Barthélémy de Saizieu 1994; Maréchal 1995.

27 As Michel Serres says of the emergence of Greek geometry, 'conditions of a religious or metaphysical nature are more decisive than economic or social reasons' (Serres 1993: 307).

28 Eliade 1984: 55.

29 In Egyptian hieroglyphs, the sign of the circle represents the placenta. Analogous significations are found in other cultural regions, see for example Griaule and Dieterlen 1991: 132, where the internally divided circle holds for the Dogon of Mali the same significance of the placenta.

30 The earliest pictographic writing in Mesopotamia in the fifth millennium traced a rectangle to signify the house.

31 Perhaps because at this stage it was still a matter of 'aiding' nature rather than dominating it.

32 There is no proof, it is true to say, in the whole of the aceramic Neolithic of the Levant (nor anywhere else) that the symbolic matriarchy may have been made concrete in the functioning of society by means of a female domination, even if women appear probably to have enjoyed a particular prestige. Cf. Cauvin, J. 1985.

33 Cauvin, J. 1978: 136.

Chapter 13 The problem of diffusion

1 Zohary 1992. Elsewhere, recent attempts to propose a local domestication of wild lentils found at Franchthi (Greece) and at Abeurador (Hérault, France) have been rejected by botanists (see for Franchthi, Hansen 1992; for Abeurador, Willcox 1991). Notably Hansen has shown that the lentils cultivated at Franchthi derive from the wild lentil of the Near East (*Lens orientalis*) and not an indigenous species gathered in the Mesolithic.

2 Digard 1990.

3 Helmer 1992: 98.

4 Ammermann and Cavalli-Sforza 1984: Cavalli-Sforza 1996.

5 Gamkrelidze and Ivanov 1985.

6 Renfrew 1987.

7 Renfrew 1991. See also Renfrew 1996.

8 For the origin of this hypothesis, see Renfrew 1991: 6–7.

9 A theory already suggested by Sherratt and Sherratt 1988.

10 Zohary and Hopf 1988.

11 Cauvin, J. 1972b.

12 Demoule 1989.
13 *Ibid.*
14 Perlès 1990.
15 See notably Zvelebil and Zvelebil 1988.
16 Perlès 1990.
17 Dennell 1985.
18 That would explain why the Proto-Indo-European 'lexicon' includes terms designating the wagon, riding animals, and the wheeled cart and its accoutrements, which on the evidence available could not have arrived with the first wave of Neolithic diffusion.
19 Renfrew 1987.
20 Dennell 1985; Zvelebil and Zvelebil 1988: 579.

Chapter 14 The completion of the Neolithic process

1 Periods 4 and 5 in the Maison de l'Orient system. See Hours *et al.* 1996.
2 The notion of a 'Levantine nucleus' appears to us to be more pertinent here than the term 'nuclear zone' used by R. Braidwood. This may continue to designate the climatic band with wild cereals which stretches from the Mediterranean to the Iranian plateau, but it has scarcely any general significance for the origins of agriculture, which only concerns, as we have seen, its western, Levantine part.
3 Contenson 1967. It is the second phase of Ramad that is relevant; the first phase conserves the local tradition of round houses.
4 Lechevallier 1978.
5 Gebel *et al.* 1988.
6 Aurenche and Calley 1988.
7 Cauvin, J. 1978: 61; Aurenche 1981.
8 At Masad Mazzal: Taute 1981.
9 Balfet *et al.* 1969; Le Mière and Maréchal 1985.
10 An example has recently been published of a plastered skull painted in red from Kfar Ha Horesh, in lower Galilee, near Nazareth (Goring-Morris 1991a). This PPNB site is not precisely dated but, taking account of the presence of axes with polished blades, it is almost certainly late PPNB.
11 Cauvin, J. 1972a: 100–1.
12 Thus Byblos (Lebanon) and the Palestinian culture of Shaar ha Golan-Munhata in the seventh millennium and the Ubaid culture of lower Mesopotamia in the sixth millennium. Cf. Cauvin, J. 1972a.
13 Helmer 1992.
14 Le Mière 1986.
15 The only site excavated on the coast, Ashkelon, has produced only hearths, pit-silos and huts in pits, and has no pottery. Cf. Perrot 1968: 408.
16 *Ibid.*: 403.
17 Period 6 in the Maison de l'Orient scheme. This is the so-called Shaar ha Golan-Munhata culture.
18 [Translator's note] Along with the French author, I have retained the literal French spelling of Assouad, in order to distinguish this site from the other Neolithic Tell Aswad, near Damascus.
19 If Gritille (Voigt 1985) was indeed a village, Hayaz may have been a nomadic encampment. See below, p. 197.
20 Moore *et al.* 1975: this was the Aceramic Neolithic 2 phase.
21 Aurenche 1981: 199.
22 For example at Tell Assouad (Cauvin, J. 1972b) and in the late PPNB of Halula (Molist, pers. comm.).

23 Cauvin, J., 1974; see below, note 30.

24 Le Mière 1979.

25 Braidwood and Braidwood 1960.

26 The first appearance of naked wheat on the Euphrates, however, dates back to the middle PPNB at Halula (Willcox 1996).

27 Buitenhuis 1985. Hayaz was a workshop for flint-knappers beside the Euphrates (Roodenberg 1979/80), perhaps frequented by nomadic groups in the late PPNB (see below). The herding of pigs there remains uncertain, while it is quite certain at Kumar Tepe, a slightly later site further north. For Halula, see Helmer and Sana in Molist 1996.

28 Copeland 1979; Copeland and Moore 1985.

29 Akkermans 1979, 1990.

30 For example at Damishliyya, sounded by Akkermans (1990). If, as Akkermans thinks, Tell Assouad and Damishliyya were more or less contemporary, that is, not earlier than 7000 BC, that puts in doubt the much earlier ^{14}C dates that were obtained for Tell Assouad (Cauvin, J. 1974).

Chapter 15 Arrival of farmers on the Mediterranean littoral

1 On 'Les Sables de Beyrouth': the collections are in the Université Saint-Joseph, Beirut. For the inventory of Natufian sites in Lebanon, see Copeland 1991.

2 See the 'Tell aux Scies', near Beirut, and Dik el Mahdi (Cauvin, J. 1968: 219–29).

3 Kirkbride 1969. See also, still in the Beqaa, the site of Saayideh (Hours 1969).

4 Contenson 1992.

5 Helmer 1989, 1992.

6 Compare Contenson 1992: Fig. 125: 12 with Moore *et al.* 1975: Fig. 9: 14, 17.

7 Tell Assouad, see chapter 14.

8 From the phase 'Amuq A' of Tell Judeideh: Braidwood and Braidwood 1960.

9 Levels 33–28: Garstang 1953.

10 Tabbat el Hamman: Hole 1959.

11 Upper level of Labwe (Kirkbride 1969), Nebaa Faour in the Beqaa (Copeland 1969), and Nebi Mend in the Homs gap itself (Parr 1983).

12 Dunand 1973.

13 Cauvin, J. 1968.

14 Dunand 1973: 24–25.

15 The unique example of this that is found at Byblos is much later: it marks the end of the 'Early Neolithic', when a new population arrives at the site from the east around 5800 BC, having retained this type of practice. Cf. the 'house of the dead' of the Middle Neolithic, Cauvin, J. 1972a: 95–6.

16 Dunand 1973: 29–32.

17 A third type of burial only involves very young children, who were placed in pottery vessels buried inside the houses.

18 Cauvin, J. 1968: 83.

19 Forest 1983.

20 As is perhaps the case, for example, when some burials of infants, who have not had the time to acquire merit, are nevertheless richly provided (Forest 1983). We must not forget that individual burials, provided with grave goods to different degrees, already existed in non-stratified societies of the Epi-palaeolithic of the Levant. Also, on Neolithic funerary symbolism of the eighth and seventh millennia in Pakistan, see Barthelemy de Saizieu 1989, 1991.

21 French *et al.* 1972.

22 Mellaart 1967.

23 Bordaz 1970.

24 Aurenche 1981.

25 In contrast with Suberde, where ovicaprids, especially sheep, seem already to have been intensively herded.

26 We have already mentioned the bone needles with incised eyes whose presence was discovered at Can Hasan (Stordeur, pers. comm.).

27 Simmons 1989. Archaeological sites in Cyprus are conventionally named according to the village in whose lands they are situated (Akrotiri) plus the name of the locality (*Aetokremnos*) in italics. The convention is not always observed, and some sites, like Khirokitia, are known by a single name.

28 Guilaine *et al.* 1995.

29 According to Guilaine (pers. comm., 1996), there are four dates of 8800/8600 BP and one earlier than 9000 BP.

30 For Halula, see Molist 1996; for Tell Assouad in the Jezirah, see Cauvin, M.-C. 1972.

31 Dikaios 1953; Le Brun 1984, 1989, 1995.

32 Guilaine *et al.*, 1995: Fig. 6.

33 Cauvin, M.-C., in Le Brun 1984; Coqueugniot in *ibid*.

34 Stordeur, in Le Brun 1984.

35 Le Brun 1987: 294.

36 Le Brun 1984, 1987, 1989, 1995; and also Cauvin, J., in the first edition (1994) of the present book.

37 One also cannot exclude an embarkation from the coast of Cilicia, even closer to Cyprus than the coast of Syria. This region is still today very poorly known, much like the north coast of Cyprus itself. However that may be, the narrow coastal plain of Syro-Cilicia certainly communicates very easily with northern Syria as well as the Anatolian plateau itself. The study of the lowest strata at Mersin, near Adana, now in the process of excavation by I. Caneva, will be very interesting from this point of view.

38 Cauvin, J. 1992b; Helmer 1989.

39 That could be the case in the neolithisation of the Middle East by diffusion from the Levant.

40 But we have here the same chronological problem as for the domestication of the bovids. If we accept the radiocarbon dates of Shillourokambos, we must suppose that pastoral nomadism had begun in the Near East before 7500 BC, which is not impossible, but is not yet documented on the mainland.

41 Le Brun 1986: 7.

42 Abraham Ronen (1995) does not hesitate to speak of 'sects' in order to describe the generally ossified and quasi-regressive attitude of Cypriot ideology at this period. In every case it is a matter of a sort of cultural isolation and slower-paced evolution, perhaps for lack of more regular contacts with the more dynamic human environment of the Levantine mainland.

Chapter 16 The sedentary peoples push east

1 Included here on account of the presence of wild cereals through the whole of the 'nuclear zone' according to Robert Braidwood, that is the climatic band with open forest with between 250 mm and 500 mm of rainfall per year.

2 At Karim Shahir or M'lefaat (Howe 1983).

3 At Zawi Chemi Shanidar (Solecki 1981), and now also at Hallan Çemi Tepesı (Rosenberg and Davis 1992).

4 Watkins 1990. Qermez Dere is on the plain south of the Jebel Sinjar.

5 Kozłowski 1990a, 1990b; Kozłowski and Kempisty 1990. Nemrik is between the Jebel Sinjar and the western Zagros, on a terrace of the Tigris.

6 From the beginning at Qermez Dere and only in the final phase at Nemrik.

7 At least in this elaborate form, for it is not certain that traces of white plaster found by Jean Perrot in the Natufian site of 'Ain Mallaha (Eynan) but not analysed were indeed made of lime, long before the Levantine PPNB when this material is developed (Maréchal 1980).

8 This is also the case for sites in the western Zagros (Cf. Zawi Chemi Shanidar, Karim Shahir). At Hallan Çemi Tepesi, there were vessels of polished stone dating to the twelfth millennium (Rosenberg and Davis 1992). Moreover the presence of bracelets of polished stone, both at Karim Shahir and at Nemrik, show that this is indeed part of the same indigenous tradition as that postulated for the Taurus and thought to have 'received' the PPNB immigration.

9 For Nemrik the presence of domesticated pig, inferred from a clay figurine and a single fragment of bone (Kozłowski 1990a), needs a good deal more support.

10 Watkins 1990; see chapter 18.

11 Present also but in small numbers in the Levant (Gilgal, Mureybet).

12 Solecki 1977.

13 We know (see chapter 4), especially since the discovery of Jerf el Ahmar, that this 'oriental' bestiary (raptors and snakes) was not absent from the Mureybetian of the middle Euphrates. With the 'abnormal' abundance, as at Zawi Chemi Shanidar, of bones of raptors in certain phases of Mureybet (Pichon 1985a), that could attest to a certain pre-Neolithic 'common background' across all of upper Mesopotamia.

14 Bader 1989.

15 Accounting for three-quarters of the chipped stone industry at the beginning of the occupation but decreasing thereafter until it becomes the minority (Bader 1989: 350), in a trend that is the reverse of what we find at Cafer Höyük and Çayönü, where obsidian replaced flint little by little. Where new populations are concerned, it seems to be a matter of progressive disaffection for the familiar material of their region of origin under the influence of a new environment.

16 Bader 1989: pl. XXXIX.

17 Helmer, pers. comm. It is also the case in the upper levels of Çayönü, which also belong without doubt to the late PPNB, but whose context still remains unpublished.

18 Merpert *et al.* 1978; Bader 1989.

19 Kirkbride 1973, 1975.

20 See below, pp. 000–0.

21 In which there also figure biconical sling bullets of clay for the first time (at Umm Dabaghiyah), which are found in all the following prehistoric cultures of Mesopotamia.

22 Helmer, pers. comm.

23 This concerns only the eastern Jezirah south of the Jebel Sinjar. To the north, the site of Ginnig with pottery of the same period (Campbell and Baird 1991) still conserves a chipped stone industry in the Nemrikian tradition. An attenuated PPNB influence however makes itself felt in the rectangular (although rather irregular) plans of the semi-subterranean houses and in the presence of skulls of wild cattle.

24 Akkermans *et al.* 1983. Bouqras lasted from about 7400 to 6800 BC.

25 Le Mière in Akkermans *et al.* 1983.

26 Roodenberg 1986.

27 *Ibid.*: Fig. 43: 2–6.

28 Cauvin, M.-C. 1988.

29 Cf. El Kowm, below.

30 Emmer wheat, einkorn, durum wheat, two-row barley and naked barley. Cf. Van Zeist in Akkermans *et al.* 1983.

31 Clason in Akkermans *et al.* 1983. We now know (1998) that cattle were domesticated for the first time a little earlier in the Middle PPNB of Halula. See below, Postscript.

32 Besançon and Sanlaville 1991.

33 Dornemann 1986.

34 Stordeur 1989b; Stordeur *et al.* 1991; Stordeur, in press (2).

35 Maréchal 1982.

36 The first mention of water channels inside a house was at Bouqras (Contenson and Van Liere 1966: 184).

37 Stordeur 1989b: 104.

38 The analogy was noted by Stordeur 1989b: 104.

39 Cauvin, M.-C., pers. comm.

40 Stordeur, pers. comm.

41 These can show themselves, not at the level of the flint object itself, but at that of its integration in ever more ingenious techniques of mounting that are sometimes difficult for the archaeologist to reconstruct. The hafting of 'scrapers' as adzes at Mureybet thus entirely reforms their traditional function without in any way modifying their typological ordinariness.

42 Van Zeist in Dornemann 1986: 6–7. If there is one place where irrigation might have been invented, it is surely in the El Kowm oasis. The artesian springs rise not at the lowest points in the area but at the top of natural hillocks, and the water could have been led away from them into the plain by gravity, at the price of some minor works (Besançon and Sanlaville 1991).

43 Helmer 1992: 144.

44 See in Fig. 63: 2 the possible indication of the ears of the bull in the protuberances that are quite difficult to interpret if they are situated in the armpits of human figures.

45 Kirkbride 1975: pl. VIIIa.

46 Akkermans *et al.* 1983: 346.

47 Kirkbride 1975: pl. VIIa.

48 The very Anatolian inspiration of a figurine from Sotto gives rise to this reservation. Compare Cauvin, J., 1989: Fig. 3 with Bader 1989: pl. LXXIII–1.

Chapter 17 Pastoral nomadism

1 This is the meaning adopted notably by Digard 1981.

2 Khazanov 1984; Francfort 1990.

3 See Hole 1980; Digard 1981; Aurenche 1984; Francfort 1990.

4 Among the Gebelya Bedouin of Sinai (Bar-Yosef 1981) or the Bakhtiari of the Zagros (Digard 1981.).

5 Besançon and Sanlaville 1991; Cauvin, J. 1990.

6 In the Wadi Dhobaï, Waechter and Seton-Williams 1938.

7 See below, pp. 193–4. Technically these are angle burins on concave truncations (cf. Fig. 68: 6).

8 Bar-Yosef 1981.

9 Well dated around 7200 BC, therefore late PPNB. Subterranean, bell-shaped silos, like those at Ashkelon (see chapter 14, note 15) also existed on this site. The presence of these silos, easily hidden during any absence, is an index not of sedentism but simply of periodic returns to a place as far as these cultures are concerned.

10 They are only distinguished by their horns. The fauna of Wadi Tbeik, studied by E. Tchernov, did not include them, in contrast with that of Ujrat el Mehed, where there were plenty of ibex (Tchernov and Bar-Yosef 1982).

11 Bar-Yosef 1981.

12 Goring-Morris and Gopher 1983.

13 The stations are therefore called 'burin sites' by A. Betts (1984: 27). Arrow-heads may be totally absent.

14 At Azraq site 31: Garrard *et al.* 1987.

15 Bounni and Al Assad 1987.
16 Aurenche and Cauvin, M.-C. 1982; Cauvin, J. 1990.
17 Stordeur and Taha 1996; Stordeur, pers. comm.
18 Helmer 1992: 143; and pers. comm.
19 Based on micro-wear analysis by P. Anderson (pers. comm.).
20 They are also found in Syria on a burin site in the Palmyra oasis (Locality 79, Hanihara and Sakaguchi 1978) and as far as northern Arabia (Field 1960).
21 Calley 1986b.
22 It is not impossible that this intensive production of weapons, close to the sources that produced an excellent flint, may have exceeded the needs of their own community, and that some of their products were disseminated among other groups. At present there is no evidence expressly supporting this view, for the 'commercial' function of workshops at this time is established only in the case of obsidian (Cauvin, M.-C., pers. comm.) and doubtless also for polished marble vases that were then made on the Euphrates (Stordeur 1998b).
23 While that of El Kowm has not been found elsewhere than at El Kowm itself.
24 Whether the excavation of the corresponding hillock remains to be done, or whether the stopping-places of nomads have not coincided with the formation of a hillock around a spring, for lack of appropriate ecological conditions.
25 See Cauvin, J.
26 This Syrian nomadism that has been specially studied in the interior of and around the oasis of El Kowm, where each survey campaign has brought its batch of new stations, seems also to be present in the interior of and around the oasis of Palmyra: cf. Hanihara and Sakaguchi 1978; Cauvin, J. 1990.
27 Lattimore 1967. For the Levant, see Lees and Bates 1974.
28 Oates and Oates 1976; see on this subject Cauvin, J. 1981.
29 Kühn 1990: 393.
30 See chapter 14.
31 Roodenberg 1979/80: 8.
32 According to Buitenhuis: cf. Helmer 1992: 95.
33 Cauvin, J., in Lichardus *et al.* 1985.
34 Cauvin, J. 1992b.

Chapter 18 Hypotheses for the spread of the Neolithic

1 For the Neolithic of Ganj Dareh (Smith 1975), the oldest in the eastern Zagros, whose beginnings (Level E) seem to be marked by the arrival of nomads already practising agriculture and no doubt also herding (cf. Helmer 1992), the ^{14}C dates have been revised (Hole 1987; Stordeur 1994). Some aberrant dates having been eliminated, the remainder favour a date for the whole of the occupation, all levels treated together, between 7800 and 7300 BC, with a strong concentration of dates around 7500. Some traits that definitely originate in south-east Anatolia are quite identifiable in its bone industry (Stordeur 1994), if not in the architecture and the chipped stone industry, which is too bland and lacking in characteristics to be compared with anything else. Note also the anthropomorphic and bull figurines that are very much inspired by the Levant (Eygun 1992: Fig. 2). Finally, the presence of notched shoulder-blades also at Çayönü, recently noted by Özdoğan (1995), may signal that the first occupation of Ganj Dareh, where they were first noted by D. Stordeur, is not earlier than the cell-plan phase of Çayönü where these tools also appear. That implies a date not earlier than 8000 BC, and in the middle of the middle PPNB period of the Levant.
2 According to the discoveries at the village of Mehrgahr, which Jarrige and Lechevallier (1980) suggest should be dated to the seventh millennium bc (uncalibrated), that is, the eighth millennium BC. The sequence of ^{14}C dates seems to lack coherence, and a problem

exists at the level of the carbon samples submitted for analysis. In any case, nothing is very clear on this matter at Mehgahr, but, for the theoretical reasons already discussed, nothing excludes a Near Eastern origin for this neolithisation, mediated through the Zagros.

3 That is, when pottery was already known in the Levant, even if certain migrant groups, echoing the case of the nomads of the Levantine final PPNB, seem for their part to lack pottery.

4 The earliest in date were evidently the diffusion of *Homo erectus* and then of *Homo sapiens* from Africa throughout the whole of the Old World.

5 Pollen diagrams produced from cores of Lake Huleh show a quite continuous decrease of trees in the southern Levant between 9500 and 6200 BC, but that reflects a steady increase in temperature rather than a reduction in precipitation (Van Zeist and Bottemma 1982). Nothing particular appears in any case for the more restricted period that we are concerned with here.

6 Cauvin, J. 1992b.

7 Schaeffer 1948.

8 Allegre 1987; Helly and Pollino 1984.

9 Sanlaville 1989.

10 See chapter 1 and Rognon 1982.

11 Capart and Capart 1986.

12 Deep sea cores from the eastern Mediterranean testify to the arrival of fresh water attributable to the outflows from the Black Sea (Capart and Capart 1986).

13 Helly 1991.

14 Capart and Capart 1986.

15 Cauvin, J. 1986.

16 Sahlins 1972.

17 Parrot 1952.

18 Diodorus V 47, cited by Capart and Capart 1986: 61.

19 The rise in sea-levels did not begin in the Neolithic, but on the contrary was completed at that period. Rossignol-Strick *et al.* (1982) consider that this unloading of melt-water into the Black Sea, which was quickly filled up, through the Bosphorus and towards the Mediterranean was already essentially complete around 16,500 BC. The level of the Mediterranean only reached that of the bottom of the Bosphorus (at -30 m) at around 8000 and a discharge channel has therefore linked these two stretches of water, which are at different levels, for a long time. Every earthquake affecting, let us say, Istanbul could have accentuated these discharges to a quite major degree. But that remains in the domain of hypothesis and geomorphology has not yet got a simple answer to this problem (pers. comm., P. Sanlaville).

20 The remainder of the interpretation of the biblical story by A. and D. Capart does not escape this danger.

21 See chapter 1.

22 Notably at Ganj Dareh: cf. Eygun 1992.

23 In Neolithic sites of the eighth millennium in Armenia and Georgia (Chataignier 1995: 185–9).

24 Masson and Sarianidi 1972 (see Fig. 7 and *passim*): this is the first Neolithic culture, called the Jeitun culture.

25 Dennell 1985.

Conclusion

1 Hodder 1990; Watkins 1992.

2 The problem could be posed in terms of the first Natufian silos at 'Ain Mallaha (Eynan). It is precisely at the level of the appropriation of the foodstuffs by some that social inequality begins to manifest itself in more recent societies (Testart 1982). But the presence of

storage facilities does not of itself imply anything of their inegalitarian usage, which is not suggested in other ways at 'Ain Mallaha.

3 That is to bring closer together at the time of their invention both the new technology in general and the strongly ritualised aspect. Cf. Cauvin, J. 1978: 136–8.

4 Serres 1969: 26.

5 *Ibid.*: 34.

6 Marx 1843: 59.

7 Cf. Morin 1986. Belief in 'matter' is one of them, while physicists today have a great deal of difficulty defining it.

8 Atlan 1986.

9 Marx and Engels 1982: 87. This speculative instinct, unfettered by sufficient factual information, seems to be widely deployed in the *The Origins of the Family*, a publication by Engels alone, simply because the prehistoric past was then so poorly known.

10 *Ibid.*: 103.

Postscript

1 Particularly noteworthy are the Acts of an important colloquium at Laval University in Quebec (Fortin and Aurenche 1998), the *Proceedings of the Second Workshop on the PPN Chipped Stone Industries* at Warsaw (Kozłowski and Gebel 1996), and finally, for Anatolia, the collective work offered as a Festschrift for Halet Çambel (Aksebük *et al.* 1998).

2 *Paléorient* 23/2. 1997.

3 Sanlaville 1997.

4 Watkins 1997.

5 Goring-Morris and Gopher 1998.

6 Bar-Yosef and Gopher 1997.

7 Especially Stordeur 1998; Stordeur, in press (1) and (2).

8 Willcox and Roitel in prep.

9 Schmidt in press.

10 Caneva *et al.* 1996

11 Watkins 1997: 267.

12 Cauvin 1998: 208, and see chapter 3 above.

13 Özdoğan 1997: 34.

14 Van Zeist and de Roller 1994.

15 Moulins 1993.

16 Cf. Cauvin, J. 1998: 211.

17 Cauvin, J. 1978.

18 We are entirely in agreement with Özdoğan (1997) when he emphasises a northern origin (especially for pressure flaked debitage and bullet cores) present in the Çayönü Neolithic. For us they form part of an 'indigenous base' with which the influences from the middle Euphrates were married in the Neolithic.

19 Schmidt in press.

20 Van Zeist and de Roller 1995.

21 Coqueugniot 1998.

22 Helmer *et al.* 1998: 29.

23 Molist 1998.

24 Helmer *et al.* 1998: 28–9.

25 The absence of domestication at Cafer Höyük, on the upper Euphrates within the Taurus mountains, means that we cannot seek this zone of initial herding at too high an altitude.

26 Schmidt in press.

27 Özbaşaran 1997: 2.

28 Cauvin, M.-C. *et al.* 1998.

BIBLIOGRAPHY

Abbes, F., 1994 'Techniques de débitage et gestion du silex sur le Moyen Euphrate (Syrie) au PPNA final et au PPNB ancien', in H. G. Gebel and S. Kozłowski (eds.), *Neolithic Chipped Stone Industries of the Fertile Crescent: Subsistence and Environment*, 1, pp. 299–312.

Akkermans, J. A. K. *et al.*, 1983. 'Bouqras revisited: preliminary report on a project in eastern Syria', *Proceedings of the Prehistoric Society*, 49: 335–72.

Akkermans, P. M. M. G., 1990. *Villages in the Steppe: Later Neolithic Settlement and Subsistence in the Balikh Valley, Northern Syria*, Amsterdam, University of Amsterdam.

Akkermans, P. M. M. G. (ed.), 1979. *Excavations at Tell Sabi Abyad*, Oxford, BAR International Series 468.

Aksebük, G., Mellink, M. J. and Schirmer, W. (eds.), 1998. *Light on Top of the Black Hill: Studies presented to Halet Çambel*, Istanbul, Ege Yayinlari.

Allegre, C., 1987. *Les fureurs de la terre*, Paris, Odile Jacob.

Ammerman, A. J. and Cavalli-Sforza, L. L., 1984. *The Neolithic Transition and the Genetics of Populations in Europe*, Princeton, Princeton University Press.

Anderson-Gerfaud, P., 1983. 'A consideration of the uses of certain backed and lustred stone tools from late Mesolithic and Natufian levels of Abu Hureyra and Mureybet (Syria)', in M.-C. Cauvin, (ed.), *Traces d'utilisation sur les outils néolithiques du Proche-Orient*, Lyons, Maison de l'Orient, Travaux de la Maison de l'Orient 5, pp. 77–106.

Anderson, P., 1991. 'Harvesting of wild cereals during the Natufian as seen from experimental cultivation and harvest of wild einkorn wheat and microwear analysis of stone tools', in O. Bar-Yosef and F. R. Valla (eds.), *The Natufian Culture in the Levant*, Ann Arbor, International Monographs in Prehistory, Archeological Series 1, pp. 521–56.

Anderson, P. (ed.), 1992. *Préhistoire de l'agriculture: nouvelles approches expérimentales et ethnographiques*, Paris, Editions du CNRS, Monographies du CRA 6.

Anderson, P., Deraprahamian, G. and Willcox, G., 1991. 'Les premières cultures de céréales sauvages et domestiques au Proche-Orient néolithique: résultats préliminaires d'expériences à Jalès (Ardèche)', *Cahiers de l'Euphrate*, 5–6: 191–232.

Anderson, P. C. and Valla, F., 1994. 'Use and hafting patterns of glossed tools at Hayonim Terrace. Are they sickles ?', in S. Kozłowski and H. G. Gebel (eds.), *Neolithic Chipped Stone Industries of the Fertile Crescent and their Contemporaries in Adjacent Regions: Studies in Near Eastern Production, Subsistence and Environment*, Berlin, Ex Oriente.

Antoniewicz, W., 1968. 'Le motif de l'orant dans l'art rupestre de l'Afrique du Nord et du Sahara central', in D. de Sonneville-Bordes (ed.), *La Préhistoire: problèmes et tendances*, Paris, Editions du CNRS, pp. 1–10.

Atlan, H., 1986. *À tort et à raison: intercritique de la science et du mythe*, Paris, Editions du Seuil.

Aurenche, O., 1977. *Dictionnaire illustré multilingue de l'architecture du Proche-Orient ancien*, Lyons, Maison de l'Orient, Travaux de la Maison de l'Orient 3, série archéologique 2.

1980. 'Un exemple de l'architecture domestique au VIIIᵉ millénaire: la maison XLVII de Mureybet', in J. Margueron (ed.), *Le Moyen Euphrate, zone de contacts et d'échanges*, Leiden, E. J. Brill, pp. 35–54.

1981. *La Maison orientale*, 3 vols., Paris, Geuthner.

1982a. 'La tradition architecturale dans les hautes vallées du Tigre et de l'Euphrate aux VIIIe-VIIe millénaires', in *Archéologie du Levant* (recueil Roger Saidah), Lyons, Maison de l'Orient, Travaux de la Maison de l'Orient 12, série archéologique 9, pp. 69–78.

1982b. 'A l'origine du temple et du palais dans les civilisations de la Mésopotamie ancienne', *Ktema*, 7, Université des Sciences Humaines de Strasbourg: 237–59.

Aurenche, O. (ed.), 1984. *Nomades et sédentaires: perspectives ethnoarchéologiques*, Mémoires du centre Jean Palerne 40, Paris, Editions recherche sur les civilisations.

Aurenche, O. and Calley, S., 1988. 'L'architecture de l'Anatolie du Sud-Est au Néolithique acéramique', *Anatolica*, 15: 1-24.

Aurenche, O. and Cauvin, J. (eds.), 1989. *Néolithisations*, Oxford, BAR International Series 516.

Aurenche O., Cauvin, J., Cauvin, M.-C., Copeland, L., Hours, F. and Sanlaville, P., 1981. 'Chronologie et organisation de l'espace dans le Proche-Orient de 12 000 à 5 600 avant J.-C.', in J. Cauvin and P. Sanlaville (eds.), *Préhistoire du Levant*, Paris, Editions du CNRS, pp. 571–601.

Aurenche O. and Cauvin, M.-C., 1982. 'Qdeir 1, campagne 1980. Une installation néolithique du VIe millénaire', *Cahiers de l'Euphrate*, 3: 51–77.

Aurenche, O., Cauvin, M.-C. and Sanlaville, P. (eds.), 1990. *Préhistoire du Levant: processus des changements culturels*, Colloque international, CNRS Lyon, juin 1988, Paris, Editions du CNRS-Paléorient.

Aurenche, O., Evin J. and Hours, F. (eds.), 1987. *Chronologies du Proche-Orient*, CNRS international symposium, Lyons, 1986. Oxford, BAR International Series 379.

Bader, N. O., 1989. *Earliest Cultivators in Northern Mesopotamia*, Moscow, Nauka (Russian with English summary).

Balfet, H., Lafuma, H., Longuet, P. and Terrier, P., 1969. 'Une invention néolithique sans lendemain. Vaisselles précéramiques et sols enduits de quelques sites du Proche-Orient', *Bullétin de la Société préhistorique française (CRSM)*, 66/6: 188–92.

Balkan, N., 1990. 'L'industrie lithique de Boytepe (Turquie)', in O. Aurenche, M.-C. Cauvin, and P. Sanlaville (eds.), *Préhistoire du Levant: processus des changements culturels*, Paris, Editions du CNRS, pp. 409–12.

Balkan-Atli, N., 1991. 'The chipped stone industry of Aşıklı Höyük: a general presentation', *Anatolica*, 17: 145–74.

1994. *La néolithisation de l'Anatolie*, Istanbul, Institut français d'études anatoliennes.

Balkan-Atli, N., Cauvin, M.-C., Deprahamian, G. and Kuzucuoglu, C., 1997. 'Rapport sur l'obsidienne cappadociennes et sa diffusion: campagne 1996', *Anatolia Antiqua*, 5: 263–74.

Barnett, R. D., 1986/7. 'Six fingers in art and archaeology', *Bulletin of the Anglo-Israel Archaeological Society*, 6: 5–12.

Barthélémy de Saizieu, B., 1989. *Les sépultures néolithiques de Mehrgarh: réflexion sur les cultes funéraires anciens*, thesis, Université de Paris X–Nanterre.

1991. 'Stabilité et évolution des pratiques funéraires néolithiques à Mehrgarh (Période 1: ca 7 000–5 800 B.C.)', *Paléorient*, 17/2: 21–50.

1994. 'Eléments de géométrie préhistorique à partir des parures funéraires au Néolithique ancien de Mehrgarh (Indus)', *L'Anthropologie*.

Bar-Yosef, O., 1981. 'Neolithic sites in Sinaï 2', *Beiträge zur Umweltgeschichte der Vorderen Orient*, Beihefte zum Tübinger Atlas des Vorderen Orients, Reihe A8, Wiesbaden, pp. 217–35.

1985. *A Cave in the Desert: Nahal Hemar*, Jerusalem, The Israel Museum.

1986. 'The walls of Jericho: an alternative interpretation', *Current Anthropology*, 27/2: 157–62.

1990. 'The PPNA in the Levant', in O. Aurenche, M.-C. Cauvin and P. Sanlaville (eds.), *Préhistoire du Levant: processus des changements culturels*, Paris, Editions du CNRS-Paléorient, pp. 297–308.

Bar-Yosef, O. and Gopher, A. (eds.), 1997. *An Early Neolithic Village in the Jordan Valley*. I: *The Archaeology of Netiv Hagdud*. American School of Prehistoric Research Bulletin 43, Peabody Museum of Archaeology and Ethnology, Cambridge, Mass.

Bar-Yosef, O. and Kra, R. S. (eds.), 1994. *Late Quaternary Chronology and Paleoclimates of the Eastern Mediterranean*, The University of Arizona, Tucson, Radiocarbon.

Bar-Yosef, O. and Valla, F. R. (eds.), 1991. *The Natufian Culture in the Levant*, Ann Arbor, International Monographs in Prehistory, Archaeological Series 1.

Belfer-Cohen, A., 1990. 'The Natufian graveyard in Hayonim Cave', in O. Aurenche, M.-C. Cauvin and P. Sanlaville (eds.), *Préhistoire du Levant: processus des changements culturels*. Editions du CNRS-Paléorient, pp. 297–308.

Besançon, J. and Sanlaville, P., 1991. 'Une oasis dans la steppe syrienne: la cuvette d'El Kowm au Quaternaire', *Cahiers de l'Euphrate*, 5–6: 11–32.

Betts, A., 1984. 'Black Desert Survey, Jordan: second preliminary report', *Levant*, 16: 25–36.

Bienert, H.-D., 1990. 'The Er-Ram stone mask at the Palestine Exploration Fund, London', *Oxford Journal of Archaeology*, 9/3: 257–61.

Binford, L. R., 1972. *An Archaeological Perspective*, New York and London, Seminar Press.

Binford, S. and Binford, L. R., 1968. *New Perspectives in Archaeology*, Chicago, Aldine.

Bordaz, J., 1970. 'The Suberde excavations, Southwestern Turkey. An interim report', *Türk Arkeoloji Dergisi*, 17: 43–70.

Bouchud, J. (ed.), 1987. *La faune du gisement natoufien de Mallaha (Eynan) Israel*, Paris, Association Paleorient, Mémoires et Travaux du CRFJ 4.

Bounni, A. and al-Assad, Kh., 1987. *Palmyre: Histoire, monuments et musée* (2nd edn), Damascus.

Braidwood, L. S. and Braidwood, R. J. (eds.), 1982. *Prehistoric Village Archaeology in South Eastern Turkey*, Oxford, BAR International Series 138.

Braidwood, R. J. and Braidwood, L. S., 1960. *Excavations in the Plain of Antioch: 1. The Earlier Assemblages Phases A–J*, Chicago, University of Chicago Press, Oriental Institute Publications 56.

Broman Morales, V., 1990. *Figurines and Other Clay Objects from Sarab and Çayönü*, Chicago, University of Chicago Press, Oriental Institute Communication 25.

Buitenhuis, H., 1985. 'Preliminary report on the faunal remains of Hayaz Hüyük from the 1979–1983 seasons', *Anatolica*, 12: 61–74.

Byrd, B. F., 1989. 'The Natufian: settlement variability and economic adaptations in the Levant at the end of the Pleistocene', *Journal of World Prehistory*, 3/2: 159–97.

Byrd, B. F., and Banning, E. B., 1988. 'Southern Levant pier-houses: intersite architectural patterning during the Pre-Pottery Neolithic B', *Paléorient*, 14/1: 65–72.

Calley S., 1985. 'Les nucléus en obsidienne du Néolithique de Cafer Höyük (Turquie). Etude préliminaire sur les techniques de taille', *Cahiers de l'Euphrate*, 4: 87–108.

1986a. *Technologie du débitage à Mureybet, Syrie IXe–VIIIe millénaires*, Oxford, BAR International Series 312(i).

1986b. 'L'atelier de Qdeir 1 en Syrie: exploitation des nucléus naviformes à la fin du PPNB, VIe millénaire', *Paléorient*, 12/2: 49–67.

Çambel, H. and Braidwood, R. J., 1980. *Prehistoric Research in Southeastern Anatolia*, Istanbul, University of Istanbul, Faculty of Letters Press.

Campbell, S. and Baird, D., 1991. 'Excavations at Ginnig. The aceramic to early ceramic Neolithic sequence in North Iraq', *Paléorient* 16/2: 66–78.

Caneva, I., Conti, A. M., Lemorini, C. and Zampetti, D., 1994. 'The lithic production at Çayönü: a preliminary review of the aceramic sequence', in H.-G. Gebel and S. Kozłowski (eds.), *Neolithic Chipped Stone Industries of the Fertile Crescent*, Berlin, Ex Oriente, pp. 253–66.

Capart, A. and Capart, D., 1986. *L'homme et les déluges*, Brussels, Hayez.

Caquot, A., Szycer, M. and Herdner, A., 1974. *Textes ougaritiques: 1. Mythes et légendes*, Paris, Editions du Cerf.

Cassirer, E., 1972. *La philosophie des formes symboliques: 2. La pensée mythique*, Paris, Les Editions de Minuit.

Cauvin, J., 1968. 'Les outillages néolithiques de Byblos et du littoral libanais', in *Fouilles de Byblos*, 4, Paris, Librairie d'Amérique et d'Orient, Jean Maisonneuve.

1972a. *Religions néolithiques de Syro-Palestine*, Paris, Librairie d'Amérique et d'Orient, Jean Maisonneuve.

1972b. 'Sondage à Tell Assouad (Djezireh, Syrie)', *Annales archéologiques arabes syriennes*, 22: 85–9.

1974. 'Les débuts de la céramique sur le Moyen Euphrate', *Paléorient*, 24: 199–205.

1977. 'Les fouilles de Mureybet (1971–1974) et leur signification pour les origines de la sédentarisation au Proche-Orient', *Annual of the American Schools of Oriental Research*, 44: 19–48.

1978. *Les premiers villages de Syrie-Palestine du IXe au VIIe millénaire avant Jésus-Christ*, Lyons, Maison de l'Orient, Travaux de La Maison de l'Orient 4, série archéologique 3.

1980. 'Mureybet et Cheikh Hassan', in J. Margueron (ed.), *Le Moyen Euphrate, zone de contacts et d'échanges*, Strasbourg, Université des Sciences Humaines, pp. 21–34.

1981. 'Le problème de l'eau au Proche-Orient. De l'homme prédateur aux premières sociétés hydrauliques', in J. Métral and P. Sanlaville (eds.), *L'Homme et l'eau en Méditerranée et au Proche-Orient*, Lyons, Maison de l'Orient, Travaux de la Maison de l'Orient 2, pp. 20–30.

1982. 'Nouvelles stations néolithiques dans la cuvette d'el Kowm', *Cahiers de l'Euphrate* 3: 79–92.

1983. 'Typologie et fonctions des outils préhistoriques: apports de la tracéologie à un vieux débat', in M.-C. Cauvin (ed.), *Traces d'utilisation sur les outils néolithiques du Proche-Orient*, Lyons, Maison de l'Orient, Travaux de la Maison de l'Orient 5, pp. 259–74.

1985. 'La question du "matriarcat préhistorique" et le rôle de la femme dans la préhistoire', in A.-M. Vérilhac (ed.), *La femme dans le monde méditerranéen: 1. Antiquité*, Lyons, Maison de l'Orient, Travaux de la Maison de l'Orient 10, pp. 7–18.

1986. 'Mémoire d'Orient: la sortie du Jardin d'Eden et la néolithisation du Levant', *Cahiers de l'Institut catholique de Lyon*, 17: 25–40.

1987. 'L'apparition des premières divinités', *La Recherche*, 194: 1472–80.

1988. 'La néolithisation de la Turquie du sud-est dans son contexte proche-oriental', *Anatolica*, 15: 70–80.

1989. 'La néolithisation du Levant et sa première diffusion', in O. Aurenche and J. Cauvin (eds.), *Néolithisations*, Oxford, BAR International Series 516, pp. 3–36.

1990. 'Les origines préhistoriques du nomadisme pastoral dans les pays du Levant: le cas de l'oasis d'El Kowm (Syrie)', in H.-P. Francfort (ed.), *Nomades et sédentaires en Asie centrale: apports de l'archéologie et de l'ethnologie*, Paris, Editions du CNRS, pp. 69–80.

1992a. 'Problèmes et méthodes pour les débuts de l'agriculture: le point de vue de l'archéologue', in P. Anderson (ed.), *Préhistoire de l'agriculture: nouvelles approches expérimentales et ethnographiques*, Paris, Editions du CNRS, pp. 265–8.

1992b. 'A propos de l'ouvrage de Renfrew *L'énigme indo-européenne: le modèle oriental de la diffusion néolithique*', *Topoï*, 2: 91–106.

1996. 'Le taureau, l'homme, la guerre', *Le Cheval de Troie*, Bordeaux, 14: 15–24.

1998. 'La néolithisation d'Anatolie', in G. Aksebük, M. J. Mellink and W. Schirmer, (eds.), *Light on Top of the Black Hill: studies presented to Halet Çambel*, Istanbul, Ege Yayinlari, pp. 207–14.

in press. 'The symbolic foundations of the Neolithic Revolution in the Near East', in I. Kujit (ed.), *Social Configurations in the Near Eastern Neolithic*, University of California, Berkeley.

Cauvin, J. and Aurenche, O., 1982. 'Le Néolithique de Cafer Höyük (Malatya, Turquie). Fouilles 1979–1980', *Cahiers de l'Euphrate*, 3: 123–38.

Cauvin, J. and Cauvin, M.-C., 1984. 'Origines de l'agriculture au Levant: facteurs biologiques et socio-culturels', in T. C. Young Jr., P. E. L. Smith and P. Mortensen (eds.), *The Hilly Flanks and Beyond*, Chicago, University of Chicago Press, pp. 43–55.

Cauvin, J. and Sanlaville P. (eds.), 1981. *Préhistoire du Levant: chronologie et organisation de l'espace depuis les origines jusqu'au VIᵉ millénaire*, Colloque international, Lyon, juin 1980, Paris, Editions du CNRS.

Cauvin, M.-C., 1972. 'Note préliminaire sur l'outillage lithique de Tell Assouad (Djézireh)', *Annales archéologiques arabes syriennes*: 90–103.

1979. 'Tello et l'origine de la houe au Proche-Orient', *Paléorient*, 5: 193–206.

1988. 'L'industrie lithique en Turquie orientale au VIIe millénaire', *Anatolica*, 15: 25–36.

1991a. 'Du Natoufien au Levant nord? Jayroud et Mureybet (Syrie)', in O. Bar-Yosef and F. R. Valla (eds.), *The Natufian Culture in the Levant*, Ann Arbor, International Monographs in Prehistory, Archaeological Series 1, pp. 295–314.

1991b. 'L'obsidienne au Levant préhistorique: provenance et fonction', *Cahiers de L'Euphrate*, 5–6: 163–90.

1995. 'L'industrie lithique de Tell Aswad en Damascène (Syrie)', in H. de Contenson (ed.), *Aswad et Ghoraifé, sites néolithiques en Damascène (Syrie) aux VIIe et VIe millénaires avant notre ère*, Beirut, IFAPO.

1996. 'L'obsidienne dans le Proche-Orient préhistorique: état des recherches en 1996', *Anatolica*, 22: 3–31.

Cauvin, M.-C. (ed.), 1983. *Traces d'utilisation sur les outils préhistoriques du Proche-Orient*, Lyons, Maison de l'Orient, Travaux de La Maison de l'Orient 5.

Cauvin, M.-C., and Coqueugniot, E., 1989. *Techniques d'échantillonnage et analyse spatiale: le campement epipaléolithique de Nadaouiyeh 2 (El Kowm, Syrie)*, Oxford, BAR International Series 522.

Cauvin, M.-C., Gourgaud, A., Gratuze, B., Arnaud, N., Poupeau, G., Poidevin, J.-L. and Chataignier, C. (eds.), 1998. *L'obsidienne au Proche-Orient: du volcan á outil*, Oxford, BAR International Series 738.

Cauvin, M.-C. and Stordeur, D., 1978. 'L'outillage lithique et osseux de Mureybet, Syrie (fouilles Van Loon 1965)', *Cahiers de L'Euphrate*, 1.

Cavalli-Sforza, L. L. 1996. 'The spread of agriculture and nomadic pastoralism: insights from genetics, linguistics and archaeology', in D. J. Harris (ed.), *The Origins and Spread of Agriculture and Pastoralism in Eurasia*, London, UCL Press, pp. 51–69.

Chataigner C., 1995. *La Transcaucasie au Néolithique et au Chalcolithique*, Oxford, Tempus Reparatum, BAR International Series, 624.

Chevallier, J. and Gheerbrandt, A., 1982. *Dictionnaire des symboles*, Paris, Laffont/Jupiter, Bouquins series.

Contenson, H. de, 1967. 'Troisième campagne de fouilles à Tell Ramad, 1966. Rapport préliminaire', *Annales archéologiques arabes syriennes*, 117: 17–24.

Contenson, H. de (ed.), 1992. *Préhistoire de Ras Shamra*, 2 vols., Paris, Editions recherche sur les civilisations.

1995. *Aswad et Ghoraifé, sites néolithiques en Damascène (Syrie) aux VIIe et VIe millénaires avant notre ère*, Beirut, IFAPO.

Contenson, H. de, Cauvin, M.-C., Van Zeist, W., Bakker-Heeres, J. A. H. and Leroi-Gourhan, A., 1979. 'Tell Aswad (Damascène)', *Paléorient*, 5: 153–6.

Contenson, H. de, and Van Liere, W. J., 1966. 'Premier sondage à Bouqras en 1965. Rapport préliminaire', *Annales archéologiques arabes syriennes*, 16/2: 181–92.

Copeland, L., 1969. 'Neolithic village sites in the south Beqaa, Lebanon', *Mélanges de l'université Saint-Joseph*, 45/5: 83–114.

1979. 'Observations on the prehistory of the Balikh Valley, Syria, during the VIIth to IVth millenium B.C.', *Paléorient*, 5: 251–75.

1991. 'Natufian sites in Lebanon', in O. Bar-Yosef and F. R. Valla (eds.), *The Natufian Culture in the Levant*, Ann Arbor, International Monographs in Prehistory, Archaeological Series 1, pp. 27–42.

Copeland, L. and Moore, A., 1985. 'Inventory and description of sites', in P. Sanlaville (ed.), *Holocene Settlement in North Syria*, Oxford, BAR International Series 238, pp. 41–98.

Coqueugniot, E., 1983. 'Analyse tracéologique d'une série de grattoirs et herminettes de Mureybet, Syrie (IXe–VIIe millénaires)', in M.-C. Cauvin, (ed.), *Traces d'utilisation sur les outils néolithiques du Proche-Orient*, Lyons, Maison de l'Orient, Travaux de la Maison de l'Orient 3, pp. 139–72.

1994. 'L'industrie lithique de Dja'dé el Mughara et le début du PPNB sur l'Euphrate syrien (sondages 1991 et 1972)', in H. G. Gebel and S. Kozłowski (eds.), *Neolithic Chipped Stone Industries in the Fertile Crescent*, Berlin, Ex Oriente, pp. 313–30.

1998. 'Dja'dé el Mughara (Moyen Euphrate), un village néolithique dan son environnement naturel à la veille de la domestication', in M. Fortin and O. Aurenche (eds.), *Espace naturel, éspace habité en Syrie du Nord (10e–2e millénaires avant J. C.)*, Actes du Colloque tenté à l'Université Laval, Québec, Mai 1997, The Canadian Society for Mesopotamian Studies (Bulletin 33) and Lyons, Maison de l'Orient Méditerranéen, Travaux de la Maison de l'Orient 28, pp. 109–14.

Crawford, O. G., 1957. *The Eye-Goddess*, London, Phoenix House.

Crowfoot-Payne, J., 1984. 'The flint industries of Jericho', in K. M. Kenyon and T. A. Holland (eds.), *The Pottery Phases of the Tell and other Finds* 3, London, British School of Archaeology in Jerusalem, Appendix C, pp. 622–759.

Demoule, J.-P., 1989. 'La colonisation néolithique de la France tempérée', in O. Aurenche and J. Cauvin (eds.), *Néolithisations*, Oxford, BAR International Series 516, pp. 255–96.

Dennell, R., 1983. *European Economic Prehistory*, London, Academic Press.

1985. 'The hunter/gatherer cultural frontier in prehistoric temperate Europe', in S. Green and S. Pelman (eds.), *The Archaeology of Frontiers and Boundaries*, New York, Academic Press, pp. 113–40.

Digard, J.-P., 1981. *Techniques des nomades Baxtyâri d'Iran*, Paris, Editions de la Maison des Sciences de l'Homme.

1990. *L'homme et les animaux domestiques: anthropologie d'une passion*, Paris, Fayard.

Dikaios, P., 1953. *Khirokitia*, Oxford, Oxford University Press.

Dornemann, R. H., 1986. *A Neolithic Village at Tell el Kowm in the Syrian Desert*, Chicago, The Oriental Institute of the University of Chicago, Studies in Ancient Oriental Civilizations 43.

Ducos, P., 1968. *L'origine des animaux domestiques en Palestine*, Bordeaux, Delmas.

Dunand, M., 1973. 'L'Aarchitecture, les tombes, le matériel domestique des origines néolithiques à l'avènement urbain', in *Fouilles de Byblos*, 5 (in 2 vols.), Paris, Librairie d'Amérique et d'Orient, Jean Maisonneuve.

Durand, G., 1984. *Les structures anthropologiques de l'imaginaire*, Paris, Bordas.

Echegaray, J. G., 1964. 'Excavations in El Khiam', *Annual of the Department of Antiquities of Jordan*, 8/9: 93–4.

Eliade, M., 1984. *De l'âge de la pierre aux mystères d'Eleusis: histoire des croyances et des idées religieuses*, 1, Paris, Payot.

Esin, U. 1991. 'Salvage excavations at the Pre-Pottery site of Aşıklı Höyük in Central Anatolia', *Anatolica*, 17: 124–74.

1996. 'Aşıklı, ten thousand years ago: a habitation model from central Anatolia', in *Housing and Settlement in Anatolia: A Historical Perspective* (Turkish and English), Istanbul, Tarih Vakfı, pp. 31–42.

Eygun, G., 1992. 'Les figurines humaines et animales du site néolithique de Ganj Dareh (Iran)', *Paléorient*, 18/1: 109–17.

Ferembach, D., 1970. 'Etude anthropologique des ossements humains néolithiques de Tell Ramad (Syrie)', *L'Anthropologie*, 74/3–4: 247–54.

Ferembach, D., and Le Chevallier, M., 1973. 'Découverte de crânes surmodelés dans une habitation du VIIe millénaire à Beisamoun, Israël', *Paléorient*, 1/2: 223–30.

Field, H., 1960. *North Arabian Desert Archaeological Survey*, Papers of the Peabody Museum 45/2, Harvard.

Flannery, K. V., 1972. 'The origins of the village as a settlement type in Mesoamerica and the Near East: a comparative study', in P. J. Ucko, R. Tringham and G. W. Dimbleby (eds.), *Man, Settlement and Urbanism*, London, Duckworth, pp. 23–54.

Forest, J.-D., 1983. *Les pratiques funéraires en Mésopotamie du Ve millénaire au début du IIIe millénaire*, Paris, Editions recherche sur les civilisations, mémoire 19.

1993. 'Çatal Hüyük et son décor: pour le déchiffrement d'un code symbolique', *Anatolica Antiqua*, 2: 1-42.

Fortin, M. and Aurenche, O. (eds.), 1998. *Espace naturel, espace habité en Syrie du Nord (10e–2e millénaires avant J.C.)*, Actes du Colloque tenté à l'Université Laval, Québec, Mai 1997, The Canadian Society for Mesopotamian Studies (Bulletin 33) and Lyons, Maison de l'Orient Méditerranéen, Travaux de la Maison de l'Orient 28.

Francfort, H.-P. (ed.), 1990. *Nomades et sédentaires en Asie centrale: apports de l'archéologie et de l'ethnologie*, Paris, Editions du CNRS.

French, D. H. Hillman, G. C. Payne, S., and Payne, R. J., 1972. 'Excavations at Can Hasan III, 1969-1970', in E. S. Higgs (ed.), *Papers in Economic Prehistory*, Cambridge, Cambridge University Press, pp. 181–94.

Gamkrelidze, T. V. and Ivanov, V. V., 1985. 'The migrations of tribes speaking Indo-European dialects from their original homeland in the Near East to their historical habitations in Eurasia', *Journal of Indo-European Studies*, 13: 49–91.

Gardin, J.-C., 1993. 'Les embarras du naturel', *Archives européennes de sociologie*, 3/4: 152–65.

Garfinkel, Y., 1987. 'Yiftahel: a Neolithic village from the VIIth millenium B.C. in Lower Galilee, Israel', *Journal of Field Archaeology*, 14/2: 199–212.

Garrard, A., Betts, A., Byrd, B. and Hunt, C., 1987. 'Prehistoric environment and settlement in Azraq Basin: an interim report on the 1985 excavation season', *Levant*, 17: 1-28.

Garrod, D. A. E. and Bate, D. M. A., 1937. *The Stone Age of Mount Carmel*, 1, Oxford, Clarendon Press.

Garstang, J. 1953. *Prehistoric Mersin: Yümük Tepe in Southern Turkey: the Neilson Expedition in Cilicia*, Oxford, Clarendon Press.

Garstang, J. and Garstang, J. B. E., 1940. *The Story of Jericho*, London, Hodder and Stoughton.

Gebel, H. G. and Kozłowski, S. (eds.) 1994. *Neolithic Chipped Stone Industries of the Fertile Crescent: Subsistence and Environment*, 1, Berlin, Ex Oriente.

Gebel, H. G., Muhesen, M. S., Nissen, H. J., Quadi, N. and Starck, J. M., 1988. 'Preliminary report on the first season of excavations at the Late Aceramic Neolithic site of Basta', in A. N. Garrard and H. G. Gebel (eds.), *The Prehistory of Jordan*, Oxford, BAR International Series 396, pp. 101–34.

Gopher, A. and Gophna, R. 1995. 'Ein Qades I: a Pre-Pottery Neolithic B occupation in Eastern Sinai', *Atiqot*, 27: 23–32.

Goring-Morris, N., 1991a. 'A PPNB settlement at Kfar Hahoresh in Lower Galilee', *Journal of the Israel Prehistoric Society*, 24: 77–101.

1991b. 'The Harifian of the Southern Levant', in O. Bar-Yosef and F. Valla (eds.), *The Natufian Culture in the Levant*, Ann Arbor, International Monographs in Prehistory, pp. 173–216.

Goring-Morris, N. and Gopher, A., 1983. 'Nahal Issaron: a Neolithic settlement in the southern Negev', *Israel Exploration Journal*, 33/3–4: 149–62.

1998 'The articulation of cultural processes and late Quaternary environmental changes in Cisjordan', *Paléorient*, 23/2: 71–93.

Goring-Morris, A. N., Goren, Y., Horowitz, L. K., Herskowtz, I., Lieberman, R., Sarel, J. and Bar-Yosef, O., 1994. 'The 1992 season of excavations at the Pre-Pottery Neolithic-B Settlement of Kfar Hahoresh', *Journal of the Israel Prehistoric Society*, 26: 74–121.

Griaule, M. and Dieterlen, G., 1991. *Le renard pâle*, Paris, Institut d'ethnologie.

Guilaine, J., Briois, F., Coularou, J. and Carrère, I., 1995. 'L'établissement néolithique de Shillourokambos (Parekklisha, Chypre), premiers résultats', *Reports of the Department of Antiquities, Cyprus, 1995*: 11–31.

Hanihara, K. and Sakaguchi, Y. (eds.), 1978. *Paleolithic Site of Douara Cave and Paleogeography of Palmyra Basin, Syria*, Tokyo, The University Museum.

Hansen, J., 1992. 'Francthi Cave and the beginnings of agriculture in Greece and the Aegean', in P. C. Anderson (ed.), *Préhistoire de l'agriculture: nouvelles approches expérimentales et ethnographiques*, Paris, Editions du CNRS, pp. 231–48.

Hauptmann, H., 1988. 'Nevalı Çori: Architektur', *Anatolica*, 15: 99–110.

1993. 'Ein Kult Gebaüde in Nevalı Çori', in M. Frangipane, H. Hauptmann, M. Liverani, P. Matthiae and P. Mellink (eds.), *Between the Rivers and over the Mountains*, Rome, Universita di Roma La Sapienza, pp. 37–69.

Helbaek, H., 1966. 'Pre-Pottery Neolithic farming at Beidha, a preliminary report', *Palestine Exploration Quarterly*, 98/1: 61–6.

Helly, B., 1991. 'Les premiers agriculteurs de Thessalie. Mythe des origines à la lumière de la philosophie', in M.-C. Cauvin (ed.), *Rites et rythmes agraires*, Lyons, Maison de l'Orient, Travaux de la Maison de l'Orient 20, pp. 135–47.

Helly, B. and Pollino, A. (eds.), 1984. *Tremblements de terre: histoire et archéologie*, Valbonne, Editions ADPCA, IVe rencontres internationales d'archéologie et d'histoire d'Antibes.

Helmer, D., 1989. 'Le développement de la domestication au Proche-Orient de 9 500 à 7 500 B.P.: les nouvelles données d'El Kowm et de Ras Shamra', *Paléorient*, 15/1: 111–21.

1992. *La domestication des animaux par les hommes préhistoriques*, Paris, Masson.

Helmer, D., Roitel, V., Saña, M., and Willcox, G. 1998. 'Interprétations environnementales et archéobotaniques en Syrie du Nord de 16000 BP à 7000 BP, et les débuts de la domestication des plantes et des animaux', in M. Fortin and O. Aurenche (eds.), *Espace naturel, éspace habité en Syrie du Nord (10e–2e millénaires avant J.C.)*, pp. 9–33.

Henry, D. O. (ed.), 1995. *Prehistoric Cultural Ecology and Evolution: Insights from Southern Jordan*, New York and London, Plenum Press.

Hesse, B., 1984. 'These are our goats: the origins of the herding in west central Iran', in J. Clutton-Brock and C. Grigson (eds.), *Animals and Archaeology: 3. Early Herders and their Flocks*, Oxford, BAR International Series 202, pp. 243–64.

Hijara, I., 1978. 'Three graves at Arpachiyah', *World Archaeology*, 10/1: 125–8.

Hillman, G. C., Colledge, S. M. and Harris, D. R., 1989. 'Plant food economy during the Epipaleolithic period at Tell Abu Hureyra, Syria', in D. R. Harris and G. C. Hillman (eds.), *Foraging and Farming: Evolution of Plant Exploitation*, London, Unwin and Hyman, pp. 240–68.

Hodder, I., 1990. *The Domestication of Europe*, London, Basil Blackwell.

Hodder, I. (ed.), 1982. *Symbolic and Structural Archaeology*, Cambridge, Cambridge University Press.

1989. *The Meanings of Things: Material Culture and Symbolic Expression*, London, Unwin and Hyman.

Hole, F., 1959. 'A reanalysis of basal Tabbat al-Hammam, Syria', *Syria*, 336/3–4: 149–83.

1980. 'The prehistory of herding: some suggestions from Ethnography', in *L'archéologie de l'Iraq au début de l'époque néolithique à 333 avant notre ère*, Paris, Editions du CNRS, pp. 119–30.

1987. 'Chronologies in the Iranian Neolithic', in O. Aurenche, J. Evin and F. Hours (eds.), *Chronologies du Proche-Orient*, Oxford, BAR International Series 379, pp. 353–79.

Holland, T. A., 1982. 'Figures and miscellaneous objects', in K. M. Kenyon and D. T. A. Holland (eds.), *Excavations at Jericho. IV The Pottery Type and Series and Other Finds*, London, British School of Archaeology in Jerusalem, Appendix C, pp. 551–63.

Hopf, M., 1983. 'Jericho plants remains', in K. M. Kenyon and T. A. Holland (eds.), *Excavations at Jericho*, V, London, British School of Archaeology in Jerusalem, pp. 576–621.

Hours, F., 1969. 'Saayideh et le Néolithique pré-poterie au Liban', *Mélanges de l'université Saint-Joseph (Beyrouth)*, 45: 31–41.

Hours, F., Aurenche, O., Cauvin, J., Cauvin, M.-C., Copeland, L., and Sanlaville, P., 1996. *Atlas des sites du Proche-Orient (ASPRO)*, Lyons, Maison de l'Orient.

Howe, B., 1983. 'Karim Shahir', in L. S. Braidwood, R. J. Braidwood, B. Howe, Ch. A. Reed and P. J. Watson (eds.), *Prehistoric Archaeology along the Zagros Flanks*, Chicago, The University of Chicago Press, Oriental Institute Publications, 105, pp. 23–154.

Huot, J.-L., 1990. 'Des sanctuaires orientaux: à propos de quelques idées reçues', in *Mélanges Pierre Levêque, Annales littéraires de l'université de Besançon*, 413, pp. 209–19.

Inizan, M.-L., 1990. 'Le débitage par pression: des choix culturels', in *Vingt-cinq ans de technologie*, Colloque d'Antibes, Juan-les-Pins, APDCA, pp. 367–78.

Jarrige, J.-F. and Lechevallier, M., 1980. 'Les fouilles de Mehrgahr, Pakistan: problèmes chronologiques', *Paléorient*, 6: 253–8.

Kenyon, K. M., 1957. *Digging Up Jericho*, London, Ernest Benn.

1979. *The Archaeology of the Holy Land*, 3rd rev. edn, London, Benn.

1981. *Excavations at Jericho: The Architecture and Stratigraphy of the Tell*, III, London, British School of Archaeology in Jerusalem.

Khazanov, A. M., 1984. *Nomads and the Outside World*, Cambridge, Cambridge University Press.

Kirkbride, D., 1966. 'Five seasons at the Pre-Pottery Neolithic village of Beidha in Jordan. A summary', *Palestine Exploration Quarterly*, 98/1: 8–61.

1968. 'Beidha 1967: an interim report', *Palestine Exploration Quarterly*, 99: 90–6.

1969. 'Early Byblos and the Beqa'a', *Mélanges de l'université Saint-Joseph (Beyrouth)*, 45: 45–60.

1973. 'Umm Dabaghiyah 1972: a second preliminary report', *Iraq*, 35: 1–7.

1975. 'Umm Dabaghiyah 1974: a fourth preliminary report', *Iraq*, 37: 3–10.

Kislev, M. E., 1992. 'Agriculture in the Near East in the VIIth millenium b.c.', in P. Anderson (ed.), *Préhistoire de l'agriculture: nouvelles approches expérimentales et ethnographiques*, Paris, Editions du CNRS, pp. 87–93.

Kozłowski, S. K., 1990a. *Nemrik 9. Prepottey Neolithic Site in Iraq*, Warsaw, Wydawnictawa University Warsawskiego.

1990b. 'Nemrik 9, a PPN site in Northern Iraq', in O. Aurenche, M.-C. Cauvin and P. Sanlaville (eds.), *Préhistoire du Levant: processus des changements culturels*, Paris, Editions du CNRS, pp. 347–53

Kozłowski, S. K. and Gebel, H. G. (eds.), 1996. *Neolithic Chipped Stone Industries of the Fertile Crescent and the Contemporaries in Adjacent Regions: Studies in Early Near Eastern Production, Subsistence and Environment*, Berlin, Ex Oriente.

Kozłowski, S. K. and Kempisty, A., 1990. 'Architecture of the prepottery neolithic settlement in Nemrik, Iraq', *World Archaeology*, 21/3: 348–62.

Kühn, T. S., 1990. *La tension existentielle: tradition et changement dans les sciences*, Paris, Gallimard. (*The Structure of Scientific Revolutions*, 2nd rev. edn 1970. Chicago, University of Chicago Press.)

Laplantine, F., 1987. *Clefs pour l'anthropologie*, Paris, Seghers.

Lattimore, O., 1967. *Inner Asian Frontiers of China*, Boston, Beacon Press.

Le Brun, A., 1985. 'Le niveau 12 de l'Acropole de Suse: mémoire d'argile, mémoire du temps', *Paléorient*, 11/2: 31–8.

1986. 'Khirokitia: une civilisation originale?', *Acts of the International Symposium Cyprus between the Orient and the Occident*, Nicosie: 1-11.

1987. 'Le Néolithique précéramique de Chypre', *L'Anthropologie*, 91/1: 283–316.

Le Brun, A. (ed.), 1984. *Fouilles récentes à Khirokitia (Chypre): 1977–1981*, 2 vols., Paris, Editions recherche sur les civilisations.

1989. *Fouilles récentes à Khirokitia (Chypre): 1983–1986*. Paris, Editions recherche sur les civilisations.

Le Goff, J., Cauvin, J., Marin, L., Peter, J.-P., Perrot, M., Auguet, R., Durand, G. and Cazenave, M., 1986. *Histoire et imaginaire*, Paris, Poiesis, diffusion Payot.

Le Mière, M., 1979. 'La céramique préhistorique de Tell Assouad, Djezireh, Syrie', *Cahiers de l'Euphrate*, 2: 4–76.

1986. 'Les premières céramiques du moyen Euphrate', thèse de troisième cycle, université Lumière-Lyon 2 (unpublished dissertation).

Le Mière, M., and Maréchal, C., 1985. 'L'expansion des arts du feu: chaux, plâtre et céramique', *Le grand atlas de l'archéologie*, Paris, Encyclopoedia Universalis, pp. 170–1.

Lechevallier, M., 1978. *Abou Gosh et Beisamoun*, Paris, Association Paléorient, Mémoires et travaux du centre de recherche de Jérusalem, 2.

Lechevallier, M., and Ronen, A., 1994. *Le gisement de Hatoula en Judée occidentale, Israel*, Paris, Association Paléorient.

Lees, S. H. and Bates, D. G., 1974. 'The origins of specialized nomadic pastoralism: a systemic model', *American Anthropology*, 39/2: 187–93.

Lefort, 1978. 'Capitalisme et religion au XVI siècle: le problème de Weber', in *Les formes de l'histoire*, Paris, Gallimard.

Legge, A. 1996. 'The beginning of caprine domestication in southwest Asia', in D. J. Harris (ed.), *The Origins and Spread of Agriculture and Pastoralism in Eurasia*, London, UCL Press, pp. 238–62.

Leroi-Gourhan, André, 1965. *Préhistoire de l'art occidental*, Paris, Mazenod.

Leroi-Gourhan, Arlette, 1974. 'Etude palynologique des derniers 11,000 ans en Syrie semi-désertique', *Paléorient*, 2/2: 443–51.

Lévi-Strauss, C., 1989. *Des symboles et leurs doubles*, Paris, Plon.

Lichardus, J., Lichardus-Itten, M., Bailloud, G. and Cauvin, J., 1985. *La protohistoire de l'Europe: Le Néolithique et le Chalcolithique*, Paris, Presses universitaires de France, Nouvelle Clio series.

McClellan, T. L., Motixam, M. and Porter, A., in preparation. 'The Tishreen Salvage excavations 1989', *Annales archéologiques arabes syriennes*.

McLaren, F. S., Evans, J. and Hillman, G. C., 1990. 'The identification of charred seeds from Epipaleolithic sites of South-West Asia', in E. H. Pernicka and G. A. Wagner (eds.), *Archaeometry no. 90*, Proceedings of the 26th International Symposium on Archaeometry, Heidelberg, pp. 797–806.

Mallowan, M. E. L., 1946. 'Excavations in the Balikh Valley, 1938', *Iraq*, 8: 111–59.

Maréchal, C., 1980. 'Utilisation de la chaux et du plâtre au Proche-Orient du VIIIe au début du Ve millénaire avant J.-C.', Université de Paris 1, Panthéon-Sorbonne (unpublished dissertation).

1982. 'Vaisselles blanches du Proche-Orient: El Kowm (Syrie) et l'utilisation du plâtre au Néolithique', *Cahiers de l'Euphrate*, 3: 218–51.

1985. 'Les bracelets néolithiques en pierre de Cafer Höyük (Turquie)', *Cahiers de l'Euphrate*, 4: 109–15.

1991. 'Eléments de parure de la fin du Natoufien: Mallaha niveau I, Jayroud 3, Jayroud 9,

Abu Hureyra et Mureybet I A', in O. Bar-Yosef and F. R. Valla (eds.), *The Natufian Culture in the Levant*, Ann Arbor, International Monographs in Prehistory, Archaeological Series 1, pp. 589–612.

    1995. 'Les éléments de parure de Tell Aswad (Syrie)', in H. de Contenson (ed.), *Aswad et Ghoraifé, sites néolithiques en Damascène (Syrie) aux VIIIe et VIIe millénaires avant notre ère*, Beyrouth, IFAPO.

Margueron, J., 1991. *Les Mésopotamiens: le temps et l'espace*, Paris, Armand Colin.

Marx, K. 1843. 'Contribution to a Critique of the Philosophy of Law by Hegel', in *Œuvres philosophiques*, Editions Champ Libre, 1981.

Marx, K. and Engels, F. 1982. *L'idéologie allemande*, Paris, Editions Sociales.

Masson, V. M. and Sarianidi, V. J., 1972. *Central Asia: Turkmenia before the Achaemenids*, London, Thames and Hudson.

Mellaart, J., 1967. *Çatal Hüyük: A Neolithic Town in Anatolia*, London, Thames and Hudson.

    1970. *Excavations at Hacılar*, 2 vols., Edinburgh, Edinburgh University Press.

Merpert, N., Munchaev, R. and Bader, N., 1978. 'Soviet investigations in the Sinjar Plain 1975', *Sumer*, 34: 27–51.

Molist, M., 1989. 'Problématique des structures de combustion fermées au Proche-Orient néolithique précéramique (10,000–6000 bc.)', *Mémoires du musée de préhistoire de l'Ile-de-France*, 2, Nemours, APRAIF; Actes du colloque de Nemours 1987, pp. 303–12.

    1998. Espace collectif et espace domestique dans le Néolithique des IXe et VIIIe millénaires BP au nord de la Syrie: apports du site de Tell Halula (Vallée de l'Euphrate), in M. Fortin and O. Aurenche (eds.), *Espace naturel, espace habité en Syrie du Nord (10e–2e millénaires avant J.C.)*, Actes du Colloque tenté à l'Université Laval, Québec, Mai 1997, the Canadian Society for Mesopotamian Studies (Bulletin 33) and Lyons, Maison de l'Orient Méditerranéen, Travaux de la Maison de l'Orient 28, pp. 115–30.

Molist, M. (ed.), 1996. *Tell-Halula (Syria): un yacimiento neolitico del valle medio del Euphrates. Campagnes de 1991 y 1992*, Madrid, Instituto del Patrimonio Historico Espanol.

Molist, M. and Cauvin, J., 1991. 'Les niveaux inférieurs de Cafer Höyük (Malatya, Turquie). Stratigraphie et architectures (fouilles 1984–86)', *Cahiers de l'Euphrate*, 5–6: 85–113.

Molleson, T., Comerford, G. and Moore, A. M. T., 1992. 'A Neolithic painted skull from Tell Abu Hureyra, Northern Syria', *Cambridge Archaeological Journal*, 2/2: 231–6.

Moore, A. M. T. and Hillman, G. C., 1992. 'The Pleistocene to Holocene transition and human economy in Southwest Asia: the impact of the younger Dryas', *American Antiquity*, 57/3: 482–94.

Moore, A. M. T., Hillman, G. C. and Legge, A. J., 1975. 'The excavations at Tell Abu Hureyra in Syria: a preliminary report', *Proceedings of the Prehistoric Society*, 41: 50–77.

Morin, E., 1986. *La méthode. III: La connaissance de la connaissance*, Paris, Editions du Seuil.

Moulins, D. de, 1993. 'Les restes de plantes carbonisées de Cafer Höyük', *Cahiers de l'Euphrate*, 7: 191–234.

Muzzolini, A., l991 'Masques et thériomorphes dans l'art rupestre du Sahara central', *Archéo-Nil*, 1: 17–42.

Neuville, R., 1951. *Le Paléolithique et le Mésolithique du désert de Judée*, Paris, Masson and Cie, Archives de l'Institut de paléontologie humaine, mémoire 24.

Noy, T., 1986. 'Seated clay figurines from the Neolithic period, Israel', in A. Bonano (ed.), *Archaeology and Fertility Cult in the Ancient Mediterranean*, First Conference on Archeology of the Ancient Mediterranean, The University of Malta, September 1985, Amsterdam, B. R. Grimer, pp. 63–7.

    1991. 'Art and decoration of the Natufian of Nahal Oren', in O. Bar-Yosef, O. and F. Valla (eds.), *The Natufian Culture in the Levant*, Ann Arbor, International Monographs in Prehistory, pp. 557–68.

Noy, T., Legge, A. J. and Higgs, E. S., 1973. 'Recent excavations at Nahal Oren, Israel', *Proceedings of the Prehistoric Society*, 39: 75–99.

Noy, T., Schulderein, J. and Tchernov, E., 1980. 'Gilgal I, a Pre-Pottery Neolithic A site in the Lower Jordan Valley', *Israel Exploration Journal*, 30: 63–82.

Oates, D. and Oates, J., 1976. 'Early irrigation in Mesopotamia', in G. Sieveking, I. H. Longworth and K. E. Wilson (eds.), *Problems in Economic and Social Archaeology*, London, Duckworth, pp. 109–35.

Özbaşaran, M., 1997. 'Aşıklı'dan sonra Musular'. *Prehistorya* (Istanbul) 1997: 1–26.

Özbek, M., 1976. 'Etude anthropologique d'ossements humains néolithiques du VIIIe millénaire avant J.-C. provenant de Mureybet', *Annales archéologiques arabes syriennes*, 26: 161–80.

1988. 'Culte des crânes humains à Çayönü', *Anatolica*, 15: 127–38.

Özdoğan, A., 1995. 'Life at Çayönü during the Pre-Pottery Neolithic Period', in *Readings in Prehistory: Essays for Halet Çambel*, University of Istanbul, pp. 75–86.

Özdoğan, M., 1997. 'Anatolia from the Last Glacial Maximum to the Holocene Climatic Optimum: cultural formations and the impact of the environmental setting', *Paléorient*, 23/2: 249–62.

Özdoğan, M. and Özdoğan, A., 1990. 'Çayönü, a conspectus of recent work', in O. Aurenche, M.-C. Cauvin and P. Sanlaville (eds.), *Préhistoire du Levant: processus des changements culturels*, Paris, Editions du CNRS, pp. 68–77.

Parr, P. J., 1983. 'Nebi Mend 1982', *Lettre d'information d'archéologie orientale* (Centre de recherches archéologiques, Valbonne), 6: 31.

Parrot, A., 1952. *Bible et archéologie*, Paris, Delachaux et Niestlé.

Perlès, C., 1983. 'Circulation de l'obsidienne en Méditerranée orientale. Peut-on appliquer les modèles?', in A. Leroi-Gourhan (ed.), *Circulations et échanges, séminaire sur les structures de l'habitat*, Paris, Collège de France, pp. 128–39.

1990. *Les Industries lithiques taillées de Franchthi (Argolide, Grèce), t.II: les industries du Mésolithique et du Néolithique initial*, Bloomington, Indiana University Press.

Perrot, J., 1966a. 'Le gisement natoufien de Mallaha (Eynan), Israël', *L'Anthropologie*, 70/5–6: 437–83.

1966b. 'La troisième campagne de fouilles à Munhata (1964)', *Syria*, 43, pp. 1–2: 49–63.

1968. 'Préhistoire palestinienne', in *Dictionnaire de la Bible*, supplément 43: pp. 286–446.

1978. *Syrie-Palestine I*, Genève, Nagel (Archaeologia mundi).

Perrot, J., Ladiray, D., Soliveres-Massei, O. and Ferembach, D., 1988. *Les Hommes de Mallaha*, Paris, Association Paléorient, Mémoires et travaux du CRFJ, 7.

Pichon, J., 1985a. 'Les rapaces de Tell-Mureybet, Syrie. Fouilles, J. Cauvin 1971–1976', *Cahiers de l'Euphrate*, 4: 229–59.

1985b. 'A propos d'une figuration aviaire à Mureybet (phase-IIIa), 8 000–7 700 avant J.-C.', *Cahiers de l'Euphrate*, 4: 261–4.

1991. 'Les oiseaux au Natoufien: avifaune et sédentarité', in O. Bar-Yosef and F. R. Valla (eds.), *The Natufian Culture in the Levant*, Ann Arbor, International Monographs in Prehistory, Archaeological Series 1, pp. 371–80.

Renfrew, C., 1987. *Archaeology and Language: The Puzzle of Indo-European Origins*. London, Jonathan Cape. (French edition, 1990, *L'Enigme européenne*, Paris, Flammarion.)

1991. 'Before Babel: speculations on the origins of linguistic diversity', *Cambridge Archaeological Journal* 1/1: 3–23.

1996. 'Language families and the spread of agriculture', in D. J. Harris (ed.), *The Origins and Spread of Agriculture and Pastoralism in Eurasia*, London, UCL Press, pp. 70–92.

Rognon, P., 1982. 'Modifications des climats et des environnements en Afrique du Nord et au Moyen-Orient depuis 20 000 B.P.', in J. L. Bintliff and W. Van Zeist, *Paleoclimates, Paleoenvironments and Human Communities in the Eastern Mediterranean Region in Later Prehistory*, Oxford, BAR International Series 133 (i), pp. 67–91.

Rollefson, G. O., 1983. 'Ritual and ceremony at Neolithic Ain Ghazal (Jordan)', *Paléorient*, 9/2: 29–38.

1989. 'The aceramic Neolithic of the Southern Levant: the view from Ain Ghazal', *Paléorient*, 15/1: 135–40.

Rollefson, G. O., Simmons, A. H. and Kafafi, Z., 1992. 'Neolithic cultures at 'Ain Ghazal, Jordan', *Journal of Field Archaeology*, 19: 443–70.

Ronen, A., 1995. 'Core, periphery and ideology in Aceramic Cyprus', *Quartär* 45/46: 177–206.

Roodenberg, J.-J., 1979/80. 'Premiers résultats de recherches archéologiques à Hayaz Höyük', *Anatolica*, 7: 3–19.

1986. *Le mobilier en pierre de Bouqras: utilisation de la pierre dans le Néolithique du Moyen Euphrate*, Istanbul, Nederlands Historisch-Archaeologisch Instituut.

Rosenberg, M. and Davis, M. K., 1992. 'Hallan Çemi Tepesi, an early aceramic neolithic site in Eastern Anatolia', *Anatolica*, 18: l-18.

Rossignol-Strick, M., 1995. 'Sea–land correlations of pollen records in the eastern Mediterranean for the glacial–interglacial transition: biostratigraphy versus radiometric time-scale', *Quaternary Science Reviews*, 14: 893–915.

Rossignol-Strick, M. *et al.* 1982. *Nature* 295: 105–9.

Sahlins, M., 1972. *Age de pierre, âge d'abondance: l'économie des sociétés primitives*, Paris, Gallimard. (English edition, 1972. *Stone Age Economics*, Chicago, Aldine.)

Sanlaville, P., 1989. 'Considérations sur l'évolution de la Basse Mésopotamie au cours des derniers millénaires', *Paléorient*, 15/2: 5–27.

1996. 'Changements climatiques dans la région levantine à la fin du Pléistocène supérieur et au début de l'Holocène. Leurs relations avec l'évolution des sociétés humaines', *Paléorient*, 22/1: 7–30.

1997. 'Les changements climatiques au Moyen Orient de 20000 BP à 8000 BP', *Paléorient*, 23/2: 249–62.

Schaeffer, C. F. A., 1948. *Stratigraphie comparée et chronologie de l'Asie occidentale (IIIe et IIe millénaires)*, Oxford, Oxford University Press.

Schirmer, W., 1990. 'Some aspects of building at the "aceramic-neolithic"', *World Archaeology*, 21/3: 363–87.

Schmandt-Besserat, D., 1978. 'Les plus anciens précurseurs de l'écriture', *Science*, (French edition) 10: 12–22. ('The earliest precursor of writing', *Scientific American*, June 1978.)

1996. 'Neolithic symbolism at 'Ain Ghazal', *American Journal of Archaeology*, 100/3: 516–17.

Schmidt, K., 1988. 'Nevalı Çori: zum Typenspektrum der Silexindustrie und die übrigen Kleinfunde', in J. Roodenberg (ed.), *Aceramic Neolithic in South-East Turkey, Anatolica*, 15. Table ronde, Istanbul, June 1986, pp. 161–201.

1995. 'Investigations in the Upper Mesopotamian Early Neolithic: Göbekli Tepe and Gürcütepe'. *Neolithics*, 2: 9–10.

'Gürcü tepe and Göbekli tepe 1995–1997', *Kazi Sonuçlari Toplantasi* (Turkish Annual Excavation Symposium, Tarsus, 1998).

Schroeder, B., 1991. 'Natufian in the Central Beqaa Valley, Lebanon', in O. Bar-Yosef and F. Valla (eds.), *The Natufian Culture in the Levant*, Ann Arbor, International Monographs in Prehistory, pp. 43–80.

Serres, M., 1969. *Hermès I: la communication*, Paris, Editions de Minuit.

1993. *Les origines de la géométrie*, Paris, Flammarion.

Servello, F., 1976. 'Nahal Divshon: a Pre-Pottery Neolithic hunting camp', in A. Marks (ed.), *Prehistory and Paleoenvironment in the Central Negev, Israel*. I: *The Advat Aquer Area*, Dallas, SMU Press, pp. 349–70.

Sherratt, A. and Sherratt, S., 1988. 'The archaeology of Indo-European: an alternative view', *Antiquity*, 62: 584–95.

Silistreli, U., 1989. 'Kösh Höyük'te bulunan Kabartma insan ve hayvan figürleriyle bezeli vazolar', *Belleten*, C.53: 361–74.

Simmons, A., 1989. 'Preliminary report on the 1988 test excavations at Akrotiri-Aetokremnos', *Report of the Department of Antiquities, Cyprus, 1989.*

Smith, P. E. L., 1975. 'Ganj Dareh Tepe', *Iran*, 13: 178–80.

Solecki, R. S., 1977. 'Predatory bird rituals at Zawi Chemi Shanidar', *Sumer*, 33: 42–7.

1981. *An Early Village Site at Zawi Chemi Shanidar*, Malibu, Undena Publications.

Solecki, R. L. and Solecki, R. S., 1970. 'Grooved stones from Zawi Chemi Shanidar, a proto-neolithic site in Northern Iraq', *American Anthropologist*, 72: 831–41.

Stanley-Price, N. P., 1977. 'Khirokitia and the initial settlement of Cyprus', *Levant*, 9: 66–89.

Stekelis, M. and Yizraely, T., 1963. 'Excavations at Nahal Oren. Preliminary report', *Israel Exploration Journal*, 13/1: 1-12.

Stordeur, D., 1983. 'Quelques remarques pour attirer l'attention sur l'intérêt d'une recherche commune entre tracélogues du silex et technologues de l'os', in M.-C. Cauvin (ed.), *Traces d'utilisation sur les outils de pierre néolithiques du Proche-Orient*, Lyon, Maison de l'Orient, pp. 231–9.

1988. *Outils et armes en os du gisement natoufien de Mallaha (Eynan), Israel*, Paris, Association Paléorient, Mémoires et travaux du centre de recherche français de Jérusalem, 6.

1989a 'Vannerie et tissage au Proche-Orient néolithique: IXe–Ve millénaire', in J.-L. Fiches and Stordeur, D. (eds.), *Tissage, corderie, vannerie: approches archéologiques, ethnologiques, technologiques*, Juan-les-Pins, APDCA, IXe rencontres internationales d'archéologie et d'histoire d'Antibes, October 1988, pp. 19–39.

Stordeur, D. 1989b. 'El Kowm 2 – Caracol et le PPNB', *Paléorient*, 15/1: 102–10.

1994. 'Outils et parures en os de Ganj Dareh (Iran, VIIe millénaire B.C.)', *Cahiers de l'Euphrate*, 7: 245–96.

1998a. 'Espace naturel, espace contraint à Jerf el Ahmar sur l'Euphrate', in M. Fortin and O. Aurenche (eds.), *Espace naturel, espace habité en Syrie du Nord (10e–2e millénaires avant J. C.)*, Actes du Colloque tenté à l'Université Laval, Québec, Mai 1997, The Canadian Society for Mesopotamian Studies (Bulletin 33) and Lyons, Maison de l'Orient Méditerranéen, Travaux de la Maison de l'Orient 28, pp. 93–108.

1998b. 'Jerf el Ahmar et l'horizon PPNA en Haute Mésopotamie, 9e millénaire avant J.-C.', in M. Lebeku (ed.) *Subartu IV. About Subartu: Studies Devoted to Upper Mesopotamia, I. Landscape, Archaeology, Settlement*, Turnhout, Brepols, pp. 13–29.

in press (1). 'Organisation de l'espace construit et organisation sociale dans le Néolithique de Jerf el Ahmar (Syrie, Xᵉ–IXᵉ millénaire av. J. C.)' in *XIVᵉ Rencontre Internationale d'Archéologie et d'Histoire d'Antibes. 22–24 Octobre 1998.*

in press (2). *Une île dans le désert: El Kowm 2 (Néolithique précéramique 8000–7500 BP)*. Paris, Editions CNRS.

Stordeur, D., Helmer, D., Jammous, B. and Willcox, G., 1996. 'Jerf-el Ahmar: a new Mureybetian site (PPNA period) on the Middle Euphrates', *Neolithics*, 2.

Stordeur, D., and Jammous, B., 1995. 'Pierre à rainure à décor animal trouvée dans l'horizon PPNA de Jerf el Ahmar, Syrie', *Paléorient*, 21/1: 129–30.

Stordeur, D., Maréchal, C. and Molist, M., 1991. 'Stratigraphie générale du tell néolithique d'El Kowm-Caracol (Syrie)', *Cahiers de l'Euphrate*, 5–6: 33–45

Stordeur, D. and Taha, A., 1996. 'Ressemblances et dissemblances entre les sites nomades et sédentaires de la steppe syrienne au VIe millénaire', in *Annales archéologiques arabes syriennes*, The International Colloquium on Palmyra and the Silk Road, Palmyra, April 1992, pp. 85–98.

Strouhal, E., 1973. 'Five plastered skulls from Pre-Pottery Neolithic B, Jericho. Anthropological study', *Paléorient*, 1/2: 231–47.

Taute, W., 1981. 'Masad Mazzal, ein Siedlungsplatz des präkeramischen Neolithikums südlich des Toten Meeres', in W. Frey and H. P. Suerpmann (eds.), *Beihefte zum Tübinger Atlas des Vorderen Orients*, Tübingen, Institut für Urgeschichte der Universität Tübingen, pp. 236–56.

Tchernov, E. and Bar-Yosef, O., 1982, 'Animal exploitation in the Pre-Pottery Neolithic B period at Wadi Tbeik, Southern Sinaï', *Paléorient*, 8/2: 17–31.

Testart, A., 1982. *Les chasseurs-cueilleurs ou l'origine des inégalités*, Paris, Société d'ethnographie.

Ucko, P. J., 1968. *Anthropomorphic Figurines of Predynastic Egypt and Neolithic Crete with Comparative Material from the Prehistoric Near East and Mainland Greece*, London, Andrew Szmidla.

Valla, F. R., 1984. *Les industries de silex de Mallaha (Eynan)*, Paris, Association Paléorient, Mémoires et travaux du centre de recherche français de Jérusalem, 3.

1987. 'Les Natoufiens connaissaient-ils l'arc ?', in D. Stordeur (ed.), *La main et l'outil: manches et emmanchements préhistoriques*, Lyons, Maison de l'Orient, Travaux de la maison de l'Orient, 15, pp. 165–74.

1988. 'La fin de l'Epipaléolithique au Levant: les industries à microlithes géométriques', *L'Anthropologie* 92/3: 901–25.

1990. 'Le Natoufien: une autre façon de comprendre le monde?', *Mitekufat Haeven*, 23: 171–5.

Van Loon, M., 1968. 'The Oriental Institute Excavations at Mureybit, Syria: preliminary report on the 1965 campaign', *Journal of Near Eastern Studies*, 27: 265–90.

Van Zeist, W. and Bakker-Heeres, J. A. H., 1982 (1985). 'Archaeobotanical studies in the Levant. 1, Neolithic sites in the Damascus Basin: Aswad, Ghoraïfé, Ramad', *Palaeohistoria*, 24: 166–255.

1984a (1986). 'Archaeological studies in the Levant. 2, Neolithic and Halaf levels at Ras Shamra', *Palaeohistoria*, 26: 151–70.

1984b (1986). 'Archaeobotanical studies in the Levant. 3, Late Paleolithic Mureybit', *Palaeohistoria*, 26: 171–99.

Van Zeist, W. and Bottema, S., 1982. 'Vegetational history of the Near Eastern Mediterranean and the Near East during the last 2000 years', in J. L. Bintliff and W. Van Zeist (eds.), *Palaeoclimates, Paleoenvironments and Mediterranean Region in Later Prehistory*, Oxford, BAR International Series 133, pp. 277–321.

Van Zeist, W., and de Roller, G. 1994. 'The plant husbandry of aceramic Çayönü, SE Turkey', *Palaeohistoria*, 33/34: 65–96.

Van Zeist, W. and Woldring, H., 1980. 'Holocene vegetation and climate of Northwestern Syria', *Palaeohistoria*, 22: 112–25.

Vernant, J.-P., 1990. *Figures, idoles et masques*, Paris, Julliard.

Vialou, D., 1987. *L'art des cavernes: les sanctuaires de la préhistoire*, Paris, Editions du Rocher.

Voigt, M., 1985. 'Village on the Euphrates', *Expedition*, 27/1: 10–24.

Waechter, J. d'A. and Seton-Williams, V. M., 1938. 'The excavations at Wadi Dhobaï 1937–1938 and the Dhobaian industry', *Journal of the Palestine Oriental Society*, 18: 172–86.

Walker-Tubb, K., 1985. 'Preliminary report on the Ain Ghazal statues', *Mitteilungen des Deutschen Orient-Gesellschaft*, 117: 117–34.

Watkins, T., 1980 'The aceramic neolithic of Cyprus: economic status and cultural origins' *Journal of Mediterranean Anthropology and Archaeology* 1: 139–49.

1990. 'The origins of house and home', *World Archaeology*, 21/3: 336–47.

1992. 'The beginning of the Neolithic: searching for meaning in material culture change', *Paléorient*, 18/1: 63–75.

1997. 'The human environment', *Paléorient*, 23/2: 263–70.

Watkins, T., Baird, D. and Betts, A., 1990. 'Qermez Dere and the early aceramic Neolithic of Northern Iraq', in O. Aurenche, M.-C. Cauvin and P. Sanlaville (eds.), *Préhistoire du Levant: processus des changements culturels*, Paris, Editions du CNRS, pp. 341–6.

Willcox, G., 1991. 'La culture inventée, la domestication inconsciente: le début de l'agriculture au Proche-Orient', in M.-C. Cauvin (ed.), *Rites et rythmes agraires*, Lyons, Maison de l'Orient, Travaux de la Maison de l'Orient, 20, pp. 9–29.

1992. 'Archaeobotanical significance of growing Near Eastern progenitors of domestic plants at Jalès (France)', in P. Anderson (ed.), *Nouvelles approches expérimentales et ethnographiques*, Paris, Editions du CNRS, pp. 159–78.

1996. 'Evidence for plant exploitation and vegetation history from three Early Neolithic pre-pottery sites on the Euphrates (Syria)', *Vegetation History and Archaeobotany*, 5: 143–52.

Zohary, D., 1992. 'Domestication of the Neolithic Near Eastern crop assemblage', in P. Anderson (ed.), *Préhistoire de l'agriculture: nouvelles approches expérimentales et ethnographiques*, Paris, Editions du CNRS, pp. 81–6.

Zohary, D. and Hopf, M., 1988. *Domestication of Plants in the Old World*, Oxford, Oxford University Press.

Zvelebil, M. and Zvelebil, K. V., 1988. 'Agricultural transition and Indo-European dispersals', *Antiquity*, 62: 574–83.

INDEX

NEW STUDIES IN ARCHAEOLOGY

Series editors

Clive Gamble, *University of Southampton*
Colin Renfrew, *University of Cambridge*
Jeremy Sabloff, *University of Pennsylvania Museum of Anthropology and Archaeology*

Ian Hodder and Clive Orton: *Spatial analysis in archaeology*
Keith Muckelroy: *Maritime archaeology*
R. Gould: *Living archaeology*
Stephen Plog: *Stylistic variation in prehistoric ceramics*
Patrick Vinton Kirch: *Evolution of the Polynesian chiefdoms*
Dean Arnold: *Ceramic theory and cultural process*
Geoffrey W. Conrad and Arthur A. Demarest: *Religion and empire: the dynamics of
    Aztec and Inca expansion*
Graeme Barker: *Prehistoric farming in Europe*
Daniel Miller: *Artefacts as categories*
Rosalind Hunter-Anderson: *Prehistoric adaptation in the American Southwest*
Robin Torrence: *Production and exchange of stone tools*
Bo Graslund: *The birth of prehistoric chronology*
Ian Morris: *Burial and ancient society: the rise of the Greek city state*
Joseph Tainter: *The collapse of complex societies*
John Fox: *Maya postclassic state formation*
Alasdair Whittle: *Problems in Neolithic archaeology*
Peter Bogucki: *Forest farmers and stock herders*
Olivier de Montmollin: *The archaeology of political structure: settlement analysis in a
    classic Maya polity*
Robert Chapman: *Emerging complexity: the later prehistory of South-East Spain,
    Iberia and the West Mediteranean*
Steven Mithen: *Thoughtful foragers: a study of prehistoric decision making*
Roger Cribb: *Nomads in archaeology*
James Whitley: *Style and society in Dark Age Greece: the changing face of a pre-literate
    society 1100–700 BC*
Philip Arnold: *Domestic ceramic production and spatial organization*
Julian Thomas: *Rethinking the Neolithic*
E. N. Chernykh: *Ancient metallurgy in the USSR: the early Metal Age*, translated by
    Sarah Wright
Lynne Sebastian: *The Chaco Anasazi: sociopolitical evolution in the prehistoric
    Southwest*
Anna Maria Bietti Sestieri: *The Iron Age community of Osteria del'Osa: a study of
    socio-political development in central Tyrrhenian Italy*
Christine A. Hastorf: *Agriculture and the onset of political inequality before the Inca*
Richard E. Blanton, Stephen A. Kowalewski, Gary Feinman and Laura Finsten:
    Ancient Mesoamerica: a comparison of change in three regions, second edition
Richard Bradley and Mark Edmonds: *Interpreting the axe trade: production and
    exchange in Neolithic Britain*

Dean E. Arnold: *Ecology and ceramic production in an Andean community*
Anne E. Yentsch: *A Chepseake family and their slaves: a study in historical archaeology*
Paul K. Wason: *The archaeology of rank*
Roland Fletcher: *The limits of settlement growth: a theoretical outline*
Christopher Tilley: *An ethnography of the Neolithic: early prehistoric societies in Southern Scandinavia*
Jerry D. Moore: *Architecture and power in the ancient Andes: the archaeology of public buildings*
Michael Shanks: *Art and the Greek City state: an interpretative archaeology*
Kristian Kristiansen: *Europe before history*
Lisa Nevett: *House and society in the ancient Greek world*

Lightning Source UK Ltd.
Milton Keynes UK
29 January 2011

166596UK00004B/8/A

9 780521 039086